Literature in English

for Cambridge International AS & A Level

COURSEBOOK

Elizabeth Whittome

Second edition

CAMBRIDGE
UNIVERSITY PRESS

University Printing House, Cambridge CB2 8BS, United Kingdom

One Liberty Plaza, 20th Floor, New York, NY 10006, USA

477 Williamstown Road, Port Melbourne, VIC 3207, Australia

314–321, 3rd Floor, Plot 3, Splendor Forum, Jasola District Centre, New Delhi – 110025, India

79 Anson Road, #06 -04/06, Singapore 079906

Cambridge University Press is part of the University of Cambridge.

It furthers the University's mission by disseminating knowledge in the pursuit of education, learning and research at the highest international levels of excellence.

Information on this title: www.cambridge.org

First published 2014

Second edition 2019

20 19 18 17 16 15 14 13 12 11 10 9 8 7 6 5 4 3 2 1

Printed in Malaysia by Vivar Printing

A catalogue record for this publication is available from the British Library

ISBN 978-1-108-45782-8 Paperback
ISBN 978-1-108-45791-0 Cambridge Elevate edition (2 years)
ISBN 978-1-108-45792-7 Digital edition

This is the second edition of your coursebook, packed with new material and features designed specially to help you to succeed in your study of literature in English at more advanced levels.

The emphasis in this book is on skills; the development of your capabilities as a literary critic and commentator. In addition to many varied exercises in reading, analysis, writing and discussion, there are features in every unit here which encourage self-assessment and progress. In this respect, the book is a significant improvement on the first edition. Any advanced student, no matter what your particular syllabus, will find the tools here to help them to success in handling any text confidently. The book is primarily designed for the Cambridge International AS & A Level syllabuses, but is equally applicable to others. However, do check your own specification for its particular requirements. Any good syllabus will certainly contain the basic elements of poetry, prose and drama, including Shakespeare, however.

What this book does not do is clear. It does not refer to the set texts on the syllabus in a particular year. Set texts come and go on a regular basis and your coursebook would soon be out of date if all the examples in the book were from a particular year's set texts. You will discover that the range of activities can be transferred to any text you are studying, so that you benefit from all the examples given, developing your skills and confidence progressively.

Additionally, there are many new examples of student writing in this coursebook, which have been annotated with comments (written by the author). These exemplars guide and encourage you to good writing as well as giving you an idea of how not to write an essay. The popular final section of the book, on essay skills, techniques and problem-solving has been enhanced in this second edition, with further examples.

The ability to read and analyse closely material which has not been pre-prepared is a core skill of the subject at advanced level. Your coursebook emphasises this core skill of unseen, now one of the compulsory examination elements at AS level in the new Cambridge International AS & A Level Literature in English syllabus and often a feature in other specifications. (Students looking to further develop their skills with responding to unseen passages would find units 22, 25 and 28 particularly useful.) These exercises also offer some elements of wider reading. The works cited in the coursebook as a whole come from the widest range of different national backgrounds from across the world, all writing in English. You won't necessarily find these on any particular year's set text list. They also span some 650 years and include Chaucer, Milton, the Metaphysicals, novels of the Indian subcontinent, Restoration drama and contemporary poetry, for example. These, and others, are all introduced by means of close analysis of poems or short passages, with further reading suggested after each.

I hope you enjoy the 'new look' edition. I've certainly enjoyed putting it together!

Elizabeth Whittome

Assessment overview and key concepts

Assessment overview

The assessment for the revised Cambridge syllabus is very clear and straightforward. You do two papers for the AS Level (Papers 1 and 2) and two more for the A Level (Papers 3 and 4); each paper lasts two hours. All papers are compulsory: there are no optional papers.

AS Level	A Level
Paper 1: Drama and poetry	**Paper 3:** Shakespeare and drama
Paper 2: Prose and unseen	**Paper 4:** Pre-/Post-1900 poetry & prose

You have a choice of questions with each set text: either a critical essay or a passage-based question, and you'll need to spend an hour on each one. Altogether, then, you'll be studying three set texts for the AS Level and four for the A Level, so seven set texts in all for the full A Level, as well as preparation for the unseen question in AS Level Paper 2, which is a new element. Each question carries equal marks.

The unseen question will allow you to choose between two passages printed on the exam paper: a poem/piece of prose, or poem/drama or prose/drama. There will be different combinations each time, so you will need to practise unseens in all three forms.

The set and unseen texts will all be written in English originally, but they come from different periods and cultures.

This book gives you practice in all aspects of analysis of poetry, prose and drama, with special chapters on the approach to unseens and examples of assessed student work. The poetry, prose and drama examples given in this book are designed to extend your reading and illustrate the basic principles of study of the subject at this level. They are not guides to your set texts, but a means of exploring the subject in detail and developing your skills of close reading, analysis and communication.

Assessment objectives

The assessment objectives show clearly the different but interconnected abilities needed for writing a literature essay at this level.

AO1	The ability to respond with understanding to literary texts in a variety of forms, from different cultures; with an appreciation of relevant contexts that illuminate readings of the texts.
AO2	The ability to analyse ways in which writers' choices of form, structure and language shape meanings and effects.
AO3	The ability to produce informed, independent opinions and interpretations of literary texts.
AO4	The ability to communicate a relevant, structured and supported response appropriate to literary study.
AO5	The ability to discuss and evaluate varying opinions and interpretations of literary texts (Cambridge International A Level only).

Key concepts

The key concepts of any subject are the essential underpinning ideas that characterise it. Knowing what they are helps students to appreciate the subject and to work productively within it. Each unit in this book shows which key concepts are incorporated. The key concepts are focused on three areas: the subject of Literature, the craft of the writer and the reading and writing of the student.

First of all, literature is an imaginative art form with written texts in distinctive forms such as poetry, prose and drama, and there are different conventions for these forms which have been established over hundreds of years. There is also a wide variety of genres, such as comedy, tragedy or satire. Students need to know about these forms and how they communicate their interpretations. Specifically, you should remember:

- The context in which literature is written and received is an important part of the background to a text.
- In detail, the language, style and structure of a text do not just inform the meaning – they are intrinsic to it. A writer makes language choices and these have effects on the reader.
- The student reads and reacts, analyses and interprets the language choices made by writers to communicate their concerns. Students should take note, particularly at A level, of what other readers and critics think.

When an essay is written, it is a response to a particular question which is framed to focus on the skills of the writer. It must be relevant to the question, structured and supported with reference to the text. Appropriate terminology should be used. The student should be aware of the effects of a work on the readers and the audience (in the case of drama).

Pathways

Although specifically designed for the Cambridge International AS & A Level, the activities in this book are all suitable for other Advanced students. The book contains a great deal of advice on undertaking passage-based questions which combine the skills of close reading with wider reference to the text. Part 1 begins with the basics of the subject and is very suitable for revision or for those who have not taken an earlier qualification such as O Level or GCSE or IGCSE in Literature, moving on to Part 2's more Advanced studies later. However, you should look closely at the specific requirements of your own syllabus, because there will be slight differences.

	AS Level Poetry	AS Level Prose	AS Level Drama	A Level Poetry	A Level Prose	A Level Drama	Essay skills and techniques
I am a Cambridge AS Level student	Units 1–6 provide core teaching	Units 7–11 provide core teaching	Units 12–17 provide core teaching	Of future interest	Of future interest	Of future interest	Useful advice for all
I am a Cambridge A Level student	Units 1–6 provide foundation teaching and revision	Units 7–11 provide foundation teaching and revision	Units 12–17 provide foundation teaching and revision	Units 18–20 provide core teaching	Units 21–23 provide core teaching	Units 24–26 provide core teaching	Useful advice
I am a Cambridge Pre-U student	Units 1–6 provide some of the core teaching required	Units 7–11 provide some of the core teaching required	Units 12–17 provide some of the core teaching required	Units 18–20 provide some of the core teaching required	Units 21–23 provide some of the core teaching required	Units 24–26	Useful advice
I am an AS/A Level student on another syllabus	Relevant background and basics	Relevant background and basics	Relevant background and basics	All useful activities	All useful activities	All useful activities	Useful advice
I am an adult on an Access to HE course or just interested	Relevant background and basics	Relevant background and basics	Relevant background and basics	All useful activities	All useful activities	All useful activities	Useful advice
I am a teacher	Good for less experienced students and revision	Good for less experienced students and revision	Good for less experienced students and revision	Many useful activities including passage questions and unseens	Many useful activities including passage questions and unseens	Many useful activities including passage questions and unseens	Useful advice – whole unit on Troubleshooting

How to use this book

This book contains a number of features to help you in your study.

Learning objectives appear at the start of each unit to outline what you will have covered and understood by the end.

Learning objectives

In this unit you will:

- Examine the structures and themes of poems
- Consider in detail the layout of poems on the page and the effect this has
- Remind yourself of some important technical vocabulary
- Identify and describe two traditional forms of the sonnet

Before you start activities are designed to activate the prior knowledge you need for each unit.

Before you start

- Review your checklist of poetry elements (see Figure 5.1 in Unit 5) and discuss them with your partner. See if you can both write the list down from memory!

KEY CONCEPTS

The effects of the First World War and of the patriarchal society are elements that could validly be developed as a contextual background.

Key concepts summarise the key concepts relevant to each unit with explanatory reminders for understanding different texts featuring throughout the book.

Self-assessment checklist features at the end of each unit make sure you are fully confident of the work of the unit before you move on.

Self-assessment checklist

Reflect on what you've learnt in this unit and indicate your confidence level between 1 and 5. If you score below 3, revisit that section. Come back to this list later in your course. Has your confidence grown?

	Confidence level	Revisited?
I can distinguish between character and characterisation		
I am more knowledgeable about types of character and their function		
I can acknowledge the relationship between character and symbol		
I see and discuss the value of parallels and contrasts of character		

Activities accompany the exercises, some for you to complete on your own as self-study, others to share with a friend or classmate. They include reading, writing and discussion, as well as watching films and video clips.

ACTIVITY 14.2

Look closely at the pairing of characters in the play you are studying, whether related by family or by function in the drama. They may seem at first to be opposites, but when you study them more closely, they may be more ambiguous, with parallels as well as contrasts.

Reflection boxes encourage active thinking about what you are studying.

Reflection: Think of a favourite poem and how different it would be if you made it into a normal prose order.

FURTHER READING

Any novel by Thomas Hardy; *Silas Marner* by George Eliot; *The Handmaid's Tale* by Margaret Atwood (recently made into a very successful TV series with the involvement of the author); *To the Lighthouse* and *Mrs Dalloway* by Virginia Woolf. I enjoy many works of speculative fiction: try *Children of Men* by P.D. James and of course *Never Let Me Go* by Kazuo Ishiguro.

Further reading suggestions in each unit give advice on developing your range of understanding.

Sample response boxes are annotated responses to essay questions where you can analyse the response, make improvements or compare with your own work.

SAMPLE RESPONSE

In *Mountain Lion*, the word *men* is repeated three times in one- and two-word sentences with exclamation marks to emphasise their destructiveness. The third stanza uses parallelism in *They hesitate. / We hesitate.* and *They have a gun. / We have no gun.* Both parties are uncertain, but only one group has a weapon.

Enjambments are used as part of the natural description at the beginning and end of the extract, lending an emphatic quality to the words *sounds* and *still* in the first section and *snow and inwardness* in the last. Additionally, the first lines of the first and fifth stanzas do not contain a finite verb, giving a sense that the actions of *climbing* and *emerging* are still continuing, helped by the enjambment. If read aloud, the pauses between lines give a dramatic significance to the encounter being described, and the final line of the extract is a direct question, which also lends dramatic emphasis.

Student response boxes are actual student responses to essay questions, with marker comments (written by the author) to help you to appreciate good practice in the subject and to improve your own work.

STUDENT RESPONSE

The poem begins with a very surprising, indeed paradoxical, statement: *Home is so Sad*, seemingly the reverse of what most people may feel. But the poem goes on to express the pathos of the home environment, emphasising how the passage of time has left it sterile and unchanged. Time has passed and stolen the family away so that home has no *heart to put aside the theft* and go back to being a more vibrant place. The objects in the house seem pathetic, mere relics of a past time that was better: *You can see how it was.*

Although the language used is relatively simple, it is very effective. The poet uses a kind of personification for the house, or at least makes it seem alive, with its persuasions to the family to return *as if to win them back*, but it has now wither[ed] in its abandonment. There is a strong contrast between the diction used in stanza 1 (sad,

The essay goes straight into a comment on the printed poem.

COMMENT

The most obvious repetition is in the final four lines of each stanza where most of the words are the same (and this continues through the poem to the final stanza). Lines 2, 3 and 4 of the final quatrain (four lines) are exactly the same, but in quatrain 1 she says *My life is dreary* and in quatrain 2 she says *The night is dreary*. This pattern is found with *The day is dreary* used in other stanzas in alternation. The use of a line or lines repeated in this way is typical of certain kinds of poem, such as the ballad, and it is known as a refrain.

Her tears fell is repeated in lines 1 and 2 of the second stanza and there is a mention of the dews, although this is worded slightly differently.

Comment boxes provide additional feedback and guidance.

KEY TERM

Parallelism: a device in which parts of the wording of a sentence are the same, repeating or paralleling each other for emphasis.

Key terms are important terms in the topic you are learning. They are highlighted in **black bold** and defined where they first appear in the book.

Part 1
AS Level

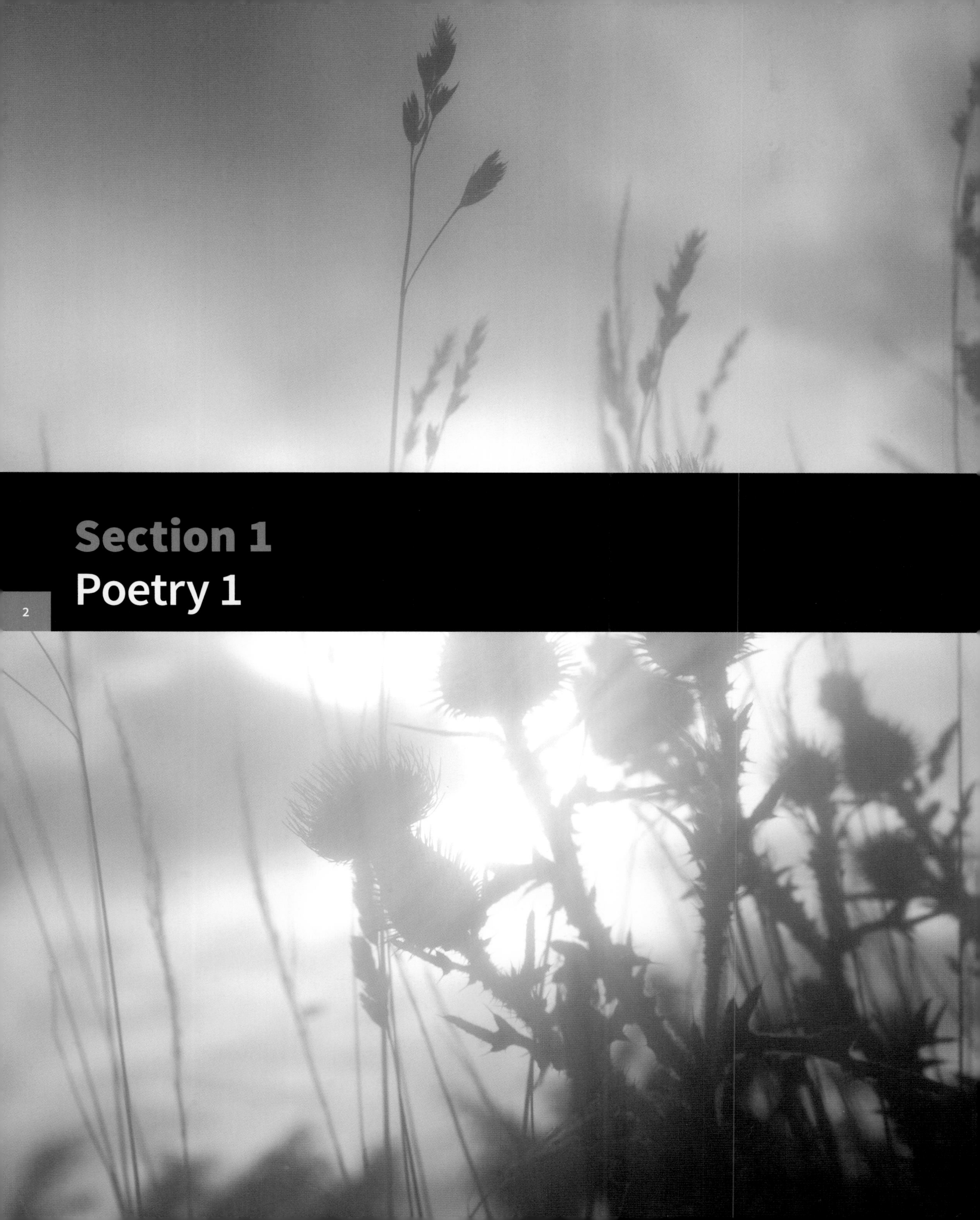

Section 1
Poetry 1

Introduction to poetry

Learning objectives

In this unit you will:

- enjoy reviewing the basics of poetry
- reflect on poems you already know and what you think about them
- consider any difficulties you may have experienced in discussing or writing about them
- remind yourself of the importance of words, their meaning and sound.

KEY CONCEPTS

Language, form, structure, genres, context, style, interpretation.

Before you start

- Remember that you are the reader and your personal response is vital! Get ready to read, concentrate and enjoy yourself. This is Unit 1 and it's always reassuring to go back to basics.
- Have your pens and notebook (whether paper or electronic) at your side. Some activities demand your undivided attention, but some can be enjoyed with a friend. If you are working alone, best to switch your phone to silent. You can share afterwards!

Responding to poetry and writing about it

This section of the book will help you to express your thoughts and feelings about poetry. The units on this topic are designed to help you to enjoy poetry to the full and to feel more secure about expressing your responses, formulating your own interpretations and supporting your ideas with examples. When you come to a poem you have never seen before (such as an examined unseen exercise), you will feel confident and alert, able to use everything you've learnt. All your reading experience will help you.

Poetry can stretch words to their limit to record unique, direct impressions of experience. A word can achieve its full potential when a skilled poet combines it with other carefully selected words. The elements of a word – its meaning, associations, context, history, sound, even its shape and length – all combine with other words to produce the distinctive qualities of a poem. No wonder that many writers see poetry as the ultimate achievement of any language, the utterance that can never really be translated without losing some of its magic. Read any poem aloud to savour its sounds and rhythms; critical appreciation will follow with practice.

All syllabuses focus on a very important Assessment Objective that reminds us that every writer chooses forms, structures and words to shape meanings. Both the writer selecting the words and the reader absorbing their effects are important in this process. You are the reader, whose close listening and reading, personal experience and enjoyment are most significant for your appreciation. You may find that you observe and give emphasis in a different way from your classmate. Providing that both of you can express your feelings, identify the evidence from the poem you are discussing and argue your case, then neither of you is wrong, necessarily. Both of you are literary critics.

Reflection: Consider why you came to this conclusion.

ACTIVITY 1.1

Discuss with your group, or teacher if possible, what qualities you think a poem should have in order to be defined as a poem and make a list. If you are working on your own, think particularly of short fragments and any texts you've come across before which didn't seem very 'poetic' (perhaps rhymes in birthday cards). Consider whether song lyrics can be called poems, since they need the music to complete their effect.

What makes a poem?

Here's a table for you, which shows where various points are discussed in the following poetry units. You may have come up with some of these points in your discussion about the qualities that define poems.

Possible qualities of a poem	Where these are discussed
A: Reading a poem out loud can be very exciting/thrilling/funny/ sad even if you don't understand all of it completely.	
B: It is usually 'about' something – a theme; but it doesn't have to tell a story.	Later in Unit 1
C: The writer is expressing her/his thoughts on a particular subject, so it can be full of humour or emotion such as anger or sadness.	Later in Unit 1
D: The meaning can sometimes be difficult at first reading because: • the words aren't in the usual order • some of them even seem to be missing • they appear to be new words not in the dictionary, or don't have their usual meaning • the language is concentrated or ambiguous.	Unit 2
E: The language can have lots of figures of speech (such as metaphor and personification) and be very descriptive.	Unit 2
F: Sometimes words or phrases or ideas are repeated.	Unit 2
G: It is written in lines and the sentences don't reach the end of the page.	Unit 3
H: There is a pattern to the way it is laid out (e.g. in verses, stanzas or groups of lines).	Unit 3
I : Sometimes it is very rhythmical and there are rhymes or other sound effects such as alliteration.	Unit 4

Of all the points in the list, it's probably D, with its range of challenges for readers, that worries students the most, especially when they have never studied poetry before or are looking at a poem for the first time. Try not to be too worried about what you see as difficulties of interpretation. Some students spend too much time trying to chase the 'meaning' of a poem and forget about the real words that *are* the poem. It's important to remember that the poet has made choices to create particular effects, and considering these in detail – their sounds, their rhythm, their combination together – often clarifies meaning where it has seemed tricky.

Unit 5 gives you hints and tips for tackling an unseen poem, helping you to interpret and to write about a poem you've never seen before. You will have more confidence in your work. There are examples of students' essays on an unseen poem, with the marker's comments showing what is good and what could be improved, which you'll find helpful.

Then, in Unit 6 you focus on writing essays on set texts for an exam, with two different examples of questions. Throughout the units you will have Study and Revision tips. The examples used are from past Literature texts on Cambridge syllabuses, as well as others that are especially memorable or appropriate to illustrate particular points. This book uses texts from writers across the world writing in English.

ACTIVITY 1.2

Look again at the table of qualities that could characterise a poem. How many of them can be seen in the following short poetic text?

> The apparition of these faces in the crowd;
> Petals on a wet, black bough.

Ezra Pound *In a Station of the Metro* (1913)

SAMPLE RESPONSE

At first there do not seem to be enough qualities to make this into a poem as such. It has only two lines, which are not of the same length; there is no distinctive rhythm or rhyme and there is not even a verb to give action to the situation and point to a theme. (Some students think this is too fragmentary to be classed as a poem and you may have some sympathy with that view.) But it is a very descriptive fragment and it uses two different images – one in each line – to capture the poet's experience of seeing people in a crowded station. (The Metro is the Paris underground system. If you do not have an underground train system where you live, imagine crowds pouring off a train.) The poem's title is important because it places the poet's observation and allows the reader to conjure up similar experiences.

The first image is that the faces are an *apparition*, a word that means 'appearance', but also 'ghost', suggesting that they do not look like living beings and perhaps are pale and sad. The second image develops the idea by the metaphor of their faces being like petals on a wet black bough: perhaps the poet is suggesting spring when the trees have blooms, but no leaves and the weather is still rainy; the petals are white or pale pink and delicate, easily blown away. Both images suggest helplessness and transience: there is nothing substantial or robust in the description at all. So although the poet has only offered us images, they are suggestive ones, haunting even, and the experience of seeing people as vulnerable in the hurly-burly of modern urban life has been communicated in two lines and two evocative images.

Reflection: Did the poem's images have this effect on you? Look at some crowds emerging from a station or underground train. Do they look cheerful and lively?

KEY TERM

Imagists: a group of early 20th-century poets who believed that experience was most effectively communicated through images of the senses. This approach is an important element in appreciating *what* a poet is expressing by considering *how* it is expressed. Sense images do not have to be metaphors. The senses are sight, hearing, touch, taste and smell; to these we can add the 'sense' of energy or movement, which could be termed the kinetic sense.

Reflection: If possible, with your partner or in a group, discuss in more detail how each theme develops as the poems progress.

The poem is a good example of Imagism. Ezra Pound was one of a group of poets called **Imagists**.

Here is another example of a short poem with vivid images by Singaporean poet Ong Teong Hean. Tai-chi was originally a training for Chinese martial arts but is now considered a very valuable exercise regime. There are some effective rhymes and half-rhymes at the ends of the lines, features that you will discuss in Unit 4.

the man of tai-chi
with such sequestered ease
creates a clean calligraphy
of graceful peace;
a centre of concentration
to pump his heart and arteries
with measured arm-motion
and steps of gnarled artistry.

Ong Teong Hean *The Tai-chi Man* (2010)

What are poems usually about?

Poets can express thoughts and feelings about anything, so poems can have as their subject matter anything in the world you can think of, such as the Underground or exercising in the morning! There are great poems created about apparently trivial objects like a lock of hair, insects such as a flea or mosquito, or growing things such as thistles or mushrooms. Major life dramas such as love, treachery and war do of course also feature. What the poet does with the subject matter, and how these ideas are developed, is the poem's theme, or it can be expressed as 'the poet's concerns'. These ideas are not separate from the words they are expressed in: the words *are* the poem.

Your exam syllabus for AS Level does not set longer narrative poems for study, so all the examples used in this part of the book will be of shorter lyric poems with distinct themes; you will find that length is not necessarily a criterion for excellence. Poems used in an unseen exam question will also be of this kind.

ACTIVITY 1.3

Write down the names of five poems you have studied and, in one or two sentences, say what they are about.

Themes in poetry

It is often easier to summarise the theme of a poem than it is to analyse the poet's methods and the effects of the language used. This poem is about the waste and futility of war, you might say, or the sadness of death, or the passage of time, or how relationships can be difficult, or how some people in power can make others suffer dreadfully.

Perhaps the poet gives a different example in each **stanza** and then concludes by emphasising his point, or uses a little anecdote that illustrates the issue. Or possibly the poet chooses images which are suggestive of a thought but don't express the thought directly, but we still grasp the gist of the argument. You'll look more closely at this in Unit 3.

KEY TERM

Stanza: an Italian word that means 'room', a place to stop. Poetic stanzas can be irregular as well as regular (see Unit 3, Verse and stanza).

ACTIVITY 1.4

Before you read the next poem, *Egrets* (1962) by Australian poet Judith Wright, see if you can find a picture of these graceful white birds, perhaps on the internet. Then, in one sentence, say what you think the poem is about. When you have answered, consider what other elements in the poem could affect the expression of this theme and your appreciation of it.

Once as I travelled through a quiet evening,
I saw a pool, jet-black and mirror-still.
Beyond, the slender paperbarks* stood crowding;
each on its own white image looked its fill,
and nothing moved but thirty egrets wading –
thirty egrets in a quiet evening.

Once in a lifetime, lovely past believing,
your lucky eyes may light on such a pool.
As though for many years I had been waiting,
I watched in silence, till my heart was full
of clear dark water, and white trees unmoving,
and, whiter yet, those thirty egrets wading.

(*A paperbark is an Australian tree with white bark which resembles strips of paper)

Judith Wright, *Egrets* (1962)

SAMPLE RESPONSE

The poet speaks of the beauty of some birds she sees at a pool as she is walking one evening and how she is affected by this memorable experience.

What is missing from this response?

This answer interprets the theme of the poem quite successfully, but to focus on theme alone is to neglect other aspects of the poem that influence the theme powerfully. Wright uses images of silence and the stillness of everything except the birds. There is effective colour contrast in the dark pool and the white birds and trees. She uses repetition of words and phrases for emphasis, and the poem's two-stanza structure takes the reader from a single incident (*Once as I travelled through a quiet evening*) to the idea that this is a special *Once in a lifetime* experience which anyone would be lucky to have. When she says *my heart was full / of clear dark water* she is using language metaphorically to express the way that experiences can overwhelm the mind. The rhymes and half-rhymes skilfully enhance the theme. You will revise these in more detail in the next three units.

ACTIVITY 1.5

Another well-known poet has written a poem about white egrets and has a collection of poems with this title, which was first published in 2010 when he was 80 years old. See if you can find out who he is!

In a Station of the Metro, that little fragmentary poem, showed the importance of style in interpretation. You are reminded similarly by Wright's poem that the way a theme is expressed is vital to its meaning: all the work you do on analysis of style will help you to refine your ideas about theme and you will be able to return to your initial statement about the writer's concerns and make it more subtle and comprehensive.

TIP

The words make the poem: its meaning doesn't exist as a separate entity underneath or inside the words like a nut whose shell has to be cracked to find the kernel inside. If you changed some of the words to others with similar meanings but different sounds, the poem would disappear and become something else.

Students usually write about a poem's theme and say little about the poet's style and methods. Any close analysis of the language of a poem will enhance the quality of an essay.

FURTHER READING

1 The website 'Poemhunter' is a useful source for poems on particular topics (such as nature, animals, cities and so on).

2 *Language for a New Century: Contemporary Poetry from the Middle East, Asia and Beyond,* edited by Ravi Shankar and Nathalie Handal (Norton, 2008).

Self-assessment checklist

Reflect on what you've learnt in this unit and indicate your confidence level between 1 and 5. If you score below 3, revisit that section. Come back to this list later in your course. Has your confidence grown?

	Confidence level	Revisited?
I can appreciate and discuss the different elements that may make a poem		
I understand what the Imagists were aiming to do		
I can identify aspects other than theme in Wright's poem about the birds		
I acknowledge the importance of style		

The language of poetry

Learning objectives

In this unit you will:

- remind yourself of metaphorical and other non-literal language, with examples to clarify
- revise and consider the effect of language with unusual word order and syntax
- review the importance of repetition and parallelism in poems and their effect.

Language, form, structure, genres, context, style, interpretation.

Before you start

- Look back at the poem by Judith Wright in Unit 1 and see if you can find any similes or metaphors. This will put you in the right frame of mind for reviewing figures of speech.

This unit will help you to appreciate and deal with some of the poetic uses of language: first, the figurative language that characterises many poems and expands their imaginative range; second, the uses of language that challenge your understanding.

The meaning of lines of poetry can sometimes be difficult to unravel because the words are new to you, they are not in the usual order, or perhaps some are missing, making the utterance ambiguous. It's important to remember that a poet's style is not seeking difficulty for its own sake but striving for freshness of presentation and thought, so that when you study the poem you will be engaged by it and remember it with pleasure as a unique utterance.

Metaphorical language

The language of poetry can be very concentrated. One of the reasons for this intensity of expression is the use of **metaphor**. Literal language – the language of fixed predictable meaning – is relatively straightforward, but as soon as language becomes figurative (filled with **figures of speech**) then it becomes highly suggestive and open to imaginative interpretation. Look at the difference between *My love is eighteen years old and has black hair* (literal) and *My love is like a red, red rose* (a figurative comparison).

Metaphor is a broad term which encompasses all the comparative figures of speech (**simile** and **personification**, for example) rather as the term 'mammal' includes a wide range of animals. It is based on comparison. In the hands of a skilled poet, metaphor can extend and enrich meaning, often working at more than one level of comparison and extending through several lines or a whole poem.

KEY TERMS

Figures of speech: Don't be put off by the fact that many words for figures of speech are unusual, often deriving from ancient Greek. This shows that using them has been an essential feature of language since ancient times. There are literally scores of them, but the following list gives you the most common ones.

Imagery: the images of any of our senses (sight, hearing, touch, taste, smell) produced in the mind by descriptive language. These images are often being compared with something else, so frequently associated with specific figures of speech.

Metaphor: the most important and widespread figure of speech. It is a comparison in which unlike objects are identified with each other so that some element of similarity can be found between them. Here a comparison is made by identifying one thing with another, but without using *as* or *like*. In its identification of one thing with another it goes further than a simile. For example:

If music be the food of love, play on (Shakespeare *Twelfth Night*): music to a lover is like food to a hungry person, feeding and sustaining.

The slings and arrows of outrageous fortune (Shakespeare *Hamlet*): life's blows are like missiles thrown at us, but note that fortune is also personified here.

Her skills have blossomed since she started lessons: her skills are growing like a plant – a bud has grown and has gradually become a beautiful flower.

Extended metaphor: where the identification of similar qualities is elaborated over a number of lines, and may run throughout a poem or paragraph of prose.

Simile: a figure of speech (really a kind of metaphor) in which two things are compared using *as* or *like*. A good simile will be clear and economical, but also suggestive; for example, *My love is like a red, red rose* (Robert Burns): beautiful, with soft skin like petals.

Personification: a form of metaphor in which the qualities of a person are transferred to non-human things or abstract qualities, to 'humanise' them and make them easier to understand; for example, *the street lamp muttered* (T.S. Eliot): the environment is just as alive as the person walking down the street.

Hyperbole: exaggeration – an over-statement, used for effect. It isn't used to disguise the truth, but to emphasise. It can be an ingredient of humour too; for example, *An hundred years should go to praise thine eyes* (Andrew Marvell, praising his lover).

Litotes: an understatement used for effect, often using a double negative (such as *not bad*); for example, Wordsworth uses *not seldom* to mean 'quite often' in *The Prelude*.

Antithesis or **contrast:** places contrasting ideas next to each other for effect; often they are in balanced phrases or clauses. This placing can also be termed **juxtaposition** (see Unit 14). You will find many examples of this throughout the book.

Climax: (from a Greek word meaning 'ladder') is the point of highest significance which is gradually reached; for example, *to strive, to seek, to find and not to yield* (Alfred Lord Tennyson). Its opposite, **anti-climax** or **bathos**, suddenly undercuts the climax (and may be humorous); for example, from a poem describing the survivors of a shipwreck (the cutter is the ship carrying foodstuffs): *they grieved for those that perished with the cutter / and also for the biscuit casks and butter* (Lord Byron).

Paradox: two apparently contradictory ideas placed together which make sense when examined closely; for example, *the child is father of the man* (William Wordsworth). If the contradiction is expressed in words in close proximity, it is called an **oxymoron**. In Shakespeare's *Romeo and Juliet*, Romeo makes a whole speech using them (e.g. *Feather of lead, bright smoke, cold fire, sick health*).

Repetition: extremely common for emphasis. The word **parallelism** is used for similar structures, phrases or clauses placed together. You will find many examples of this throughout the book; for example, Tennyson's *Mariana* (see the section on repetition and parallelism later in this unit).

Anaphora: repetition of introductory phrases.

Irony: in its simplest form, irony involves a discrepancy between what is said by a writer and what is actually meant, or a contrast between what the reader expects and what is actually written. More complex forms of irony are dealt with in Part 2 of this book. The word **sarcasm** refers to speech rather than writing, although it would be appropriate for a character speaking in a play.

Sarcasm: The use of a mocking or scornful tone of voice. If analysing a writer's tone you should use the word 'irony', but a character's direct speech can be called sarcastic.

Examples

1 In Wilfred Owen's poem *Exposure*, the poet vividly depicts the experience of men in the trenches in winter, waiting for something to happen. The pattern of comparisons here is mostly one of personification, making the inanimate alive, and thereby emphasising the cruelty of the cold weather: *the merciless iced east winds that knive us*; *the mad gusts tugging on the wire*; *Dawn massing in the east her melancholy army*; the frost which will be *shrivelling many hands and puckering foreheads crisp*. At one point, Owen imagines home and its fire, with its *crusted dark-red jewels*: here he compares the shape of the glowing coals to red jewels, precious by virtue of their warmth and beauty.

2 When South African poet Dennis Brutus describes in his poem *Nightsong: City* the way that police cars rush about the city at night, he says they *cockroach* through the *tunnel* streets. A cockroach is a hard-shelled insect associated with heat and dirt, which scuttles around in the dark, viewed with distaste by everyone. *Tunnel* has connotations of darkness and danger. He continues the insect imagery when he describes violence in a simile: *Violence like a bug-infested rag is tossed*... This gives the impression of a grim city life in which lower life forms have taken over; nonetheless, he loves his city and his country. *My land, my love, sleep well* is how he ends the poem.

3 Caribbean poet Grace Nicholls also uses an insect image in her poem *Up My Spine*, where she sees the old woman *twist-up and shaky like a cripple insect*. In spite of seeming old and feeble, the old woman has great power in the poem. You can find it on the internet.

4 In *Sonnet 73* by William Shakespeare, a series of related extended metaphors is used. It is a typical Shakespearean sonnet (see Unit 3) with three sections of four lines followed by a couplet at the end, making 14 lines in all. The speaker of the poem is feeling his age, and he relates his physical self to three extended metaphors: the season of the year, the time of day and the progress of a fire. You will notice that the unit of comparison gradually diminishes, down to the 'ashes', which are his last remains.

5 Here are some lines filled with very visual metaphors and similes from the poem *After Midnight* by Indian poet Amit Chaudhuri (born 1962):

> Last night, the medallion moon was caught oddly
> between sleek, glowing channels of telephone wire.
> No one stirred, but a Pacific of lights went on burning
> in the vacant porches ...
> Twice, I sensed hands,
> behind windows, strike a match, and a swift badge of flame
> open and shut like a hot mouth.

An extract from *After Midnight* (2008), by Amit Chaudhuri

The *medallion moon* is silver, round, like a jewel printed with significant words, the lights are a vast sea like the Pacific Ocean, and the match is the same colour and shape as a red badge. *Like a hot mouth* is a personification, as if the flame speaks and is then quiet.

ACTIVITY 2.1

Look closely at the metaphors in the poems you are studying; then analyse some of them by writing clearly what things are being compared and what effects these comparisons have. If you like drawing, try making a visual representation of them instead together with a friend.

Reflection: What effects do these comparisons have?

KEY TERMS

Diction: the writer's choice of vocabulary. (You may also come across the word *lexis*, which is a term from the field of Linguistics.) Not to be confused with diction meaning style of pronunciation in speaking.

Neologism: a newly coined word or expression, usually by poets or writers to draw attention to the meaning they are conveying.

Neologisms: One difference between most prose and poetry is that poets sometimes create new words (or neologisms) to draw attention to the meaning they are conveying. You need to work out what the effect of the new word is in its context. Here is an example:

Thomas Hardy wrote many poems when his first wife died, remembering the love they had shared in earlier, happier days. In his poem *The Voice*, he imagines hearing her voice as he is out walking by himself and wishes he could see her as she once was, but she is *ever dissolved to wan wistlessness*. This last word is one coined by Hardy. *Wist* is an archaic word for 'know' and was old when Hardy was writing too. So *wistless* means 'unknowing' and *wistlessness* is the state of not knowing or unconsciousness. All together the word suggests someone who is gone, part of the past, no longer a thinking, feeling person; its sounds are soft, sad and *wistful*, a word very similar in sound which means 'longing'. In both sound and meaning, therefore, the word chosen by Hardy focuses the sense of loss when the living reflect on the absence of the longed-for dead. You don't need to worry about the meaning of unusual or archaic words when you are practising for the unseen paper, as these words will always be given to you.

ACTIVITY 2.2

Try to identify some poems in which new words have been created for a particular effect. Your teacher will help you here. You may need a dictionary to help you find the basic building-block words used by the poet.

KEY TERM

Syntax: the arrangement of words into sentences so that the relationship of each word to the others can be appreciated. (Each language has its own conventions of syntax.) The Ezra Pound poem in Unit 1 was not a complete sentence as it didn't have a finite verb (a verb which has a subject doing the action), appropriate for an utterance that records a fleeting impression rather than an action.

Unusual syntax and omission of words (sometimes called 'deviation')

An important way in which the language of poetry can differ from the language of prose is in its occasionally unusual syntax; word order can be altered and some words omitted to create an interestingly different effect. In this way, the reader is forced to become more attentive to the words and is not able to skim the surface.

The well-known poem by W.H. Auden (1907–1973) *Musée des Beaux Arts* begins by saying *About suffering they were never wrong, / The Old Masters*, rather than *The old masters were never wrong about suffering*. This is known as an inversion; here, the inversion stresses the suffering which is the poet's main concern by placing it directly at the beginning. The poetry of Emily Dickinson (1830–1886) is filled with inversions. For example:

> A solemn thing – it was – I said –
> A woman – white – to be – …
> A hallowed thing – to drop a life.

Landscape with the Fall of Icarus by Pieter Bruegel the Elder. This painting is described in W.H. Auden's poem *Musée des Beaux Arts*, which is named after the museum in Belgium which holds the painting.

ACTIVITY 2.3

Discuss with a partner the word order and syntax in some poems you are studying. In almost every one you will find deviations from the 'normal' word order, and you will find words omitted. Try to consider the effect these have. A good way to point out the difference is to put the lines into sentences in the usual prose order, adding any words you need to make the meaning clear. The first thing you will notice is how much longer your version is, a reminder that poetry can often be very concentrated compared with prose. The Dickinson stanza would begin *I said it was a solemn thing to be a woman.*

Reflection: Think of a favourite poem and how different it would be if you made it into a normal prose order.

This feature is not confined to poetry. In the play *Death of a Salesman*, Linda speaks of her husband to her sons, saying: *Attention, attention must be finally paid to such a person.* The word *attention* is emphasised by its position and by its repetition (rather than the more usual *You should pay attention to a person like that*).

ACTIVITY 2.4

Here is another example: a poem by Gerard Manley Hopkins (1844–1889) that uses unusual syntax and omits words to create specific effects. Analyse how Hopkins does this. Whether on your own or with a partner, use a highlighter to pinpoint those areas of the poem where words are in an unusual order or words have apparently been left out.

Glory be to God for dappled things –
For skies of couple-colour as a brinded cow;
For rose-moles all in stipple upon trout that swim;

Fresh-firecoal chestnut-falls; finches' wings;
Landscape plotted and pieced – fold, fallow, and plough;
And all trades, their gear and tackle and trim.
All things counter, original, spare, strange;
Whatever is fickle, freckled (who knows how?)
With swift, slow; sweet, sour; adazzle, dim;
He fathers-forth whose beauty is past change:
Praise him.

Gerard Manley Hopkins *Pied Beauty* (1877)

SAMPLE RESPONSE

Hopkins omits words and writes very concentratedly in this poem praising God's creation. One characteristic method he uses is to create double-barrelled words such as *couple-colour*, *rose-moles*, *fresh-firecoal* and *fathers-forth*, each of which would require many more words to paraphrase their meaning in prose. The four words *fresh-firecoal chestnut-falls* delightfully sum up the beauties of autumn when chestnuts fall, and fires are made to warm us up and to roast the chestnuts. *Fathers-forth* suggests a loving and enabling parent who cares deeply but is not possessive. Hopkins also uses lists of words, whose meaning and sound work together to image the great variety of multicoloured and multicharactered things and people in the world: *counter*, *original*, *spare*, *strange* ... *swift*, *slow*; *sweet*, *sour*; *adazzle*, *dim*. He does not need to spell out with unnecessary extra words what he is referring to. The images of the senses (sight, sound, touch, taste, smell and movement are all implied here), together with the sounds of the words, combine to create a picture of a great creation iridescent with change, and a great creator whose beauty, in contrast, depends upon his unchanging nature. Hopkins's poetry is rich with similar examples.

Repetition and parallelism

KEY TERM

Parallelism: a device in which parts of the wording of a sentence are the same, repeating or paralleling each other for emphasis.

Poetic method often includes exact repetition of words and phrases, or whole lines, in order to intensify effects. **Parallelism** is repetition which may have some subtle differences. The first example for you to consider is from Tennyson's poem *Mariana*. Here are the first two stanzas:

With blackest moss the flower-pots
   Were thickly crusted, one and all:
The rusted nails fell from the knots
   That held the pear to the gable-wall.
The broken sheds look'd sad and strange:
   Unlifted was the clinking latch;

Weeded and worn the ancient thatch
    Upon the lonely moated grange.
She only said, 'My life is dreary,
    He cometh not,' she said;
She said, 'I am aweary, aweary,
    I would that I were dead!'
Her tears fell with the dews at even;
    Her tears fell ere the dews were dried;
She could not look on the sweet heaven,
    Either at morn or eventide.
After the flitting of the bats,
    When thickest dark did trance the sky,
She drew her casement-curtain by,
    And glanced athwart the glooming flats.
She only said, 'The night is dreary,
    He cometh not,' she said;
She said, 'I am aweary, aweary,
    I would that I were dead!'

An extract from Alfred Lord Tennyson
Mariana (1830)

Mariana in the Moated Grange by John Everett Millais.

ACTIVITY 2.5

See if you can find examples of exact repetition in the two stanzas from *Mariana*. Then look to see if you can find parallelism, where the repeated phrase or construction has a slight variation. Don't include the rhyme at this stage, although it is, of course, a kind of parallelism.

COMMENT

The most obvious repetition is in the final four lines of each stanza where most of the words are the same (and this continues through the poem to the final stanza). Lines 2, 3 and 4 of the final quatrain (four lines) are exactly the same, but in quatrain 1 she says *My life is dreary* and in quatrain 2 she says *The night is dreary.* This pattern is found with *The day is dreary* used in other stanzas in alternation. The use of a line or lines repeated in this way is typical of certain kinds of poem, such as the ballad, and it is known as a refrain.

Her tears fell is repeated in lines 1 and 2 of the second stanza and there is a mention of the dews, although this is worded slightly differently.

▶

There are other examples of parallelism, such as nearly every object being given a descriptive word (an adjective) to qualify it: *blackest moss*, *rusted nails*, *broken sheds*, *clinking latch*, *ancient thatch*, *lonely moated grange*, *sweet heaven*, *thickest dark*, *glooming flats*.

There is a relentless pattern here, which is very appropriate for the repetitive, doomed existence of Mariana, waiting for the man who never comes. Her environment is dark and gloomy, and only the *heaven* (which she cannot face) is *sweet*. By the final stanza of the whole poem, the refrain's changes reveal a climax of desperation:

Then, said she, 'I am very dreary,
He will not come,' she said;
She wept, 'I am aweary, aweary,
O God, that I were dead!'

We shall now look at an example of a shorter poem by W.B. Yeats that depends equally upon these features. The whole poem follows Activity 2.6.

TIP

By paying close attention to the words in poems – their implications, their sounds and their arrangement – you will gradually become a skilled and responsive literary critic.

ACTIVITY 2.6

See if you can identify the repetition and parallelism in this poem by Irish poet W.B. Yeats: *An Irish Airman Foresees His Death*, written about Yeats's friend Major Robert Gregory who died in the First World War.

I know that I shall meet my fate
Somewhere among the clouds above;
Those that I fight I do not hate,
Those that I guard I do not love;
My country is Kiltartan Cross,
My countrymen Kiltartan's poor,
No likely end could bring them loss
Or leave them happier than before.
Nor law, nor duty bade me fight,
Nor public men, nor cheering crowds,
A lonely impulse of delight
Drove to this tumult in the clouds;
I balanced all, brought all to mind,
The years to come seemed waste of breath,
A waste of breath the years behind
In balance with this life, this death.

W.B. Yeats *An Irish Airman Foresees His Death* (1919)

COMMENT

You should have had no difficulty in finding parallel and antithetical (contrasting) phrases and constructions here. Note also its regular metre and rhyme. (You will find discussion of regular rhythms and rhymes in Unit 4.)

What effect does it have that the poem is written using such parallels and contrasts? Remember the 'I' of the poem is not Yeats: he is imagining the thoughts of his friend. What sort of person is the 'I' of the poem? What are his feelings about the war in which he is engaged? Think about the word 'balance', which is used twice towards the end.

Reflection: Discuss with a friend or in class what you think about the lines: *A lonely impulse of delight / Drove to this tumult in the clouds*. I find them very memorable and moving (and they stand alone without repetition and parallelism in other lines). Compare this insight with other war poems you have studied.

●●● FURTHER READING

1 The website www.poets.org is a useful resource for studying poetry.
2 *100 Best Loved Poems*, edited by Philip Smith (Dover Thrift, 1995).

Self-assessment checklist

Reflect on what you've learnt in this unit and indicate your confidence level between 1 and 5. If you score below 3, revisit that section. Come back to this list later in your course. Has your confidence grown?

	Confidence level	Revisited?
I know how to discuss and write about the difference between literal and figurative language	1	
I can provide some examples of metaphor	4	
I understand what the effects of unusual syntax and omission of words may be in poetry	3	
I can see how important the effects of repetition and parallelism are in poetry	5	

Poetic structures and themes

Learning objectives

In this unit you will:

- examine the structures and themes of poems
- consider in detail the layout of poems on the page and the effect this has
- remind yourself of some important technical vocabulary
- identify and describe two traditional forms of the sonnet.

Language, form, structure, genres, context, style, interpretation.

Before you start

- Think of two short poems you know well and consider how their different sections are put together. You could look back at Unit 1 and Judith Wright's poem about the egrets. How do the two stanzas relate to each other? Is one a development of the other? What did you discover about the two short poems you chose for yourself?

In this unit, you will study the ways in which poetic structures enhance themes, and how the layout of poems differs from prose layout. You will also learn some of the technical vocabulary for discussing the way that lines of poetry are organised.

Theme and structure

The development of a poem's ideas will be made possible by the underpinning structure of the poem as a whole. Where does the poem start, how does it continue and in what way does it reach its conclusion? What relationship do the different sections of the poem have to each other? What effect does this have on the unfolding of the theme of the poem? Always ask these questions about structure, about how the poem is built.

Here are some common poetic structures.

- The poet remembers the past and compares it with the present (e.g. Caribbean poet Olive Senior in *Ancestral Poem*).
- The poet recounts an experience or tells a little anecdote in the first few sections of the poem, and the final stanza or line is a philosophical reflection on the significance of the experience (e.g. many of Philip Larkin's poems).
- The poet speaks directly to the reader, adopting the persona of another person and expressing that person's thoughts in character (e.g. some of Robert Browning's or John Donne's poems).
- The poet expresses many innermost feelings, sharing them with the reader in an intimate way (e.g. many of Sylvia Plath's poems).
- The poet addresses something directly in the second person (*you*), and praises its qualities in an emotional, lyrical way (e.g. John Keats's *Odes*).
- The poem presents two sides of an argument, sometimes with two different voices, sometimes reaching a conclusion (e.g. poems by Andrew Marvell or Christina Rossetti).

- The poem is a description – of a person, place or event – moving from a particular experience to generality, or from general experience to the particular (many poets).

ACTIVITY 3.1

Take three poems that you are studying and summarise the structure of each one.

Reflection: Think about some poems you know and see if you can add any categories to this list.

Layout

Here is an example of prose layout taken from a short story by Katherine Mansfield. You can see by its descriptive quality that it is literary prose, not the language of, say, a newspaper article.

> Over by the breakwater the sea is very high. They pull off their hats and her hair blows across her mouth, tasting of salt. The sea is so high that the waves do not break at all; they thump against the rough stone wall and suck up the weedy, dripping steps.
>
> Katherine Mansfield *The Wind Blows* (1920)

ACTIVITY 3.2

Compare the appearance of this piece of prose (or a page of a novel or short story, or a magazine article), with the following short poem, which is on a similar topic to *The Wind Blows:*

Whitecaps on the bay:
A broken signboard banging
In the April wind.

Richard Wright *This Other World (1998)*

TIP

The poet George Macbeth (1932–1992) said: *A poem is always laid out on the page in a way which has some significance.*

KEY TERM

Concrete poem: Concrete poetry (sometimes called shape poetry) is arranged in such a way that the words on the page form a distinct recognisable shape which adds to the poem's meaning. An example is George Herbert's *Easter Wings* in which the stanzas form the shape of angels' wings when you turn the page sideways.

SAMPLE RESPONSE

In the poem example, the writer has shaped or patterned the words on the page deliberately, making choices for effect. Some of the lines are longer, some are shorter, but none of them use the whole space as the prose example does.

Concrete poems

Poets can sometimes use extreme methods when they lay out a poem on the page, knowing that we will be reading it and assimilating its 'shape'. Here is an example from a poet whose work often deviates from the normal conventions of punctuation and layout. The arrangement of the words symbolises the meaning they express, and thus describes the poem's character. This sort of poem is known as a **concrete poem**.

Reflection: See if you can find some other examples of poems where the layout is significant in the way it creates shapes or patterns on the page. Try writing a descriptive poem yourself in which you vary the size and layout of the words to give a visual image of the subject of the poem.

```
                        e
                   n  o  r  t
Steve is almost    i  c  h  en  .
David talks Good Sense.
Jane is often  v e r y   v a g u e
Lucy. VERY DENSE.
Catty Cora's fffffull of sssspite.
                   O
Dick is rather     D
                   D.
                 a    l
                  n  e
Liz is quite an    G    , but
Alan thinks he's GOD.
```

Attributed to e e cummings

End-stopped lines, open lines, enjambment and caesura

The poem that follows, *Piano* (1918) by D.H. Lawrence, shows that a less extreme layout can be very expressive.

The poet, or his persona, is an adult sitting listening to a singer being accompanied on the piano, probably at a concert. But the experience reminds him of his childhood, when he used to sit under the piano enjoying his mother playing and singing. You need to imagine an old-fashioned wooden upright piano (not a keyboard) with a small child curled up near his mother's legs and feet, sheltered by the wooden keyboard above. (My own son used to do just this when he was small and I was practising!) The poet is deeply affected by the memory of his mother and of being a child, loved and protected; the past overcomes him so that he cannot contain his sense of loss. The singer, in the present time of the poem with the great big black piano, can sing as loudly as she likes, but it is 'in vain'. She cannot affect him. It is his memory of childhood that overcomes his mind. The poet's use of contrasts of the two different pianos and singers representing the past and the present is very effective. He is aware that the experience has un-manned him by reminding him of his childhood and he admits in the final poignant line *I weep like a child for the past*.

You are now going to look and see whether the arrangement of the words into lines helps to communicate his feelings to you. You'll learn some useful technical terms too.

ACTIVITY 3.3

Look carefully at the definitions and then at the poem to find further examples. Discuss them with your friend.

Softly, in the dusk, a woman is singing to me;
Taking me back down the vista of years, till I see
A child sitting under the piano, in the boom of the tingling strings
And pressing the small, poised feet of a mother who smiles as she sings.

In spite of myself, the insidious mastery of song
Betrays me back, till the heart of me weeps to belong
To the old Sunday evenings at home, with winter outside
And hymns in the cosy parlour, the tinkling piano our guide.

So now it is vain for the singer to burst into clamour
With the great black piano appassionato. The glamour
Of childish days is upon me, my manhood is cast
Down in the flood of remembrance, I weep like a child for the past.

D.H. Lawrence *Piano* (1918)

The presence of run-on lines or **enjambments** are very significant in this poem. The reader feels that the poet's control of his thoughts and feelings is gradually breaking down and his emotion is getting the better of him. At first the enjambment is calm and reflective: *till I see / A child sitting under the piano*; then it becomes more emotional: *the insidious mastery of song / betrays me back.* When we reach the final stanza, the floodgates are opened: *the glamour / of childish days is upon me* and finally *my manhood is cast / down in the flood of remembrance*, culminating in the final, simple sentence which admits his overwhelming emotion: *I weep like a child for the past.* (Note that the word 'glamour' has evolved into something different today. If you look it up in a good dictionary you will find the old word meant 'magic'. It has a more superficial meaning today, linked with make-up, women's magazines and fashion.)

There is much more to say about this poem; for example, the use of the present tense throughout, even when he is describing past childhood experiences. This adds to the immediacy of his memory. I also like his use of sound words such as *singing, tingling, boom, tinkling.* The upright acoustic piano is an instrument quite capable of sounding tinkling as well as producing a boom or tingling effect if you are right next to it, especially for a child sitting close. The use of aabb rhyme is very skilful too. (For more on rhyme and sound effects, see Unit 4.) You could consider the contrast of the hymns that the family sings around the old upright piano with the dramatic grand piano at the concert, with a completely different sort of music – almost certainly not religious. His life has changed so much, but he still recalls his childhood experiences with intense emotion.

KEY TERMS

End-stopped line: a line that expresses a complete thought. The second line, although it makes sense on its own, needs the third line to complete it and is therefore an **open line**.

Enjambment: (from a French word meaning 'straddling' or getting its leg into the next line): a run-on line where the meaning crosses a line break.

Caesura: The slight natural pause in a line. Most lines of poetry, unless they are very short, have such a pause. Sometimes this is emphasised by a punctuation mark to indicate where you might take a breath if you were reading.

ACTIVITY 3.4

Read the whole poem again and try to consider what effect this arrangement of the lines has. Discuss this with a partner or in a group.

COMMENT

If the poem was being read out loud to an audience who did not have the text in front of them, the reader would have to be very skilful to create the same effects that you grasp visually.

KEY TERMS

The difference between a **verse** and a **stanza** is that a verse is usually the regular unit of structure within a hymn, song or rhymed poem. As these units can also be called stanzas, the term 'stanza' is extremely useful, as it describes both regular and irregular units. (The word 'verse' can also be used to mean poetry in general, for example US writer Maya Angelou's verse means her poetic works.)

Sonnet: a 14-line poem with particular variations of rhyme, rhythm and structure.

Volta: a change of idea or mood in a sonnet, usually at line 8 or line 12.

Verse and stanza

Regular **verses** or **stanzas** of different lengths have special names as follows:

Number of lines	Name
2	couplet
3	triplet or tercet
4	quatrain
5	quintain
6	sestet
7	septet
8	octave or octet

Larger groupings than this are much more unusual, and might even be called a verse paragraph if there are no breaks.

The sonnet

Poets sometimes follow a traditional pattern in the structures they adopt, and there are many such traditional forms. The one you are most likely to encounter at this stage is the **sonnet**, a 14-line poem with particular variations of rhyme, rhythm and structure. The sonnet is derived from two main varieties: the Petrarchan (or Italian) sonnet and the Shakespearean (or Elizabethan) sonnet. Shakespeare's *Sonnet 73*, whose metaphors you looked at in Unit 2, is a perfect example of a Shakespearean sonnet.

Many poets have adjusted the strict rhyme scheme of the Petrarchan sonnet to suit themselves, but usually they follow one of two structures. The first form is an octave (eight lines) followed by a sestet (six lines), which generally groups the ideas or reflections into these two sets of lines. At this point, there can be a change of idea or mood, known as a **volta**.

A volta can be seen in the following sonnet, *Upon Westminster Bridge* by the Romantic poet William Wordsworth.

Earth has not any thing to shew more fair:
Dull would he be of soul who could pass by
A sight so touching in its majesty:
This City now doth like a garment wear
The beauty of the morning; silent, bare,
Ships, towers, domes, theatres, and temples lie
Open unto the fields, and to the sky;
All bright and glittering in the smokeless air.
Never did sun more beautifully steep
In his first splendour valley, rock, or hill;
Ne'er saw I, never felt, a calm so deep!
The river glideth at his own sweet will:
Dear God! the very houses seem asleep;
And all that mighty heart is lying still!

William Wordsworth *Upon Westminster Bridge* (1802)

An early 19th-century engraving of Westminster Bridge.

The first eight lines (the octave) are linked in sound not only by their rhyming pattern, but also in meaning, all being one sentence. The poet describes the beauty and majesty of the city of London as equalling any natural scene (surprisingly, you may think, for a nature-loving Romantic poet). The final six lines (the sestet) are also linked in their intertwined rhymes and the way in which they become more personal and exclamatory in their tone of wonder and awe. (Note, too, the inversions that emphasise: *Never did sun*, *Ne'er saw I*).

This beautiful poem is not just a good example of a Petrarchan sonnet structure, but worthy of further study of its language and imagery; for example, its use of extended personification and cumulative lists, abstract nouns, parallel phrases and inversions, all of which express and emphasise the meaning with great delicacy.

TIP

The shaping and arrangement of lines in a poem reinforce and support its ideas. You could express this in another way: **form is essential to meaning.**

Here are two examples.

1. The poem *Rules for Beginners* by Carol Rumens uses the same words to end each line but in a different order in each stanza. Look this poem up on the internet – you will be amused by how cleverly she uses the same words at the end of each line: *mother, disco, O level, children, nice* and *adult* in a different order and with a different effect each time.
2. Indian poet Debjani Chatterjee writes a regular villanelle in *Words Between Us*. This is a very old conventional form, with extremely regular patterns of repeated lines, very suitable for poems about love going wrong – all those arguments!

Words Between Us

Language breaks down and sounds have no meaning.
Words splutter, dialogues die in mid air;
you and I cross and there is no meeting.
Eyes do not glance, there is no encounter,
postures are hidden and gestures are bare;
language breaks down and sounds have no meaning.
Even masques expose the fading actor
curtains are drawn but invite no fanfare.
You and I cross and there is no meeting.
We are less than strangers in theatre,
playing separate parts in solitaire.
Language breaks down and sounds have no meaning.
Silence replays the role of the jester.
No more are we one, no longer a pair.
You and I cross and there is no meeting.
Too many scenes have started to fester,
too many pauses are mimes that ensnare.
Language breaks down and sounds have no meaning.
You and I cross and there is no meeting.

Debjani Chatterjee *Words Between Us* (2008)

ACTIVITY 3.5

Look up Shakespeare's sonnets on the internet and note how in each case the 14 lines are divided up (3 quatrains and a couplet.) Sonnet numbers 18, 33, 29, 64, 71, 104, 106 and 138 are recommended as not too tricky!

Reflection: Never forget that the poet's choice of form, structure and language shapes meaning.

This is the second form that traditional sonnets often take: the Shakespearean division of three sets of four lines followed by a final couplet that clinches the main idea of the poem. The brevity and self-contained perfection of the sonnet form are very effective for expressing the poet's thought. You will study closer analysis of the rhythmical and rhyming patterns of poems such as these in Unit 4.

FURTHER READING

1 The Poetry Foundation website is another good source for studying poetry.
2 *Poems of the Great War*, edited by Christopher Navratil (Running Press, 2014).

Self-assessment checklist

Reflect on what you've learnt in this unit and indicate your confidence level between 1 and 5. If you score below 3, revisit that section. Come back to this list later in your course. Has your confidence grown?

	Confidence level	Revisited?
I am able to identify and discuss some common poetic structures	✓	
I can explain the differences in layout between poetry and prose	✓	
I am completely familiar with technical terms such as enjambment, end-stopped and open lines	✓	
I am able to discriminate between the two traditional sonnet forms (Petrarchan and Shakespearean)	✓	

Unit 4

Working with rhythms, sounds and movement

Learning objectives

In this unit you will:

- review and investigate scansion of rhythm, metre, rhyme and pace
- consider sound effects of words and lines
- apply and practise what you've learnt
- analyse the effects of verse forms.

KEY CONCEPTS

Language, form, structure, genres, context, style, interpretation.

Before you start

- Think of two poems which use rhyme at the ends of lines and seem to have a steady, regular rhythm. Now find two which don't use rhyme and whose lines seem to be of different lengths. See if you can describe the different effects of each with a friend and then let your friend have their turn. In this unit, you'll learn the technical vocabulary for discussing these effects.

KEY TERMS

Scansion: the analysis of poems into stanzas, lines and pauses. This includes rhythm and rhyme, and the effects of sound and pace.

Rhythm: The measured flow of words and phrases in verse or prose as determined by the relation of long and short or stressed and unstressed syllables.

The analysis of poems into stanzas, lines and pauses is part of a process called **scansion**. This includes rhythm and rhyme and the effects of sound and pace. Your work here will help you to appreciate the way that word sounds affect meaning. Make sure you're ready!

Sometimes the words 'versification' and 'prosody' are used. Look them up. These are technical terms which cover the area of analysis of verse forms in poetry.

Rhythm

Rhythm comes from an ancient Greek word meaning 'flow'. Nothing could be more familiar to us: all around us, natural and human-made rhythms – repeated and regular – give movement and shape to our lives. The seasons follow each other in a regular pattern; night and day alternate in regular succession; inside our bodies, our hearts and lungs work rhythmically. Clocks strike, car engines tick over and music throbs, all switching between one state and another (tick-tock-tick-tock, dark-light-dark-light and so on).

Reflection: Discuss with a partner or in a group some other examples of rhythms at work in our lives.

Syllables

We dance and sing and make music, creating our own rhythms in an obvious sense, but our language too has its own rhythmical patterns, flowing in an undulating or wave-like arrangement of stronger and weaker elements. Individual words have their own rhythms, depending on how many syllables they have. A syllable is one sound and each word we utter is made up of one or more syllables.

red
know
find
Each has one syllable.

better
pencil
movement
Each has two syllables.

poetry
computer
advising
Each has three syllables.

In each of these words, some of the syllables are stressed, or emphasised, when you say them out loud, and some are not stressed. It is the pattern created by the alternation of the stressed and unstressed syllables that creates the rhythmical effect of words and, in turn, the sentences or lines of poetry that they form. (You may come across the words 'strong' or 'weak' used instead of 'stressed' or 'unstressed'.)

Marking stressed syllables

If you are analysing rhythm and want to show that a syllable is emphasised or stressed, use the mark ´ or ¯ on top of the syllable. If the sound is not stressed, the accepted notation is a ˘ or ° shape. Later, when you become more experienced, you won't need to use these: you'll be able to glance at a poem, speak it in your head and hear at once what the pattern of rhythm is.

The rhythms of poetry are easiest to see when the lines have a regular pattern, and this is your next area for study. Later in this unit, you'll analyse some less regular lines and what is known as **syllabic verse**.

Metre

Metre means 'measure' and you already use it to measure length (centimetre) and distance (kilometre). (In the USA it is spelt *meter.*) In poetry, metre is the measurement of an arrangement of rhythms, and it has its own terminology – which is traditional and common to many languages. When you analyse the pattern of stressed and unstressed syllables in a line of poetry, you are identifying the characteristic metre, especially if it's regular. This is part of the process known as scansion, one aspect of which you are familiar with already – line division. Another aspect of scansion to consider is the rhyme scheme, which you will study later in this unit.

KEY TERMS

Metre: the name for the organisation of rhythms into regular and recurring patterns, such as you find in poetry.

Foot: where two or three syllables recur in a pattern to form a metrical unit of rhythm (the plural is feet).

Trochee: a metrical foot consisting of a stressed syllable followed by an unstressed one. The names of the other feet are on the next pages.

ACTIVITY 4.1

How to scan a regular line of poetry

Identify the syllables in each word and decide whether they are stressed or unstressed, marking them on top with a ¯ or ˘ as you go. Use your common sense about the sound of the word, then read it aloud, exaggerating the whole line slightly to identify the beat.

Count the number of **feet** in the line, marking the divisions between the feet with a vertical line. Marking syllable divisions with a line when you start is helpful, but this won't be necessary when you become more experienced. Similarly, you will soon be able to count the number of feet without using the line divisions, or even marking the stresses, although this will take a little more practice.

Here are some examples for you to try. I've done the first line for you as a guide and marked the syllables (but not the feet). Copy the extract and mark the syllables and feet.

Heard a carol, mournful, holy,
Chanted loudly, chanted lowly,
Till her blood was frozen slowly,
And her eyes were darkened wholly …

An extract from Alfred Lord Tennyson *The Lady of Shallot* (1751)

In this stanza, the recurring pattern (or foot) is ¯ ˘, repeated four times in each line. This pattern is called a **trochee** (pronounced *tro-kee*) or you can call it a trochaic foot. It has a falling rhythm – try reading it out to yourself and listening to the regular rhythms of each line and the way it dies away.

ACTIVITY 4.2

Copy the following verses. Divide the lines into syllables, marking those which are stressed and those which are unstressed. Remember they are all regular patterns.

1

The Curfew tolls the knell of parting day,
The lowing herd wind slowly o'er the lea,
The ploughman homeward plods his weary way,
And leaves the world to darkness and to me.

An extract from Thomas Gray *Elegy Written in a Country Churchyard* (1751)

2

The Assyrian came down like the wolf on the fold,
And his cohorts were gleaming in purple and gold;
And the sheen of their spears was like stars on the sea,
When the blue wave rolls nightly on deep Galilee.

An extract from Lord Byron *The Destruction of Sennacherib* (1815)

3

Touch her not scornfully;
Think of her mournfully,
Gently and humanly;
Not of the stains of her –
All that remains of her
Now is pure womanly.

An extract from Thomas Hood *The Bridge of Sighs* (1844)

A useful verse

More than 200 years ago, the poet Samuel Taylor Coleridge wrote a little verse for his son to teach him the basic feet which you've just been working out. Here it is; I've marked the stresses for you.

> Trōchĕe trīps frŏm lōng tŏ shōrt;
> From long to short in solemn sort
> Slōw **spōndēe** stālks; strōng fōot! yet ill able
> Ēvĕr tŏ cōme ŭp wĭth dāctȳl trĭsȳllăblĕ.
> Ĭāmbĭcs mārch frŏm shōrt tŏ lōng;
> Wĭth ă leāp ănd ă bōund thĕ swĭft ānăpāests thrōng.
>
> Samuel Taylor Coleridge *Metrical Feet – a lesson for a boy* (1834)

If you count the number of feet in the extracts you've analysed, you'll find the following: in your examples there are four feet in the Byron, five feet in the Gray and two in the Hood. Here are the technical names for this analysis:

1 foot = monometer
2 feet = dimeter
3 feet = trimeter
4 feet = tetrameter
5 feet = pentameter
6 feet = hexameter

Longer lines of seven, eight and nine feet are sometimes, but rarely, found. Now you know the correct terminology to describe the metre of a particular regular line: **dactylic tetrameter** or **iambic pentameter**, for example.

Iambic monometer is extremely rare, but an example follows:

Thus I
Passe by,
And die:

This is the first stanza from *Upon His Departure Hence* by Robert Herrick. Most lines of poetry are longer than this, although these spare, depressive lines are very effective for the poet's wretched mood.

The most common regular metre in English poetry is iambic pentameter, which has been used by every great traditional poet in English. Those parts of Shakespeare's plays that are in verse are in iambic pentameter, which is known as **blank verse** when it has no rhyme at the end of each line. You'll see more examples of Shakespeare's language in Sections 3 and 6 of this book. A line of iambics with 6 feet (in other words 12 syllables in all) is known as an **Alexandrine**. The poet Alexander Pope (see Unit 22 for one of his poems) famously characterised the Alexandrine's potential to slow or speed the flow of a poem in a rhyming couplet consisting of an iambic pentameter followed by an Alexandrine:

KEY TERMS

Spondee: an occasional foot with two stressed syllables; obviously you couldn't have a whole poem made up of them. (Why not?)

Iambus: this foot (˘ ¯) is known as an iambus or you can call it an iambic foot. It has a rising rhythm.

Anapaest: this is another rising rhythm, but the pattern here of two unstressed syllables followed by a stressed one (˘ ˘ ¯) is called an anapaest (or anapaestic foot).

Dactyl: the pattern here is known as a dactyl (¯ ˘ ˘) and these are dactylic feet. It has a falling rhythm which seems to suit very well the meaning of the poem's lines here, reflecting on a suicide: doomed and melancholy.

KEY TERMS

Alexandrine verse: a line of iambics with 6 feet – 12 syllables in all.

Blank verse: written in iambic pentameter but has no rhyme at the end of each line.

TIP
Don't confuse blank verse with free verse – see later in the unit. This is one of the commonest mistakes made in student essays on poetry!

Reflection: Knowing the technical vocabulary is helpful and interesting, but your knowledge must always be directed towards appreciation of the effects of what you have observed. It is the means to an end, not an end in itself.

A needless Alexandrine ends the song
That like a wounded snake, drags its slow length along.

Alexander Pope *An Essay on Criticism* (1711)

In this unit, you've moved quickly from the rhythms of individual words to their measurable flow in regular lines of poetry. The terminology you've learnt applies usefully to many older poems, although you will find little irregularities within basically regular pieces.

Variations in the pattern

If you speak lines of poetry out loud and listen to their sound, the natural, conversational rhythms of the words being used to express particular thoughts are obvious. These may not fit a perfectly regular pattern, and you'd have to distort the natural pronunciation and stress of the words to force them into one. If every foot and every line in poetry were perfectly regular, or exactly like all the others, it would be precise in a mathematical sort of way, but it would be monotonous and inflexible.

Now that you know the basic metres, you will be in a position to appreciate variations and feel their effects. Even in lines you consider to be basically regular, there are some small deviations from the basic pattern where the meaning or natural pronunciation demands it.

Some of the most effective lines of poetry contain skilful variations which emphasise important words. The reader's attention is caught because a potentially smooth rhythm has been disrupted.

ACTIVITY 4.3

Analyse the metre of the poem *Piano* by D.H. Lawrence, printed in full in Unit 3. Try scanning it and discuss your analysis with a classmate or your teacher.

It's important to realise that where the stresses come may be a matter of opinion, not scientific fact; in line 5, the word *green* could be unstressed or stressed, for example: if unstressed, that would have been another iambic foot. If both *green* and *fields* are emphasised, it draws attention to their similar sound and lengthens the phrase effectively. Look at the way in which the meaning of the final line is also enhanced by its length: on—on—and out of sight.

The following example is a poem written in basic iambic pentameter with many skilful and effective irregularities. These enhance the poet's emotional state as well as emphasising particularly important words. The poet is Sir Thomas Wyatt, who was writing in the 1530s and 1540s, and the subject is his rejection by women, one in particular, who used to love him. You will note that the passage of centuries has not affected certain basic human themes, although more recent feminist critics might have something to say about his attitudes. The spelling has been modernised and you are given the meaning of words now out of date.

ACTIVITY 4.4

Scan the following poem and see where the stressed syllables are.

They flee from me, that sometime did me seek
With naked foot, stalking in my chamber.
I have seen them gentle, tame, and meek,
That now are wild, and do not remember
That sometime they put themselves in danger
To take bread at my hand; and now they range
Busily seeking with a continual change.

Thanked be fortune it hath been otherwise
Twenty times better; but once, in special,
In thin array, after a pleasant guise,
When her loose gown from her shoulders did fall,
And she me caught in her armes long and small,
Therewith all sweetly did me kiss
And softly said, 'Dear heart, how like you this?'

It was no dream; I lay broad waking:
But all is turned, through my gentleness,
Into a strange fashion of forsaking;
And I have leave to go of her goodness,
And she also to use newfangledness.

But since that I so kindly am served,
I would fain know what she hath deserved.

Sir Thomas Wyatt *They Flee from Me* (1503–1542)

sometime = once
array = clothing
guise = masked ball
small = slender
newfangledness = liking new things

The rhythms of this are complex and subtle. Your scansion will show some regular lines and others where variations occur. Here are three examples, although you probably found more than this.

COMMENT

1 *They flee from me, that sometime did me seek / With naked foot, stalking in my chamber.*

Line 1 is regular iambic pentameter, establishing an overall pattern at the beginning. Line 2 begins within the pattern, with the first two feet iambic. But the word *stalking* upsets this pattern, emphasising the strong determined movement referred to (and emphasising the wild animal images used).

2 *And she me caught in her armes long and small*

At the time of writing the word *armes* would have two syllables, not one as *arms* does today. Imagine this line made regular:

She caught me in her armes long and small.

The line as written by Wyatt has a completely different emphasis: the phrase *she me caught* with its three stresses focuses powerfully on the action and creates a pause after the word *caught* (the caesura) before the delicate description of her long slender arms.

▶

3 *It was no dream; I lay broad waking:*

The line begins regularly enough, but after the caesura pause (*dream*) there are four stressed syllables: I, lay, broad, wak-(ing). (Even if you decide that 'I' should be unstressed, there are still three together.) The poet is reminding himself that he is wide awake, not daydreaming or asleep; these experiences were real and in sharp contrast to his present state of dejection because he has been forsaken. The stressed syllables draw attention to this.

ACTIVITY 4.5

Look in an anthology and see if you can find any poems that don't seem to fit a traditional metrical form. If it's obviously a more modern piece, try counting the syllables. If it appears to have no regular structure at all, is not syllabic and has no rhyme, then it is probably **free verse**.

Syllabic verse

You may have noticed that all the examples of basically regular poetry here were written centuries ago. Of course, there are more recent examples, but it's certainly true that modern and contemporary poets don't use those traditional forms as consistently as their predecessors. More modern poets may have written regular poems in which the regularity is achieved only in the number of syllables per line: this is known as **syllabic verse**. You might well find it easier to scan this more recent verse that doesn't fit the traditional metrical patterns. You count the syllables *whether they are stressed or not* and see whether each line has the same number.

ACTIVITY 4.6

Try counting the syllables in the following lines by Derek Walcott and you will see how easy it is to scan this kind of poetry.

Days thick as leaves then, close to each other as hours
and a sunburnt smell rose up from the drizzled road

The cloud passes high like a god staying his powers – the
pocked sand dries, umbrellas re-open like flowers

Derek Walcott *Midsummer (XVII* and *XXVI)* (1984)

Each line has 12 syllables.

ACTIVITY 4.7

The following poem is complete. Its title, *Metaphors*, is a reference to a figure of speech with which you are familiar, and the poem is a kind of riddle.

I'm a riddle in nine syllables,
An elephant, a ponderous house,
A melon strolling on two tendrils.
O red fruit, ivory, fine timbers!
This loaf's big with its yeasty rising.
Money's new-minted in this fat purse.
I'm a means, a stage, a cow in calf.
I've eaten a bag of green apples,
Boarded the train there's no getting off.

Sylvia Plath *Metaphors* (1966)

Reflection: Count the syllables and the number of lines and guess the riddle!

Reflection: Discuss with a friend what some of the metaphors suggest. I like *Boarded the train there's no getting off*, which is a very apt metaphor for becoming a parent – a lifetime commitment!

COMMENT

The poet, Sylvia Plath, is writing a poem about pregnancy. The nine syllables and nine lines are particularly appropriate in this case, suggesting in their form the length of time in months her physical being is affected and combining well with some very descriptive metaphors.

Haiku

Haiku is a kind of syllabic verse that is great fun to write yourself. It was originally a Japanese verse form consisting of 17 syllables altogether in three lines of five, seven and five syllables. Because it's so short, it can only express one idea, feeling or image, but this can be very effective: it is like a snapshot in words.

Provided that you can count syllables, it isn't difficult to write a haiku of your own. A class were given a list of subjects and here are three of the results, for the titles *Memory, Food* and *Summer*.

The smell of roses	5 syllables
Reminds me of my mother	7 syllables
Filled the house with love	5 syllables
Bring me a coffee,	5 syllables
Chocolate fudge cake with cream!	7 syllables
(Diet starts Monday)	5 syllables
Dust swirls on the road.	5 syllables
The sun has yellowed the fields.	7 syllables
Summer haze floats down.	5 syllables

Free verse

At first sight, free verse has no apparent regularity in its form, but it is in fact designed cunningly in the cadences and breath groups of the speaking voice. It is given shape by the use of repetition, parallelism, enjambment (run-on lines) and pauses, and is as carefully designed as regular iambic pentameters.

ACTIVITY 4.8

Identify examples of repetition, parallelism, enjambment and pauses in the following poems and discuss their effect. The first is an example from D.H. Lawrence, who wrote many free verse poems in contemplation of animals.

Climbing through the January snow, into the Lobo canyon
Dark grow the spruce-trees, blue is the balsam, water sounds
still unfrozen, and the trail is still evident.

Men!
Two men!
Men! The only animal in the world to fear!

They hesitate.
We hesitate.
They have a gun.
We have no gun.

Then we all advance, to meet.

Two Mexicans, strangers, emerging out of the dark and snow
and inwardness of the Lobo valley.
What are you doing here on this vanishing trail?

D.H. Lawrence *Mountain Lion* (1923)

The second example of free verse is from *The First Breakfast: Objects*, by Indian poet Dilip Chitre (born 1938).

This morning is tasteless, colourless, odourless:
I sit alone at the big table.
The waiter is watching me.
In the deadly white dish
lie two fried eggs.
Two containers of salt and pepper.
A bowl of butter. A bowl of jam.
Two oranges. A heap of toast.

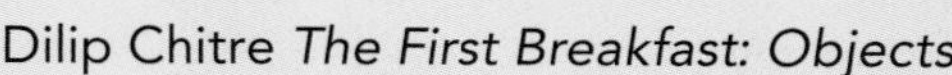

Dilip Chitre *The First Breakfast: Objects*

SAMPLE RESPONSE

In *Mountain Lion*, the word *men* is repeated three times in one- and two-word sentences with exclamation marks to emphasise their destructiveness. The third stanza uses parallelism in *They hesitate. / We hesitate.* and *They have a gun. / We have no gun.* Both parties are uncertain, but only one group has a weapon.

Enjambments are used as part of the natural description at the beginning and end of the extract, lending an emphatic quality to the words *sounds* and *still* in the first section and *snow and inwardness* in the last. Additionally, the first lines of the first and fifth stanzas do not contain a finite verb, giving a sense that the actions of *climbing* and *emerging* are still continuing, helped by the enjambment. If read aloud, the pauses between lines give a dramatic significance to the encounter being described, and the final line of the extract is a direct question, which also lends dramatic emphasis.

The First Breakfast: Objects has an apparently simple construction, but there are a number of repetitions and parallel phrases. Here most of the lines are end-stopped apart from the run-on line about the eggs. Objects are listed without verbs – they just sit there on the table. The verse form makes the simple matter of eating breakfast into something strange and menacing.

TIP

Always try to identify the effects of layout, rhythm and pace in the poems you are analysing, relating them as closely as possible to the development of the poet's thoughts and observations.

Pace

In some poems, the **pace** is regular and steady, and in others there is a perceptible speeding up or slowing down. This affects the meaning of the poem and its atmosphere. In *Mountain Lion*, for example, the section where the poet and his companions meet the strangers is slowed by the short lines and brief repetitive sentences. The Byron poem *The Destruction of Sennacherib* (see the earlier section on Metre) has a swift flowing pace, which drives through the poem, aptly mirroring the movement of advancing troops.

KEY TERM

Pace: a word used to denote the speed at which a verse moves.

KEY TERMS

Rhyme: the agreement in sound between words or syllables. These words rhyme: *night*, *sight*, *fight*; so do these: *flying*, *dying*, *implying*.

KEY TERMS

Internal rhyme: when words within the same line rhyme.

Rhyme and sound effects

When people are asked what gives poetry its special quality, nine out of ten will mention **rhyme** first. This is not only because we remember the nursery rhymes and poems of our childhood, it's also because we know instinctively that sounds are an integral part of the meaning of words in poems.

This echoing of sounds can give pleasure to the hearer and is probably associated with the pleasure we have in music. Even tiny children love rhyme: their delight in nursery rhymes such as *Humpty Dumpty* is largely because the words 'go together' in sound – and, of course, the rhythms are usually very regular too.

Rhyme also helps to structure or shape poetry, organising the verse, binding it together and intensifying the meaning, because words that rhyme are more noticeable than words that don't rhyme. This is an effect similar to a random visual pattern where you would notice a repeated motif immediately.

Some poets never use rhyme, but it is the commonest and one of the oldest forms of metrical device, even so. Your analysis of metre or scansion will therefore often include the consideration of rhyme. It is usually thought of as occurring at the ends of lines of poetry, but it can also occur within lines, in which case it is known as **internal rhyme**.

How to indicate a rhyme scheme

The accepted method of indicating a rhyme scheme is to use small letters of the alphabet to denote the rhyming sounds at the ends of lines. Remember, it's the sound not the spelling of the words which is important; you'll need to say the words over to yourself to see if they rhyme. After all, English spelling being what it is, *cough* rhymes with *off*!

Here is a pair of rhyming couplets:

A mighty creature is the germ, a
Though smaller than the pachyderm. a
His customary dwelling place b
Is deep within the human race. b

Ogden Nash *The Germ* (1902–1971)

If you were to use the terminology you already know, together with this new information, you might say something like this:

The regular iambic tetrameter together with the rhyming couplets aabb create a comic effect here. The pairing of *germ* with *pachyderm* (elephant) is particularly incongruous.

Although accurate, it wouldn't be very helpful just to say 'This poem rhymes aabb' without any analytical comment.

ACTIVITY 4.9

Now try these two stanzas from *The Rime of the Ancient Mariner* by Coleridge. On a copy, mark the metre (it's a regular one) and indicate the rhyme by underlining rhyming words and putting a, b, c, and so on.

And now there came both mist and snow,
And it grew wondrous cold:
And ice, mast-high, came floating by,
As green as emerald.

And through the drifts the snowy clifts
Did send a dismal sheen:
Nor shapes of men nor beasts we ken—
The ice was all between.

Samuel Taylor Coleridge *The Rime of the Ancient Mariner* (1834)

Reflection: Did you notice the internal rhyme in line 3 of the first stanza and lines 1 and 3 of the second? You still say 'It rhymes abcb', but also 'There are internal rhymes in lines 1 and 3 in the second stanza'. The rhythmical and rhyming effects are very obvious in these two stanzas; say them out loud to hear what a thrilling effect they have.

Different rhyme schemes

ACTIVITY 4.10

Look at the following poems, or extracts from poems, and note the rhyme schemes using the alphabetical notation you've learnt.

1

I was angry with my friend:
I told my wrath, my wrath did end.
I was angry with my foe:
I told it not, my wrath did grow.

William Blake *A Poison Tree* (1794)

wrath = anger

2

I have come to the borders of sleep,
The unfathomable deep
Forest where all must lose
Their way, however straight,
Or winding, soon or late;
They cannot choose.

Edward Thomas *Lights Out* (1917)

3

Side by side, their faces blurred,
The earl and countess lie in stone,
Their proper habits vaguely shown
As jointed armour, stiffened pleat,
And that faint hint of the absurd –
The little dogs under their feet.

Philip Larkin *An Arundel Tomb* (1964)

4

These, in the day when heaven was falling,
The hour when earth's foundations fled,
Followed their mercenary calling
And took their wages and are dead.
Their shoulders held the sky suspended;
They stood, and earth's foundations stay;
What God abandoned, these defended,
And saved the sum of things for pay.

A.E. Housman *Epitaph on an Army of Mercenaries* (1914)

5

What passing-bells for these who die as cattle?
Only the monstrous anger of the guns.
Only the stuttering rifles' rapid rattle
Can patter out their hasty orisons.
No mockeries now for them; no prayers nor bells,
Nor any voice of mourning save the choirs,—
The shrill, demented choirs of wailing shells;

And bugles calling for them from sad shires.
What candles may be held to speed them all?
Not in the hands of boys, but in their eyes

▶

Shall shine the holy glimmers of good-byes.
The pallor of girls' brows shall be their pall;
Their flowers the tenderness of patient minds,
And each slow dusk a drawing-down of blinds.

Wilfred Owen *Anthem for Doomed Youth* (1917)

A soldier from the First World War.

COMMENT

Some of these rhyme schemes are simple and others are more complex in the way that the rhyming sounds are interwoven.

1 aabb
2 aabccb
3 abbcac
4 abab (with the a rhymes **feminine** and the b rhymes **masculine**)
5 ababcdcd; effegg

The final example's rhyme scheme is typical of the sonnet form in which the poem is written. (The sonnet is discussed in Unit 3.)

KEY TERMS

Feminine rhyme: a rhyme on two syllables, as Housman uses on *falling* and *calling* and *suspended* and *defended*.

Masculine rhyme: a rhyme on one syllable only, as used by Blake, Thomas and Larkin here.

Half-rhyme or pararhyme

Half-rhyme is widely used in modern and contemporary poetry. Wilfred Owen, whose sonnet you have just analysed for full rhyme, used half-rhyme extensively in other poems he wrote. Half-rhyme and pararhyme are the most common names but there are others, such as near, approximate and slant rhyme.

The effect of half-rhyme

The extract from *An Arundel Tomb* you looked at in activity 4.10 has full rhymes throughout, until its very final lines, where the poet uses a half-rhyme in conclusion.

Time has transfigured them into	a
Untruth. The stone fidelity	b
They hardly meant has come to be	b
Their final blazon, and to prove	c (half-rhyme)
Our almost-instinct almost true:	a
What will survive of us is love.	c (half-rhyme)

Sometimes the last line of this poem is taken out of its context and quoted to prove a point (an optimistic point about human nature), but it can't be read in such a way. The poet's use of the two *almosts* in the penultimate (second to last) line warns the reader that the statement is being subtly qualified and this is enhanced by the poet's use of the half-rhyme on *prove* and *love*. You'll notice that the half-rhyme here takes the form of an **eye-rhyme**. In the following stanza (the beginning of *Strange Meeting* by Wilfred Owen), the half-rhymes are mostly not eye-rhymes.

KEY TERMS

Ear-rhyme: a true rhyme when spoken aloud, but looks as if it shouldn't be by its spelling. *Choirs* and *shires* in Owen's poem are like this (as are the words *cough* and *off* mentioned earlier).

Eye-rhyme: a rhyme that looks as if it should rhyme from the spelling but doesn't – there are no examples of this in these poems, but the words *rough* and *cough* would be eye-rhymes.

Half-rhyme: repeats the final consonant sound in words without the vowel sound corresponding. Where the use of a full rhyme may give an impression of confidence and completeness, a half-rhyme can help to create a sense of unease or disturbance. You may also come across the terms *imperfect*, *near*, *oblique*, *off* and *slant rhyme* – they mean the same.

ACTIVITY 4.11

Find the words which half-rhyme at the ends of these lines:

It seemed that out of battle I escaped
Down some profound dull tunnel, long since scooped
Through granites which Titanic wars had groined.
Yet also there encumbered sleepers groaned,
Too fast in thought or death to be bestirred.
Then, as I probed them, one sprang up, and stared
With piteous recognition in fixed eyes,
Lifting distressful hands as if to bless.
And by his smile, I knew that sullen hall;
By his dead smile I knew we stood in Hell.

Wilfred Owen *Strange Meeting* (circa 1918)

The half-rhyme here runs aabb, as it does throughout this war poem in which the poet imagines meeting someone in the afterlife who turns out to be the enemy he had killed on the battlefield. The sombre tone of the poem depends on the skilful use of pararhyme, where perfection and clarity are always out of reach and the dreamlike atmosphere is central.

ACTIVITY 4.12

Here is the middle stanza of a poem by Elizabeth Jennings called *The Enemies*, where the mysterious, disturbing quality of the invasion is enhanced by the use of loose half-rhymes. You might not notice them unless you look closely. Find the half-rhymes and note the rhyme scheme in the usual way (using a, b, c, and so on).

Now in the morning all the town is filled
With stories of the swift and dark invasion;
The women say that not one stranger told
A reason for his coming. The intrusion
Was not for devastation:
Peace is apparent still on hearth and field.

Elizabeth Jennings *The Enemies*

The pattern of half-rhymes runs ababba.

Look back at the short poem about the man practising tai-chi in Unit 1 and you will find many half-rhymes at the ends of lines.

Other effects of sound

Rhyme is only one of several features of language in poetry which use the sounds of words to influence or reflect their meaning. Among these features are **alliteration**, **assonance**, **consonance** and **onomatopoeia**.

Alliteration

Alliteration is the repetition of consonant sounds, especially at the beginning of words; poets have used it for centuries. In Old English verse (before the Norman invasion of 1066), alliteration was an essential part of the metrical scheme of poems and even more important than rhyme. It is still used widely for particular effects. A modem poet such as Ezra Pound, whose poem *In a Station of the Metro* you have already studied in Unit 1, wrote a version of an Old English poem called *The Seafarer* and he included all the alliteration from the original; you can appreciate its flavour without having to learn the old language. Here's part of it (the letters which alliterate are underlined):

KEY TERMS

Alliteration: the repetition of consonant sounds, especially at the beginning of words.

Assonance: the repetition of vowel sounds within words that have different consonants. There is assonance in the long 'o' sound in the following words: *home*, *road*, *bone* and *foe*.

Consonance: identical consonants but different vowels, such as *slip* and *slop*, *creak* and *croak*. The kind of half-rhyme used by Wilfred Owen in *Miners* (see Unit 6) is largely a kind of consonance.

Onomatopoeia: There are a number of words whose sound seems to imitate their meaning, so that the sound reflects the sense of the word. That is the definition of onomatopoeia, or echoism as it is sometimes called. English is a very onomatopoeic language and perfectly suited to poetry.

May I, for my own self, song's truth reckon,
Journey's jargon, how I in harsh days
Hardship endured oft.
Bitter breast-cares have I abided, …

Ezra Pound *The Seafarer* (1915)

The first lines of James Elroy Flecker's poem *The Old Ships* (1915) alliterates evocatively:

I have seen old ships sail like swans asleep …

Alliteration can also be an essential ingredient of the fun in comic verse or tongue-twisters such as *Peter Piper picked a peck of pickled pepper* or *She sells sea shells on the sea shore*.

The effect of individual sounds

There's more to analysing the effect of these sound patterns than just underlining sounds that are the same as each other. The speech sound itself which is being repeated may well have a particular effect, and you should try to identify this. Here are examples of some of the sounds:

- ***k***, ***g***, ***ch***, ***qu***, ***st***, ***ts*** These can be hard, violent sounds, noisy and harsh: try saying *crag*, *clock*, *biggest*, *stick*; a similar effect can be found in t and d.
- ***m***, ***n***, ***ng*** These are humming, singing, musical sounds that can also have a gently sinister effect: *humming*, *moaning*, *murmuring*.
- ***f***, ***w*** These sound soft and light: *flow*, *fly*, *winnow*, *furrow*.

You could continue in this vein: *z* sounds harsh and *sh* sounds soothing; long vowels sound slower and more peaceful, while short ones give the impression of quick movement.

You may feel that such close examination of English sounds is slightly ridiculous. Certainly, if you've never really considered the sounds of our words, some of the claims made here may seem far-fetched. But when several groups of students were asked which ten words they thought were the most beautiful-sounding in the English language, some words seemed to be on everyone's list. They were all words whose sound reflected and intensified their meaning: words like *cool*, *moon*, *velvet*, *softness* and *mellow*. So it seems that some words have a powerful effect when meaning and sound coincide.

Reflection: What would your ten words be?

ACTIVITY 4.13

Review what you've learnt in this unit and the previous one, then read and enjoy the sounds and rhythms of the following lines, the first stanza of T.S. Eliot's poem *Preludes*:

The winter evening settles down
With smell of steaks in passageways.
Six o'clock.
The burnt-out ends of smoky days.
And now a gusty shower wraps
The grimy scraps
Of withered leaves about your feet
And newspapers from vacant lots;
The showers beat
On broken blinds and chimney-pots,
And at the corner of the street
A lonely cab-horse steams and stamps.

And then the lighting of the lamps.

T.S. Eliot *Preludes* (1917)

Under timed conditions, you do not have time for extensive comment on rhythms, rhymes and sound effects. But a few well-chosen examples will enhance your work immensely.

FURTHER READING

1. The www.haikupoetry.org has many enjoyable examples of this form.
2. *Stressed Unstressed: Classic Poems to ease the mind*, edited by Jonathan Bate and Paula Byrne (Harper Collins, 2016).

Self-assessment checklist

Reflect on what you've learnt in this unit and indicate your confidence level between 1 and 5. If you score below 3, revisit that section. Come back to this list later in your course. Has your confidence grown?

	Confidence level	Revisited?
I understand the effect of syllables, stressed and unstressed, and know how to indicate them		
I can discuss and write about the effects of different metres		
I am able to explain the different rhyme schemes used in poetry		
I realise the effect of individual sounds and sound patterns in poetry		

Poetry unseens

Learning objectives

In this unit you will:

- clarify how you can prepare to approach unseen poetry questions with confidence
- study the poetry unseen checklist
- develop critical ideas by annotating passages
- compare the work of students and the assessments of it, adding your own thoughts.

KEY CONCEPTS

Language, form, structure, genres, context, style, interpretation.

Before you start

- Review Unit 1, which takes you back to basics. Remember how much you've learnt since then and feel confident!

If you are taking the 9695 AS Level course, you will now have a compulsory unseen paper, which has poetry in it. In this unit, you have some guidelines to help you to frame your responses so that you feel confident about answering on a poem you haven't seen before. First you have to read and appreciate the poem, then to write on it, so there are two different kinds of activity here: considering the elements of the poem and how they fit together; and writing a successful essay incorporating these ideas.

It's natural to feel apprehensive. You may be thinking 'What if I don't understand the poem?', but remember, what has been set will be just right for you at your level, and all the other students are in just the same situation. If there are any unusual words, the meanings will be given to you. Examiners are not trying to catch you out, they want to give you the best opportunity to show what you can do. You won't be expected to know about the historical context or the writer's life – what is being tested is the effect of the words and forms chosen by the poet. All the work you've done on your poetry set texts and all your previous reading of poems will help you too.

In this unit, you will have reminders of the different aspects of a poem that should be considered in any critical appreciation and examples of students' essays on unseen poems at different levels.

Take an active approach to analysis

An unseen exercise tests close reading, so you need to annotate the poem: underlining, highlighting, linking, commenting in the margin. It becomes a working document and will be the basis of your answer.

Use a highlighter and coloured pens to pick out and underline different aspects of the poem; for example, metaphors, repetition, rhyme and so on. You will immediately have a sense of entering into the word choices made by the poet.

Every poem is different, so you need to be flexible

Figure 5.1 will remind you of what you need to think about, but each poem creates its own little world and sometimes you'll want to say more about the figures of speech because it is a very metaphorical poem; at other times you feel the very regular metre and rhyme are overwhelming, and you'll try to foreground that and the sorts of effect it has. The examples later in this unit demand this different approach, as you'll see.

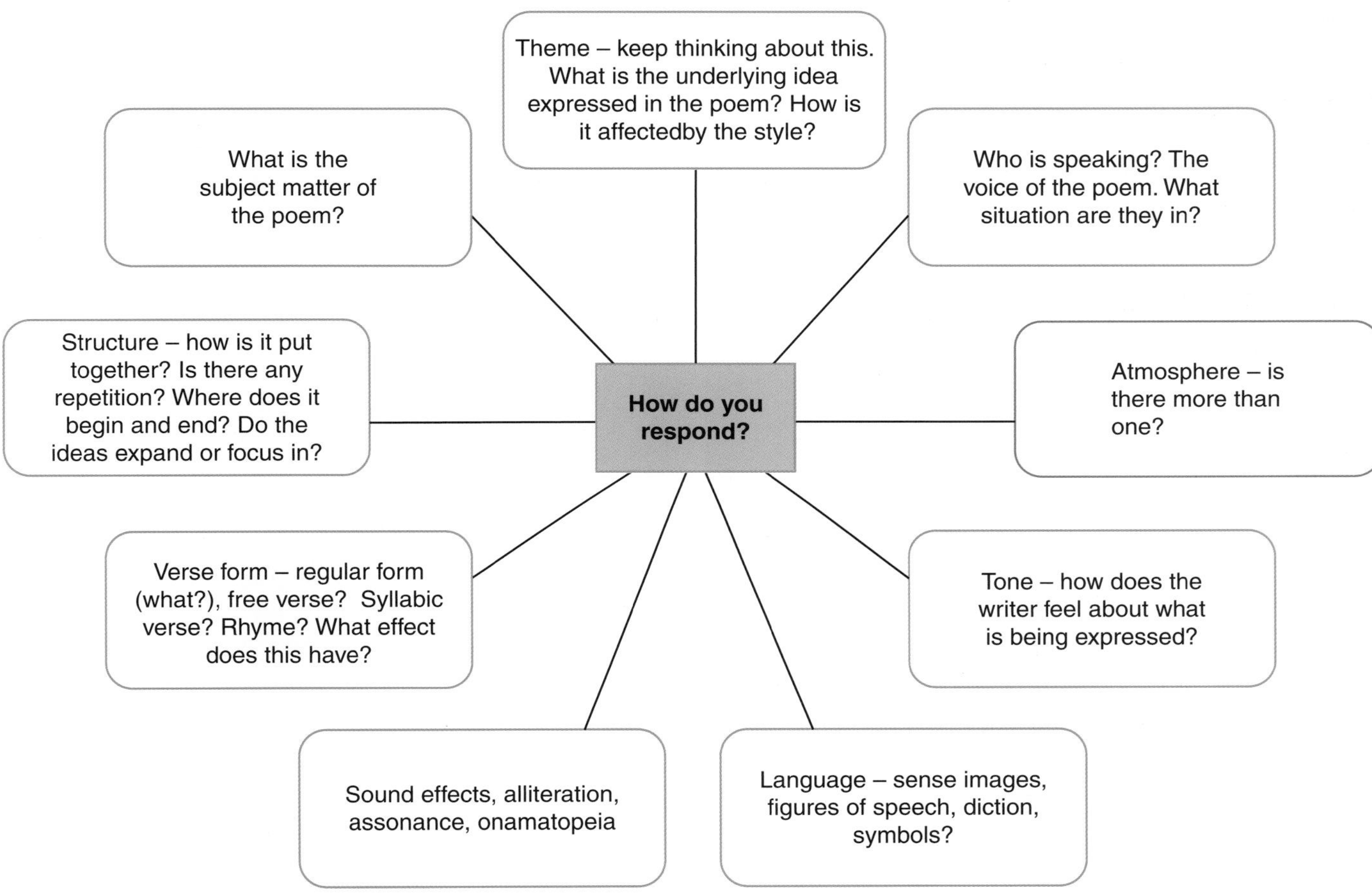

Figure 5.1: Checklist for analysing poetry.

ACTIVITY 5.1

Make a copy of the following poem by Thomas Hardy if you want to keep your textbook clean! Read the poem three times and then, using your highlighter and coloured pens, pinpoint any repetitions, the rhyme and the use of alliteration and assonance. I have done a few for you, but there are many examples throughout. Thomas Hardy is well-known for his use of sound effects which link words in meaning as well as sound – you won't find many poems these days with as many sound effects as this one. Make notes on other aspects as you go.

Beyond the Last Lamp *(Near Tooting Common)*

I

While rain, with eve in partnership, a
Descended darkly, drip, drip, drip, a
Beyond the last lone lamp I passed b
    Walking slowly, whispering sadly, c
    Two linked loiterers, wan, downcast: b
Some heavy thought constrained each face, d
And blinded them to time and place. d

II

The pair seemed lovers, yet absorbed
In mental scenes no longer orbed
By love's young rays. Each countenance
    As it slowly, as it sadly
    Caught the lamplight's yellow glance,
Held in suspense a misery
At things which had been or might be.

III

When I retrod that watery way
Some hours beyond the droop of day,
Still I found pacing there the twain
    Just as slowly, just as sadly,
    Heedless of the night and rain.
One could but wonder who they were
And what wild woe detained them there.

Makes it sound real

Rhyme (same throughout)

first person poem

What do you notice about this line?

but the poet isn't blind to them

dark, miserable evening – pathetic fallacy?

the two people don't seem to be young

He's wondering what they are talking about

when he comes back they are still there

keeps repeating slowly and sadly

IV

Though thirty years of blur and blot
Have slid since I beheld that spot,
And saw in curious converse there
        Moving slowly, moving sadly
        That mysterious tragic pair,
Its olden look may linger on –
All but the couple; they have gone.

V

Whither? Who knows, indeed... And yet
To me, when nights are weird and wet,
Without those comrades there at tryst *
        Creeping slowly, creeping sadly,
        That lone lane does not exist.
There they seem brooding on their pain,
And will, while such a lane remain.

Thomas Hardy *Beyond the Last Lamp (Near Tooting Common)* (1911)

he tells us this happened 30 years ago

They could be dead by now; the place is the same

Questioning

* a secret meeting of lovers

Association of the place, the people, + the poet

KEY TERM

Pathetic fallacy: the term used to describe the literary presentation of inanimate objects in nature as reflecting human feelings. Here the writer uses it to link state of mind and weather.

ACTIVITY 5.2

Here are two student analyses of the poem. Read them carefully and then have a look at the marginal comments made on each as well as the summative comment at the end.

STUDENT RESPONSE A

This poem by Thomas Hardy is about the poet seeing lovers together in a place and then at the end of the poem they have gone and he still doesn't know what they were talking about. They seem worried. He uses a lot of alliteration in the poem and it rhymes all the way through with a regular verse form. The rhyme goes aa bb cc with a line in the middle that doesn't rhyme.

The poem is a sort of narrative as Hardy tells the story of the sad lovers but we don't really know all the details as he never tells us what they are saying. However he uses a lot of words which suggest sadness such as *'misery'*, *'woe'* and *'sadness'*, he also says they are a *'tragic pair'* so we know there is some sad love story going on. He also says *'brooding on their pain'*.

He watches them and then suddenly jumps 30 years to when he goes back and they aren't there of course, but he does associate them with the place.

There are quite a few repetitions in the poem and some odd old fashioned words such as *'wither'* and *'tryst'* so you can tell it was written a long time ago – also there are is no traffic which there certainly would be today, although there is a street light.

I think the poem has a sad tone and atmosphere, but I would like it better if I knew what they were sad about.

The student has identified some elements of the poem such as diction associated with sadness, with some useful examples. The idea that this is a story – a narrative – is right, but perhaps it's a narrative about the poet as well as the lovers. The writer has little to say about the voice of the poem.

The same is true here. The student has noticed the time shift, but does not relate it to the poet's experience. This could be developed to a comment about the poet and the place itself and our relationship with places and their associations for us.

There are many repetitions, but no examples are given and there is no discussion of them. This observation should be in a separate paragraph, not with the contextual points which follow.

'Tone' and 'atmosphere' are important aspects of poems which are worth more development than they are given in this hasty summing up, although there is some personal response to the poem.

Some historical context is hinted at here, which could be developed into further personal response to the situation – perhaps a timeless one.

Making a comment on the rhyme and alliteration is not the most convincing introduction to a poetry essay, although what is said is a valid observation. The student has noticed that the line in the middle of each stanza doesn't rhyme, and it would be worth exploring this in more detail, but in a later paragraph.

Reflection: Read the poem again, revisit the checklist in Figure 5.1 and think about ways in which this writer's essay could be improved.

COMMENT

The essay shows some close attention and observation of elements of style, but dashes them down rather randomly without considering their effect or exploring them in detail. Closer use of examples from the poem would help.

STUDENT RESPONSE B

Hardy writes a poem about two lovers in a specific place (near Tooting Common) and from the very beginning we feel that this is an experience he himself had; the voice of the poem is his own and he gives us an insight into his own thoughts and feelings, although the lovers – the subject of this poem – are never given a voice. He is full of sympathy for them and the tone of the poem is mournful throughout.

The poem's structure takes us from the initial sighting of the two lovers under the lamplight on a dark and miserable evening ('drip, drip, drip') to another sighting of them a few hours later when he comes past again, to thirty years later when he goes back to the place and remembers them, though they of course are no longer there. There is a sort of cyclical pattern where the poet feels that the lane '*does not exist*' unless the lovers are there – they are linked to that place forever in his mind.

This is a poem with a very regular scheme of rhymes and sounds and they are used to enhance the sense of repetition of the action. The rhyme scheme, which is aa bb dd, is completely regular but the middle line of each stanza does not rhyme (c) but has the repeated idea of '*slowly*' and '*sadly*' in each stanza. This is very effective. It's as if the regular action contains the slow sad movements of the lovers as they walk. As well as rhyme, the poem is full of alliteration, which is a dominant feature of the language, linking the words in a wistful sound right through the poem, creating the sad tone and mood.

The language creates a kind of pathetic fallacy with the rain and the evening producing just the right setting for a sad tale. The rain and the evening are personified as '*in partnership*' and the light of the street lamp is also personified '*the lamplight's yellow glance*' Everything around the lovers is in sympathy with them.

I find it very touching that we do not know why the lovers are there and what they are discussing. Hardy calls them '*mysterious*' and '*tragic*' and this is what he achieves in the poem – we often observe people who we will never meet and never know their lives but can feel sympathy for them. It is also true that some places are forever associated with people who were there at one time and like ghosts continually haunt the place. Hardy shows great sympathy, but he has also made a story out of these lovers and shared his feelings with us. A very sympathetic poem with beautiful sounds.

A good introduction which focuses clearly on the poet's experience as well as the two lovers. The mention of the tone in the introduction is apt as this is such a dominant feature.

The comment on structure picks up the focus on the poet and shows the time structure of the poem and its development. The 'cyclical structure' is a perceptive point and could be developed further.

This is a concise paragraph with a number of related points. It effectively interprets meaning relative to sound effects and rhyme, although it would be helpful to have further brief examples of these. In a poem such as this, there are many examples of alliteration but only a few need to be used as illustration to confirm the point. More general comment, with illustration, on the metre/rhythm and verse form of the poem would be helpful here.

Effective comment on language and pathetic fallacy. A few more word choices could be explored, with examples.

Strong personal response to the poem, related to the theme of people in time and place.

COMMENT

This essay has a very good overview of the poem and an appreciation of the way in which the elements work together to produce an effect. Some further examples of suitable text and the metrical form of the poem could have been used, but the essay is coherently structured and well-expressed and is a strong answer.

ACTIVITY 5.3

This poem by Indian poet Sampurna Chatterji is very different in its setting and theme. Copy it and annotate it as you have done before. You'll find your notes are very different from the ones on Hardy's poem!

Her balcony bears an orchid smuggled in a duffle bag from Singapore. Its roots cling to air. For two hours	third person, not first is the orchid a symbol? What of?
every morning the harsh October sun turns tender at its leaves. Nine steps from door to balcony and already she is a giant insect fretting in a jar.	metaphor
At one side of her one-room home, a stove, where she	physical description of the room
cooks dal* in an iron pan. The smell of food is good. Through the window bars the sing-song of voices high then low in steady arcs. With his back to the wall, a husband, and a giant stack of quilts, threatening to fall. Sleeping room only, a note on the door should have read, readying you for cramp. Fall in and kick off your shoes.	*soup made from lentils, beans or peas has two meanings! Rhyme here, also two meanings Uses the second person here
Right-angled to this corridor with a bed, trains make tracks to unfamiliar sounding places. Unhidden by her curtains, two giant pigs lie dead, or asleep, on a dump.	Vivid visual images
Every day the city grows taller, trampling underfoot students wives lovers babies. The boxes grow smaller. The sea become a distant memory of lashing wave and neon, siren to seven islands*, once. The sky strides inland on giant stilts, unstoppable, shutting out the light.	internal rhyme No commas in this list personification of sky Paradox? Sky shut out light?

Sampurna Chattarji *Boxes* (2008)
*siren = a mythical creature who lured sailors to their deaths
seven islands = islands south of Mumbai, now part of the city

ACTIVITY 5.4

Read the following critical account of the poem.

SAMPLE RESPONSE

The poem *Boxes* creates an image of a couple being shut into a small flat in a city – Mumbai – hardly able to move and cut off from the natural world, just as if they were imprisoned in a box, so the title is very apt. The descriptions are very vivid with sense impressions and the atmosphere is claustrophobic.

The poem is structured in four stanzas, beginning with the narrative of her and her husband. The first one suggests that they have only just arrived from Singapore, from where she has smuggled an *orchid* in her bag. She is finding the lack of space confining and dehumanising, as we can see from the metaphor that she is *a giant insect fretting in a jar*. She then describes in stanzas 2 and 3, using sense images, the environment of the *one-room home, nine steps from door to balcony*. The only good sense is the smell of the food she is cooking, but there are sounds of other people and trains, the sight outside of two pigs, possibly dead, on a dump and a sense of terrible restriction of space affecting her and her husband. The room is really more of a *corridor*, their bedding doesn't fit in and the window bars on the windows make it seem like a prison. In the final stanza, the poem moves beyond the flat and their personal lives into a wider realisation that everyone in the city is in a similar situation, cramped and cut off from natural space and living. This has the effect of broadening the theme so that the reader feels the poet's concern with cities as horrible places for any human being to live in.

As far as language goes, the poet does not write in the first person 'I', which is effective because it makes her observations seem more objective and reasonable. For just two lines at the beginning of stanza 3, she uses the second person 'you' which involves the reader directly. We too would have to *kick off* our shoes if we were there. The orchid is a beautiful flower and a symbol of beauty from somewhere else – perhaps of herself, because its roots *cling to air*, perhaps as she is having to do, to stay alive in this horrible box. The insect simile is a contrast with the orchid. The city is personified as trampling all kinds of people, effectively showing its evil intentions. The final image of the sky is interesting as it is a paradox – how can the sky be shutting out the light instead of letting it in? It seems like a huge giant taking all the light with it inland away from the city by the sea.

The poem has four five-line stanzas that have usually 12 or 13 syllables in each line, so it is not free verse. There are few rhymes: *wall* and *fall* in stanza 2 show the link between being confined and life collapsing and the internal rhyme of taller and smaller in stanza 5 draws attention to the way that the increasing size of the city affects the living space of the inhabitants. The second line of the last stanza gives us a list of people with no commas, making them seem like a vast mass of different kinds of people all thrown together.

This is a very descriptive poem which makes me think about city life and how hard it can be for the inhabitants. However, the poet does not make over-emotional statements but uses language skilfully to show us the realities of life in a cramped flat.

Reflection: Now discuss with a partner the good points of the essay and any ways you think it could be improved.

ACTIVITY 5.5

Look back at Figure 5.1. Using different colours for each element on the checklist (theme, voice of the poem, structure, and so on) underline in the chosen colour those parts of the essay that refer, however briefly, to each element. Then use a highlighter to highlight each quotation from the poem. You will easily be able to see coverage of points and illustrations.

FURTHER READING

1. The Poet's Corner section of 'theotherpages.org' (www.theotherpages.org/poems) is a good text resource.
2. *Great Short Poems*, edited by Paul Negri (Dover Thrift, 2000)

Self-assessment checklist

Reflect on what you've learnt in this unit and indicate your confidence level between 1 and 5. If you score below 3, revisit that section. Come back to this list later in your course. Has your confidence grown?

	Confidence level	Revisited?
I know the requirements of the unseen poetry question		
I have assimilated the checklist of important elements for discussion in Figure 5.1		
I have studied carefully the two essays on the Thomas Hardy poem and the marker's notes and can learn much from them		
I have read and discussed the sample response to the question (Activity 5.4) on the poem Boxes		

Unit 6
Timed poetry essays, critical and passage type

Learning objectives

In this unit you will:

- recognise how you can be prepared to answer questions on your poetry set texts under timed conditions
- organise your work into helpful categories
- engage with sample and students' answers
- account for the marginal comments made.

KEY CONCEPTS

Language, form, structure, genres, context, style, interpretation.

Before you start

- Review your checklist of poetry elements (see Figure 5.1 in Unit 5) and discuss them with your partner. See if you can both write the list down from memory!

Choice of questions

If you are taking the Cambridge AS level course, you normally have a choice between two kinds of questions: the critical essay on your set text and the passage question, or close critical commentary, on a poem taken from it. In this unit, you will be given some guidelines on both alternatives, so that you feel confident about answering either type under timed conditions. You may be studying a particular poet whose work has characteristic features that you have discussed as part of your preparation. You may be using an anthology, a collection of poems, some of which have ideas, or themes, in common. In either case, you have the advantage that you will have studied the poems beforehand and so you will be writing from a position of knowledge and understanding.

If you are in the first year of any advanced course such as A Level or the Pre-U, you will often have exercises of this kind to give you practice in poetry criticism, so the examples here are just as helpful for you.

Studying an anthology

An anthology is a collection of poems that will not be by the same writer or even necessarily on the same topic. However, there will be some links between them and it is these that the question setter will exploit.

Studying an individual poet

The work of an individual poet will vary, but there will be some concerns that the writer constantly returns to, and you will be able to find these once you know the whole work well. Additionally, there will be characteristic features of style that you come to identify as typical of your particular poet. So with Ted Hughes, for example, you would consider poems about animals, weather and the violence of nature among other topics together with elements of style such as close observation, powerful imagery and careful attention to poetic form.

Study techniques

Whether you are studying an anthology or a collection by one poet, the techniques described here will be helpful.

Begin with individual poems

It is best to read, discuss and analyse individual poems first so that you appreciate each one before you embark on attempting to find links between them. Once you have studied and enjoyed a range of poems, you will begin to see that they have thematic or stylistic links. For example, your anthology may contain a number of poems about an aspect of nature or use the natural environment as a background; there may be poems about childhood, love, death, time or age, or even something as apparently mundane as an insect. Your poet may typically use regular verse forms and rhyme, or syllabic forms or free verse.

Active learning: create headings

List the poems that could be used if there is a question on a particular topic. In the anthology *Songs of Ourselves, Vol 2* for example, you could begin your list with some obvious topics as follows, going on later to more complex ones:

Love and family

The Uncles; On My First Daughter; Sons, Departing; Ode on Melancholy; The Forsaken Wife; I Find No Peace; Amoretti; Verse written on her Death-bed

Travel, migration and society

These Are The Times We Live In; The Border Builder; The Migrant; The White House

Sleep and death

I Dream of You, to Wake; Care-charmer Sleep; To Sleep; This is My Play's Last Scene; Last Lines; Requiem

Reflection: Consider what other categories you could create from this selection.

ACTIVITY 6.1

If you are studying an anthology, create a list or matrix of poem topics. Be prepared to find a poem that doesn't seem to fit the mould, as well as one or two that appear in two or three lists. In the case of an individual poet, try to divide the poems into topics and also identify recurrent features of style.

Poetry critical essay

ACTIVITY 6.2

Here is an example of a critical essay question and a sample response. Before you read the essay, read the two poems *Esther's Tomcat* and *The Jaguar* by Ted Hughes. Extracts from the poems are provided here.

Daylong this tomcat lies stretched flat
As an old rough mat, no mouth and no eyes,
Continual wars and wives are what
Have tattered his ears and battered his head.

Like a bundle of old rope and iron
Sleeps till blue dusk. Then reappear
His eyes, green as ringstones: he yawns wide red,
Fangs fine as a lady's needle and bright.

Ted Hughes *Esther's Tomcat* (1960)

The apes yawn and adore their fleas in the sun.
The parrots shriek as if they were on fire, or strut
Like cheap tarts to attract the stroller with the nut.
Fatigued with indolence, tiger and lion
Lie still as the sun. The boa-constrictor's coil
Is a fossil. Cage after cage seems empty, or
Stinks of sleepers from the breathing straw.
It might be painted on a nursery wall.

Ted Hughes *The Jaguar* (1957)

Ted Hughes (1930–1998).

SAMPLE RESPONSE

Essay: Several poems in your Ted Hughes selection are about animals. Referring to two poems, discuss how they explore this subject.

The two animal poems I have chosen are both by Ted Hughes and both are about cats: the first a domestic cat who spends his days sleeping inside and his nights roaming around outside; and the second a wild member of the cat family, a jaguar, who is in a cage at the zoo. Although at first sight their lives are very different, they share a kind of fierce intensity which, in the poet's eyes, lifts them beyond the everyday world and physical context in which they spend their lives.

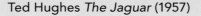

> A clear introduction to both poems, showing a link between them.

The structure of the poem *Esther's Tomcat* introduces the cat asleep in the house with vivid, visual similes, looking like *an old rough mat* or *like a bundle of old rope and iron*, but when he wakes in the evening, another identity appears – one with legendary qualities: *fangs fine as a lady's needle*; *eyes, green as ringstones*.

> Good use of textual detail throughout.

The poet tells a legend about a fierce tomcat before describing this particular cat's nocturnal activities: fighting, killing and mating, always somehow managing to escape danger. The final stanza images the cat on the rooftops, *his mind on the*

> Textual detail continues.

Helpful consideration of structure, figures of speech and diction, with examples.

moon stalking over the round world as it sleeps. This structure emphasises the range of environments related to the cat: its apparently innocent domestic life, sleeping during the day; its historical antecedents – the legendary story of the vicious tomcat that attacked a knight; the present cat's aggression and dominance; and ends with an image which suggests its mysterious, universal qualities: crying out and asserting its individuality while the world sleeps. These environments are contrasted throughout. Far from being an ordinary old pussy cat, it is something quite different: The poet's language is very rich in similes and metaphors which enhance the image of the cat: the diction of *old rope and iron* sounds tough but uncouth; as soon as his glowing eyes open the image of jewels is used, and his fangs are like a lady's needle, a medieval image which links with the legend of the cat and the knight in the next stanza, a legend which is somehow made more real in the reference to an actual place, *Barnborough*, and the fact that the bloodstain is still there *after hundreds of years*. The onomatopoeic word *grallochs* (which means disembowels) sums up the vicious nature of the tomcat's aggression; his superiority over any dog is unquestionable.

Close attention to the poem's sound effects.

The poet uses four-line stanzas which vary in length between eight and ten syllables, although the longest line goes to 11 syllables – appropriately the line describing the knight trying desperately to fight off the cat. There are occasional rhymes such as *bright*, *knight* and *bite*, which link the images of the cat in sound as well as meaning, biting the knight with his sharp bright teeth, and there are a number of half-rhymes such as *quiet* and *pullet*, *moon* and *men*, the first emphasising the cat's slyness, the second expanding the range of the cat's activities at night. Hughes makes much use of enjambments throughout the poem which give weight to the words that follow the pause, most notably in the gap between stanzas 4 and 5 which climaxes with the phrase *Is unkillable*, an explicit statement of fact – no metaphor here, although perhaps some hyperbole (exaggeration). *Esther's Tomcat* is an ironical title because it reminds us that although we think we own animals they are individuals with their own integrity, their own lives and perhaps a significance beyond the normal.

Useful discourse marker.

The Jaguar also has a structure which moves from the everyday world – here the zoo – to the globe itself in the final stanza. Contrasts between the different environments are also emphasised: the other animals are described vividly in metaphorical language as shallow, noisy or lazy, with none of the intense vitality of the jaguar, which attracts visitors to its cage. The parrots are like *cheap tarts*, the apes *yawn*, the lion and tiger *lie still as the sun* – powerful but unmoving. The whole is like a picture *painted on a nursery wall* – colourful but static, childish. The people are like children too – the crowd stares *like a child at a dream*. In contrast, the jaguar is imaged in intense paradoxical images, *the drills of his eyes*, *on a short fierce fuse*, the *eye satisfied to be blind in fire*, *by the bang of blood in the brain deaf the ear* – this last line illustrates the powerful one-syllable words linked by alliteration of the *b* sound, which so contrast with the leisurely lines describing the other animals such as *fatigued with indolence* …. The jaguar's pacing does not draw attention to his caged state, but rather the opposite: *there's no cage to him* as he strides, *his stride is wildernesses of freedom*, an evocative metaphor of space and liberty which contrasts entirely with the closed world of cage and zoo. The poet compares him to a *visionary* in a cell, a holy man whose imagination takes him way beyond the narrow space in which he is confined. Indeed, it seems that his stride makes the world itself turn, so intense is he: *Over the cage floor the horizons come*, a conclusion which has strong similarities with *Over the roofs go his eyes and outcry.*

Both poems use very vivid images to create the animals and their different environments, making us think again about the lives of other living beings and how they exist separately, even though they intersect with ours. Our imaginations are stirred beyond normal, everyday experience: in the first poem taking us back to a land of legends, knights and ladies, and in the second to the life of the mind which can transcend physical confinement. I especially like the contrast between the old tomcat sleeping at home and what he does outside; but the image of the jaguar whose intensity cannot be controlled by physical confinement is even more fascinating, and the pace and sound effects in this poem are very evocative.

Refers to both poems and makes personal comment on them.

FURTHER READING

In his poem *Stray Cats*, the Indian poet E.V. Ramakrishnan describes the way the cats *monitor the world from treetops / and hold their weekly meetings in the graveyard*, further developing ideas about cats at night that Hughes introduces in *Esther's Tomcat*.

ACTIVITY 6.3

Research the poetry of Seamus Heaney on the internet. See if you can find copies of *The Skunk, The Otter* and *Clearances*. Extracts are reproduced here.

And there she was, the intent and glamorous,
Ordinary, mysterious skunk,
Mythologized, demythologized,
Snuffing the boards five feet beyond me.

It all came back to me last night, stirred
By the sootfall of your things at bedtime,
Your head-down, tail-up hunt in a bottom drawer
For the black plunge-line nightdress.

Seamus Heaney *The Skunk* (1998)

Seamus Heaney (1939–2013).

I loved your wet head and smashing crawl,
Your fine swimmer's back and shoulders
Surfacing and surfacing again
This year and every year since.
…
And suddenly you're out,
Back again, intent as ever,
Heavy and frisky in your freshened pelt,
Printing the stones.

Seamus Heaney *The Otter* (1998)

And don't be dropping crumbs. Don't tilt your chair.
Don't reach. Don't point. Don't make noise when you stir.

Seamus Heaney *Clearances II* (1986)

When all the others were away at Mass
I was all hers as we peeled potatoes.

Seamus Heaney *Clearances III* (1986)

ACTIVITY 6.4

The essay title for the two essays which follow was: *Discuss some of the ways in which Heaney's poetry explores love*. This is a critical essay.

Read carefully the following student responses and the marker's notes made in the margin and at the end.

STUDENT RESPONSE A

In the selected poetry, Heaney explores in various ways the idea of love, love of people and romance. I will use the poems The Skunk, The Otter and Clearances to talk about his exploration of love. Generally Heaney's presentation of love is personal and true as opposed to a sense of infatuation.

In The Skunk Heaney explores his love for his wife in the context of his absence as he goes to America. He presents the skunk as a recurring figure who appears every night. This sense of certainty between Heaney and the skunk reminds him of his wife and the way that his love for her is certain and recurring. The context of the poem being a poem home to his wife after a fairly long marriage so far 'after eleven years' is that he misses his wife and is reminded of her by the skunk. Also Heaney uses the metaphor of the skunk raising its tail and compares it to the action of his wife looking for the black slip dress in their bedroom drawers. The projection of this image presents his love as ▶

The introduction does make the poems sound entirely autobiographical, which simplifies Heaney's achievement as a poet. Poems should be able to develop personal experience into something others can appreciate and share.

This is factually wrong – the poem describes a nightdress.

fond, memorable and simple as he remembers beautiful moments in their relationship. *The Skunk*'s use of metaphor, imagery and language shows that his love for his wife is very strong, true and displays stability between them.

In The Otter, Heaney uses a more physical approach to describe his love towards the woman in the poem. It could be interpreted as Heaney's wife in which case it is loving and meaningful or it could be a stranger in which case it feels more sexual and voyeuristic. Heaney describes the woman being held by the water she is swimming in and also states that he is '*holding her*' which suggests support and security and that he feels the woman is precious. His description of the movement and rhythm suggests physical possibilities between them. Critics have said he is a poet of the home and family, so this could suggest a more voyeuristic approach to love and shows a different exploration of love by Heaney.

Finally Heaney presents a more family oriented expression of love in Clearances where he describes his relationship with his mother, saying 'I was X and she was O' this could show his complications with his mother as they are opposites and conflicting. When he says they stood 'silent' and that the water dripped like 'drops dripping off a soldering iron'. This describes the way they peeled potatoes together and shows an awkward and tense relationship. On the other hand when they fold the sheets and cross and come together it shows the bond and collaboration between them. Therefore Clearances as a whole can show Heaney's love for his mother as an often unspoken but still deep and meaningful relationship. Similar to The Skunk Heaney remembers small but meaningful moments between him and his mother.

In conclusion Heaney presents a very strong and long-lasting image of love and also explores it through marriage (The Skunk, The Otter), romance and family (Clearances) All the love presented here seems personal and private and long lasting with the examples of his wife and his mother.

It's best to avoid the word 'simple' at this level!

So far there are no direct examples from the text.

The essay is becoming more complex, but there are still no examples.

Uses examples more successfully here.

A clear conclusion, but again the emphasis on the personal and autobiographical.

The essay has flashes of more complex thought and is clearly organised, but the lack of close reference is an important area for improvement.

STUDENT RESPONSE B

Heaney explores the theme of love through his depictions of his own relationships through different settings, times and places. The varied forms of love that he experiences as a child, then later as a husband and father, are expressed in both his observations of his loved ones, shown in The Otter and The Skunk and his relationships and responses to mutual family love, shown in Changes and Clearances.

Heaney describes his experience of witnessing a skunk parading across the verandah in a garden in California as 'beautiful, invitational and dreamlike'. His communications of his love and desire for his wife are demonstrated through the focus on the physical distance between him and the skunk, the use of the words 'beyond me' connotes how he wishes to etherealise this depiction of his wife. The setting employed by Heaney also accentuates the themes of romantic love, as he describes 'the oranges looming in the orange trees' and the 'beautiful useless bark of eucalyptus' The images and sensual mixtures of sight and smell also contribute to the idea of her intangibility as the oxymoronic use of ▶

A well-expressed, clear introduction that suggests a thoughtful approach.

Uses text in support.

Helpful consideration of verse form.

Argument develops.

Compares poems thoughtfully.

Interesting ideas that could be developed further.

Clear, straightforward ideas about the son/ mother relationship.

A clear summing up in the conclusion. The student has tried to show different types of love.

'beautiful, useless' indicates how Heaney feels his wife is remote and 'beyond him' as he details that the scent 'spelt her absence'. The use of setting can also be seen in The Otter. Heaney evokes the intensity of the memory of him and his wife in Tuscany, again using sense experiences. Similarly to the 'tang of eucalyptus' and the 'oranges that loomed in the orange tree' The Skunk, the 'grape-deer air' which Heaney recalls in The Otter amplifies how his adoration for his wife is awakened from the memory of his senses. The form of the poem, with the use of variable line lengths in each quatrain, suggests a wave-like movement connoting first their separation and then their intimacy. This is reflected in the poem as Heaney depicts how his wife is at first 'beyond him' but now they 'close and deep as the atmosphere on water', unlike his position just as a watcher in The Skunk. He is seen to undercut the idea of himself as the observer admiring his wife by describing how they are together with the closeness of the atmosphere on water.

Heaney's exploration of parental love can be contrasted with this discussion of his love for his wife in The Otter and The Skunk. In Changes, he uses biblical imagery to express how he is compelled to stand sentinel and watch over his son as he grows, detailing that he had 'a bird's eye view of a bird'. In the earlier poems discussed, he focuses on his love for his wife by separating himself from her, while the opposite can be said for his love for his son in 'Changes'. As he says, 'we walked through the fields to the pump in the long grass' augmenting the idea that his love is based on his reflections on their relationship, rather than seeing his child as a separate entity. The structural differences between the poems also show the differences in the poet's experience of love. In Changes, the regular couplets and unvarying line lengths connote constancy and reliability, pointing the difficulty in accepting the changes taking place as his son prepares to leave home, while the variation in line length and stanzas in The Otter suggest the poet's enthralment with the unpredictable nature of his love for his wife. As he details his wife 'surfacing and resurfacing' from the water, the combination of sibilance and fricatives intensifies how her behaviour can catch him by surprise and captivate him. In contrast in Changes, his insistence on protecting his son sees him employ a gravity, almost lecturing in tone, 'remember this, you may wish to retrace this path,' which shows his love for his son is rooted in familiarity and reliability.

Heaney also explores how the patterns of parental love and its overpowering nature repeat across the generations. In Clearances, Heaney is seen to unearth all of his feelings towards his mother at the different stages of his professional and personal life, and does this by envisaging her entire character as a mother rather than an individual. Heaney is shown to reduce his mother to her domestic role, listing the instructions she gave to her children such as 'Don't be dropping crumbs, Don't tip your chair.' He depicts her as an archetypal country wife, referring to the women as like birds 'rippling their feathers', showing his love of her as a mothering figure. This is matched by his own love as a parent which accentuates the sense of instinctive protection – the simplistic, unconditional love of a parent.

Heaney's poetry about love is wide-ranging, incorporating the close intimacy of husband-and-wife relationships, especially when they are apart, and the bond between parent and child, both from his experience as a child with his mother and as a father with his son. He is characteristically honest and observant in all of these different situations.

Well-organised and expressed, with some good use of the text to support the argument.

Poetry passage question

ACTIVITY 6.5

Comment closely on the poet's concerns and methods in the poem *Miners* by Wilfred Owen.

There was a whispering in my hearth,
A sigh of the coal,
Grown wistful of a former earth
It might recall.

I listened for a tale of leaves
And smothered ferns,
Frond-forests, and the low sly lives
Before the fawns.

My fire might show steam-phantoms simmer
From Time's old cauldron,
Before the birds made nests in summer,
Or men had children.

But the coals were murmuring of their mine,
And moans down there
Of boys that slept wry sleep, and men
Writhing for air.

I saw white bones in the cinder-shard,
Bones without number.
For many hearts with coal are charred,
And few remember.

I thought of all that worked dark pits
Of war, and died
Digging the rock where Death reputes
Peace lies indeed:

▶

Comforted years will sit soft-chaired,
In rooms of amber,
The years will stretch their hands, well-cheered
By our life's ember;

The centuries will burn rich loads
With which we groaned,
Whose warmth shall lull their dreaming lids,
While songs are crooned
But they will not dream of us poor lads
Lost in the ground.

Wilfred Owen *Miners* (1918)

SAMPLE RESPONSE

A striking opening sentence in a relevant and well-focused opening paragraph.

Few poems range in time and space as widely as *Miners*. The poet imagines the very beginnings of earth's history when dense vegetation fell and was compressed into what is now dug out and burnt as coal; he thinks of the miners who risk their lives to do this work and it reminds him of the soldiers in the trenches who dig *pits of war*. Both risk their lives so that unthinking people can sit safely and comfortably at home in front of a coal fire, never dreaming of the poor lads *lost in the ground* who work to keep them safe and warm. These very different settings and atmospheres are fully evoked by the language of the poem.

Emphasis on poem's structure.

The poem's structure – seven regular four-line stanzas and a final longer one of six lines – has a kind of circular effect, beginning with the poet sitting in front of his fire at home and imagining the coal whispering to him of the distant past, but realising that the coal speaks of the mine and the men working there, suffering deep below the ground in the airless pits: these four stanzas form the first half of the poem. There is then one stanza about soldiers in the trenches suffering similarly, until the return in the two final stanzas to the domestic fireside, where now no-one remembers the suffering that has gone into providing such warmth and security.

Poetic methods with illustration.

The poet makes very effective use of figures of speech and diction. Personification of the coal itself *whispering, murmuring*; of Time, like an old witch with a cauldron producing *steam-phantoms*; of Death; of the years sitting *soft-chaired* and stretching their hands to the fire: all these take abstract or inanimate objects or ideas and give them a kind of sinister life and vitality.

Personifying the years as sitting by the fire and being warmed is much more effective than just saying that people did it. The poet's diction is similarly evocative: thinking of the far distant past *before the birds made nests in summer / Or men had children*, he imagines the life forms as *low* and *sly*; the ferns have been *smothered* to create coal and this links with the men who are gasping for air in the mine. He uses the physical sensory qualities of a coal fire – its hissing and its cinders – to imagine

▶

the coal speaking or creating ghosts from Time's cauldron and the white remains of the fire when it has burnt down remind him of the numberless bones of those who have died in the mine.

Interestingly, he begins in the first-person singular as himself or his persona sitting by the fire and imagining where the coal comes from in past and present and its voice speaking to him: *I listened*, *I saw*. But by the time he gets to the final two stanzas this has developed into the first-person plural *our life*, *we groaned*, as if he has associated himself entirely with the miners, culminating in *us poor lads*. This empathy gives the poem a very poignant quality. Indeed, the tone of the poem parallels its structure, moving from a reflective musing at the beginning to a sense of anger and sadness that the miners and the soldiers have been forgotten.

Sensitive to the tone of the poem.

The use of half-rhyme in an abab pattern throughout links the words effectively in meaning as well as sound; for example, *hearth* and *earth*, where one depends on the other, or *mine* and *men* similarly. This reaches a climax in the final longer stanza where there are two sets of three rhymed words: *loads*, *lids*, *lads*, and *groaned*, *crooned* and *ground*. The contrast between the domestic scenes where people are dozing and babies are being sung to and the wretched conditions suffered by those who have provided their comfort is very striking.

An apt comment on half-rhyme, linking it to the poem's theme.

Owen is known as a war poet of the First World War, and this poem does refer in stanza 6 to conditions in the trenches. If you called this a war poem, as some do, then the mines would symbolise the trenches and the miners the soldiers. However, the very vivid description of the prehistoric world, and the images of thoughtless people enjoying the warmth of their coal fires, and the conditions in the mine itself suggest that this is a poem about miners, as the title makes clear. The reference to the soldiers in the trenches supports the poem's theme of sacrifices made by some on behalf of others who don't even think of them, the kind of sacrifices we still see in the world today, such as cheap clothes being stitched by children or the poor on behalf of wealthier countries.

Aware of different possible interpretations.

Personal response which emphasises the continuing relevance of the poem.

TIP

Make sure that your answer relates theme and style throughout, and that you use examples to support the points you make. You will not have time to say everything.

ACTIVITY 6.6

What other points could you make about the three poems analysed here? Discuss with your class what other effective points could be made, or examples given. Go to Unit 29 in Part 3 of this book for a checklist to remind you of what to consider when writing under timed conditions.

FURTHER READING

1. The 'Reading Poetry' page on the University of Pennsylvania website (www.english.upenn.edu/~mgamer/Teaching/Handouts/readingpoetry.html) is all about reading poetry with more pleasure and understanding.
2. The poem *Introduction to Poetry* by Billy Collins takes you back to the final tip in Unit 1!

Self-assessment checklist

Reflect on what you've learnt in this unit and indicate your confidence level between 1 and 5. If you score below 3, revisit that section. Come back to this list later in your course. Has your confidence grown?

	Confidence level	Revisited?
I realise what studying a poetry anthology entails		
I appreciate the issues involved in dealing with an individual poet		
I know how best to organise my poetry work		
I can evaluate and discuss sample answers on poetry		

Section 2
Prose 1

Unit 7
Studying a novel or short story

Learning objectives

In this unit you will:

- approach work on the novel with confidence
- identify types of narrator in the novel or short story
- recognise free indirect speech
- review themes and settings in the novel
- consider fictional presentation of experience.

KEY CONCEPTS

Language, form, structure, genres, context, style, interpretation.

Before you start

- Remind yourself of novels or short stories you have recently studied and enjoyed. Consider who tells the story and what effect this has.

This section of the book will help you to think about and discuss your prose set texts, which are likely to be novels or short stories as this is a Literature course. It will also help you to think critically and analytically about any unseen passage from a novel or short story that you read and write on in an exam. In this unit, you will look at narrative approach, themes and settings, and briefly at whether a particular novel or short story is more concerned with concrete description or the creation of consciousness. In Unit 8, you will examine some openings of novels or short stories and what they show. Other units discuss structure (Unit 9), characterisation (Unit 10), commenting on an unseen piece of prose (Unit 11) and answering a passage question or writing an essay on a prose work (Unit 12).

Approaching a novel

Every novel is unique, but for each one there will be a writer, of a particular gender and age, who lived or is living at a particular time and in a particular place. This individual has ideas and attitudes to life that will be expressed in the novel because she or he wrote it. For each novel there is a reader too – you – with your own facts of biography and preference. The text itself has a **narrator** (or narrators) to tell the story, a setting or settings, and characters. The novel is written in language which is structured into sentences, paragraphs and (probably) chapters.

KEY TERM

Narrator: the person who tells the story – not the author.

The interaction between these elements creates an incomparable experience for the reader, an experience that might last several days or weeks, depending on the length of the novel and how much time you have to read. Unlike many poems, which can easily be read at one sitting, a novel becomes part of the very fabric of your daily life as you snatch a couple of chapters on the bus or before going to sleep. Sometimes you are fortunate enough to have time to read the whole thing without interruption, for example when on holiday or recovering from an illness. These units are designed to help you to express in words your experience of reading and enjoying a novel, as well as developing a critical framework for appreciating any other work of prose that you read.

Approaching the short story

Much of what is true of the novel can also be applied to the short story. However, the short story is intended to be read in one sitting, and has much less time to make an impression. Its setting and characters must be delineated skilfully and economically, its structure sculpted with great care. It can't afford to be leisurely in its approach. In some ways, it is similar to a poem; for example, it may use **symbols** to elaborate elements of the piece and build deftly to a climax which sums up the theme concisely.

KEY TERM

Symbol: a physical object that represents an idea or abstract concept. For example, a heart or rose may conventionally represent romantic love.

Narrative and telling stories

The telling of stories is as old as human society. In the past, many stories were not recorded in written words but spoken, passed down from one generation to the next (the oral tradition). Everyone loves stories and much of our conversation consists of telling other people about our experiences: what happened, who said what and to whom, and how we felt about it. We listen avidly to other people's accounts of their doings. Beyond our own domestic and social world, we tune in to the news stories of the world, the public narratives. We also create narratives within our own minds, rehearsing conversations, imagining events and dreaming by day and night.

ACTIVITY 7.1

If possible, tell a partner the story of one of your dreams, or an event which happened over the weekend. Discuss the potential this has for a short story. Your dream is likely to be **surrealistic**, perhaps more difficult to craft into a short story without a lot of editing.

The narrator

Every narrative has at least one narrator: the person who tells the story. In most everyday situations, the narrator is easy to spot: she or he is a reporter being her/himself in an easily defined context. However, in a work of prose fiction, the writer chooses a narrator to present her/his story in a way that will be effective. This may involve writing in her/his own voice or it may mean adopting the voice of someone else – a character in the story – or a mixture of both. So any writer may begin as narrator by using her/his own voice, then introduce a person to tell the story, a story in which there are characters who also have their own voices and who may tell part of the story, or write a letter or diary. This is known as **multiple narration**.

In the novel *Wuthering Heights* (1845–1846) by Emily Brontë, the novelist does not speak in her own voice at all, but uses two very different narrators to tell the story. Within their telling of the story, further characters speak, write letters and contribute their own points of view. This may sound complicated, but it is very effective in presenting different views of the same events (and in that sense is much closer to our own real-life experience where different people take a range of views of the same event). Another writer who does this very effectively is US writer William Faulkner in *The Sound and the Fury* (1929).

KEY TERMS

Surrealism: a movement originating in the visual arts, but when applied to writing it means combining realistic details with unlikely dreamlike images.

Persona: comes from a Latin word meaning 'mask' and is the 'I' who speaks in a novel, short story or poem: the writer's own identity is hidden by the mask of the chosen narrator.

First-person narrative

When a character tells the story in the first person ('I') this is known as first-person narrative. You can say that the writer adopts the **persona** of that particular character; so, for example, in *Wuthering Heights*, Emily Brontë adopts the persona first of Mr Lockwood, then of Nelly Dean. Later, when another character writes a letter or tells a substantial part of the story, another persona is being used, for example Isabella.

ACTIVITY 7.2

Find and make a list of some novels written in the first person. Identify who the 'I' of the story is. Can you find a story where the 'I' changes and becomes another person?

Omniscient narrator

Not all stories are told in the first person. Sometimes the narrator's viewpoint is that of the writer; if the writer moves from character to character freely, knowing everybody's thoughts and feelings and showing that they have all the information about what has happened and is going to happen, then obviously the narrative isn't restricted to one person's point of view. It is told in the third person ('he', 'she', 'it' or 'they') and may range widely, seeing all the different parts of the narrative with equal clarity. This kind of storyteller is known as an **omniscient narrator** because they know everything. The word *omniscient*, meaning 'all-knowing', is often used to describe God and, in a sense, this kind of storyteller is god-like; after all, a character can be born or married or killed at the stroke of a writer's pen! This is probably the commonest approach for a writer to adopt and it has been used successfully for centuries.

ACTIVITY 7.3

What are the advantages and disadvantages of:

a) the first-person narrative method?

b) the omniscient narrator?

KEY TERMS

Omniscient narrator: see definition on this page.

Unreliable narrator: one whose views can't be fully trusted by the reader, perhaps because the narrator is too young to understand events fully, or is biased in some way, or doesn't know everything, or is perhaps a liar or exaggerator. You may sometimes find the term 'imperfect' narrator.

SAMPLE RESPONSE

When a writer creates a character who tells a story in the first person, the reader is able to understand and appreciate the innermost thoughts and feelings of that person, often noticing their flaws and idiosyncrasies, as well as the narrowness of their vision of the world. Perhaps what they say is **unreliable**, and the reader is given the opportunity by the writer to spot this, which creates many interesting, ironic effects. The omniscient narrator style, in contrast, gives the possibility of many different perspectives, and comments across a range of characters and situations.

ACTIVITY 7.4

Here are two short paragraphs, one from *North and South* (1855) by Elizabeth Gaskell, and one from *The Great Gatsby* (1925) by F. Scott Fitzgerald. Read them and see if more than one point of view is being given. In extract 1, try to identify any moments where the narrator seems to know more than the character does, and is letting the reader know about it. In extract 2, the narrator of the story, Nick Carraway, is describing his first encounter with Gatsby, who is 50 feet away looking at the stars. Try to identify any moments where the writer is trying to overcome the disadvantage of having a first-person narrator.

Extract 1

Margaret opened the door and went in with the straight, fearless, dignified presence habitual to her. She felt no awkwardness; she had too much the habits of society for that. Here was a person come on business to her father; and, as he was one who had shown himself obliging, she was disposed to treat him with a full measure of civility. Mr Thornton was a good deal more surprised and discomfited than she. Instead of a quiet middle-aged clergyman, a young lady came forward with frank dignity – a young lady of a different type to most of those he was in the habit of seeing.

Elizabeth Gaskell *North and South* (1855)

Extract 2

I decided to call to him. Miss Baker had mentioned him at dinner, and that would do for an introduction. But I didn't call to him, for he gave a sudden intimation that he was content to be alone – he stretched out his arms toward the dark water in a curious way, and, far as I was from him, I could have sworn he was trembling.

F. Scott Fitzgerald *The Great Gatsby* (1925)

SAMPLE RESPONSE

Extract 1

First of all, there are two characters, and we are shown the thoughts of both of them. (This would be impossible if Margaret were telling the story in the first person – how would she know that Mr Thornton was not used to seeing young women like her?) The narrator seems more interested in Margaret than Mr Thornton, at least at this point in the story. Some of what Gaskell writes shows Margaret's own thoughts and consciousness of herself, but there are moments when Gaskell gives the reader more about Margaret than the character knows herself: is she aware, for example, that she is straight, fearless and dignified, and that this is *habitual to her*? Probably not. She does know that she feels no awkwardness, and that she wants *to treat him with a full measure of civility*, but then *frank dignity* seems to be the writer again, making sure that we know clearly how Margaret is behaving. It is possible, therefore, for the writer to use the omniscient narrator method and still get close to the innermost thoughts of a character.

Extract 2

Fitzgerald's presentation of Nick's character seems from this short passage to suggest he is friendly and also tactful. His description of Gatsby shows him to be sensitive and observant. It is central to the novel that the main character, Gatsby, who is not the narrator, is watched and described by someone, the narrator Nick, who is observant, otherwise how would the reader find out about him? However, Fitzgerald makes sure that the disadvantage of the single viewpoint is lessened by adding in some observation for us that goes further than Nick's viewpoint. Would it be possible to see someone trembling if they were 50 feet away, and in the dark? I think not, but the reader accepts this additional detail from the author and gains their first impression of a lonely but romantic and passionate man, trembling in the dark.

Mixed narrative

A writer can enjoy the benefits of both kinds of narrative approach by adopting an essentially third-person structure and then having lengthy passages or even whole chapters within it where a character or characters tell part of their story in the first person. A striking example of this method is *Bleak House* by Charles Dickens, where there is one omniscient voice who has much knowledge and a strong social conscience, and another, Esther Summerson, who tells her own story and makes observations on those around her, but is limited by her point of view and situation.

KEY TERMS

Focalization: the limited point of view of one character in the story without using the first-person narrative approach.

The narrator can also adopt the limited point of view of one character in the story without having to use a first-person narrative style. A good example of this is in *Disgrace* by J.M. Coetzee, a novel written in the third person throughout ('he') but **focalized** upon the thoughts and feelings of the main character, David Lurie. It is also written in the present tense, making its experiences very immediate and vivid (see Unit 25 for a passage from *Disgrace* for analysis).

Jane Austen and James Joyce are well-known exponents of this kind of narrative. What it allows is a kind of double perspective – the words seem to come from both inside and outside the character's mind at once, and this can be very effective. The contemporary American novelist Paul Auster makes use of **free indirect speech** extensively throughout his long novel *4-3-2-1*. Here are two examples, one from Jane Austen's *Emma* and one from a story in *Dubliners* by James Joyce.

Extract 1

'Let me entreat you,' cried Mr Elton; 'it would indeed be a delight; let me entreat you, Miss Woodhouse, to exercise so charming a talent in favour of your friend. I know what your drawings are. How could you suppose me ignorant? Is not this room rich in specimens of your landscapes and flowers! and has not Mrs Weston some inimitable figurepieces in her drawing-room, at Randalls?'

<u>Yes, good man!—thought Emma—but what has all that to do with taking likenesses? You know nothing of drawing. Don't pretend to be in raptures about mine. Keep your raptures for Harriet's face.</u> 'Well, if you give me such kind encouragement, Mr Elton, I believe I shall try what I can do. Harriet's features are very delicate, which makes a likeness difficult; and yet, there is a peculiarity in the shape of the eye, and the lines about the mouth which one ought to catch.'

Jane Austen *Emma* (1816)

The **free indirect speech** in Extract 1, which I've marked with underlining, is between two passages of **direct speech** and is very effective for showing the difference between what a person says out loud and what they are actually thinking.

KEY TERMS

Indirect speech: reports speech without quotation marks and puts control back into the hands of the omniscient narrator, as in the following simple example:

'Where are you going?' asked Olwethu angrily.

'I thought I might go and visit Thandeka,' replied Tshepo.

(Direct speech)

Olwethu asked Tshepo angrily where she was going.

She replied that she was going to visit Thandeka.

(Indirect or reported speech)

Free indirect Speech (as used in literary works): a mixed form where it is difficult to separate the voice of the narrator from the voice of the character. Some parts will sound like indirect or reported speech, but others sound very close to the voice of the character.

KEY TERM

Direct speech: in a novel or short story told by an omniscient narrator this gives the narrator a chance to allow characters some words of their own, which they will be enclosed in quotation marks.

Extract 2

A few light taps upon the pane made him turn to the window. It had begun to snow again. He watched sleepily the flakes, silver and dark, falling obliquely against the lamplight. The time had come for him to set out on his journey westward. <u>Yes, the newspapers were right: snow was general all over Ireland.</u> It was falling on every part of the dark central plain, on the treeless hills, falling softly upon the Bog of Allen and, farther westward, softly falling into the dark mutinous Shannon waves. It was falling, too, upon every part of the lonely churchyard on the hill where Michael Furey lay buried.

James Joyce *Dubliners* (1914)

Themes in the novel

Now that you have thought about who tells the story (the narrator), it is time to consider some of the typical themes of the novel. The **coming-of-age** experience, the influence of family, gender issues, love and marriage, money, class and culture, journeys, town and country, the individual and society, education, crime – these all feature prominently in the history of the novel. A concern of the novel which has emerged consistently in the latter half of the 20th century and up to the present is writing itself. This is known as **metafiction**. It is not a new idea, however, since Laurence Sterne's novel *Tristram Shandy* (1760–1767) tells a story, but interrupts and reflects on it.

Reflection: Whether a writer uses a first-person, third-person or mixed narrative approach, there will always be artistry in its handling so that particular effects can be achieved, as you will see in later examples. Writers make deliberate choices.

KEY TERMS

Coming-of-age or **growing-up novel:** (sometimes called the *bildungsroman*): has a young person as its main character. It may be in either first- or third-person form.

Metafiction: narrators comment on their own writing in a self-reflexive manner, or play games with the readers, reminding them that writing a novel is a process, and the end result is not real life. The finished article is a construct of the writer. Some examples of this are to be found in the work of John Fowles (*The French Lieutenant's Woman*), Salman Rushdie (*Midnight's Children*) and Ian McEwan (*Atonement*). Two novels by Chimamanda Adichie, *Half of a Yellow Sun* and *Americanah*, have major characters whose writings become part of the novel and contribute to its social analysis and characterisation.

Background and setting

The novelist or short story writer chooses to set their novel or short story in a particular society at a specific time, which may not be contemporaneous with the novelist's own life. It may be set in a country different from the one in which you live. It may be in the far or not so distant past, or even, in the case of a science fiction work, set in the future.

As part of your preparation, work with a friend to make notes on the novel or short stories you are studying, focusing particularly on:

- Where and when are the novel or stories set.
- What kind of society is depicted?
- Is there more than one setting/society? If so, are they used as contrast with one another, so that one emphasises distinctive features of the other?
- What effect does this have on the narrative/creation of characters?
- Is the setting a background for the action, or does it assume greater importance in the structure of the novel as a whole?

The moors above Haworth, in the north of England, familiar to Emily Brontë.

> **KEY TERMS**
>
> **Colonial** and **post-colonial literature:** written in English from a number of societies which were governed in the past by Britain as a colonial power. Post-colonial works explore the issues of personal and national identity and displacement, often using particular narrative techniques to do so.
>
> **Back story:** a set of events leading up to the main plot – background information that can be revealed during the main narrative.

Some examples of setting

Some novels have as a title the name of a place, a house even, or different geographical areas, for example, *Brick Lane* (Monica Ali), *Wuthering Heights* (Emily Brontë), *Bleak House* (Charles Dickens), *The Mill on the Floss* (George Eliot), *Northanger Abbey* (Jane Austen), *Barchester Towers* (Anthony Trollope), *The Famished Road* (Nigerian writer Ben Okri) or *Brideshead Revisited* (Evelyn Waugh). A house is usually the centre for a family with its culture and attitudes as well as an economic unit, so money is almost always a concern – indeed, it is one of the most important themes in the English novel, together with class. *Northanger*

Abbey is in part a parody of Gothic novels that are often set in old medieval buildings, ruined abbeys and the like. In *North and South* by Elizabeth Gaskell, the distinctive geographical settings and cultural oppositions give the novel its title and central concern. *Americanah* is a contemporary novel with a range of settings: Nigeria, North America and England, and the word is one coined by characters talking about attitudes to the United States. The Indian, New Zealand and Western Australian settings of *Games at Twilight*, *The People Before* and *On Her Knees*, to give just three examples from *Stories of Ourselves 1*, are essential for an appreciation of the stories' themes and characterisations. Equally, the South African, Nigerian and French backgrounds of *The Woman's Rose, The Plantation* and *Showing the Flag* from *Stories of Ourselves 2* (CUP) are vital elements in the tales.

Insights into **colonial** and **post-colonial** societies depend upon their particular settings, as do the stories from North America in *Stories of Ourselves*, for example *The Moving Finger* by Edith Wharton and *The Contest* by Annie Proulx. *A Fistful of Colours* by Suchen Christine Lim is a novel set in Singapore with **back stories** from old colonial times as well as debates on current issues in the modern city state. There is a student essay on Nigerian author Chinua Achebe's novel *Things Fall Apart* in Unit 12.

Reflection: Look at the stories or novels you are studying and consider carefully how far the setting adds to the writer's expression of their main concerns. How would this be different if the setting was elsewhere? You may find that certain themes are universal – such as relationships between family members, or the individual's struggles within particular social groups, or the desire of one person to have power over another, or loss or love or regret, and so on. However, setting the fictional exploration of these themes in a particular world will add depth or poignancy to its effects.

ACTIVITY 7.5

See if you can find some other novels whose titles are the name of a house or a place or a geographical setting. If you have read one of them, consider why the novelist has chosen to focus upon the setting rather than a character or a theme.

Concrete creation or stream of consciousness?

Some novels are concrete and realistic in their descriptions of places, attempting to replicate in words the sense impressions of the physical world they focus on. Other works try to create the complex impression of a character's response to that world by giving an impression of the ebb and flow (stream) of their **consciousness**. It is possible to combine the two approaches; this has been particularly evident in more contemporary works of fiction.

KEY TERM

Stream of consciousness: writing that tries to express the very complicated thoughts and feelings which pass through the mind at any one time. Virginia Woolf and James Joyce are famous examples of writers in this form.

ACTIVITY 7.6

These two extracts are both concerned with a character. Decide which kind of writing each is: concrete and realistic, or inwardly responsive. Try re-writing each one in the style of the other. Discuss the different effects created with a classmate.

Original	Rewritten
Extract 1 has concrete and sensory descriptions of the experiences and actions of the main characters, presented as external to themselves (They are at a writers' workshop and the narrator does not know their names, only what country they come from).	It is rewritten as if focused on the interior thoughts of one of the party – the Senegalese who has to read part of her story to the group.

(Continued)

(*Continued*)

Original	Rewritten
The next day they did not talk about the previous evening. They talked about how fluffy the scrambled eggs were and how eerie the jacaranda leaves that rustled against their windows at night were. After dinner the Senegalese read two pages of a funeral scene, stopping often to sip some water, her accent thickening as she became more emotional… From Chimamanda Ngozi Adichie *Jumping Monkey Hill* (2008)	No-one took any notice of me last night. All they can talk about is the breakfast – who cares about the scrambled eggs? And I like the sound of the tree's leaves rustling against my window – it reminds me of home. Oh, why did I come? Now I've got to read part of my story. I chose the funeral scene, but it's upsetting. I hope I can do it without crying.
Extract 2, also in the third person 'he', is focused internally on the stream of the character's consciousness.	It is rewritten to emphasise what he is doing and the things which surround him.
How trifling it all is, how boring it all is, he thought, compared with the other thing – work. Here he sat drumming his fingers on the table-cloth when he might have been – he took a flashing bird's eye view of his work. What a waste of time it all was to be sure! Yet, he thought, she is one of my oldest friends. I am by way of being devoted to her. Yet now, at this moment her presence meant absolutely nothing to him: her beauty meant nothing to him; her sitting with her little boy at the window – nothing, nothing. He wished only to be alone and to take up that book. Virginia Woolf *To the Lighthouse* (1927)	He sat and drummed his fingers on the red checked table-cloth. He glanced at his wife and son sitting at the window that looked out onto the sea. The old book he was reading was on the table next to his steaming cup of coffee, together with the used crockery, scraps of food and the coffee pot.

Using metaphor to express setting

Here is an example from *The White Tiger* by Indo-Australian writer Aravind Adiga. The urban setting is given horrific metaphorical life in the comparison with the hens, the writer making it explicit in the last sentence of the extract. This is also a post-colonial novel.

> Look at the way they keep chickens there in the market. Hundreds of pale hens and brightly coloured roosters, stuffed tightly into wire-mesh cages, packed as tightly as worms in a belly, pecking each other and shitting on each other, jostling just for breathing space; the whole cage giving off a horrible stench – the stench of terrified, feathered flesh. On the wooden desk above this coop sits a grinning young butcher, showing the flesh and organs of a recently chopped-up chicken, still oleaginous with a coating of dark blood. The roosters in the coop smell the blood from above. They see the organs of their brothers lying around them. They know they're next. Yet they do not rebel. They do not try to get out of the coop.
>
> The very same thing is done with human beings in this country.
>
> Aravind Adiga *The White Tiger* (2008)

In the next example, a particular setting is used which is neither concrete nor internalised, but expressed with such vivid metaphorical language that the reader is in no doubt of the writer's strength of feeling. It is not directly connected with a character.

> It was a town of red brick, or of brick that would have been red if the smoke and ashes had allowed it; but, as matters stood it was a town of unnatural red and black like the painted face of a savage. It was a town of machinery and tall chimneys, out of which interminable serpents of smoke trailed themselves for ever and ever, and never got uncoiled.
>
> Charles Dickens *Hard Times* (1854)

ACTIVITY 7.7

Look closely at the novel or short stories you are studying to identify its/their main concern/s, narrative method/s, approach to setting and distinctive presentation of experience. The next unit will give you further practice in identifying these aspects, using the openings of novels or stories to do so.

FURTHER READING

1. Many older works of fiction are available free of charge on the internet on www.gutenberg.org. This is a wonderful resource for readers, especially for classics like the works of Dickens or Hardy.
2. Try *The Interpreter of Maladies,* by Bengali writer Jhumpa Lahiri (short stories which explore people displaced from their birthplace) and *Catcher in the Rye*, by US writer J.D. Salinger (first-person novel about adolescence).

Self-assessment checklist

Reflect on what you've learnt in this unit and indicate your confidence level between 1 and 5. If you score below 3, revisit that section. Come back to this list later in your course. Has your confidence grown?

	Confidence level	Revisited?
I recognise types of narrator with ease		
I am able to analyse the use of free indirect speech		
I appreciate the importance of themes and setting in the novel or short story		
I am interested in, and able to discuss, the presentation of experience in prose works		

Unit 8
Prose – opening paragraphs

Learning objectives

In this unit you will:

- understand the importance of the opening of a story
- study different openings and respond to their effects
- reflect on the implications for unseen work.

Language, form, structure, genres, context, style, interpretation.

Before you start

- Find three novels or short stories, preferably ones that you've never seen before. Look closely at the opening paragraph of each and then list some of the things you feel could possibly develop as a result of what you've observed in it. Discuss these with a friend and reflect on whether you might like to carry on reading. Ask your teacher what actually happens! Were your predictions right? (If your teacher isn't available, you can probably find a summary of the plot on the internet.)

This unit is going to look at some different openings of novels and short stories, how they have been created by their authors, and what effects they produce. You can often guess what sort of work is going to unfold from the first few paragraphs of the narrative. It is really important for the writer to get the opening right, so that you, the reader, are intrigued from the beginning. You long to enter this world, with its distinctive social or natural background, its ideas and characters. Each of the following passages is also an unseen prose passage, however brief, so look closely at the sample response to each one, to get a sense of some of the ways in which you can write about unseen extracts.

Openings from novels and short stories

ACTIVITY 8.1

Look closely at each numbered opening paragraph and write two paragraphs about its setting and characters, as well as what sort of novel or short story it might turn out to be. The language, as well as the narrator's position, may be helpful clues to you. There are seven examples here, but each one is quite different. Sample responses are given after the final extract.

Extract 1

Mr Beverley Metcalfe tapped the barometer in the back hall and noted with satisfaction that it had fallen several points during the night. He was by nature a sun-loving man, but he believed it was one of the marks of a true countryman to be eternally in need of rain. He had made a study and noted the points of true countrymen. Had he been of literary habit and of an earlier generation, his

▶

observations might have formed a little book of aphorisms. The true countryman wore a dark suit on Sundays unlike the flannelled tripper from the cities; he loved a bargain and would go to any expense to do his marketing by private treaty instead of through the normal channels of retail trade; while ostensibly sceptical and conservative he was readily fascinated by mechanical gadgets; he was genial but inhospitable, willing to gossip for hours across a fence with any passing stranger, but reluctant to allow his closest friends into his house.. These and a hundred other characteristics Mr Metcalfe noted for emulation.

Evelyn Waugh *An Englishman's Home* (1938) – short story

Extract 2

My father's family name being Pirrip, and my Christian name Philip, my infant tongue could make of both names nothing longer or more explicit than Pip. So, I called myself Pip, and came to be called Pip. I give Pirrip as my father's family name, on the authority of his tombstone and my sister, – Mrs Joe Gargery, who married the blacksmith. As I never saw my father or my mother, and never saw any likeness of either of them (for their days were long before the days of photographs), my first fancies regarding what they were like, were unreasonably derived from their tombstones. The shape of the letters on my father's, gave me an odd idea that he was a square, stout, dark man, with curly black hair. From the character and turn of the inscription, 'Also Georgiana Wife of the Above,' I drew a childish conclusion that my mother was freckled and sickly. To five little stone lozenges, in a neat row beside their grave, and were sacred to the memory of five little brothers of mine, – who gave up trying to get a living, exceedingly early in that universal struggle, – I am indebted for a belief I religiously entertained that they had all been born on their backs with their hands in their trousers-pockets, and had never taken them out in this state of existence.

Ours was the marsh country, down by the river, within, as the river wound, twenty miles of the sea.

My first most vivid and broad impression of the identity of things seems to me to have been gained on a memorable raw afternoon towards evening. At such a time I found out for certain, that this bleak place overgrown with nettles was the churchyard; and that Philip Pirrip, late of this parish, and also Georgiana wife of the above, were dead and buried; and that Alexander, Bartholomew, Abraham, Tobias, and Roger, infant children of the aforesaid, were also dead and buried; and that the dark flat wilderness beyond the churchyard, intersected with dykes and mounds and gates, with scattered cattle feeding on it, was the marshes; and that the low leaden line beyond was the river; and that the distant savage lair from which the wind was rushing, was the sea; and that the small bundle of shivers growing afraid of it all and beginning to cry, was Pip.

Charles Dickens *Great Expectations* (1860–1861) – novel

▶

Extract 3

Two elderly women sat knitting on that part of the veranda which was screened from the sun by a golden shower creeper; the tough stems were so thick with flower it was as if the glaring afternoon was dammed against them in a surf of its own light made visible in the dripping, orange-coloured clusters. Inside this coloured barrier was a darkened recess, rough mud walls (the outer walls of the house itself) forming two sides, the third consisting of a bench loaded with painted petrol tins which held pink and white geraniums. The sun splashed liberal gold through the foliage, over the red cement floor, and over the ladies. They had been here since lunchtime, and would remain until sunset, talking, talking incessantly, their tongues mercifully let off the leash. They were Mrs Quest and Mrs Van Rensberg; and Martha Quest, a girl of fifteen, sat on the steps in full sunshine, clumsily twisting herself to keep the glare from her book with her own shadow.

Doris Lessing *Martha Quest* (1952) – novel

Extract 4

May in Ayemenem is a hot, brooding month. The days are long and humid. The river shrinks and black crows gorge on bright mangoes in still, dustgreen trees. Red bananas ripen. Jackfruits burst. Dissolute bluebottles hum vacuously in the fruity air. Then they stun themselves against clear windowpanes and die, fatly baffled in the sun.

Indian writer Arundhati Roy *The God of Small Things* (1997) – novel

Extract 5

The white hair was trapped in the tweezers. I pulled it taut to see if it was gripped tightly, then plucked it.

'Aaah!' grimaced Daddy. 'Careful. Only one at a time.' He continued to read the *Times of India*, spreading it on the table.

'It is only one,' I said, holding out the tweezers, but my annoyance did not register. Engrossed in the classifieds, he barely looked my way. The naked bulb overhead glanced off the stainless-steel tweezers, making a splotch of light dart across the Murphy Radio calendar. It danced over the cherubic features of the Murphy Baby, in step with the tweezers' progress on Daddy's scalp. He sighed, turned a page, and went on scrutinising the columns.

Each Sunday the elimination of white hairs took longer than the last time.

Indian writer Rohinton Mistry *Of White Hairs and Cricket* from *Tales from Firozsha Baag* (1987) – short story

Extract 6

Once upon a time and a very good time it was there was a moocow coming down along the road and this moocow that was coming down along the road met a nicens little boy named baby tuckoo.

▶

His father told him that story: his father looked at him through a glass: he had a hairy face.

He was baby tuckoo. The moocow came down the road where Betty Byrne lived: she sold lemon platt.

O, the wild rose blossoms

On the little green place.

He sang that song. That was his song.

O, the green wothe botheth.

When you wet the bed first it is warm then it gets cold. His mother put on the oilsheet. That had the queer smell.

His mother had a nicer smell than his father. She played on the piano the sailor's hornpipe for him to dance. He danced:

Tralala lala,

Tralala tralaladdy,

Tralala lala,

Tralala lala.

Uncle Charles and Dante clapped. They were older than his father and mother but Uncle Charles was older than Dante.

Irish writer James Joyce *A Portrait of the Artist as a Young Man* (1914–1915) – novel

James Joyce (1882–1941).

Extract 7

On a sticky August evening two weeks before her due date, Ashima Ganguli stands in the kitchen of a Central Square apartment, combining Rice Krispies and Planter's peanuts and chopped red onion in a bowl. She adds salt, lemon juice, thin slices of green chili pepper, wishing there were mustard oil to pour into the mix. Ashima has been consuming this concoction throughout her pregnancy, a humble approximation of the snack sold for pennies on Calcutta sidewalks and on railway platforms throughout India, spilling from newspaper cones. Even now that there is barely space inside her, it is the one thing she craves. Tasting from a cupped palm, she frowns; as usual, there's something missing. She stares blankly at the pegboard behind the countertop where her cooking utensils hang, all slightly coated with grease. She wipes sweat from her face with the free end of her sari. Her swollen feet ache against speckled gray linoleum. Her pelvis aches from the baby's weight.

Bengali writer Jhumpa Lahiri *The Namesake* (2003) – novel

SAMPLE RESPONSE

Extract 1
It is clear from this opening paragraph that the writer is interested in the way that his main character, Mr Metcalfe, is trying to be what he is not – a *true countryman*. Metcalfe is trying to integrate himself into a social set in the country to which he does not quite belong, although he would very much like to. *These and a hundred other characteristics Mr Metcalfe noted for emulation*. The writer's list of examples is based on antithesis, for example the contrast between the countryman's suit and the *flannelled tripper*; *private treaty / retail trade*; *ostensibly sceptical / fascinated by mechanical gadgets*; *willing to gossip for hours across a fence / reluctant to allow his closest friends into his house*. These help to create a humorous, satirical tone from the very first paragraph. The story revolves around outsiders in the close-knit social set to which Mr Metcalfe aspires and wittily exposes the social hierarchies in a Cotswold village.

Extract 2
The opening of *Great Expectations* establishes that it is a first-person narrative with Pip as the protagonist. His description of the graves of his family is both macabre and humorous, and this is a feature of Dickens's tone throughout the novel. Pip's vivid imagination is also evident in the next paragraph with its evocative depiction of the raw afternoon in the bleak graveyard on the marshes and his sense of fear: an apt prelude to the sudden appearance of the convict who terrifies him by his appearance, the convict who is to have such an impact on his life. The final sentence of this second paragraph is noteworthy as an example of Dickens's style: the parallel clauses with their incremental repetition gradually focusing through time and space; the long, slow build-up to a climax (Pip, the *bundle of shivers*, the centre of the novel); and, typically of Dickens, the bathos of the name Roger after the biblical and mythological-sounding names of the other children adding a touch of humour. (This sentence is one of my favourites in the whole of literature and reminds us that Dickens is as poetic in his use of language as anyone working in lines and stanzas.)

Extract 3
This third-person narrative begins with a setting of the scene on a veranda bright with colourful flowers. Before the characters are even introduced, the rich beauty of the flowers and the contrasts between shadow and brightness are emphasised. There are some indications of the setting, such as the mud walls and the petrol tins with geraniums and the red cement floor, which do not sound like England today. (It is in fact set in Africa about 60 years ago.) The two ladies are very talkative: the word *talking* is repeated and the word *incessantly* sounds like a criticism from the narrator. Their tongues have been *let off the leash;* a metaphor which suggests that they are like dogs kept under control most of the time but are now able to run free. This might give the impression that they are normally supposed to keep quiet (perhaps while their husbands do most of the talking – they are both referred to with their husband's names, not their first names). Martha is introduced right at the end of the paragraph and her age immediately suggests a character with whom a younger reader can sympathise. (Which of us has not sat as a child trying to amuse ourselves while our elders talk and talk behind us?) The writer's use of light and shade images is so extensive that it perhaps suggests that metaphorically Martha's story will be one of striking contrasts. The sentences are long and richly descriptive.

▶

Extract 4
This short opening paragraph is extremely descriptive with many adjectives of colour and texture. The combination of this with short sentences and present tense verbs (*is*, *are*, *shrinks*, *gorge*, *hum*) creates an immediacy and dramatic impact for a scene in which, as yet, no people have made an appearance. The reader expects an exotic setting (it is India) and the author's voice in the third-person narrative sounds authoritative. However, although the images are exotic and colourful, there are also many words that suggest over-ripeness to the point of rottenness (*brooding*, *humid*, *gorge*, *ripen*, *burst*, *fruity*) and the flies *stun themselves* and *die*.

Extract 5
This first-person narrative begins in a most unusual way, with the description of the main character plucking hairs from his father's head. He is evidently not very old as he calls his father *Daddy*, yet he is old enough to be relied on to do this job every Sunday (we find out later that he is 14). The vivid opening engages our interest immediately – what can be the reason for this activity? There is a clue in the third paragraph: Daddy is scrutinising the classified section of the newspaper. In combination with the final line of the extract, it suggests that Daddy is removing his white hairs so that he looks younger and more eligible for any job that he may spy in the classified adverts. The first-person narrator is observant and imaginative: he describes the effect of the light bulb on the tweezers and the calendar with its Baby picture. This observation helps to set the scene – they are not a rich family if the bulb is bare, and the father is seeking work. We feel the son's irritation and distaste at having to do this job every Sunday. Although a short story, this is a miniature coming-of-age narrative. By the end of the story, his criticisms of his parents and his limited viewpoint have broadened into an appreciation of his family and an awareness of time passing, change and mortality. Note the very naturalistic conversation that opens the story of personalities interacting in a family.

Extract 6
The narrator uses the voice and limited speech register of a very small child, suggesting that this will be an autobiographical novel, beginning at the very beginning of the life in question. It is in the third person, but the narration is very close to the sense impressions of the small child, with references to the smell of the oilcloth, wetting the bed, to the implied feel of a hairy beard, the taste of lemon platt (lemon-flavoured sweets), the sounds of music and clapping. Childish words are used such as *moocow*, *nicens*, *tuckoo*, and simple sentence structures of subject, verb and object, with no subordinate clauses, to emulate the immature thought processes of the child. Older people have particular associations for the small child: his mother smells nicer than his father, and he seems closer to her; Betty Byrne is notable for what she sells that is a treat for the child; he notices that his uncle is older than Dante.

Extract 7
The woman in the passage is in the final stage of her pregnancy. She is making herself something to eat, mixing the ingredients that are nearest to those she remembers from the place she came from – India. The prose is written in the third person, but the narrator is very close to Ashima's thoughts and action, enhanced by her use of the present tense. We can envisage her little concoction of food (a craving she experiences because of her pregnancy) even as she is making it. The images of food and cooking activity are clear and precise, but the passage takes us way

▶

Reflection: Compare this with the opening of *Great Expectations*. Pip is only a child, but his thoughts are expressed in long, complex, rhythmical sentences by Dickens – there is no attempt to imitate the speech patterns of a young child.

beyond her apartment in Central Square with its kitchen and its neat countertop and hanging utensils into the Calcutta pavements and railway platforms: images of space and travel far away, where the food she is trying to emulate is sold outdoors for a few coins and presented to you in a piece of newspaper. The contrast between the two worlds is made very striking (suggested in the small phrase *Calcutta sidewalk*: a place in India coupled with the US word for 'pavement'). Her ingredients are American ones, named by the writer: *Rice Krispies and Planter's peanuts*, and they are not quite sufficient for what she craves – a taste of the old country from which she came. Ethnic food is often a symbol in post-colonial fiction for what is missing in the immigrant experience – the basic stuff of life with all its traditional connotations, the ingredients of which are difficult to find in the new country.

In addition to the food preparation, the writer stresses the woman's physical discomfort: *craves*, *sweat*, *swollen*, *ache*. This novel beginning with a pregnancy, close to the time of the child's birth, takes the reader back even further in the main character's life than the previous example. The protagonist is about to be born, into a household the roots of whose culture are elsewhere, trying to adapt to the new country which has taken the family in. The importance of names, of suffering, of displacement: these are the very concerns of the novel as it unfolds.

Reflection: Even the smallest section of a novel can give you a sense of the writer's concerns and methods of working. Pay attention to the detail, and the larger picture will emerge clearly. You will find that this is true for drama as well: one scene can tell you a great deal.

ACTIVITY 8.2

Choose one of the prose works whose first paragraph has interested you and try reading the complete work. Are your first impressions borne out in the novel or story as a whole?

Take five novels or volumes of short stories and read the first paragraph. Would they interest you enough to carry on reading?

FURTHER READING

Two novels with engaging openings:

1. *1984* by George Orwell (1949)
2. *Paradise* by Toni Morrison (1997)

Self-assessment checklist

Reflect on what you've learnt in this unit and indicate your confidence level between 1 and 5. If you score below 3, revisit that section. Come back to this list later in your course. Has your confidence grown?

	Confidence level	Revisited?
I acknowledge the importance of the opening paragraph in prose fiction		
I value and can demonstrate close reading as a skill for unseen work		
I am open to the significance of varied approaches		

Unit 9

The novel – structure

Learning objectives

In this unit you will:

- consider the different ways in which events can be arranged in a novel
- evaluate the effects of these on the reader
- remind yourself of some important technical vocabulary useful for discussing prose fiction
- examine the different short story structures commonly seen.

KEY CONCEPTS

Language, form, structure, genres, context, style, interpretation.

Before you start

- Remind yourself of what a story is by thinking back on books you have studied or read for pleasure. You might find it helpful to think about films you have seen and how they structure their plots – some of them use flashbacks, for example. Discuss these with a friend and try to find some examples where you have found this technique particularly successful or, on the other hand, very difficult to follow!

A story is not just a series of events; how these are arranged and communicated is very important to the effect the novel or short story has on the reader. The **plot** may be complicated in a novel, but telling this story or summarising the narrative is not considered to be an important skill in exams at the more advanced level.

KEY TERMS

Plot: the series of events and actions that occur in a story.

Chronological: following the order of events as they actually happen.

Chronological arrangement

How the events of the story are arranged is part of the structure of the novel or short story. If you consider the events of your own life, they take place in time and therefore in a particular order. If you try to describe the order in which events actually happened, then you try hard to put first things first and culminate in the final event, as it happened. You might do this if you were describing a car accident to a policeman and trying to be precise. This description can be denoted using letters of the alphabet: **a** followed by **b**, **c**, **d**, **e** and so on.

Some novels and short stories are written in this way. At no time is there any irregularity in such works: events happen in the order in which they would occur in real life. If events go from A to Z without deviation, then this may create an atmosphere of regularity and completeness: the story proceeds evenly throughout. Many light novels, intended for whiling away an afternoon in a not very challenging way, are written in such a manner. The 'airport novel' is called this because it is something for reading on the beach or on holiday and tossing aside when it is finished. It is more difficult to see what people are reading these days as they use electronic readers – a pity for people like English teachers who are always interested in what the world is reading!

However, the kinds of novel that are set for study at more advanced levels are often more complex in their structure than this. Every time a writer begins the story in the middle and then goes back to an earlier point in the hero's life, or a character describes a memory of the past in detail, then the **chronological** pattern is altered and this is bound to have an effect on the reader's understanding and appreciation of the novel as a whole.

TIP

Never tell the story of a novel! You will waste valuable time and add no value to your answer. The marker of your essay knows the story well and does not want to hear it again!

Reflection: What effect does each method of structuring your story have on your narrative? Discuss each one with your friend and then do the same with their story.

KEY TERM

Frame device: giving a narrative the same beginning and end, within which the main narrative takes place – sometimes the finding of a manuscript or a letter, for example.

ACTIVITY 9.1

If possible, recount to a friend an interesting incident that happened to you one weekend. Tell the events in the order in which they actually happened. Then try beginning with the climax of the story and working back to the start. Now see if you can pick an incident from the middle of the story and work backwards to the start and forwards to the end.

COMMENT

You have probably found that some stories are more effective told in one of the suggested ways than others. A dramatic story with tension and a climax may be spoilt if you know the ending first.

Non-chronological arrangement

Order: putting Z first

In the novel *The Unbearable Lightness of Being* by Milan Kundera, the reader is told almost straight away that the central characters, a young couple, are killed in an accident. Everything that follows about their earlier life together is coloured by the reader's knowledge of their untimely deaths. This has a poignant effect on the reader, who can never forget for a moment the fleeting nature of their physical and emotional lives, so vividly portrayed by the writer, but doomed to end early. If you know Shakespeare's play *Romeo and Juliet*, you will remember that the Chorus tells us in the first moments of the play that the lovers are *star-cross'd* and *take their life*, with similar effect. We appreciate the intensity and liveliness of the fated characters much more than we would do if they were to live to an old age and die in their beds. The novel *The White Tiger* by Aravind Adiga begins at the end, with the first-person narrator gradually getting to the point of telling his story. This may give the effect of a **frame device**, a favourite literary method used in poetry as well as prose (Keats's *The Eve of St Agnes*, for example) and in memory plays, discussed in Unit 15 of this book. It is a metaphor that comes from the concept of framing a painting, and as a frame improves a picture, a framing device helps to enhance the main narrative. Two examples are *The Reluctant Fundamentalist* by the Pakistani novelist Mohsin Hamid and *The Strange Case of Dr Jekyll and Mr Hyde* by British writer Robert Louis Stevenson.

Changing the order completely

ACTIVITY 9.2

Read the following passages from *The Third Policeman* by Flann O'Brien and work out what the order of the events was, using a, b, c and so on. Try to consider the effect of this.

Not everybody knows how I killed old Phillip Mathers, smashing his jaw in with my spade; but first it is better to speak of my friendship with John Divney because it was he who first knocked old Mathers down by giving him a great blow in the neck with a special bicycle-pump which he manufactured himself out of a hollow iron bar. Divney was a strong civil man but he was lazy and idle-minded. He was personally responsible for the whole idea in the first place. It was he who told me to bring my spade. He was the one who gave the orders on the occasion and also the explanations when they were called for.

I was born a long time ago. My father was a strong farmer and my mother owned a public house.

Flann O'Brien *The Third Policeman* (1968)

COMMENT

The events that take place in this extract could be ordered like this:

a birth

b friendship with Divney

c the idea

d Divney knocking old Mathers down

e smashing the jaw in

f the explanations

But they are arranged in the following order: e, b, d, b, c, f, a. The impression created is of a conversation where the ideas are repeated and events do not always come out in the right order. The character speaking sounds as if he takes after his father for strength and has spent much time at his mother's, having many stories to tell of his exploits!

Frequency: a single event told several times

In *The Collector*, a novel by John Fowles, a young woman is kidnapped. The first section of the story is a first-person narrative told by the girl, describing what happens to her. There is a sudden shift in the second section of the novel and the same events are told by the kidnapper, also in the first person. The final section returns to the girl's point of view. This has the effect at first of involving the reader's imagination and empathy with the girl, then creating a profound shock by involving us in the inner life of the kidnapper, enhanced by the use of the first-person narrative twice over. When we return to the girl's viewpoint in the third section, we feel a sense of hopelessness because we know, with the benefit of hindsight into the kidnapper's mind, that she will never escape.

In Emily Brontë's *Wuthering Heights*, the same narratives are told by different characters, creating a richly complex effect. Different points of view of the same events help to develop the characterisation of Heathcliff and Catherine, as well as Nelly Dean, one of the narrators, with her common-sense view of events. Brontë sometimes delays the second telling of an incident so that our initial assumptions, based on the first person's account, are challenged. This is particularly used for creating an aggressive image of Heathcliff at first, then making him more sympathetic. It also reminds us that the 'truth' is very difficult to define and depends upon the person telling the story as well as the person listening or reading. Similar effects are created in the modern African novels *Americanah* (Adichie) and *A Grain of Wheat* (Ngũgĩ).

Duration of events

Sometimes a novel seems to slow down and at other times speed up. A few years can pass in one sentence. An apparently brief, chance meeting can take a whole chapter to describe. Here is a passage from *The Secret Agent* (1907) by Joseph Conrad, which describes the murder of Mr Verloc, an event that, in real time, would take only a moment or two.

ACTIVITY 9.3

Look at the pace of the description of this event and try to identify those aspects which slow it down.

He was lying on his back and staring upwards. He saw partly on the ceiling and partly on the wall the moving shadow of an arm with a clenched hand holding a carving knife. It flickered up and down. Its movements were leisurely. They were leisurely enough for Mr Verloc to recognise the limb and the weapon.

They were leisurely enough for him to take in the full meaning of the portent, and to taste the flavour of death rising in his gorge. His wife had gone raving mad – murdering mad. They were leisurely enough for the first paralysing effect of this discovery to pass away before a resolute determination to come out victorious from the ghastly struggle with that armed lunatic. They were leisurely enough for Mr Verloc to elaborate a plan of defence involving a dash behind the table, and the felling of the woman to the ground with a heavy wooden chair. But they were not leisurely enough to allow Mr Verloc the time to move either hand or foot. The knife was already planted in his breast.

Joseph Conrad *The Secret Agent* (1907)

COMMENT

Conrad repeats the phrase *they were leisurely enough* again and again. Ironically the word *leisurely* itself slows the pace, and the repetitive structure builds suspense until the climax of *they were not leisurely enough* and then it is too late – the knife is in his breast. Conrad's technique of focusing on Verloc's consciousness slows the events down – one can have many thoughts in just a moment. (Compare this effect with the use of parallelism and repetition in poetry in Unit 2.)

Contrast this with the brisk details of the opening sentence of this detective story (designed to make you want to read on):

> On November the 21st, the day of her forty-seventh birthday, and three weeks and two days before she was murdered, Rhoda Gradwyn went to Harley Street to keep a first appointment with her plastic surgeon....
>
> (from *The Private Patient* by P.D. James, 2008)

The connections in a complex narrative

Sometimes the writer will draw attention to the structural links in the story. The following passage, which comes from *Bleak House* (1852–1853) by Charles Dickens, is an example that reveals the vast and seemingly never-ending material the novelist has at her/his disposal to shape into a novel. The choice will be made to suit her/his theme.

> What connexion can there be, between the place in Lincolnshire, the house in town, the Mercury in powder, and the whereabouts of Jo the outlaw with the broom, who had that distant ray of light upon him when he swept the churchyard-step? What connexion can there have been between many people in the innumerable histories of this world, who, from opposite sides of great gulfs, have, nevertheless, been very curiously brought together?
>
> Charles Dickens *Bleak House* (1853)

And the novelist is, of course, doing the bringing together. Victorian novelists, of whom Dickens is one, were very fond of coincidences, not merely to make the plot more engaging, but also to suggest the complex networks of social connections and responsibilities that people try to ignore.

At other times, structural links are made by the creation of characters who, placed next to one another – or juxtaposed – bring out the writer's concerns very clearly by contrast. Repetition of image or symbol can also help to create structural links in a novel. (This is discussed further in Unit 10.)

Reflection: Why do you think novelists are so attracted to writing stories about children or young people growing up? Do you find them more interesting to read than other kinds of novel? What challenges do they pose for the writer? (For example, should they be first- or third-person narratives?)

Stories of development or coming-of-age

This is a structure where the main character is shown developing through the work, making mistakes and learning until she/he is educated, sometimes morally, into realisation of her/his own shortcomings and sometimes into greater maturity. *Martha Quest* by Doris Lessing is a novel of this kind set in colonial Africa, as are *Great Expectations* by Charles Dickens and *Emma* by Jane Austen. Such novels often show the society in which the novel is set as hostile to the aspirations of the character, although not in the latter case. In Nigerian novelist Adichie's *Half of a Yellow Sun*, for example, Ugwu, one of the three protagonists, is shown growing up against the terrible background of the Biafran war.

Emma is very carefully constructed, with the main character, Emma, making errors of judgement and wrong suppositions that gradually unfold and are resolved when she learns the truth. Characters are introduced at just the right moments for advancing Emma's progress, and public events – such as balls and picnics – punctuate the narrative regularly and helpfully for the reader's appreciation of the social setting.

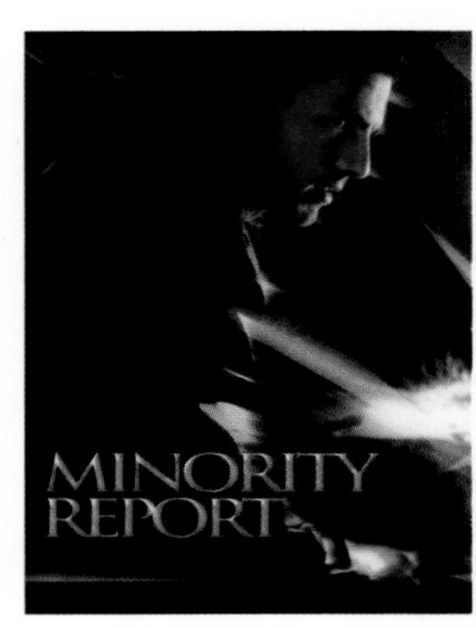

The film *Minority Report* is based on a short story by Philip K. Dick.

Short story structures

A short story has, by its nature, less space to create complex narrative structures. Nonetheless, the story will form a satisfying whole and its climax, often expressed in the final paragraph or sentence, will sum up the experiences that have been explored in the story. A 'twist' in the final moments of a short story is often asserted as a feature of the short story genre, but there are many stories, for example in *Stories of Ourselves*, a popular set text, where there is no such twist. Instead, a more gradual realisation of its concerns and characters takes place and is no less satisfying. Some short story writers are capable of incorporating complex narrative methods into a relatively short space of time: one such is the Canadian writer Alice Munro, whose stories often involve quite complicated 'stories within stories' that have more in common with *Wuthering Heights* than with most short stories.

KEY TERM

Ambiguity: means being open to more than one meaning or interpretation. Different points of view create **irony** from ambiguity. What one character sees as good may be disastrous for another, so irony is inevitable. Ambiguity and the irony that springs from it are among the most significant effects in literature.

ACTIVITY 9.4

Read the short stories you are studying and work out their structure. Do they have a sudden 'twist' at the end where all is revealed, or not at all? Or do they have a more gradual revelation of theme and character, or a resolution that is ambiguous?

Other writers create a book of short stories that are each complete and satisfying within themselves, and in fact all relate to each other, with shared characters and events, but seen in different timescales and from different points of view. A good example of this is *The Turning* by Tim Winton (included in the anthology *Stories of Ourselves*). *Go Down, Moses* by the American writer William Faulkner is another. The Wyoming tales of Annie Proulx are a more recent American example. This allows a kind of novelistic development of character, theme and language features through individual stories which are complete and satisfying in themselves too.

TIP

When answering passage questions, make sure that you consider the place of the extract within the novel's or story's structure. Is this one of the many moments when the heroine/hero is faced with her/his own mistake and has to learn to be more careful? Is this one of the descriptions of the place that regularly punctuate the narrative, drawing attention to a particular theme? Always try to analyse the writer's skill and artistry.

Two examples from *Stories of Ourselves* where there is a 'twist in the tail' are *Meteor* (John Wyndham), a story which has multiple narration too, and *An Englishman's Home* (Evelyn Waugh). Two stories which have a gradual revelation of the theme are *The Third and Final Continent* (Jhumpa Lahiri) and *Games at Twilight* (Anita Desai).

FURTHER READING

1. Although its length may make it seem daunting to you, try reading the great Victorian novel *Middlemarch* by George Eliot. The strands of the story are interwoven in a network of connections, motivations and sheer coincidence, all of which make the novel absolutely compelling.
2. Zimbabwean writer Tsitsi Dangerembga's *Nervous Conditions*. This is a post-colonial novel of a family set in Rhodesia (now Zimbabwe) in the 1960s.

Self-assessment checklist

Reflect on what you've learnt in this unit and indicate your confidence level between 1 and 5. If you score below 3, revisit that section. Come back to this list later in your course. Has your confidence grown?

	Confidence level	Revisited?
I understand chronological structure		
I am learning to appreciate different kinds of non-chronological arrangement in prose		
I can identify and discuss stories of development		
I know some typical short story structures and how they work		

Unit 10
Characterisation

Learning objectives

In this unit you will:

- review different kinds of character in the novel
- analyse character description in a variety of novels
- study the critical comments on each
- make the association of characters with setting and symbols
- consider contrast as a technique of characterisation.

KEY CONCEPTS

Language, form, structure, genres, context, style, interpretation.

Before you start

- With a friend, make a list of all your favourite characters from novels or short stories. Discuss why they appear on your list. Is it because they are so lovable, or, perhaps more likely, so villainous or mysterious?

Characterisation, or the making of characters, is one of the most important features of any novel and what for many readers makes a novel memorable. It is frequently the subject for homework essays and examination questions, and your work should reflect your appreciation of both what a character is like and what their place is in the ideas and structure of the novel as a whole. This is also true of the short story, although inevitably the characterisation will be less developed in a shorter work.

Reflection: Enjoying a novel thoroughly can sometimes lead you into thinking of the characters as real people. If a filmed version of your novel has been made, this is an even easier trap to fall into as you may associate a character with a particular actor who plays the part. It is important to remember that the creation of character is being employed by the writer for particular effects in the novel as a whole.

TIP

At more advanced level, a description of a character, or character sketch, is not enough; some reference to the way in which the writer creates the character (characterisation) and their contribution to the work as a whole will be essential.

In almost every novel a character or set of characters engages the reader's interest from the very outset. In the opening paragraphs looked at in Unit 8, it was clear from most of them that the story begins with a focus on a person. In this unit, you are going to look at some of the techniques used by writers to present a character in the novel as a whole.

In our lives, we meet people and respond to their age, gender and appearance, what they do and say, and how they react to us and other people. We know ourselves too, and reflect on our own consciousness, attributes and appearance, although our self-knowledge is likely to be partial and biased. In a novel, the writer selects a narrative method (see Unit 7) and then works within this first- or third-person structure to present the appearance, actions and thoughts of characters.

Rounded and flat, three-dimensional and one-dimensional characters

In creating the world of the novel with its unique and distinctive qualities, the writer has to focus on and delineate (describe precisely) the main area of interest and activity. What follows here uses a number of comparisons – some of them rather mixed, as I try to clarify the point. It is rather like a person using a pair of compasses: the sharp end is pressed into the paper and a circle is drawn with the pencil on the other end. (If you have studied John Donne's poetry, you will be aware of the potential of this image!) The circle, and everything inside it, represents the focus of the novel, with the point at the centre. Characters close to the centre of the circle may be characterised in full and complex detail, while others at the edge of the circle are simply sketched in.

Another way of describing this difference is to call the detailed characters 'rounded' because they are apparently three-dimensional, and the simple sketches 'flat' characters because they are types: one-dimensional and with perhaps a single feature or mannerism. In some comic novels, these features are so exaggerated that you could call such characters **caricatures**.

KEY TERM

Caricature: a depiction of a person whose main features are simplified and exaggerated. Some of Dickens's minor characters are caricatures.

It would not be wise to dismiss their effectiveness, though, because they might be vital to the plot, or add to the expression of the author's main concerns in the novel, or act as a contrast or parallel to one of the major characters. So the role or function of the character does not necessarily depend on the depth and detail with which it is presented.

Description of characters

The way in which a writer describes a character in a third-person narrative is very revealing, not only of aspects of the character being presented but also of the writer's attitude to the character.

ACTIVITY 10.1

Look closely at these descriptions. In what ways and how effectively does the writer introduce the character/s?

Extract 1

John Reed was a schoolboy of fourteen years old; four years older than I, for I was but ten; large and stout for his age, with a dingy and unwholesome skin; thick lineaments in a spacious visage, heavy limbs and large extremities. He gorged himself habitually at table, which made him bilious, and gave him a dim and bleared eye with flabby cheeks. He ought now to have been at school; but his mamma had taken him home for a month or two, 'on account of his delicate health.' Mr Miles, the master, affirmed that he would do very well if he had fewer cakes and sweetmeats sent him from home; but the mother's heart turned from an opinion so harsh, and inclined rather to the more refined idea that John's sallowness was owing to over-application and, perhaps, to pining after home.

Charlotte Brontë *Jane Eyre* (1847)

▶

Extract 2a

The general had yellowed eyes, which suggested to Ifemelu a malnourished childhood. His solid, thickset body spoke of fights that he had started and won, and the buck-teeth that gaped through his lips made him seem vaguely dangerous. Ifemelu was surprised by the gleeful coarseness of him. 'I'm a village man!' he said happily, as though to explain the drops of soup that landed on his shirt and on the table while he ate, or his loud burping afterwards.

Extract 2b

And then there was Cristina Tomas. Cristina Tomas with her rinsed-out look, her washy blue eyes, faded hair and pallid skin. Cristina Tomas seated at the front desk with a smile. Cristina Tomas wearing whitish tights that made her legs look like death.

Nigerian Chimamanda Ngozi Adichie *Americanah* (2013)

Extract 3

Miss Lumley rules by fear. She's short, and oblong in shape, so that her iron-grey cardigan falls straight from shoulder to hip with no pause in between for a waist. She always wears this cardigan, and a succession of dark skirts, which can't possibly be the same one. She has steel-rimmed glasses behind which her eyes are hard to see, and black shoes with Cuban heels, and a tiny lipless smile. She does not send children to the Principal for the strap, but does it herself, in front of the class, holding the hand out flat, bringing the black rubber strap down in sharp quick efficient strokes, her face white and quivering, while we watch, wincing, our eyes filling with involuntary tears.

Canadian Margaret Atwood *Cat's Eye* (1988)

Extract 4

Now Prophet Revelations Bitchington Mborro is busy thundering about Judas and Golgotha and the cross and the two thieves next to Jesus and things, making like he was there and saw it all. When Prophet Revelations Bitchington Mborro is in form he doesn't stand in one place. He paces up and down like there are hot coals under his feet. He flails his arms, sometimes waving his stick at the sky, sometimes jumping around, as if he is itching where nobody can see. Every once in a while a woman will scream Sweet Jeeeeesus, or Hmmm-hmmm-hmmm, or Glory, glory, or something like that, which means that the spirit is touching her.

Prophet Revelations Bitchington Mborro is drenched in sweat now and his robe clings to his chest….

Zimbabwean NoViolet Bulawayo *We Need New Names* (2013)

Extract 5

Lily, turning her eyes from him, found herself scanning her little world through his retina: it was as though the pink lamps had been shut off and the dusty daylight let in. She looked down the long table, studying its occupants one by one, from Gus Trenor, with his heavy carnivorous head sunk between his shoulders, as he preyed on a jellied plover, to his wife, at the opposite end of the long bank of orchids, suggestive, with her glaring good looks, of a jeweller's window lit by electricity. And between the two, what a long stretch of vacuity!

►

How dreary and trivial these people were! Lily reviewed them with a scornful impatience: Carry Fisher, with her shoulders, her eyes, her divorces, her general air of embodying a 'spicy paragraph'; young Silverton, who had meant to live on proof-reading and write an epic, and who now lived on his friends and had become critical of truffles; Alice Wetherall, an animated visiting-list, whose most fervid convictions turned on the wording of invitations and the engraving of dinner-cards; Wetherall, with his perpetual nervous nod of acquiescence, his air of agreeing with people before he knew what they were saying; Jack Stepney, with his confident smile and anxious eyes, half way between the sheriffand an heiress; Gwen Van Osburgh, with all the guileless confidence of a young girl who has always been told that there is no one richer than her father.

Edith Wharton *The House of Mirth* (1905)

SAMPLE RESPONSE

Extract 1

John Reed is one of the unpleasant Reed family who make Jane's early life a misery. The descriptive adjectives used for him suggest a pale and unhealthy complexion: *dingy*, *dim* and *bleared*, for example. He is unhealthily fat because he eats too many sweets: we are told he is *large*, *stout*, *heavy* and *flabby*. The reason for this becomes clear: he is entirely spoilt by his mother who has convinced herself that he should spend a couple of months at home instead of being at school because he has been working too hard and is homesick, although his master at school seems to have a clearer-sighted view. John is not a major character in the novel, but at this point, he is used as a contrast with Jane, who is bright but thin, undernourished and victimised. She is hated by her aunt, John's mother, and treated very badly, unlike her cousin. It is Jane's critical and judgemental eye which provides us with this little portrait, telling us of her difficult situation in the Reed household.

Extract 2

These two brief descriptions are of minor characters in the novel *Americanah*. In a few words, Adichie creates vivid portraits. The general's physical attributes are closely linked with his character: the phrase *gleeful coarseness* is particularly apt, suggesting a self-satisfied crudity of manner. The main character's aunt is his mistress and the reader is not encouraged to think positively of him here. His yellowed eyes and thickset body suggest both an unhealthy lifestyle and an aggressive nature, and his proud claim to be from the country, *I'm a village man*, does not suggest innocence or lack of sophistication, but perhaps a distance from civilised behaviour. He is strong, confident and unsubtle.

Ifemelu, the protagonist of the novel, is a black Nigerian woman and Cristina Tomas is registering her for a course. During their brief interchange, Cristina Tomas is very patronising. This brief sketch reveals through physical description her lack of vitality. Diction such as *rinsed-out washy*, *faded*, *pallid* establishes both the colour of her skin (white) and her bland colourless nature. Her *whitish tights* enhance this impression so that her legs look like those of a corpse. Adichie does not need to say that Cristina is white: the diction makes this clear, associating her pallor with an uninteresting nature.

▶

Extract 3

Although the novel is recounting past events, the passage is in the present tense, giving it an immediacy which adds to the picture of the sadistic teacher here. The sentence structure emphasises by repetition the simple confidence of her actions: she *is*, she *wears*, she *has*, she *does*; this makes her seem very determined. The colours associated with her are dark or metallic ones: iron-grey cardigan, steel-rimmed glasses, dark skirts, black shoes and, of course, a black strap with which to hit those pupils who have done something wrong. There is little of humanity about her. Atwood says that you can't see her eyes and her smile is *tiny* and *lipless*. Although her beating is undertaken in a very efficient way, the final detail of the description is particularly disturbing: when she is administering the strap, her face is *white and quivering*, from some undefined emotion – anger, perhaps, or a kind of sadistic passion. The class can only watch wincing as she hits the unfortunate miscreant. The sounds and rhythms of the final sentence are worth noting: *her face white and quivering, while we watch, wincing, our eyes filling with involuntary tears*. The use of alliteration of the 'w' sound here (*white*, *while*, *we*, *watch*, *wincing*) and assonance of *quivering*, *wincing*, *filling* is as evocative as any poet's line, and suggests, interestingly, some sort of link in meaning as well as sound, a commonality of emotion between the teacher and the class. And this is borne out at the end of the chapter where the protagonist observes:

Although Miss Lumley is not what anyone thinks of as a girl, she is also not a boy. When the brass handbell clangs and we line up outside our GIRLS door, whatever category we are in also includes her.

Extract 4

The pastor in this rural evangelical church has an improbable and amusing name, which Bulawayo repeats several times for comic effect. The description is written in the present tense, making it immediate and instantly colourful. Bulawayo's narrator – a young girl – lists the events and people in the Bible that he is talking about, linking them with 'and', but she is not is not particularly impressed with his approach *making like he was there and saw it all* and seems unmoved by the religious implications of his words. Her use of *and things* is rather dismissive of the Bible story. She is much more interested in the actions he performs, leaping around and flailing his arms, and the dramatic effect it has on his hearers. *Like there are hots coals under his feet* is a vivid simile. This is a short passage but a very lively one, capturing the child's irreverent attitude and comic alertness to sight, sound and movement.

Extract 5

This savage description of the wealthy house party as they dine is seen through the eyes of Lily, the novel's protagonist, or rather, it is seen through her eyes scanning the scene *through* [the] *retina* of another character, Selden, who is very influential in the novel in reminding her of the shortcomings of wealthy society and its values. She has earlier been trying to convince herself that she should do her best to become engaged to a wealthy but very dull young man, and a few pages previous to this passage she has been 'talking up' the group that she here criticises so sharply. We could point to the predatory images of Gus Trenor, which are to be developed later ▶

on in the novel, and of his wife looking like the *jeweller's window*, whose concern for the family's money makes her a formidable adversary later on in the novel, and to each of the other named characters, all of whom will play a part in Lily's downfall. These ironies unfold with the progress of the novel. But here, the description of these shallow, unlikeable people, each pinpointed with a sharp little comment, is a study in point of view as much as a description of character: it reveals Selden's attitude, seen through Lily's description, and behind them both, the social criticism of the novelist herself. The passage goes on to show Lily's saving grace: the intelligence which makes her aware that she has changed her mind about this social group.

Associating characters with settings or symbols

Another way in which characters can be presented is by associating them with a particular setting or symbol, a physical representation of an idea or quality.

- In *Great Expectations* (Dickens), Miss Havisham is always associated with a dark room full of dust, cobwebs and images of the past.
- The bleakness of Heathcliff's character in *Wuthering Heights* (Brontë) is emphasised by association with the moors and their wild weather, his relationship with Catherine like the rocks beneath the earth.
- In *The Great Gatsby* Fitzgerald contrasts the house of Tom and Daisy Buchanan with that of Jay Gatsby: the former being old and well-established, part of the wealth of a dynasty; the latter new and built to impress, with a library containing books whose pages have not even been cut and a cupboard full of beautiful but unworn imported silk shirts.
- In Thomas Hardy's *Tess of the D'Urbervilles*, the phases of Tess's life are enhanced by the different natural settings in which they take place.
- In Lahiri's *The Namesake*, the name Gogol, which is given to the main character, symbolises European culture, something he would like to rid himself of as the novel progresses.
- Adichie's *Americanah* uses the symbol of African hair and its springy tight curls to represent quintessential African nature: lively, untameable, distinctive. The first chapter is set in a hairdressing salon and this **motif** continues through the novel.
- In Doris Lessing's *Martha Quest*, the dress that Martha makes for the dance symbolises her independence from her parents and her rejection of her mother in particular.
- In George Eliot's *Middlemarch*, the symbols of mirror and window represent respectively the ego (the personality focused on itself) and the more altruistic and outward-looking escape from self.
- Books symbolise the mind's expansion and development in Eliot's *The Mill on the Floss*: Maggie's love for them is sadly not encouraged as she is a girl and therefore is thought not to need education, whilst her brother Tom is not at all academic and wants to do practical things but must be educated as he is the boy of the family.

ACTIVITY 10.2

Consider a novel or short story you are studying: do any of the characters have a symbol attached to them?

Reflection: What effect does this have: firstly on the characterisation, and secondly on the work as a whole? Are any of the characters associated with a particular setting?

KEY TERM

Motif: a recurrent element in a text. It is a word used in relation to music as well.

Hardy's *Tess of the D'Urbervilles* is set in rural Wessex.

Parallels and contrasts

Minor characters can contribute to the plot or enhance the themes of a novel by providing reinforcement of the qualities of a major character, or, conversely, throwing their characteristics into clear relief by the contrast they provide.

Example of main character	Parallel/contrast
Mrs Elton in *Emma* – shallow, pretentious and snobbish, interfering and spiteful.	Miss Bates – loquacious and boring but good-hearted and open, unlike Mrs Elton. Emma herself interferes, but she learns her lesson as the book develops and gains sense and judgement.
Elinor in *Sense and Sensibility*.	Her sister Marianne. Each acquires some of the characteristics of the other as the novel proceeds.
Olanna in *Half of a Yellow Sun*.	Her sister Kainene. This troubled relationship is arguably the most important one in *Half of a Yellow Sun*.
Rochester in *Jane Eyre* is used to represent the passionate nature of Jane.	St John Rivers is a more cool person and can be argued to represent order and control.

Some literary critics argue that Brontë is more successful in her creation of Jane Eyre than of these two male characters, who are criticised as unconvincing and two-dimensional. However, if you realise their structural function in the novel as contrasting with each other and intensifying Jane's nature (the novel's main concern), then they could be seen as more successful.

ACTIVITY 10.3

Add to this list by referring to the novels or short stories you are studying.

Reflection: If possible, discuss the characters on your list with a partner or a classmate. How many are created in depth? Do you find the pairing (either of similarity or difference) an effective one in each case?

FURTHER READING

1. D.H. Lawrence's *Short Stories*: these are substantial stories that are long enough to develop characterisation.
2. Canadian Margaret Atwood's *Cat's Eye* (Anchor, 1988) is a novel which explores growing up and relationships.

Self-assessment checklist

Reflect on what you've learnt in this unit and indicate your confidence level between 1 and 5. If you score below 3, revisit that section. Come back to this list later in your course. Has your confidence grown?

	Confidence level	Revisited?
I can distinguish between character and characterisation		
I am more knowledgeable about types of character and their function		
I can acknowledge the relationship between character and symbol		
I see and discuss the value of parallels and contrasts of character		

Prose unseens

Learning objectives

In this unit you will:

- clarify how you can prepare to approach unseen prose questions with confidence
- study the prose unseen checklist
- develop critical ideas by annotating passages
- compare the work of students and the assessments of it, adding your own thoughts.

KEY CONCEPTS

Language, form, structure, genres, context, style, interpretation.

Before you start

- The advice given here is very similar to the advice given in the poetry section. If you are going to have a choice of material to respond to in an unseen assessment (you will have a choice in the Cambridge examination), it's always sensible to make your decision on the day, not to go into examination thinking 'I always like the poem best', or 'I much prefer to write on prose'. Each piece is different and has a different appeal. It's important to read and choose very carefully and not to rush into it. As part of your preparation for examination, discuss with a partner how you feel about having to write on a prose unseen and the challenges you face. This unit should help you!

If you are taking the 9695 AS Level course, you will now have a compulsory unseen paper, which has a prose passage in it. In this unit, you have some guidelines to help you to frame your responses so that you feel confident about answering on a passage of prose you haven't seen before. First you have to read and appreciate it, then to write on it, so there are two different kinds of activity here: considering the elements of the passage and how they fit together; and writing a successful essay incorporating these ideas.

It's natural to feel apprehensive. You may be thinking 'There's a lot of reading in this passage' or 'Do I understand this?', but remember, what has been set will be just right for you at your level, and all the other students are in just the same situation. If there are any unusual words, the meanings will be given to you. Examiners are not trying to catch you out; they want to give you the best opportunity to show what you can do. You won't be expected to know about the historical context or the writer's life – what is being tested is the effect of the words and forms chosen by the writer. All the work you've done on your novels and short stories and all your previous reading will help you, too.

In this unit, you will have reminders of the different aspects of a prose passage that should be considered in any critical appreciation and examples of students' essays on unseen extracts at different levels.

Take an active approach to analysis

An unseen exercise tests close reading, so you need to annotate your passage: underlining, highlighting, linking, commenting in the margin. It becomes a working document and will be the basis of your answer.

Use a highlighter and coloured pens to pick out and underline different aspects of the piece; for example, different characters, passages of description in unusual sentences and direct speech, as well as metaphors and other figures of speech. You will gradually begin to appreciate the effects of the word choices made by the writer.

Every passage is different, so you need to be flexible

Figure 11.1 reminds you of what you need to think about, but each passage is part of a novel or short story that creates its own world. What has been picked for you to comment on will be complete in itself, but it will be very suggestive of the work as a whole, which you haven't got in front of you.

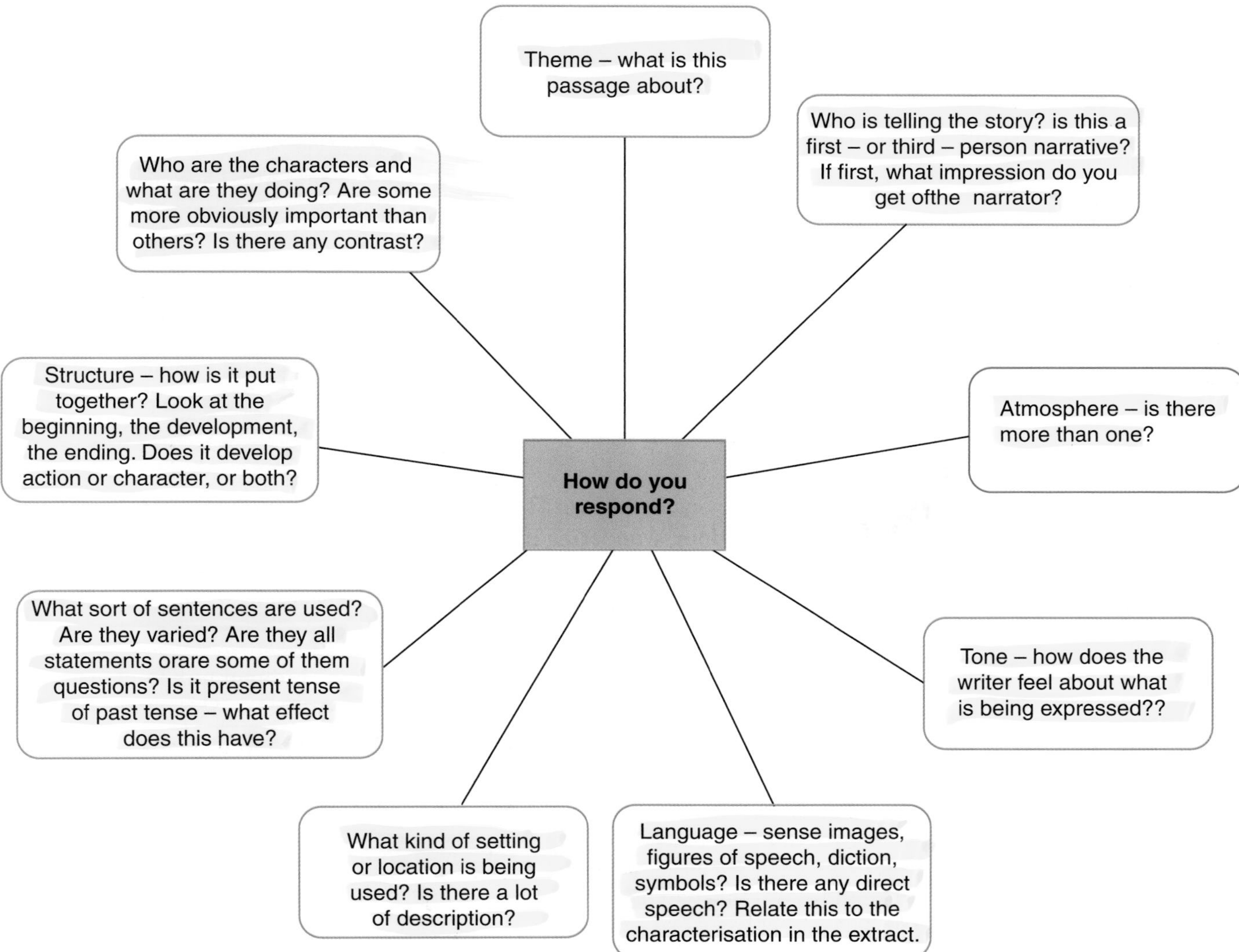

Figure 11.1: Checklist for analysing prose.

ACTIVITY 11.1

Two passages are presented here, complete with student responses. Read each passage carefully and, using your highlighters, underline and colour the different elements such as figures of speech, direct speech and character description. Do this before you read the student response to the passage.

Then look at the student responses, noting the comments made by the marker.

Essay: *Write a critical appreciation of the prose passage, commenting particularly on characterisation and creation of atmosphere.*

Passage 1

The village was now far behind. Darkness had thickened. It struck him, like a new experience, that he was alone. He listened. He seemed to hear, in the distance, steps on a pavement. The steps approached him. He walked faster and faster, away from the steps. But the faster he walked, the louder the steps became. He panted. He was hot all over, despite the cold air. Then he started running madly. His heart beat harder. The steps on the pavement, so near now, rhythmed with his pounding heart. He had to talk to someone. He must hear another human voice. Mugo. But what were mere human voices? Had he not lived with them for six years? In various detention camps? Perhaps he wanted a voice of man who would understand. Mugo. Abruptly he stopped running. The steps on the pavement receded into a distance. They would come again, he knew they would come to plague him. I must talk to Mugo. The words Mugo had spoken at a meeting two years before had touched Gikonyo. Lord, Mugo would know.

But by the time he reached Mugo's hut, the heat of his resolution had cooled. He stood outside the door, wondering if he should knock or not: what really, had he come to tell Mugo? He felt foolish, standing there, alone. Maybe he had better come tomorrow. Maybe another time he would know best how to tear his heart before another person.

At home, he found Mumbi had not yet gone to bed. She brought him food. This reminded him that he had hardly eaten anything the whole day. She sat opposite him and watched him. He tasted a little food and then pushed the rest away. He had lost his appetite.

'Make me a cup of tea,' he said between his teeth.

'You must eat,' Mumbi appealed. Her small nose shone with the light from the lamp. The appeal in her eyes and voice belied the calm face and the proud carriage of her well-formed body. Gikonyo stared at the new, well-polished mahogany table. Perhaps he should have called on Mugo for a talk between men.

'I don't want anything to eat,' he grunted.

From Ngũgĩ Wa Thiong'o *A Grain of Wheat* (1967).

[Mugo is a political associate of Gikonyo, who has experienced detention. Mumbi is Gikonyo's wife]

STUDENT RESPONSE

This passage written in third person narrative voice depicts a man who feels very anxious and isolated. He thinks he is being followed and want to get reassurance from his friend Mugo. Although he wants to communicate, something holds him back and he feels self-conscious. His anxiety makes it impossible for him to do so. He seems not to have a close relationship with his wife, either. The contrast between his desire to speak to his friend and his cool relationship with his wife is strongly shown in the passage.

A clear overview of the passage, with some reference to narrative method and the characterisation of the main character.

In the first paragraph Ngugi uses pathetic fallacy and symbolism to underline Gikonyo's isolation and anxiety. He is alone in the *'darkness'* which had *'thickened'*. He thinks he can hear footsteps and this makes him fearful. They seem to symbolise the authorities following him, as when they recede, he *'knew they would come to plague him'* another time. Perhaps as he has experienced imprisonment he is particularly nervous of being followed.

The technical terms *symbolism* and *pathetic fallacy* are aptly used. The text is quoted directly in support.

The sentence structure in the first paragraph effectively focuses on the fear of Gikonyo. His actions are presented as past tense verbs: *'he listened'*, *'he walked'*, *'he panted'* Some sentences are formed of only two words, which creates suspense. He links the footsteps to his own heartbeat: *'rhythmed with his pounding heart'*. Ngugi focuses closely on his character's thoughts and feelings by using free indirect halfway through the paragraph, giving Gikonyo's own thoughts: *'He had to talk to someone...but what were mere human voices? ...I must talk to Mugo....Lord, Mugo would know.'*

The effect of varied sentence structure is an effective point.

Notices the use of free indirect speech and its effect.

He also questions himself. These techniques allow the writer to maintain the observation of the 3rd person narrator and combine it with close involvement with his hero's thoughts and feelings of uncertainty. This technique is also used very effectively in the next paragraph 'Maybe he had better come tomorrow'. 'To tear his heart' is a metaphor showing his anguish effectively, but it also contrasts with the way he speaks to his wife in the next section.

The passage ends with a change of focus – onto the dialogue with his wife and the depiction of their relationship.

The contrast between Gikonyo's attitude towards his male friend and his wife is a feature of the passage that has been well-noted.

Mumbi seems an attractive young woman (*'small nose'*, *'well-formed body'*) and she is trying hard to be a good wife – the table is polished, she has food prepared. She too is depicted as anxious – beneath the *'calm'* exterior she *'appeals'* to him (a repeated word) but he pushes the food away and orders her to make him a cup of tea. He evidently prefers a *'talk between men'*, showing his sexist attitude to women generally as well as to his wife. Ngũgĩ successfully focuses on his main character but is still able to suggest the inner life of Mumbi his wife.

An unusual point. Mumbi is a secondary character but she is well and succinctly depicted here.

This is a well-organised and thoughtful essay that uses good technical terminology correctly and discusses its effects. The point about contrast is a good one.

Reflection: Consider if there are ways in which you could add to or improve this essay. Would it be helpful to have a conclusion summing up the student's response, for example? Do you think enough has been said about the atmosphere created?

ACTIVITY 11.2

Passage 2 has two student responses after it. Read and annotate it yourself with the help of a friend, then read the student responses and the marker comments that go with them.

Passage 2

'I'll read to you till the fire burns low and then we'll go to bed.' Holding the book in one hand and bending over me to get the light of the fire on the book, he puts his other hand over my breast, and I cover his hand with mine, and he reads from *Antony and Cleopatra*. He cannot see my face, not I his, but his low tender voice trembles as he speaks the words so full for us of poignant meaning. That tremor is my undoing. 'Don't read any more. I can't bear it.' All my strength gives way. I hide my face on his knee and all my tears so long kept back come convulsively. He raises my head and wipes my eyes and kisses them, and wrapping his greatcoat round me carries me to our bed in the great, bare ice-cold room. Soon he is with me and we lie speechless and trembling in each other's arms. I cannot stop crying. My body is torn with terrible sobs. I am engulfed in this despair like a drowning man by the sea. My mind is incapable of thought. Only now and then, as they say drowning people do, I have visons of things that have been – the room where my son was born; a day, years after, when we were together walking before breakfast by a stream with hands full of bluebells; and in the kitchen of our honeymoon cottage, and I happy in his pride of me. David did not speak except now and then to say some tender word or name, and hold me tight to him....

So we lay all night, sometimes talking of our love and all that had been and of the children and what had been amiss and what had been right. We knew the best was that there had never been untruth between us. We knew all of each other and it was right. So talking and crying and loving in each other's arms we fell asleep as the cold reflected light of the snow crept through the frost-covered windows.

David got up and made the fire and brought me some tea, and then got back into bed, and the children clambered in too, and we sat in a row sipping our tea... After breakfast, while he showed me where his account books were and what each was for, I listened calmly, and unbelievingly he kissed me when I said I, too, would keep accounts....And hand in hand we went downstairs and out to the children, who were playing in the snow....

A thick mist hung everywhere, and there was no sound except, far away in the valley, a train shunting. I stood at the gate watching him go.

From Helen Thomas *World Without End* (1972)

STUDENT RESPONSE 1

This passage outlines the distraught reaction from the first person to her husband going off to the 1st World War. The passage shows a foreshadowing of death and time being portrayed as the enemy as well.

Throughout the passage, death is foreshadowed. Pathetic fallacy of '*a thick mist hung everywhere*' mirrors the author's own misery and confusion. Through the loss of clear sight, vulnerability and isolation are emphasised, which parallels the author's own sense of being weakened. The mist clouding the atmosphere suggests the uncertainty of the future – will he return? This is especially emphasised as the mist is enveloped by '*the silence of death*,' which further emphasised a sense of doom. The repetition of words about the temperature also add to this effect. The repeated use of '*cold*' in "*the great bare ice-cold room*' and the '*cold reflected light*' and '*my heart cold with sadness*' foreshadows the death of the husband. The listing of great, bare and ice-cold accentuates the overwhelming combination of emotions felt by the narrator. Light is normally a symbol of warmth and understanding, but here ironically it is cold light.

The authors emotions are graphically portrayed throughout. She 'cannot stop crying'. Her body is 'torn with terrible sobs'. The staccato alliteration of 'cannot' and 'crying', 'torn' and 'terrible' expresses effectively the anguish she feels. She uses a simile to express this: she is engulfed in her despair 'like a drowning man at sea'. Again, listing is used to accentuate the emotion: 'holding me tightly to him, his face white, his eyes full of a fear I had never seen before' involves her husband too in the distress of the parting.

Time is suggested as the enemy here. All through the passage, there are reminders of change brought by time – the fire burning low, the night passing and dawn breaking, the train in the distance shunting, ready for the journey which will bear him away.

Death being foreshadowed is now being discussed, with quotation to support. The term 'pathetic fallacy' is correctly used.

Further textual reference supports the topic of this paragraph successfully, with symbolism being noted.

The narrator's grief is discussed with apt illustrations analysing language and sound effects.

A short introduction but two interesting points are made: one about foreshadowing of death and the other about time being the enemy.

A rather brief reference to the idea introduced in the first paragraph – that the real enemy is time.

This essay has much to commend it, although it ends rather abruptly. Some of the ideas are stated but not fully developed and it feels rushed towards the end. Paragraph 2 is a good one, with plenty of apt detail, but there isn't much sense of the love relationship at the heart of the passage. The room may be cold, but the husband-and-wife relationship is very warm. The writer started with an ambitious agenda in the first paragraph that isn't quite fulfilled. There is plenty of potential here, but time management may be a problem for this student.

STUDENT RESPONSE 2

Thomas's passage focuses on a woman whose husband is about to go off to war. She depicts this through sorrowful language in the first person and we feel very sympathetic to the situation as her children are involved as well. It is a varied passage with description and direct speech as well, to present a very sad human situation.

The language used to describe the narrator's state of mind is particularly striking. 'My body is torn with terrible sobs. I am engulfed in this despair like a drowning man by the sea. My mind is incapable of thought'. The simile and the use of alliteration make this a very moving account of her feelings. The narrator starts the passage in the present tense which makes it very immediate but then moves on to tell the story in the past.

The theme of love is presented throughout the passage and from the very beginning: 'I'll read to you till the fire burns low and then we'll go to bed'. Intimacy and warmth are symbolised from the outset. What is being read is one of the world's great love stories *Anthony and Cleopatra*, but we notice it is a tragic love story, which adds to the atmosphere. Their embraces and their physical closeness are well-portrayed ('I hide my face on his knee') and add to the poignant effect. It is getting colder, and the word cold is repeated several times, but the warmth of their love for each other is evident. 'So we lay all night, sometimes talking of our love'. This is enhanced by the writer's use of the past when they were happy, as a contrast to the present grief. She remembers when their son was born, when they walked together after picking bluebells, and on their honeymoon. The direct speech that they have with each other is another method used by Thomas to bring the situation to life. They even discuss practical matters like the household accounts, which gives authenticity to the situation.

Pathetic fallacy is used to underpin the gloomy and depressive mood of the couple. 'The snow crept through the frost-covered window', 'the cold reflected light of the snow and the thick mist' that hung everywhere' all help to create a chilled and wretched atmosphere to accompany the parting of the family. This makes it very effective, as if the whole world mourns the departure of the husband to war.

This is a sad account of a terrible situation caused by war. It effectively reminds us of the human tragedies we should avoid.

Well-illustrated with a variety of observations about language use.

Symbolism noted to illustrate the account of love in the passage.

A good point about Antony and Cleopatra.

Well-illustrated and with a sound point on the use of the past memories.

Consideration of direct speech and its effect.

Effective consideration of *atmosphere* and *pathetic fallacy*.

A brief but personal summing up.

A good overview of the passage, with personal response and awareness of narrative method.

A good essay with a strong overview of the characters' feelings portrayed in the passage and the language used to present them. Lots of points are made, the essay is well-constructed and well-illustrated throughout. This is a better essay than the first one because it has a strong appreciation of how the passage works as a whole; it is balanced in its treatment and full of good detail, as well as offering a personal response.

Reflection: Consider if there are ways in which you could add to or improve these essays. Do you agree with the marker's comments? What have you learnt from looking closely at other students' work?

FURTHER READING

Try some well-known short-story writers whose work has been translated into English: Anton Chekhov (Russian) and Guy de Maupassant (French)

Self-assessment checklist

Reflect on what you've learnt in this unit and indicate your confidence level between 1 and 5. If you score below 3, revisit that section. Come back to this list later in your course. Has your confidence grown?

	Confidence level	Revisited?
I understand the requirements of the new unseen Prose question		
I have assimilated the checklist of important elements for discussion		
I have examined the work on the Ngũgĩ passage carefully and can discuss it		
I have studied the two Thomas passages carefully and learnt from them and the marker's notes		

Unit 12
Timed prose essays, critical and passage type

Learning objectives

In this unit you will:

- recognise how you can be prepared to answer questions on your prose set texts under timed conditions
- organise your work into helpful categories if you are studying an anthology
- clarify the differences between the a) essay question and the b) passage question
- engage with sample and students' answers
- account for the marginal comments made.

KEY CONCEPTS

Language, form, structure, genres, context, style, interpretation.

Before you start

- Review Figure 11.1, your checklist of prose elements given in the last unit. Do you know what to look for in a passage? You will have seen any extract before because you have studied the novel or short story, but this will be a small extract so all your skills of observing, noting and thinking will be required!

As with poetry essays, for each set text that you study there will be two alternative questions in the Cambridge AS level examination: one is an essay on an aspect of the novel or short story anthology, such as characterisation or main concerns; the other is an extract from the work, which you have to analyse in detail – a passage question essay. These are sometimes called the a) essay and the b) essay. As you've just completed the unit on unseens, we're going to start with the passage question, which uses those skills you've just been studying.

Prose analysis – the passage question or b) essay type

In this part of the unit, you are going to work further on the skills of prose analysis so that you feel confident about tackling the passage questions on your novel and any other prose work that you study in the future. Many of the lessons learnt in unseen analysis of poetry and prose are just as useful here. You will find further reminders in Section 3 of this book.

ACTIVITY 12.1

With a partner, make a list of what you think are the points in common with poetry passage question work.

- You will be familiar with the work, whether poem or passage of prose, because you have studied the set text. So you are able to establish the subject, situation and background straight away.
- You will still need to work through the set prose text carefully to make sure you are clear about the sense of the words. As you do this, consider the structure carefully – in a poem, you will be guided by the stanza divisions (see Unit 3); in prose, although it is an extract from a larger whole, your teacher or the setter who sets the paper will have taken great care to choose a passage that has a clear, complete structure of its own.
- You will be able to identify the main concerns (or themes) of the set passage, just as you do in poetry criticism. You know the themes of the novel as a whole, but not all of them will be evident in the passage. Read carefully and don't make assumptions that aren't based on the evidence in front of you.
- Prose writers use imagery and figures of speech just as poets do, so you will be able to identify metaphor, hyperbole and so on in your prose extract, and discuss its meaning and effect in a similar way. Equally, identifying any noteworthy diction is important whether you are scrutinising a poem or a piece of prose.
- The writer's tone is an important feature of any piece of writing, whether in prose or poetic form. If you find this a difficult aspect of analysis, you might find it helpful to think of tone of voice if it were read aloud and what you are able to deduce from this.
- Finally, the atmosphere created in the prose passage is just as worthy of discussion as it may be in a poem.

Reflection: Compare your list with these ideas.

ACTIVITY 12.2

Read and consider the new skills you will need to develop.

1 When writing about a poem, you know you need to discuss its form: its distinctive rhythms, metrical scheme, rhyme and use of sound effects such as alliteration, assonance and onomatopoeia. When analysing a prose passage, you will need to look at its division into paragraphs and sentences. Don't assume that prose doesn't have any rhythms of its own. In the passages that follow, you will see that prose writers also vary their sentences, use parallels and contrasts, and build to climactic moments. Look back at the sentence from *Great Expectations* identified earlier in Unit 8 and see how it builds into a climax.

2 Prose writers also use passages of description and reflection, which poets tend not to do, and you will need to observe and comment on the effect of these.

3 Dialogue, or passages of direct speech are widely used in the novel or short story. When you come to the section of the book on drama (Section 3), you will find in Unit 17 a discussion of dialogue – because plays work only with visual effects and words spoken by characters. Dialogue in the novel is supported and contextualised by description, commentary and reflection. A character's thoughts in a play will need to be expressed in some kind of **soliloquy** or aside, but in the novel, they can be explored fully by the narrator, whether the narrative is in the first or third person. See **Soliloquy** in Unit 17.

Passage question practice

ACTIVITY 12.3

Using the skills described, and those you have seen exemplified in the last unit, analyse each passage in some detail. The first four are from novels, the fifth from a short story. Sample responses follow the passages. Note that the questions asked are typical wording based on past examination questions, although in an exam the extracts would be a little longer.

Essay: *Discuss the effects of the following passage in detail, commenting particularly on how Dickens creates sympathy for Paul.*

Passage 1

Paul had never risen from his little bed. He lay there, listening to the noises in the street, quite tranquilly; not caring much how the time went, but watching it and watching everything about him with observing eyes.

When the sunbeams struck into his room through the rustling blinds, and quivered on the opposite wall like golden water, he knew that evening was coming on, and that the sky was red and beautiful. As the reflection died away, and a gloom went creeping up the wall, he watched it deepen, deepen, deepen, into night. Then he thought how the long streets were dotted with lamps, and how the peaceful stars were shining over head. His fancy had a strange tendency to wander to the river, which he knew was flowing through the great city; and now he thought how black it was, and how deep it would look, reflecting the hosts of stars—and more than all, how steadily it rolled away to meet the sea.

As it grew later in the night, and footsteps in the street became so rare that he could hear them coming, count them as they passed, and lose them in the hollow distance, he would lie and watch the many-coloured ring about the candle, and wait patiently for day. His only trouble was, the swift and rapid river. He felt forced, sometimes, to try to stop it—to stem it with his childish hands—or choke its way with sand—and when he saw it coming on, resistless, he cried out! But a word from Florence, who was always at his side, restored him to himself; and leaning his poor head upon her breast, he told Floy of his dream, and smiled.

Charles Dickens *Dombey and Son* (1848)

ACTIVITY 12.4

Comment closely on the ways in which Woolf develops the reader's response to Mrs Ramsay in the following passage.

Passage 2

She turned the page; there were only a few lines more, so that she would finish the story, though it was past bed-time. It was getting late. The light in the garden told her that; and the whitening of the flowers and something grey in the leaves conspired together, to rouse in her a feeling of anxiety. What it was about she could not think at first. Then she remembered; Paul and Minta and Andrew had not come back. She summoned before her again the little group on the terrace in front of the hall door, standing looking up into the sky. Andrew had his net and basket. That meant he was going to catch crabs and things. That meant he would climb out on to a rock; he would be cut off. Or coming back single file on one of those little paths above the cliff one of them might slip. He would roll and then crash. It was growing quite dark.

But she did not let her voice change in the least as she finished the story, and added, shutting the book, and speaking the last words as if she had made them up herself, looking into James's eyes: 'And there they are living still at this very time.'

'And that's the end,' she said, and she saw in his eyes, as the interest of the story died away in them, something else take its place; something wondering, pale, like the reflection of a light, which at once made him gaze and marvel. Turning, she looked across the bay, and there, sure enough, coming regularly across the waves first two quick strokes and then one long steady stroke, was the light of the Lighthouse. It had been lit.

In a moment he would ask her, 'Are we going to the Lighthouse?' And she would have to say, 'No: not tomorrow; your father says not.' Happily, Mildred came in to fetch them, and the bustle distracted them. But he kept looking back over his shoulder as Mildred carried him out, and she was certain that he was thinking, we are not going to the Lighthouse tomorrow; and she thought, he will remember that all his life.

Virginia Woolf *To the Lighthouse* (1927)

Godrevy Lighthouse.

ACTIVITY 12.5

Consider the ways in which Ngũgĩ presents the character of Karanja in this extract from the novel.

Passage 3

But the rain when later it fell, did not break into violence. It drizzled continuously, varying neither in speed nor in volume. The country, it seemed, was going to plunge into one of those stinging drizzles that went on endlessly. On such days the sun never said good morning, or else good night. Without a watch, you could never guess the time.

At his mother's hut in Thabai, Karanja crammed a few clothes into a bag.

'You'll not let me make you a cup of tea?' his mother asked again. She sat on a stool near the fireplace; her right leg bent at the knee, resting on a hearthstone. She was bowed double, leaning forward, so that her chin and hands rested on the bent knee. Wairimu was wizened, with hollow eyes and protruding jaws. Her eyes now watched the silent movements of her son at the door.

'No,' Karanja said, after a pause, as if words and speech cost him pain.

'It is raining outside. A cup of hot tea will warm you inside – since you say you'll not stay here for the night.'

'I've already said I don't want tea – or anything,' he said, his voice raised with obvious irritation. The irritation was directed less at Wairimu than at the bag he handled, the smoke-ridden hut, the drizzle outside, at the life and things in general.

Ngũgĩ Wa Thiong'o *A Grain of Wheat* (1967)

ACTIVITY 12.6

Discuss the effects of description and dialogue in the following passage, commenting on how they are used to present Balram's inner conflicts.

Passage 4

As we drove, I tried hard not to look at the red bag – it was torture for me, just like when Pinky Madam used to sit in short skirts.

At a red light, I looked at the rearview mirror. I saw my thick moustache and my jaw. I touched the mirror. The angle of the image changed. Now I saw long beautiful eyebrows curving on either side of powerful, furrowed brow muscles; black eyes were shining below those tensed muscles. The eyes of a cat watching its prey.

Go on, just look at the red bag, Balram – that's not stealing, is it?

▶

I shook my head.

And even if you were to steal it, Balram, it wouldn't be stealing.

How so? I looked at the creature in the mirror.

See – Mr Ashok is giving money to all these politicians in Delhi so that they will excuse him from the tax he has to pay. And who owns that tax, in the end? Who but the ordinary people of this country – you!

'What is it Balram? Did you say something?'

I tapped the mirror. My moustache rose into view again, and the eyes disappeared, and it was only my own face staring at me now.

'This fellow in front of me is driving rashly, sir. I was just grumbling.'

'Keep your cool, Balram. You're a good driver, don't let the bad ones get to you.'

Aravind Adiga *The White Tiger* (2008)

ACTIVITY 12.7

Comment closely on ways in which the writer develops the reader's response to the main character in Passage 5.

Passage 5

I left India in 1964 with a certificate in commerce and the equivalent, in those days, of ten dollars to my name. For three weeks I sailed on the SS Roma, an Italian cargo vessel, in a third-class cabin next to the ship's engine, across the Arabian sea, the Red Sea, the Mediterranean, and finally to England. I lived in North London, in Finsbury Park, in a house occupied entirely by penniless Bengali bachelors like myself, at least a dozen and sometimes more, all struggling to educate and establish ourselves abroad.

Jhumpa Lahiri *The Third and Final Continent from Interpreter of Maladies* (1999)

SAMPLE RESPONSE 1

Passage 1

The passage, which is narrated in the third person, focuses on Paul, who is lying in bed ill, in a house which is in a city (there is mention of streets and lamps) but also near to a great river. (In fact, it is set in London and the river is the Thames.) The paragraphs trace through a day and into the evening and night as Paul lies there watching and listening to the sights and sounds, apparently not sleeping. At the end of the passage, there is a reference to telling Florence, or 'Floy' as he calls her, about his dream of the river, although to the reader it seems like a waking dream.

▶

Dickens is closely attuned to the boy's observations, thoughts and feelings throughout the passage and uses language successfully to create the world of someone very ill. He lies *quite tranquilly* during the day and at night waits *patiently* for daybreak. Some of his observations are gentle, beautiful ones, such as the sunbeams and the peaceful stars. Dickens uses onomatopoeic words to describe the effect of the sunbeams which came into Paul's room *through the rustling blinds and quivered on the opposite wall.* They are *like golden water* and the simile of water is in contrast to the inexorable dark river described later in the passage. But as night falls, the beauty falls away and as a *gloom went creeping up the wall, he watched it deepen, deepen, deepen, into night*. The repetitive structure here emphasises the night fears which afflict him. Although he tries to think of the light sources, the lamps and the *peaceful stars*, his mind keeps returning to the *resistless* dark deep river flowing towards the sea. Although Florence is described as being always at his side, Dickens so effectively evokes Paul's half-conscious state that we are barely aware of Florence and her devotion.

Dickens uses sympathetic words such as *his little bed* and *his poor head* to encourage the reader's identification with the sick child, but his description of the deep black river and its relentless flowing towards the sea suggests that the child's death is inevitable and the river symbolises this. The passage has a very sad atmosphere and the reader is moved by the child's imminent death.

The sentence structures are long and cumulative, building effectively with their repetitions a sense of the boy's reflective and compulsive thoughts: *Then he thought how the long streets ... how the peaceful stars ... now he thought how black it was ... how deep ... how steadily ...* The sentences flow rhythmically and relentlessly like the river, until one sentence near the end, whose rhythms are choppy and desperate: *He felt forced, sometimes, to try to stop it – to stem it with his childish hands – or choke its way with sand – and when he saw it coming on, resistless, he cried out!* Dickens's use of varied sentence structures is particularly striking, and not just in this novel.

Passage 2

This passage from *To the Lighthouse* is written in the third person, but centred closely on the thoughts and feelings of the main character, Mrs Ramsay, who is reading a bedtime story to her son and worrying about one of her other children coming home late from an evening walk by the sea. What is striking here is the small amount of action – turning the page, shutting the book, saying the last words of the story, looking back at the light of the lighthouse and the boy being carried out to bed by Mildred. Most of the passage is about Mrs Ramsay's thoughts, many of them imagined, feared events, using the modal verb *would* for conjecture – *he would be cut off*, he *would roll and then crash*; and later in the passage she imagines *he would ask her* about the lighthouse visit, which his severe father has already vetoed. She envisages what her son is thinking, and the final imagined thought of the passage is a *certain* one, expressed in a simple future, not *he would*, but *he will remember that all his life*. Even the direct speech used is an invented conversation. None of Mrs Ramsay's thoughts and imaginings are about herself: they are all empathetic, centred on her sons, and this is typical of the portrayal of her character throughout the novel. It is not a passage rich in metaphorical language, although there is

▶

personification in the first paragraph: *the whitening of the flowers and something grey in the leaves conspired together* – it is this that reminds her the others have not yet returned home and leads to her worrying about them. She does not allow this worry to enter her voice as she finishes the story because she does not want her son to pick up her anxiety.

Short though this passage is, it is a remarkable depiction of a mother's thoughts and feelings, centred on the welfare of her children, shot through with anxious imaginings. Even if we did not know the title of the novel, we would sense the importance of the lighthouse as some sort of symbol or motif having particular significance, with the words *wondering* and *marvel* being used and clinched finally in the short sentence: *It had been lit* at the end of the penultimate paragraph.

Passage 3

This third-person narrative deals with Karanja packing up and leaving his mother's house. It begins and ends with a description of the weather and the setting, and in the central section gives the conversation between Karanja and his mother.

Although Wairimu is described, it is clear that the narrator is closer to the character of Karanja as his thoughts and feelings are given to the reader while hers are not. The descriptions of Wairimu are external ones: *She was bowed double, leaning forward … Her eyes now watched the silent movements of her son.* Karanja's feelings are closely observed and conveyed to the reader *as if words and speech cost him pain; his voice raised with obvious irritation … at the life and things in general.*

Ngũgĩ Wa Thiong'o in 2013.

Ngũgĩ uses pathetic fallacy to enhance the feelings of Karanja, so that the dull, wretched weather reflects his own mood. The personification of the sun in the first paragraph – *the sun never said good morning, or else good night* – effectively suggests the way in which mood can be created by the weather, or weather can chime in with mood.

The dialogue is brief and concerns an everyday matter – having a cup of tea. If this were a play, the two characters would have only a brief interchange. But because it is a novel, the writer is able to explore and expand on the feelings of one of the characters in particular and use the setting of the *smoke-ridden hut, the drizzle outside* to give depth to those feelings. Ngũgĩ's style is precise and his sentences brief and elegant. It is easy to picture the scene and to appreciate the feelings of Karanja, but there is no attempt to draw sympathy for him here – this is the human condition, and we have to just get on with it.

Passage 4

This is a passage from a first-person, past-tense narrative about a chauffeur, Balram, who steals from, and eventually murders, his employer Mr Ashok. The *red bag* referred to here is filled with money for bribes. The narrator is, from the outset, candid about his obsession with the bag, just as he had been obsessively attracted to Pinky Madam sitting in the back of the car with her short skirts. The word *torture* gives insight metaphorically into these fixations.

He keeps nothing from the reader and we are entirely aware of his dissatisfaction with his lot as a humble chauffeur who just drives around all day but has a rich inner life. However, he is torn between respect for proper behaviour as a servant and his compulsive desire to break free and be independent, which is imaged frequently in the novel as two voices speaking to him, or two alternative scenarios being proposed. When he looks at himself in the mirror, he sees first of all his own simple physical reflection, and then when he moves the mirror, that of his more persuasive demonic **alter ego** with its *eyes of a cat watching its prey*. The novelist uses dialogue to present the alter ego's voice of temptation with its political persuasions about who the money belongs to: *who but the ordinary people of the country – you!*, as well as the voice of the employer asking if he has spoken. The first-person, past-tense narrative is the perfect medium for presentation of his story: the discrepancy between the ordinary interchanges of daily working life and the innermost thoughts and desires of the persona, which are entirely opaque to others. The narrator's lively descriptions and juxtapositions make the novel both humorous and shocking. We cannot help but sympathise with Balram, but the graphic description of the murder and his certain knowledge that his family will be awfully punished (even though they are an unsympathetic group) leave us with very mixed feelings. (If you are not studying this novel, it is a recommended read!)

Passage 5

At first sight, this appears to be a factual, autobiographical account of a Bengali man who has left his native country and is seeking to educate and establish himself abroad. The reader may wonder if this is a short story at all, or just a series of unimaginative facts about the writer's life. However, if one looks more closely, one can see signs of a narrator who tries to express simple facts without emotion, but who has clearly suffered. His poverty is evident – only ten dollars in his pocket, only a third-class cabin in a hot and noisy part of the ship, sharing a house in not the best part of London with 12 or more others like himself. The length of his voyage is emphasised in the list of seas he crossed over three weeks. The whole paragraph, with its apparently factual details, builds to the moment when he uses the word *struggling* to describe his experience. But he has not become self-centred in this: he identifies with all the others like himself when he says *ourselves*, not *myself*. The story reveals him to be a sensitive but reserved person trying to adapt in a different world (he moves from Britain to the United States) and in spite of finding happiness in his marriage and living in his new milieu for thirty years, still reflecting on the mysterious nature of the 'ordinary' person's 'ordinary' life: *It is beyond my imagination*.

KEY TERM

Alter ego or 'other self': a character who is similar to another in the text, or one who represents the author in some way, or, as here, a different aspect or side of the character being presented. An example of the first definition could be Orlick in *Great Expectations* as a much darker alter ego of Pip.

TIP

Attention to the detail of language, form and tone is essential in writing critical analysis of prose extracts. Always substantiate your ideas with brief supporting quotations.

Writing a critical essay on prose

ACTIVITY 12.8

If you are studying an anthology of short stories, then you need to begin by reading and analysing each story individually first so that you appreciate each one before you try to find common themes or style in them. Once you have studied a few, you will start to see these links of theme or style.

Active learning: create headings

Examples of common themes

- Husbands/wives
- Power/dominance over others
- Hostility to different races/aliens
- Supernatural occurrences
- Extreme states of mind
- Loneliness
- Remorse
- Coming-of-age

See if you and a partner can find examples of these themes and write them under these headings.

Examples of style features that may be found in a number of stories

- First-person or third-person narrative
- Structure with final twist
- Structure with more ambiguous plotless ending
- Use of symbolism, setting, atmosphere, dialogue
- Humour/irony

Again, see if you and a partner can exemplify these from your anthology

Reflection: Test yourself. Without looking at the book, would you be able to write down two or three stories which have a theme or feature of style in common so that you could answer a question using them?

If you are studying a novel

Refer to Unit 29 in Part 3 for advice on structuring your material, then read the following essays. You do not need to have studied the novels *Things Fall Apart* by Chinua Achebe or *Half of a Yellow Sun* by Chimamanda Ngozi Adichie to appreciate the essays, as their arguments are very clearly structured. It is possible to appreciate the development of the argument, use of examples and precision of expression whether or not you know the novels well.

SAMPLE ESSAY

Essay: 'Women can be seen as both superior and inferior to men in *Things Fall Apart*.' In the light of this statement, discuss your view of the position of women in the novel.

It is true that the presentation of women in *Things Fall Apart* is an apparently contrasting one. One view of them is that they are supreme; while another is that they are really outsiders in the society. The novel explores these two perspectives of women.

> A well-focused introduction which relates clearly to the essay title.

Without question, the society is intrinsically patriarchal. This is evidenced throughout in many ways, with many of the important ceremonies being 'for men'. Ibo women have no say in village matters such as legislation, village councils and war. The running of the village is done by men. Meetings in the town square are conducted by men as well. Unsurprisingly, at the highest level of the Ibo judiciary system – the *egwugwu* – it is the titled and influential men like Okonkwo behind the masks. Women are generally uninvolved. At the *egwugwu*-judging ceremony, for example, the man's wife is not even there to present her case. Her brothers-in-law represent her. This indicates the lack of a woman's case in political society.

> There is a range of apt examples here to support the point being made.

Ibo women are also treated as inferior to men; moreover, their inferiority is accepted by both men and women. For example, all Ibo society accepts wife-beating as an allowed practice. In addition, women are bargained off to suitors with a suitable dowry, which is negotiated by men. The bride is involved only in the role of serving. In general, the women seem to be outsiders in a lot of aspects of village life: socially they are considered inferior, politically they are not present. The roles they do play in the village are domestic ones – cooking, cleaning and looking after children.

> A useful marker to show where the essay is going, here another similar point.

> Further detailed examples in this paragraph.

Even in agriculture, there is a ready distinction between men and women. Okonkwo asserts that plants like coco-yam and beans are what women and children grow – *Yam was a man's plant*. The importance of yams as a subsistence product is evidenced by the New Yam Festival, so women are inferior in this respect.

> Moves to another area of activity – agriculture, for example.

Religiously too there is evidence of male and female distinction. The spirits that appeared for Ezudu's funeral are entirely men – *The most dreaded of all* [the spirits] ... *he was always alone*. The *egwugwu* are entirely male. In families, as we can see from Okonkwo, it is always the man who can set up a shrine to his own personal god. From all this, we may draw the conclusion that women were inferior to men, outsiders in their life

> Shows a further set of examples, here from religion.

> Apt quotation.

Perhaps the most important and direct representation of Ibo women as inferior societal outsiders is the recurrence of the term *agbala* throughout the novel. *Agbala* is defined very early on as a derogatory term for a titleless man, but we also find out that it means 'woman'. The equation of a woman to a titleless man, in a society where title is a judge of a man's individual worth, can hardly be a clearer indication of where women stand in Ibo society

> Directs the reader to an important point here.

> Uses the language of the text effectively.

However, the novel does not give only a one-sided presentation of women. Women do play an important part in Ibo society. Clearly, in terms of religion, there is male domination in the areas of worship, judicial ceremony and gods. However, we are introduced to two figures that assert a female role in this area – Ani and Chielo. Ani is the earth goddess representing fertility and abundance. The whole of Ibo society,

▶

The argument has a change of direction, clearly signposted.

Very impressive knowledge of the text to support the argument.

including men, respect her highly, as evidenced by the incidents of the week of peace, in which one of the village elders expresses great disapproval at Okonkwo's careless disregard for the rule against wife-beating. This incident shows two things: one, that to displease Ani would incur her wrath and was considered a genuine threat to the village's well-being; and two, that there were existing limitations on the practice of wife-beating. The latter is reinforced later with the men's verdict as *egwugwu* that *it is not bravery when a man fights a woman*. The society is collectively aware that women do have a place. We can see this also by the appropriation of titles by women, for example the eldest wife in the household.

Chielo too is a prominent figure. She is a respected and feared priestess – the Oracle. The Oracle features prominently in male decisions regarding war: for example, the Oracle was consulted over the issue of the Ibo woman killed by another clan. The Ibo respect the Oracle's words and choose the peaceful solution, believing she is the voice of Agbala, a goddess. We can see here that *agbala* is not just a derogatory name for a man but a significant religious – and female – symbol.

In short, we can see two apparently conflicting presentations of women – one that perceives women as inferior outsiders in most of Ibo society, and one that reveres their status as superior. But the two are not so much conflicting as logically complementary. The statement *mother is supreme* indicates the reverential status of women in the context of their roles in society as mothers, a role of unparalleled importance since children will grow up to take their places in the clan. This creates a new perception of how women – and men – are presented in the novel: both occupy their respective spheres. The ceremony may be for men, but women have their day too, when they take over the job of collectively cooking for the whole village. Their contributions to religion and society are of fertility (Ani) and peace (Oracle). Since we can see throughout the novel that the Ibo society is heavily agricultural, as well as typically gentle, diplomatic and peaceful, the importance of these two contributions cannot be underestimated. This complementary duality is also supported in the structure of the novel by the fact that the ones who fail – Okonkwo and Unoka – see males as superior, whilst the successful character Obierika understands the importance of both sexes throughout.

This is a particularly effective conclusion, making the final point in the argument very clear. The essay is full, carefully organised and balanced. Excellent knowledge of the text is a strength.

SAMPLE ESSAY

Essay: Discuss some of the ways in which Adichie uses food and meals *in the novel Half of a Yellow Sun.*

Food and meals are a motif that runs throughout Adichie's novel, from Ugwu's startled encounter with Master's overflowing fridge at the beginning, to the scenes of starvation in the Biafran war at the end. Meals are shared out of friendship and hospitality, but food is also imaged as a symbol of different cultures: the Westernised and the African. There is a difference between village culture and the more sophisticated city culture, too. The making of meals in a kitchen can also be a way of showing dominance of one person over another, imaging in miniature the enforced starvation of a whole people whom the enemy wish to crush in war.

This is a clear and detailed introduction, with a number of ideas outlined.

▶

Linking phrase.

Details of the contrasts between Western/African food and city/rural African food. Good close illustrations.

Useful link word for additional comment on character and theme.

New idea clearly indicated and developed in this paragraph. Good knowledge.

Apt critical vocabulary.

Aware of contrast of tone in the novel.

Links with previous paragraph and gives detailed examples of point made.

Useful comments on narrative methods and juxtaposition using appropriate vocabulary.

These contrasts are clearly seen in the narrative concerning Ugwu. Ugwu, the unsophisticated village boy who becomes Master's servant, is shown to develop and mature in the novel and this is symbolised in his learning to cook. When he first arrives and Master tells him to help himself from the fridge, he is overwhelmed by the array of food on offer and, in a humorous scene, gorges himself with cooked chicken, putting some into his pockets for later. His development is imaged in his learning from Olanna how to cook sophisticated African food, which she and the Master and their frequent house guests will enjoy, and he takes pride in this achievement. Ugwu is contrasted with Harrison, the servant who makes only Western food for Richard, although he admits he eats *native* food at home. Richard, as an expatriate character who wants to integrate further into African life, has to tell him to stop cooking *beets* in different ways – beets being a vegetable not used in Nigeria, but in Harrison's eyes a Western dish. Richard would rather eat hot pepper soup than the canapés created by Harrison for a party, because Richard is trying to steep himself in African ways. Richard's extreme physical reaction to the hot pepper is also amusingly drawn. Ironically, Harrison's Western meal, which includes lemon tart praised by Kainene as being better than the one she had in London, prefaces the scene where she and Richard have an enormous row with each other.

Ugwu's development is further revealed when he goes home to his village and we see his reaction to eating village food again: he feels *the endless gassy churning in his stomach from eating only fruit and nuts*. He has not only become a more sophisticated cook, but cannot eat traditional village food without feeling unwell. He is also taken aback when Master's mother arrives from the country and takes over the kitchen, which has become his domain.

At this point, the use of food to dominate others, already suggested in Harrison and Ugwu, is shown clearly in the character of Master's mother, only here it is a contrast between country cooking and city cooking, not Westernised food. *I want to cook a proper soup for my son*, she says and sweeps away all the new cookery techniques that Ugwu has learnt from Olanna. It is all part of her plot to get Olanna away from Odenigbo and marry him to a village girl of her choice. Although she is thwarted and the kitchen is returned to Ugwu, the girl she has brought to her son's bed becomes pregnant, and ultimately Baby is looked after by Olanna and Odenigbo, becoming a symbol of a generation of Biafran children who are affected by conflict. The search for her food and attempts to stop her from getting *kwashiorkor* are central to the later more tragic phase of the novel, when everyone is starving and deprivation becomes a weapon of war.

The gradual darkening of the tone of the novel as war approaches is reinforced by the difficulties faced by the characters in finding food. Baby is given dried egg yolk when they can get it instead of real eggs, Olanna finds herself fighting for a tin of corned beef, and the relief packages from the Red Cross with their condensed milk, Ovaltine and salt seem *luxurious*. But Ugwu *hated the relief food*. Their extreme situation is imaged in Olanna's visit to the market, where she considers: *If she bought the chicken it would be all she would buy. So she bought four medium sized snails instead.*

As well as the symbolic use of food to represent hardship, Adichie's use of a non-chronological narrative brings the situation into sharp relief. The juxtaposition of images of plenty, and feasting with friends, and images of starvation and desperate theft between neighbours reinforce the horrors of the war and the tragedy of those caught up in it, moving between the early 1960s and the late 1960s to emphasise this.

Food and meals are a constant motif in this novel, successfully used in both comic and tragic scenes, to show the maturation of individual characters, the dominance of one person over another and of one ethnic group over another, leading to the horrors of starvation in civil war, which Adichie presents graphically to readers of this novel.

Sums up clearly and aptly in this conclusion. The writer uses the texts well to illustrate the sound points made and is a carefully structured and convincing argument.

TIP

Read your set text thoroughly several times. Once is never enough. Best to turn off your phone and other electronic devices and immerse yourself in the world of the novel!
Some tips for better revision:

- Don't always start at the beginning every time you pick up the book to revise. Students often know the early parts of a novel or play more thoroughly because of this.
- Choose a chapter at random and see how well you know it.
- Can you say what happened just before and what happens just after your chapter?
- Choose a few paragraphs for close analysis. They will often reveal a great deal about the writer's themes and style.

FURTHER READING

1 The short stories of US writer Raymond Carver are models of concise writing which never waste words but are very suggestive.

2 For something completely different from Carver, try the short stories of Edgar Allen Poe – highly descriptive horror stories, often of the supernatural.

Self-assessment checklist

Reflect on what you've learnt in this unit and indicate your confidence level between 1 and 5. If you score below 3, revisit that section. Come back to this list later in your course. Has your confidence grown?

	Confidence level	Revisited?
I appreciate what is required in Prose exam questions		
I have scrutinised the elements common to them and poetry passage questions and understand them		
I can recognise the different forms of exam questions – the a) and b) alternatives		
I know how to read and annotate student responses and learn from them		

Section 3
Drama 1

Unit 13
Studying a play

Learning objectives

In this unit you will:

- enjoy reviewing the basics of drama
- reflect on plays you already know and what you think about them
- consider any opportunities they offer you for discussion and practical drama interaction
- remind yourself of the importance of the audience in drama work.

KEY CONCEPTS

Language, form, structure, genres, context, style, interpretation.

Before you start

- Remember that you are the audience as well as a reader and your personal response to what happens on the stage is vital! You will need to use your imagination. Write down or sketch what you remember of a scene from a play you have studied and consider why it has stayed in your memory. Discuss this with a friend.

Plays are written to be performed by actors and watched by an audience, and this is the single most important difference between drama and the other literary forms. When you read a novel or poem, it is usually a solitary activity except when you are in class (although, of course, novels and poems can be dramatised). The units in this section on drama are intended to help you get to grips with the dramatic form and the kinds of effects writers can achieve when they write for an audience in the theatre. The plays you are studying are theatrical pieces rather than writing for television or radio. If you have seen your set play only on DVD, or in a cinema version, you should try to imagine how it could be **staged** for live performance. The effect of seeing real people in real time enacting a drama is very exciting.

When you come to write essays on plays for exams, you will either write a critical essay on an aspect of the play such as themes, characterisation or the playwright's methods, or have a passage from your set play for close critical comment. (Shakespeare is compulsory in many syllabuses at this level, so there is wide coverage of his plays in this unit.) It's really important that when you write on plays, you consider the audience response, especially in the passage questions. If a character on the stage is about to be murdered, the audience isn't just thinking 'Oh, this shows the playwright's concern with the theme of power', they are on the edge of their seats with suspense and fear. A good answer will mention the audience reaction as well as the underlying theme. There is more on audience response throughout these units on drama.

KEY TERM

Staging: the whole process of realising a dramatic work for performance.

What to expect at a play

The experience

Full-length plays take between one and four hours and are usually watched at one sitting. They are enthralling: going to the theatre is a great experience and always involving, even if you are seeing a familiar play newly directed and performed by a different cast. This helps to account for the way enthusiasts go to see the same Shakespeare play again and again over the years. They want to experience yet another, different, interpretation and see a fresh actor bring new life to a familiar role.

ACTIVITY 13.1

Discuss and share your experience of any play you have seen, either in a theatre or acted at school. Take a scene from the play, read it and then act it out with friends.

Reflection: What aspects of the scene emerged from acting it which you hadn't realised just by reading? (Hints: it could be the action as well as the words; the relationship of characters; the presence of humour.)

The plot of the play and its structure

The experience of watching a play all at one sitting means that the work usually has a kind of dynamic, rhythmical movement; change is activated, surprising and complicating events occur, and expectancy and uncertainty are generated in the audience as they watch. There are peaks and troughs of excitement, climaxes and quieter moments. The audience may feel some satisfaction when a final resolution is reached. A strong and often complicated plot is a common feature of good drama because it must entertain and engage the audience from start to finish. Even *Waiting for Godot* by Samuel Beckett, the modern classic once criticised because nothing happens and nobody does anything, depends upon the audience's expectation that there will be a plot, and their reaction to finding out that there isn't much of one. Some contemporary drama has indeed tried to move away from the strongly plotted form and offer inconclusive, open-ended conclusions, but every drama, including *Waiting for Godot*, has its moments of climax and excitement, and endings do not have to have a wedding or a death to bring a play successfully to a close. Every play will, however, have an expressive structure by which the playwright shapes the dynamic process, communicating and exploring the major issues of the play.

The characters

Characters are often used to engage the sympathies and involvement of the audience; or they may represent ideas that the playwright would like the audience to think about. In the latter case, the characters need not be sympathetic or likeable; indeed, some dramatists have made characters deliberately unlikeable so that the audience concentrates on the ideas and not the human sympathies.

Characters speak (in verse or prose) and at times they are silent. They do things and they react to each other. As in prose writing, they may have qualities or perform actions that are paralleled or contrasted with one another to highlight particular themes. Their motivation is the mainspring of the play's plot.

When you are reading a play, rather than watching a performance, you need to try to imagine the action. Ask yourself about the characters who are not speaking: what might their reaction be to the events going on?

Reflection: Consider the following table.

Example	Details	Effect on characters/ audience
The last scene of *King Lear* (Shakespeare) – a tragedy	The king's three daughters all lie dead in front of him.	All the characters are affected by the tragedy, as is the audience.
The second act of *Absurd Person Singular* (Alan Ayckbourn) – a comedy	One of the characters is trying to commit suicide in various ways throughout. She only speaks at the very end of the act when she starts to sing.	The others are completely oblivious, missing her pill-taking, setting up a rope to hang herself, sticking her head in the gas oven, and so on. The audience's laughter grows in intensity throughout the act.

The setting/space

When you use the word *setting* to discuss a novel, it means the time(s) and place(s) in which the action of the novel is set. The meaning of *set* in drama is more specifically focused on the environment, or **space**, in which the actors perform.

KEY TERM

Stage space: used to create an illusion of the setting the playwright wants to create.

ACTIVITY 13.2

Working with a classmate, take a short sequence from a novel or short story you are studying, where characters speak to each other, and try to make it into a scene from a play. The characters' words will become dialogue, set out with the name of each character at the head of each speech. Actions will become stage directions. Read your little scene and see what is gained and lost by changing its form.

A naturalistic play creates space by using solid sets to make walls and rooms on the stage, or even trees and rocks for an outside environment, but some plays use more flexible and imaginative forms.

Whether a play is performed in a traditional theatrical space with a stage set and curtains, or in the middle of a room without scenery, or even read in class, it has a setting for its action and this will be established by the playwright, either by stage directions, which give instructions or, like Shakespeare's plays, in the language spoken by characters. It could be a dining room or a forest, a temple or a castle, an island, a bedroom or the deck of a ship. There may be special effects of lighting or music, or spectacular ones such as thunder and lightning. *The Norman Conquests* (1973) by Alan Ayckbourn is a series of three full-length plays, each depicting the same six characters over the same weekend in a different part of a house: so the setting for one is the dining room, another the living room, and the third the garden. Each play is self-contained, and they may be watched in any order, some of the scenes overlap, and on several occasions, a character's exit from one play corresponds with an entrance in another. Every playwright will make a choice of setting for the particular effect she/he is aiming at. When you are reading a play alone in your room, you have to use your imagination to envisage the setting, and when you are writing your essay, you mustn't forget that the text you are discussing is a play, meant for performance, not a text like a novel.

The issues

Drama is a very effective medium for the exploration of domestic, social, political and philosophical issues in an intense, highly charged atmosphere. Everything will be settled after a couple of hours – what Shakespeare calls 'the two hours' traffic of our stage', so it has to be presented concisely. It is worth considering why a writer, especially a contemporary one, has chosen to write a play rather than a novel, since both could theoretically engage with the same themes. A play's impact will be vivid, immediate and powerful; its main concerns will be conveyed directly by the actions and reactions of a group of characters, and there is no quiet or reflective description as there can be in a novel. There is no omniscient narrator guiding the reader's observation, nor is there the single focus of a first-person narrator, although occasionally a character will speak directly to the audience. This can make conflict on the stage particularly aggressive, love scenes extraordinarily tender and death especially poignant, especially as the audience is looking at real people in real time. Humour will make an audience laugh out loud in a way that rarely happens with even a very amusing novel.

Accepted forms

Plays, particularly those of Shakespeare or plays written earlier, are often categorised as comedy, tragedy, history, farce, and so on. They are at times given a historical category, such as Restoration comedy. These categories are helpful in a general way, but are only a guideline, since most tragedies have their humorous moments, just as every comedy has more poignant ones; many historical dramas are tragic, and many farces are satirical. Be prepared to redefine the plays you are studying, and keep an open mind.

A scene from Arthur Miller's domestic drama *Death of a Salesman*.

ACTIVITY 13.3

What sort of play are you studying? Write down where and when the action takes place, and then say whether you think it is:

- a drama of domestic or personal issues
- an analytical, perhaps critical, comment on a particular kind of society
- a play of moral dilemmas
- a play of political insights
- a play of philosophical questioning
- or perhaps all of these!

Here is a table showing some examples of different types of plays:

Type of play	Example	Comment
Domestic dramas	*Death of a Salesman* (US playwright Arthur Miller)	Complex, fragile relationships, especially between father and son
	Who's Afraid of Virginia Woolf? (US playwright Edward Albee)	A savage portrait of a marriage
	A Midsummer Night's Dream (Shakespeare)	An arranged marriage and the conflicts that result
	The Dilemma of a Ghost (Ghanaian Ama Ata Aidoo)	The suffocating influence of the family on a marriage
Plays of ideas	*After the Revolution* (US playwright Amy Herzog)	The problems of political idealism
	Top Girls (British Caryl Churchill)	Feminism
	My Children! My Africa! (South African Athol Fugard)	Apartheid in South Africa
	A Man for All Seasons (British Robert Bolt)	Conscience and integrity
	Death and the King's Horseman (Nigerian Wole Soyinka)	The importance of ritual in the cohesion of society
	The Dilemma of a Ghost (Ghanian Ama Ata Aidoo)	Conflicts of old and new in Ghanaian society
Plays of social analysis	*Mrs Warren's Profession* (British George Bernard Shaw)	Prostitution and society's hypocrisy
	The plays of Athol Fugard; (*Woza Albert!* is a name of a play by Simon, Ngema and Mtwa)	Critical presentation of South Africa pre independence, sometimes using humour and song
	Restoration comedy such as *The Country Wife* (William Wycherley) or *The Way of the World* (William Congreve)	Shrewd and comic comments on social norms and behaviour
	The Importance of Being Earnest (Oscar Wilde)	Comic exploration of social conventions

(Continued)

Reflection: Decide which kind of issue dominates the play you've chosen.

(Continued)

Type of play	Example	Comment
Historical/ political plays	*A Man for All Seasons* (Robert Bolt)	Exploration of the complexities of politics and morality
	Antony and Cleopatra (Shakespeare)	The qualities of the 'real' Thomas More and the 'real' Antony are not important here
	Henry IV i) and ii), Richard III	Historical truth is not the main point of these plays. What matters is the perception with which the playwright approaches the issues raised by the lives of the famous, and in what ways and how effectively they are expressed in dramatic form

Reflection: Take care that you do not try to categorise a play too simply. You will find that a domestic drama can be socially perceptive; that a social satire can contain serious themes; that a comedy can have very poignant moments; that a history play can be a domestic drama, and so on. (These themes are developed in more detail in Unit 14.) Think again about plays you know and see if your categories have been too one-dimensional.

FURTHER STUDY

Search online for 'Elizabethan theatre, by Joyce Sherry', a very informative short video about Shakespeare's theatre.

Self-assessment checklist

Reflect on what you've learnt in this unit and indicate your confidence level between 1 and 5. If you score below 3, revisit that section. Come back to this list later in your course. Has your confidence grown?

	Confidence level	Revisited?
I can appreciate the basics of drama		
I understand what you have to do in the exam		
I am more conscious of different types of plays		
I have accepted the importance of acknowledging audience response and can discuss this		

Unit 14
Studying the themes of a play

Learning objectives

In this unit you will:

- review common themes in drama and relate to your own experience
- engage with examples of these themes
- clarify some appropriate terminology for discussing drama.

KEY CONCEPTS

Language, form, structure, genres, context, style, interpretation.

Before you start

- Remind yourself of plays you have studied and write down, using two or three words, what they are about (for example, servants and masters; love; power; poverty; and so on).
- See how many you can select and compare with a friend's list.

Here are some common concerns explored by playwrights, vividly presented with all the resources of the theatrical context. You have already started to consider some of these ideas.

The family drama

Almost everyone belongs to a family and has parents or guardians and probably brothers and/or sisters. If you are a mature student, you may be married or have children of your own. This basic domestic and social situation is one of the great **universal** experiences that forms the basis for most Shakespearean and other dramas.

KEY TERM

Universal: that everyone can relate to the experience.

ACTIVITY 14.1

If possible, in a group, share the details of your family and where you are positioned in it. For example, are you the middle one of three children, as I am? Or are you the older brother of two? Do you have only one parent? Are you an only child? More importantly, how do you feel about it? Do you think your younger sister/brother is the favourite of your father? Does your mother or father tell you what to do? In the marriages you have observed, is there a dominant partner?

Here is a table showing some examples of plays which include family conflict:

Family relationship	Play	Type of conflict
• Married couple	• *Macbeth* (Shakespeare) • *Death and the King's Horseman* (Soyinka) • *The Comedy of Errors* (Shakespeare)	• Tragic influence • Different aspects of colonial attitudes • The comedy of the nagging wife

(Continued)

Reflection: The central issue of family life and its complexity is bound to be a dominant theme in drama. Is this one reason why we enjoy watching it?

(*Continued*)

Family relationship	Play	Type of conflict
• Siblings (brothers and sisters – sometimes twins)	• *Hamlet, King Lear, The Tempest, Much Ado About Nothing* and many others (Shakespeare) • *The Taming of the Shrew* (Shakespeare) • *Top Girls* (Churchill) • *Measure for Measure* (Shakespeare) • *Twelfth Night; The Comedy of Errors* (Shakespeare)	• A good and an evil brother or sisters; if a tragedy, the evil one does great harm; if a comedy, all is resolved in the end • Two sisters of very different character • Two sisters of very different character, here representing political attitudes as well • Brother and sister in serious conflict, although they love each other • Twins who look alike and are very close, creating comic effects
• Father and son or daughter (NB Not many mothers appear in Shakespeare's plays)	• *Hamlet, The Merchant of Venice, The Tempest, A Midsummer Night's Dream* and many others (Shakespeare) • *Death of a Salesman* (Miller) • *The Dilemma of a Ghost* (Aidoo) • *A Man for All Seasons* (Bolt)	• Fathers are domineering and controlling, often demanding the impossible and creating tension which may be tragic, or an obstacle to overcome in comedy • Thomas More and his daughter are very close and he has educated her at a time when few women were educated
• Entire family, including husbands and wives of children and the father's mistress	• *Homesick* (Singapore's Alfian Sa'at)	• A comic portrayal of family tensions against an outbreak of the contagious virus SARS

KEY TERM

Juxtaposition: the skilful placing of elements side by side so that they illuminate each other by contrast. The elements can be words, concepts or characters. It can be used in discussing poetry, prose and drama.

Shakespeare's use of balanced characterisations also reveals a love of patterns, of parallels and contrasts that illuminate each other through **juxtaposition**, and this reminds us that his plays are both poetry and drama.

Youth and age

Linked with the family drama, but not always, is the conflict between older and younger generations, also a favourite theme of the novel. 'The younger rises when the old doth fall' comes from the last scene of *King Lear* and encapsulates this theme perfectly. The older characters may be envious of the young, or moved by them and their potential; the younger characters may be respectful or scornful of their elders – these relationships are seen in many plays.

- *Romeo and Juliet* emphasises through its imagery and action the contrast between the young and the old, and the lovers' parents are all part of the older generation, as are the Nurse and the Friar.
- *My Children! My Africa!* and *The Road to Mecca* (both by Fugard) have younger characters whose honesty and idealism are in direct contrast with more mature characters.
- Aidoo's *Anowa* shows the parents in conflict with their daughter over her choice of husband.

ACTIVITY 14.2

Look closely at the pairing of characters in the play you are studying, whether related by family or by function in the drama. They may seem at first to be opposites, but when you study them more closely, they may be more ambiguous, with parallels as well as contrasts.

Reflection: Does love feature in the play that you are studying? Consider whether passion for a person or something else (such as greed for money) is an issue explored in the play.

Love

Love is a favourite theme of comedies, which often end in marriages and pairings, but it is also significant in tragedy.

- Shakespeare's *Antony and Cleopatra* and *Romeo and Juliet* are both love tragedies.
- *The course of true love never did run smooth*, as one of the characters says in *A Midsummer Night's Dream*, and most audiences expect these complications in a play.
- In Shakespeare's comedies, love is also imaged as a kind of madness, and can make people behave in bizarre and unlikely ways. The transformation of Bottom the Weaver into an ass in *A Midsummer Night's Dream* and Titania falling in love with him is a dramatic way of suggesting that love can transform us, even make fools of us, and that we can fall in love with the most unlikely others.
- In *Death of a Salesman* (Miller), Willy loves his wife, but the brief sexual affair he has had with another woman because of the loneliness of his life as a travelling salesman is a mainspring of the plot and the core of the problems between him and his elder son, Biff.

KEY TERM

Cross-dressing: this takes place when characters of one gender dress as the other. In Shakespeare's day, all the parts were played by men and boys, so a boy could be dressed as a girl who then disguises herself as a man. This reminds the audience of the complexities of human sexuality.

Gender debates

The 'battle of the sexes' is one of the great themes of literature. Gender debates fill Shakespeare's comedies, with the battle of the sexes raging in *The Taming of the Shrew and Much Ado About Nothing and* **cross-dressing** in *Twelfth Night* and *As You Like It* reminding the audience of the complexities of sexuality.

In *A Midsummer Night's Dream*, the apparently tangential (i.e. not closely connected to the main action) characters of Theseus and Hippolyta open the play with a reminder of how they came to be betrothed: *Hippolyta, I wooed thee with my sword / And won thy love doing thee injuries*, says Theseus – hardly a gentle romantic start to their relationship! This is paralleled by the savagery of the interchanges between the fairy king and queen, Oberon and Titania, and the love combats between the lovers under the influence of the love potion.

- The vulnerability of both sexes is evident throughout Shakespeare's tragedies too, with women's honour underpinning men's reputation in *Othello.*
- Honour and reputation are similarly key themes in all Restoration comedy, giving rise to much comic business.
- The feminist issue is paramount in *Top Girls* by Caryl Churchill, with the first scene establishing the theme strongly.
- The opening of Fugard's play *My Children! My Africa!* uses a debate about the genders to establish the relationship between Thami and Isabel.
- Alan Ayckbourn's comedy *Absurd Person Singular* takes three married couples and sets an act of the play in each of their kitchens in turn. There is nothing like a kitchen for bringing out the tensions in a married couple's relationship!

You will notice how many of these examples illustrate the importance of the first scene in establishing a theme that runs through the work, similar to what you explored in prose works.

TIP

Having women dressing as men gives Shakespeare the opportunity to explore gender issues and forces audiences/readers out of their conventional views of the place of women in society. This is a popular area for exam questions on comedies in particular.

Power and authority

So far, the themes mentioned have been familial or personal ones. But much drama is also concerned with power and authority, and with the nature of society and the way it is governed.

- In Soyinka's *Death and the King's Horseman*, the pressure of the colonial society, its expectations and lack of understanding is a central theme.
- Even in domestic dramas such as *Death of a Salesman* (Miller), the social pressures of the time are a powerful background to the action, and society's expectations of conventional behaviour drive Willy's actions and behaviour towards his children.
- *After the Revolution* (Herzog) depends upon strong political views and whether individuals act with integrity, in this case threatening personal and familial relationships.
- In *Top Girls*, Churchill's focus falls upon the patriarchal societies that women have had to endure throughout history.
- Arthur Miller's play *The Crucible* reveals the powerful grip of a ruling group who rule by fear and will not allow individual freedom of thought and speech.
- *A Man for All Seasons* (Bolt) takes a well-known era in English history for its portrayal of the absolute monarch Henry VIII who is determined to have his own way and ready to remove all opposition in order to satisfy his desires.
- In Fugard's plays, the apartheid era in South Africa enshrines the power of a ruling group, who are one particular race, that seeks to dominate the others. This is an important context for many works of the colonial and post-colonial eras.

All of Shakespeare's history plays, and most of his tragedies, are close examinations of politics and power, and the ambitions of those who would seek to aggrandise themselves:

nobles wanting to become kings, kings wanting to dominate or wage war, politicians wanting to manipulate or blame others. If there are such disturbances in society, then order will give way to chaos, and peace may slide into war.

- Shakespeare uses images of breakdown in nature and the wider environment to **mirror** and intensify this chaos. Under such circumstances, some followers will be treacherous, others loyal – another area of great interest to the playwright.
- He often shows that a person's mind is like a kingdom which can lose its control and become disordered, even gripped by madness. In *King Lear*, the disorder in the king's mind is mirrored in the breakdown of society in his kingdom and is given metaphorical emphasis by the huge storm. In *Macbeth,* the murder of the king is accompanied by terrible disruption in nature itself, described in Act 2 Scene 4 by Ross and the old man.

KEY TERM

Mirroring: a useful term for the symbolic reflection of one thing in another.

If you are studying *Macbeth*, consider the detailed evidence in the text that the king's death is disruptive of society and nature as a whole. Your answer to this will help you to understand what happens when Caesar is assassinated in *Julius Caesar*. In *Top Girls*, how many women reach the top in a business environment and with what effect on their attitudes to other people – men and women? In *My Children! My Africa!*, consider the effect that disenfranchisement has on the young population of a country. How can they react to this without violence?

ACTIVITY 14.3

Who wields authority in the play that you are studying? Who has power and in what way do they use it? Who shows themselves to be loyal and who acts treacherously in their own self-interest? What social pressures are shown? Make a list of your characters and then, with the help of a classmate, create a diagram showing the interaction of each person with the others and what outside pressures are acting on them.

Appearance and reality

One of the great themes of Shakespearean and Restoration drama is the contrast between the way things appear to be and what they really are. Perhaps it's not surprising that men and women of the theatre are obsessed with the deceitfulness of surfaces. For whatever reason, this dichotomy (or split) between *being and seeming* runs through the characters, the situations and the language of all of Shakespeare's plays and of the plays of the Restoration period.

Characters disguise themselves, pretend to be what they are not, act or put on a show and behave hypocritically. Apparently noble characters are revealed to have flaws, fools are shown to be wiser than clever people, and even the evil can sometimes have redeeming features. 'Don't judge at face value' seems to be a central theme of all of Shakespeare's work, and it is highly ironic that he should use that most artificial of media – the theatre – to persuade us to think more deeply about what appears before our eyes.

In *Measure for Measure* and other plays, the darkness of night allows for what is known as a **bed trick:** the substitution of one woman for another pretending to be someone else, a trick used elsewhere by Shakespeare and a favourite device of comedy and **farce**.

KEY TERMS

Bed trick: the substitution of one actor for another pretending to be someone else in bed in the dark.

Farce: comedy full of exaggerated situations and improbable twists and turns of plot. The humour is often very physical.

ACTIVITY 14.4

With the help of your teacher, find out how many of Shakespeare's plays contain cross-gender disguises and how they are used in the play. Do disguise of other kinds feature in the plays you have studied?

KEY TERMS

Mistaken identity: where characters disguise themselves, pretend to be what they are not, act or put on a show and behave hypocritically.

A comic and a tragic example

In *The Comedy of Errors*, the fact that there are two pairs of identical twins – the Antipholus brothers and their servants, the Dromio brothers – allows Shakespeare to create a chaotic world of **mistaken identity** which is hilarious for the audience but confusing for the characters, who are forced to face the issues of their own nature and identity before all is resolved.

In the tragedy *King Lear*, the characters of Kent and Edgar are forced to disguise themselves as a serving man and the mad beggar Poor Tom respectively, giving rise to many of the play's deepest insights into the human condition, so disguise and mistaken identity are not always comic features.

TIP

A playwright's use of the contrast between appearance and the reality beneath is by no means simplistic: sometimes good characters are forced to disguise themselves in order to survive in a hostile world.

ACTIVITY 14.5

Make a list of the dominant ideas or themes in the play that you are studying. Compare this with your quick starter activity response and see how far your ideas have developed over this unit. As you develop your skills of analysis, you will be able to identify the means by which the playwright explores these themes: through the play's structure and action, through characterisation, and through language and tone.

FURTHER STUDY

Search online for '*Death of a Salesman*, Hoffman'. There's plenty of family drama in this short video from Miller's *Death of a Salesman*!

Self-assessment checklist

Reflect on what you've learnt in this unit and indicate your confidence level between 1 and 5. If you score below 3, revisit that section. Come back to this list later in your course. Has your confidence grown?

	Confidence level	Revisited?
I can apply my experience as a family member to the appreciation of plays		
I am attentive to common themes that playwrights deal with		
I appreciate the significance of the themes of power and authority		
I understand and can discuss appearance and reality in drama		
I can define bed trick, farce and mistaken identity		

Unit 15
Studying play structures

Learning objectives

In this unit you will:

- define linear structure and plot
- explore exposition and action
- clarify denouement
- consider patterning devices.

KEY CONCEPTS

Language, form, structure, genres, context, style, interpretation.

Before you start

- Refer to a play you know well and write down in one paragraph what happens in the play.
- Now think of **three** complicating things that happen in the play to interfere with a simple conclusion of the story. There will probably be more than this, but it gives you a clear sense of the ways in which a relatively straightforward series of events is never as uncomplicated as it appears.
- If you are working with a friend, compare notes on your findings.

Linear structure

How a play is constructed will have a significant effect on the audience's response to its main concerns. All plays will have action and may enact a kind of linear process, as shown in the following diagram:

The beginning or **exposition** gives the background and prepares the potential for conflict, or shows the pressures that come from certain characters' motivations.

Then the central section can reveal complications developing, a counter-force operating and conflict coming out into the open.

Finally, an ending is reached, often after many climaxes in the action. This is often called the **denouement**.

KEY TERMS

Exposition: the early part of the play in which the audience receives background information about setting, events, characters and possibly themes, so that they understand what's going on.

Denouement: comes from a French word which means 'untying' and is used in relation to unravelling or resolving the complexities of the plot.

KEY TERMS

Act and Scene:
These are divisions within a play to show change and development. An act is a larger Unit, a scene is a smaller part of an act. However, it should be noted that some recent playwrights do not use them at all.

Plot: the events that make up a story. The secondary stories are known as subplots, or, if they are very important, parallel plots.

There may be a different state of affairs by the end: the world of the play may have altered, the balance of power is different, or perhaps someone has changed. There may be a resolution, a denouement or unravelling. In some plays, deaths end the action; in others, marriage or other kinds of union. This linear structure of exposition, development, complication and denouement is very dynamic and uses climaxes effectively, holding the audience in suspense and often excitement.

In some contemporary plays, the situation may seem to have gone nowhere and returned to where it began, but in fact there is always more process than first appears. In Beckett's *Waiting for Godot*, Godot has not arrived, true, but the audience is now fully acquainted with the two tramps and has experienced their personalities and obsessions, as well as gaining insight into the playwright's view of existence.

Shakespeare's plays are divided into five **acts**, each of which has a number of **scenes**. Some of these are brief – a mere ten or twenty lines – and some lengthy, with several hundred, and these scenes can themselves be divided into shorter units, although nominally one scene. More contemporary drama may have only two or three acts or just one.

Plot

All plays have a **plot** or story, although some are simpler than others. The story of a Shakespeare play is always complex, with many characters and a number of stories going on at the same time and interweaving one with the other. The main plot of a Shakespeare play never follows through scene after scene without a break, but is constantly interspersed with the sub-, secondary or parallel plots. The effect is of a rich weave of different threads, all moving onwards and interacting.

Originality

Shakespeare's plots are not original, in the sense that they use known stories by other writers, often combined. However, these stories always have a different emphasis and meaning when Shakespeare modifies or adds to them. Originality of plot was not particularly prized in his day, and his audiences would have appreciated a new slant on an old story.

Reflection: How important is originality of plot? Can you think of artistic works where the plot needs to be original? Include other forms such as prose and film.

ACTIVITY 15.1

If you are studying a Shakespeare play, research the plot or plots to find out which old stories he adapted and combined.

TIP

The complexity of the plot of some plays means that sometimes students believe they are doing something worthwhile when they tell the story of a play. Unfortunately at this level, telling the story doesn't strengthen your answer – you are expected to know it as the baseline from which you develop your critical insights into other features of the work. Get to know the story really well but never tell it in an essay: this wastes valuable time! After all, the marker already knows it. Refer to Unit 36 for further advice on this.

Exposition

All plays, of whatever era, have an exposition from which the audience will gain essential information about the world of the play. See definition of 'exposition' in the Key Terms box at the start of this unit. The playwright always has the challenge of making the exposition interesting because it could be boring if the first characters on the stage just repeated the details of the story up to that point in a long-winded or list-like way. Types of exposition include:

- Shakespearean exposition (see next section)
- beginning near the end of the story (significant back story)
- introduction of a major character
- memory (sometimes indicated by a narrator speaking directly to the audience)
- fighting talk or action
- thematic prologue
- foreshadowing (see explanation later in this unit)

Shakespearean exposition

Here are three of Shakespeare's expositions as examples:

Example 1

Theseus and Hippolyta are about to be married. They discuss their courtship and Theseus's impatience for the marriage. He tells his servant to go out and encourage sport and merriment among the youth of Athens as part of the wedding celebrations.

A Midsummer Night's Dream

(Continued)

A Midsummer Night's Dream is largely set in a magical forest.

Example 2

Three witches meet in a storm and agree that they will meet Macbeth. When the scene changes, the king is being given a report of a bloody battle that has been going on, in which his follower, the noble Macbeth, has fought bravely. The Thane of Cawdor has behaved treacherously, so the king announces that he is to be put to death and Macbeth is to receive his title.

Macbeth

Example 3

The Duke of Gloucester speaks directly to the audience. The battle is over and thoughts turn from warlike behaviour to the pleasures of love, but not for him, as he is deformed and not *shap'd for sportive tricks*. He speaks of his intention to be a villain rather than a lover, therefore, and to set Clarence and the king against each other.

Richard III

ACTIVITY 15.2

Write down your thoughts on what sort of play is going to follow in each case. What might the audience be expecting? Do you think you can already see that the ending will be tragic or comic, for example?

More examples of exposition

1 Beginning the play near the end of the story

- In Sophocles's great tragedy *Oedipus Rex,* the king has already murdered his father and married his mother long before the action of the play starts. When he demands the truth out of the old shepherd, we, and Oedipus, discover the essential facts and the crisis breaks.
- In *The Crucible* (Arthur Miller), John Proctor's affair with Abigail is over and she has been dismissed from the household before the action begins, but the consequences of that relationship are still to unravel as the play progresses.
- In *The Tempest* (Shakespeare), Prospero was ousted many years before the action of the play and he is only now able to take revenge, or at least get his own back.

- Athol Fugard gradually lets the audience know how past events have led up to the point at which *The Road to Mecca* begins.

2 Introduction of a major character

He or she often has problems that need to be resolved.

- Macbeth shows his prowess on the battlefield, but his ambitions haven't yet been satisfied, in spite of the honours that the king bestows upon him.
- The Common Man in *A Man for All Seasons* (Bolt) plays many roles, all secondary to the scenes of the main characters but vital in his commentaries and contribution to the fluency of the action.
- Jane Hopcroft is introduced cleaning the kitchen in Ayckbourn's *Absurd Person Singular* before a word of dialogue is spoken. Her obsessive housework is a source of much of the play's comedy as well as a satirical comment by the playwright on conventional attitudes to social class.

3 Memory plays

- At the beginning of Tennessee Williams's *The Glass Menagerie,* the main character Tom tells the audience it is a memory play and guides their responses and sympathies into the first scene.
- Similarly, the boy – Michael – in *Dancing at Lughnasa* (Brian Friel), now a grown man narrating the story of his sisters, speaks directly to the audience and reflects on the nature of memory.
- Less simply*, Death of a Salesman* (Miller) interweaves memories of the past into the present timescale of the play, complicating the effect with fantasy sequences. The play was originally entitled *The Inside of His Head,* reminding us that what goes on in our minds is a complex mixture of the past, the here-and-now and our imaginative flights of fancy. (Look back at the passage from Virginia Woolf's novel *To the Lighthouse* in Unit 12 to see how a novelist deals with a similar concern.)

4 Fighting talk

To begin with, dissension is exciting for an audience as well as helpful in establishing the play's concerns.

- The exposition of *The Alchemist* by Ben Jonson is a fierce quarrel between the three collaborators.
- The opening of *Romeo and Juliet* is a quarrel between the household servants of Montague and Capulet, from which the situation of the *two households, both alike in dignity* is revealed to the audience.
- The debate in Fugard's *My Children! My Africa!,* on the other hand, is a formal presentation in words of arguments about gender differences.

5 Thematic prologue

- *Top Girls* (Caryl Churchill) has as its first act a surrealistic scene set in a restaurant that is completely timeless since all the female characters in it come from down the centuries to celebrate the promotion in the office of the 20th-century woman Marlene. The scene is set with a feminist agenda, the dominant theme that will affect the rest of the play.
- *Death and the King's Horseman* (Wole Soyinka) establishes the importance of key rituals and central symbolic figures in the tribe before the main action begins.

KEY TERM

Foreshadowing: a writer will sometimes give a hint of what is to come in the play or novel.

6 Foreshadowing

A playwright will sometimes give a hint of what is to come in the play. This is known as **foreshadowing**. It can also be seen in novels.

- Situations may seem particular knotty – can they ever be resolved?
- Characters may appear to have personalities that are volatile or inflexible.
- The language and imagery has an undertone of uncertainty or even menace. Sometimes it is stated directly. The chorus in *Romeo and Juliet* says: *a pair of star-crossed lovers take their life,* so we know from the outset that a tragedy will occur.

See more about foreshadowing in *The Tempest* in Unit 28.

Reflection: Consider another play you've studied and ask yourself if there are any other ways that the play's action could have been introduced. What difference might this make to the audience's response and expectation?

ACTIVITY 15.3

Look closely at the play you are studying and note down what kind of exposition it has. Does it fit into one of these six categories? Can you think of other categories? (For example, in some of Shakespeare's plays, a couple of secondary characters are gossiping about the main interest of the play.)

KEY TERM

Action: what is happening at any given moment in the story, what people are doing. (The plot is the completed series of actions making up the whole story.)

Action

The central **action** of a play is often forged by a chain of cause and effect, which the audience can believe and be involved in.

- Sometimes one of the characters is a driving force who makes things happen; for example, Shakespeare's *Richard III* or Norman in Alan Ayckbourn's *The Norman Conquests*.
- Perhaps the hero has to face obstacles before his goals can be reached, and these struggles may be mental obstacles, something within his own nature, rather than physical or contextual. Shakespeare's tragic heroes are often in this category.
- In *Top Girls*, this pattern is ironically reversed for Marlene, who is shown as successful from the outset. The play gradually reveals her inner life and secrets, which show her to be less successful as a human being.
- In Harold Pinter's play *Betrayal,* the action runs backwards so that the final scene is the first in chronological time, making the adulterous relationship, which is its subject, both more poignant and more pointless. The climax of the play is the first meeting of the lovers, not the last.

The action can also generate tension, which the playwright sustains by withholding information from the audience or keeping them in suspense. The tension can rise and fall through the central section of the play, but its general trend is upwards. In comedy or farce, the suspense of the audience will be generated and satisfied in gradual revelations until the final unravelling reveals all.

Resolution (or denouement)

- In a comedy, the resolution often results in marriages and pairings, the unravelling of the complications in a happy ending. Remember that denouement or the French word *dénouement* ('untying') is often used for this stage. In *A Midsummer Night's Dream,* the marriages take place, the *rude mechanicals* perform their play to great amusement, and the fairy king and queen resolve their differences.

- In a tragedy, deaths will occur but there may be a sense ultimately of a new beginning.
- In more contemporary drama, the final scene may be much more open-ended than those in earlier plays, with endings that suggest further complication or even a return to the status quo of the very beginning of the play.
- The 'tying up of loose ends' can sometimes strike an audience or reader as somewhat contrived. How believable is the undeclared passion of the Dominee in *The Road to Mecca* (Fugard), for example? You may also be able to think of novels in which the ending is over-neat, for the sake of the satisfactory rounding off of the author's concerns. Iris Murdoch's novels fall into this category.

ACTIVITY 15.5

Discuss in class or with a group the ending of the plays you are studying. How satisfied are you that the ending resolves the issues raised by the play? You should jot down what you think the main issues of the play are before you start your discussion.

Patterning devices

The dynamic linear structure discussed is not the only way in which playwrights handle their material. Although the action is driving onwards, another kind of network operates simultaneously in plays, shown in the following diagram:

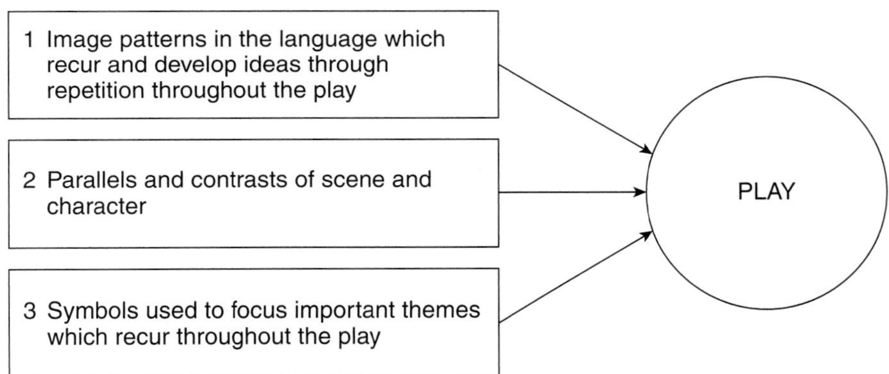

Different kinds of patterns of action and language link aspects of the play through networks of comparisons.

Imagery

Imagery is one of the most important patterning structures used in Shakespeare's plays, and is also employed by other playwrights.

ACTIVITY 15.6

Look carefully at the comparisons suggested in the three extracts and the effects they have.

You will remember from the poetry units that imagery is the word used for metaphorical language. Shakespeare's work is rich in imagery. Here are some examples of evocative metaphors and similes:

Example 1

Why strew'st thou sugar on that bottled spider
Whose deadly web ensnareth thee about?

Richard III Act 1 Scene 3

Example 2

… Here lay Duncan,
His silver skin laced with his golden blood

Macbeth Act 2 Scene 3

Example 3

But earthlier happy is the rose distilled
Than that which, withering on the virgin thorn
Grows, lives, and dies, in single blessedness.

A Midsummer Night's Dream Act 1 Scene 1

SAMPLE RESPONSE

Example 1

The image of Richard as a poisonous spider is enhanced by the use of alliteration: all the hissing 's' sounds are very effective.

Example 2

By comparing Duncan's dead skin with silver, Macbeth gives an image of pallor but also of something precious. His blood, normally red, is imaged as gold, more precious than an ordinary mortal's because he is the king, even though dead. The word *laced* gives a visual image of the tracery of blood on his skin, but *lace* is also a word associated with the clothing of the nobility. So the imagery given by Shakespeare to the guilty Macbeth is very visual in its effect, but also reveals Macbeth's awareness of the precious majesty of Duncan: the murderer is in no doubt of the enormity of his crime, and this is revealed through the imagery.

Example 3

Egeus is threatening his daughter Hermia with being sent to a nunnery if she doesn't marry Demetrius, his chosen husband. He wants her to realise that the single life of a nun in a cloister will be a waste of her beauty, so he attempts to persuade her by comparing her with a lovely rose which, if left to bloom by itself, will simply wither and die. *On the virgin thorn* sounds particularly harsh and bleak. Of course, she doesn't want to be a nun, she wants to be married – but to the man of her own choice, not her father's! What seems a conventional image (beautiful girl equals lovely rose) suits her father's conventional thinking, but it becomes more interesting as it develops through the lines.

Repeated image patterns

The individual images given in Activity 15.6 are very effective in themselves at stirring our imaginations. However, Shakespeare also uses imagery in repeated patterns.

- In the first example in this list, Richard III is constantly compared to a spider with webs of deceit and extraordinary venom in the play of that name.
- *Macbeth* is notable for image patterns of blood, from the first bloody man in Act 1 Scene 2 throughout its horrible murders to the final decapitation of the central character.
- *Romeo and Juliet* has light and darkness images; *Hamlet* has military ones. Every Shakespeare play will have its own special pattern.

Other more recent playwrights use similar techniques. The car (referred to but not seen) is an image used throughout Miller's *Death of a Salesman*, suitably enough for a travelling salesman. However, Willy is confused at times about which car he is talking about, suggesting he is losing his grip on reality. It is also a reminder of the family's struggle to make ends meet in the present, but also of a happier past as well as the means of his final suicide.

ACTIVITY 15.7

Research whether the play you are studying has recurring patterns of images. What are they? Use a library to find books on Shakespeare's imagery or search facilities on the internet to identify literature websites that will give you instances of a repeated word representing an image in a play. (For Shakespeare, you could try darkness or blood in *Macbeth*, madness in *Twelfth Night*, corruption in *Hamlet*, or storm in *King Lear*.)

Reflection: What effect do these recurring patterns have in the play as a whole? Think about atmosphere and audience response to it.

Parallels and contrasts

Parallel scenes are another effective symmetric device used for emphasis. A playwright may use a great variety of types of character and dramatic effect; however, there may also be parallel scenes which, set against one another, have an intensifying effect on the drama and point the contrasts that also exist. In every case, the play's themes are emphasised too.

- Ayckbourn's *Absurd Person Singular* has three acts and is structured around the kitchens of three different households in a succession of Christmas parties (set 'Last Christmas ... This Christmas ... Next Christmas'). The couples who live in the kitchens, and interact with each other and their visitors, are thus placed by the playwright in parallel situations at parallel times. The audience's appreciation of the social satire is precisely focused by this device.
- In *Romeo and Juliet*, there are two scenes (Act 2 Scene 5 and Act 3 Scene 2) when the Nurse brings news to Juliet: in the first, she brings the happy news of Romeo's arrangement to meet and marry her; in the second, the terrible news that Romeo has been responsible for the death of Juliet's cousin, Tybalt. In each case, the structure of the sequence is the same: the Nurse doesn't come out with her news directly and Juliet is desperate for it. The effect is to create comedy in one and tragic suspense in the other, but in both the Nurse's middle-aged slowness and common-sense approach to life contrast sharply with Juliet's vivacious and impulsive youth. The contrast of youth and age is one of Shakespeare's great themes, nowhere more obvious than in the juxtaposition of these two parallel scenes.

KEY TERM

Juxtaposition: is placing next to one another for effect of comparison or contrast. An effect which is widely used in all forms of literature! This is a very useful key term.

KEY TERM

Irony of situation: an event or occasion in which the outcome is very different from might have been expected. It is also seen in the novel.

- In Churchill's *Top Girls,* scenes at the office and at Joyce's house are strongly contrasted: one is urban and affluent, the other rural and poor. The scenes have very different tones and language, emphasising the lack of cohesion in women's roles in society and the difficulty the sisters have in communicating with each other.

Dramatic irony is a kind of **irony of situation** where one person or group of people know something that others do not. It may be the audience who can see the discrepancy between what a character thinks is true and what the situation actually is. This may give rise to comic or tragic irony, or irony of situation.

ACTIVITY 15.8

With a friend, try to identify parallels and contrasts within your set play or any others that you have read or seen. What effect does this juxtaposition of scenes have on the audience?

Symbols

The theatre is a visual medium and playwrights often use physical symbols as structural devices. They are not part of the linear structure of the play, but may represent ideas or develop characterisation, proving a constant physical reminder to the audience of what they stand for throughout the play.

- In *Candida* by George Bernard Shaw, a photograph of Candida dominates the early scenes. The characters' discussion of her looks introduces the playwright's concerns about women, and how they are viewed by men and other women.
- In *Death of a Salesman* (Miller), the wire recorder represents the world of new technology and material objects accessible to those with money to spare. (Does Howard need to hear his child's voice recorded?) By contrast, Willy's family is struggling to pay rent and repair appliances.
- *The Glass Menagerie* (Williams) is itself symbolic of the fragile world inhabited by Laura Wingfield, but Williams also intended the play to have 'legends', or key ideas and phrases, projected at the side of the stage to focus the audience's attention on the ideas of the play as they developed – a very Brechtian idea, in practice (see Unit 13; the **Distancing** or **alienation effect**). However, this has rarely been incorporated into productions of the play. The result of this has been to emphasise the naturalism of the play and to diminish its symbolic and representative qualities.
- In Caryl Churchill's *Serious Money,* the telephone represents the world of speedy communications and insider dealing.
- In *Othello,* the handkerchief is the physical 'proof' that Othello thinks he needs to show that Desdemona is unfaithful. In fact, the way he impresses the story of the handkerchief upon her shows his domination of her.
- In *King Lear,* the letter which Edmund has forged to implicate his brother represents sibling rivalry, the attempt of one brother to worm deeper into the affections of his father than his brother, whom he is trying to oust.
- In *The Road to Mecca,* the lights and candles in the room are symbolic of the luminous radiance and creativity of the central character, Miss Helen.

KEY TERM

Distancing or **alienation effect:** a feature of some plays in which the familiar is made strange so that the audience see characters and events differently and are surprised into thinking about them rather than simply identifying with or accepting them. The playwright Bertolt Brecht (1898–1956) popularised the term, initially in German *verfremdungseffekt*.

ACTIVITY 15.9

Look closely at the play you are studying and see whether any of the patterning devices described here are used by the playwright to enhance theme or characterisation.

TIP

Awareness of a play's structure and a willingness to try to discuss it are characteristic of higher-quality essay answers.

FURTHER STUDY

Search online for 'Act 1 Scene 1 *Macbeth*, G.C. Howard'. You'll find three different versions of the first scene of *Macbeth* showing the witches. Some of the images are disturbing.

TIP

When you are writing on an extract from your set play, consider its place in the development of the play as a whole: not only its place in the unfolding of the plot and the intensifying of the drama but also its relationship with any parallel scenes.

Self-assessment checklist

Reflect on what you've learnt in this unit and indicate your confidence level between 1 and 5. If you score below 3, revisit that section. Come back to this list later in your course. Has your confidence grown?

	Confidence level	Revisited?
I can recognise linear structure and plot		
I can discuss what exposition is		
I understand the definition of denouement and its effect		
I appreciate patterning devices such as imagery, parallels and contrasts and symbolism		

Characters in drama

Learning objectives

In this unit you will:

- review characterisation
- consider characters in action and stage directions
- recognise character types and chorus figures
- acknowledge the importance of conflict and persuasion
- extend understanding of parallels and contrasts
- reflect on audience sympathy and identification.

KEY CONCEPTS

Language, form, structure, genres, context, style, interpretation.

Before you start

- Make a list of characters you remember best from plays you have studied before (or from the one you are working on now). On one side of the page, put the characters' names and on the other, note down a few words to describe their character and appearance.
- Do you have a picture in your mind of what they look like? Think carefully about where this comes from – is it because you have seen the play or a film with the part played by a particular actor?

The characters in a play, whether by Shakespeare or Miller, Soyinka or Herzog, Bolt or Churchill, are often very memorable; it is not surprising that students relate immediately to them, especially if they have seen the play on stage or in a film version. As in the novel, the people who inhabit the action can be the natural focus of any reader or audience when they first encounter that work.

TIP

Many exam questions focus on character, so you need to be well-prepared for this topic. However, at AS or first-year A level, questions will not simply ask for descriptions of characters; there will always be a particular focus and you will need to direct your material carefully to that.

Created in words

Characters in a play are not real people; they are created first and foremost by language and imagery. But because actors interpret them, they can seem real and you are bound to respond to them with feeling. It's just important to make sure that you can identify the reasons for your interpretation or your powerful response by quoting the words and images that have influenced you, especially if you are answering a passage question or an essay on characterisation. The word **characterisation** means '*making* a character', and it reminds you that the writer has chosen words and tones to create a particular effect. What impressions are created of the characters described here, and of the people describing them? Sometimes they are describing themselves.

KEY TERM

Characterisation: a literally '*making* a character'; the writer has chosen words and tones to create a particular effect. Also see Unit 10.

Example	Impression created
• 1 *I'll get him a job selling. He could be big in no time. My God! Remember how they used to follow him around in high school? When he smiled at one of them their faces lit up. When he walked down the street . . . [he loses himself in reminiscences].* Willy about Biff in *Death of a Salesman*	• Willy's description of Biff at school in 1 shows more about Willy than it does about Biff perhaps: his love for his son and desire for him to do well make him unrealistic, as many parents are, about wanting their children to do the things they have done, or in this case not done.
• 2 *The truth is that I am worse than Nero feeding Christians to the lions. I feed young people to my Hope. Every young body behind a school desk keeps it alive. So you've been warned! If you see a hungry gleam in my eyes when I look at your children . . . you know what it means. That is the monster that stands here before you.* Anela Myalatya of himself in *My Children! My Africa!*	• Mr Myalatya in 2 calls himself a monster for keeping a sense of hope which drives him, but at this point neither he nor the audience believe what he says here criticising himself. Sadly, his idealism and hope are to prove tragic in the South African context of the play.
• 3 *O, she doth teach the torches to burn bright!* Romeo of Juliet in *Romeo and Juliet* Act 1 Scene 5	• Romeo's passion as well as Juliet's beauty are expressed in the imagery and tone here.
• 4 . . . *how lovely and sweet and pretty she is . . . in the eyes of others – strangers – she's terribly shy and lives in a world of her own and those things make her seem a little peculiar.* Amanda and Tom of Laura in *The Glass Menagerie*	• Amanda describes her daughter with characteristic exaggeration and optimism. Tom loves his sister no less, but is much more realistic about her personality.
• 5 *I am determined to prove a villain . . .* Richard III of himself in *Richard III* Act 1 Scene 1	• Richard III's determination *to prove a villain* does show his evil nature, but it also shows his love of play-acting and self-conscious assuming of roles for himself.
• 6 . . . *yet do I fear thy nature; It is too full o' th' milk of human kindness . . .* Lady Macbeth of Macbeth in *Macbeth* Act 1 Scene 5	• This shows the relationship of the Macbeths and their relative toughness, although later she is shown to be not as hard-hearted as she boasts here, and her unconscious mind rebels against her, as you see vividly in the sleepwalking scene.

ACTIVITY 16.1

Look closely and critically at what characters say of themselves, and what they say about each other, in the play you are studying.

Reflection: What effect does this have in the overall structure of the play?

Characters in action

KEY TERM

Stage business: activity with props (properties), that are employed for extra dramatic impact (notes, letters, cleaning materials, length of rubber hose).

There are few stage directions in a Shakespeare play. However, those that do exist, together with the words given to each character, contain enough clues for the director or the attentive reader to visualise the actions and gestures that the characters will perform. *Actions speak louder than words*, as the old saying has it, and certainly, in Shakespeare's *Othello*, the way Iago behaves towards Othello gives us a very different view from the hypocritical words he speaks to him with apparent sincerity. Other dramatists give quite full stage directions, even describing the appearance and manner of the characters when they first appear. George Bernard Shaw, for example, often gives very lengthy descriptions of characters, more in the manner of a novelist. In *Death of a Salesman*, Arthur Miller gives description as well as commentary on the action, and many hints about tone and emotional quality for the actors playing the parts.

Television, in particular, has made audiences used to very naturalistic acting; in the theatre, stronger projection and more exaggerated gestures and actions are necessary to communicate to the whole audience, even those in the back rows of the theatre.

Hand gestures work well in the theatre (*Romeo and Juliet*, National Theatre, London, 2013).

ACTIVITY 16.2

Look closely at the use of stage directions in the following sequences. How are they used to complement the words to create effects of character and theme? You can use the term **stage business**.

Extract 1

(Jane thinks that Eva is trying to clean the oven, when in fact Eva is trying to commit suicide in various ways, including putting her head in the gas oven.)

Jane: It's at times like this you're glad of your friends, aren't you? *[She goes at the oven with fresh vigour, singing cheerily] [During the above Eva writes another brief note and places it in a prominent position on the table. She now rises and goes to a chair where there is a plastic washing basket filled with clean but unironed clothes. Coiled on top is a washing line. She returns to the table. Jane, emerging for fresh water, catches sight of her]*

Sorting out your laundry? You're a terror, aren't you? You're worse than me. *[She returns to her oven and resumes her song]*

[Eva begins to pull the washing line from the basket. She finds one end and ties it in a crude noose. She tests the effectiveness of this on one wrist and, satisfied, pulls the rest of the rope from the basket. Every foot or so is a plastic clothes peg which she removes]

I think I'm beginning to win through. I think I'm down to the metal anyway, that's something. There's about eight layers on here.

[Eva comes across a pair of knickers and two pairs of socks still pegged to the line. She removes these and replaces them in the basket]

There's something stuck on the bottom here like cement. You haven't had cement for dinner lately, have you? [She laughs]

[Eva now stands with her clothes line staring at the ceiling …]

Alan Ayckbourn Absurd Person Singular (1972)

Extract 2

Linda: Just rest. Should I sing to you?

Willy: Yeah. Sing to me. *[Linda hums a soft lullaby]* When that team came out – he was the tallest, remember?

Linda: Oh yes. And in gold.

[Biff enters the darkened kitchen, takes a cigarette and leaves the house. He comes downstage into a golden pool of light. He smokes, staring at the night.]

Willy: Like a young god, Hercules – something like that. And the sun, the sun all around him. Remember how he waved to me? Right up from the field with the representatives of three colleges standing by? And the buyers I brought, and the cheers when he came out – Loman, Loman, Loman! God Almighty, he'll be great yet. A star like that, magnificent, can never really fade away!

[The light on Willy is fading. The gas heater begins to glow through the kitchen wall, near the stairs, a blue flame beneath red coils.]

Linda: *[timidly]* Willy, dear, what has he got against you?

Willy: I'm so tired. Don't talk any more [Biff slowly returns to the kitchen. He stops, stares towards the heater.]

Linda: Will you ask Howard to let you work in New York?

Willy: First thing in the morning. Everything'll be all right. [Biff reaches behind the heater and draws out a length of rubber tubing. He is horrified and turns his head toward Willy's room, still dimly lit, from which the strains of Linda's desperate but monotonous humming rise.]

▶

Willy: *[staring through the window into the moonlight] Gee, look at the moon moving between the buildings! [Biff wraps the tubing round his hand and quickly goes up the stairs.]*

Arthur Miller Death of a Salesman (1949)

SAMPLE RESPONSE

Extract 1

The contrast between the action of the two speakers is remarkable – one trying to kill herself and the other doing domestic chores. The misunderstanding is extremely comic for the audience, with Eva looking for new ways to kill herself using what is in the kitchen (drink, sleeping pills, oven, washing line, later electric wires) and Jane seeing each of Eva's actions as an indication of a housewifely desire to tidy up. Jane is the only person to speak here, and she is completely oblivious to the evidence in front of her, imagining that Eva is like her, an obsessive housewife. Her vigorous and cheerful demeanour is in complete contrast to the suicidal Eva, who is beginning, in any case, to feel the effect of having taken sleeping pills. Although the audience laugh at this sequence, there are some serious points being made: how often do we misinterpret others' actions because of our own obsessions? What does compulsive tidiness reveal about character? Are not the everyday objects which surround us all deadening in their own way?

Extract 2

The stage directions here at the end of Act 1 show Biff discovering Willy's suicide apparatus and counterpoint (a term from music which is sometimes used in place of 'juxtapose'). Willy's nostalgic and hyperbolic reminiscences of him as a youthful sportsman – *like a young god, Hercules*. Miller makes the gas fire very prominent in his stage directions, even stressing the colours of red and blue (a little like the phone box in Miller's *A View from the Bridge*), alerting the audience to its significance. The use of the stage space and the lighting here, to show both Biff and his parents separately, reminds us of the way in which the theatre has effects of ironic juxtaposition that cannot easily be replicated in filmed versions of the play. Linda's desperate humming and timid question to Willy maintain our awareness of her anxiety about him, and her ignorance of his affair with the other woman, the discovery of which, depicted later in the play, is so important in the fractured relationship between him and his son. Willy's love of the moonlight and its beauty is a reminder of his affinity with the natural world and the play's concern with the contrast of town and country life.

ACTIVITY 16.3

Take a scene from a play you are studying and note the stage directions. Then look at the dialogue and consider what prompts it offers to the action. How does this action illuminate the characterisation (and indeed the themes) in the scene? Work with a friend so that you can consider how another student might interpret the scene differently.

Character types

In his plays, Shakespeare makes frequent reference to the four humours: well-established means of delineating personality types at the time he was writing. The four types – melancholic, phlegmatic, choleric and sanguine – are based essentially on the four elements of water, earth, fire and air, and their dominant characteristics are, respectively: depression, stolid calm, anger and optimism. References to them recur throughout the plays. Greek tragedies and Roman comedies are full of characters dominated by one ruling passion or quality. Ben Jonson's plays, such as *Volpone* and *The Alchemist,* create characters who are types in this way, and their names often give the clue to their personalities: Subtle, Justice Overdo, Sir Epicure Mammon, and so on. In many Restoration comedies, a similar effect is created: Lord Foppington, Sir Fopling Flutter, Lady Fainall, Aimwell and Archer, for example. There is more on stock characters later in this book.

TIP

Although you can make reference to typical character traits, it is always helpful to show that you recognise complexity of character where it is presented in the plays you are studying.

Chorus figures

A chorus is a character or group of characters who help to tell the story of the play, and sometimes act in it as well. Chorus figures have been used from the very earliest Greek drama, and are still used today. The chorus makes the audience aware of the context and meaning of the play, and can represent the audience's point of view. Taken together, the characters of the chorus can provide a powerful communal appeal. Here are some examples:

- In *Oedipus Rex* by Sophocles, the Chorus represent a common-sense view of the tragedy.
- T.S. Eliot uses a chorus of women to represent the ordinary parishioners of Canterbury at the time of the martyrdom of Thomas à Becket in *Murder in the Cathedral.*
- In *The Fire Raisers*, Max Frisch has a chorus of firemen.
- Peter Shaffer's *Equus* uses a chorus of horses – actors wearing horse masks who do not speak but are an important part of the action and atmosphere.
- Ama Ata Aidoo uses chorus figures – the Old Man and Old Woman – in *Anowa.*
- Other examples of individual chorus figures are: The Common Man in *A Man for All Seasons* (Bolt), Michael in *Dancing at Lughnasa* (Friel), the Praise-singer in *Death and the King's Horseman* (Soyinka) and Time in *The Winter's Tale* (Shakespeare).

Motivation

Why do characters do what they do? Their behaviour should be generally believable and arise out of the situations they find themselves in. Audiences tend to accept the status quo at the beginning of the play, even if it is rather unusual, and then expect believable behaviour after that. On the whole, there are plenty of plausible reasons for characters' behaviour suggested within the text. In *Othello,* a character whose motives are discussed endlessly is Iago. Is he a 'motiveless' character who is just evil, as some have claimed, or is he fuelled by envy of Cassio or Othello, racism, revenge at being passed over for promotion, anger because he thought Othello has had sex with his wife, and so on? Your interpretation must take account of those clues in the text that you think are important, and you must be able to quote them. In *Who's Afraid of Virginia Woolf?* by Edward Albee, George and Martha are cruel to each other, but their complicated games are fuelled by their inability to have a child and the elaborate fantasy they have created, a fact not revealed until the end of the play.

ACTIVITY 16.4

If possible, discuss with a group the motivation of the characters in the play you are all studying. You will find a great variety of opinions.

Is there a difference between what characters say about themselves and what you, the audience or reader, observe? There may be irony if the character is not fully aware of their motives. In Arthur Miller's *A View from the Bridge,* Eddie is not able to face the nature of his love for his niece Catherine, and feels tortured when his wife forces him to face up to it near the play's climax. Shakespeare's King Lear, for example, is not very self-aware: *he hath ever but slenderly known himself,* says one of his own daughters. In *Much Ado About Nothing*, Benedick and Beatrice are the last to realise the powerful attraction they feel for each other.

Conflict and persuasion

It is often said that drama comes from characters in conflict, and this is certainly a valid point. Characters will often argue and try to persuade one another, and this may be a kind of suppressed conflict.

- The conflict between Thomas More and Henry VIII in *A Man for All Seasons* runs through the play, although there is only one early scene in which the two appear together. It is the many henchmen representing the desires of Henry who have the overt conflicts with More.
- The long scene between Marlene and Joyce at the end of *Top Girls* is a furious personal and political argument, and its aftermath ends the play.
- The row that erupts between Tom and Amanda after Jim leaves the apartment in *The Glass Menagerie* is the fatal one that sends Tom off into the world away from the family.
- The argument between Macbeth and Lady Macbeth in which she accuses him of being weak and unmanly pushes him into the murder of Duncan.
- The many arguments between the lovers in *A Midsummer Night's Dream* are a source of both laughter and reflection.

TIP

Make sure that you support your interpretations of character by close reference to the text. Many different interpretations are valid because the approach of Shakespeare and other playwrights allows for different emphasis and perspective.

However, in the relationships between characters depicted by Shakespeare, one of the most enduring images is of persuasion: one character whispering into another's ear, or flattering another to win a point, or speaking seductively to win a lady's hand. Here are some examples:

- Iago pouring poisonous lies into Othello's ear (*Othello*)
- Richard, Duke of Gloucester wooing Lady Anne (*Richard III*)
- Lady Macbeth urging Macbeth to murder the king (*Macbeth*).

Reflection: What effect does each conflict have on the audience and their appreciation of the unfolding drama?

ACTIVITY 16.5

Find some examples of conflict in the plays you have studied. They can be physical fights, disagreements or the force of two personalities ranged against each other.

ACTIVITY 16.6

Find some persuasion scenes in the plays you know, and read or act them with a partner, if possible. What do they add to your appreciation of the playwright's characterisation? How successfully does one character persuade the other?

Parallels and contrasts of character

As we've seen, one of the most significant structural devices used by playwrights is the juxtaposition of elements to emphasise and clarify their qualities, and characters are no exception. Sometimes a play's very framework is dependent upon opposing, or apparently opposing, characters who are often, although not always, from the same family. Consider the following:

- the sisters Marlene and Joyce in *Top Girls*: opposites who articulate between them many of the issues faced by women today.
- the brothers Biff and Happy in *Death of a Salesman*, one much more complex and tortured than the other.
- Edgar and Edmund in *King Lear*: the two sons of Gloucester, one a heroic knight, even a Christ figure, the other a villain.
- Eva and Jane, two very different wives in *Absurd Person Singular*.

Sometimes, two paired, opposing characters can be representative not only of different forms of personality, but of opposing methods of government, even the succession of one epoch to another. For example, Richard II and Bolingbroke in *Richard II* represent respectively the medieval and the new era that heralds the Tudors; Marlene in *Top Girls* is a Thatcherite but Joyce is a socialist.

ACTIVITY 16.7

Research some paired characters and consider how far they are opposite to each other. Do you find any similarities between them?

TIP

You will remember that one of drama's great themes is that one should not judge by appearances. It is always sensible to reflect on characters and whether they can be summed up as simply 'good' or 'bad'. Usually you will find some aspect of a 'good' character who is unpleasant or unappealing, and you will even feel some sympathy for villains too.

Sympathy and identification

Unless the production is a very poor one, everyone who watches a play will find themselves involved in the unfolding situation and identifying with some of the characters and the crises they face. Sympathy is only to be expected with Shakespeare's characters, such as Viola from *Twelfth Night* and Ophelia from *Hamlet,* Orlando from *As You Like It* or Claudio from

Measure for Measure. But do you always sympathise with Hamlet? (You could even harbour a sneaking sympathy for Claudius!) Or King Lear? What about Shylock? What is it about Richard III or Edmund (in *King Lear*) that fascinates and entertains even though they are such villains? Is there anything good to be said about Iago? Why do you have such mixed feelings about Caliban in *The Tempest*? What about the *old fantastical Duke of dark corners* in *Measure for Measure*? Which of the sisters do you sympathise most with in *Top Girls*? Do you think Tom was justified in leaving his mother and sister in *The Glass Menagerie*? Do you find Biff as tragic a figure as Willy in *Death of a Salesman*? And how do you respond to Cleopatra?

TIP

Try to pinpoint the evidence in the text that supports your view of a character, using brief quotation where you can, and remember: the more complex the characterisation, the more likely it is that there will be differing opinions and interpretations.

FURTHER STUDY

Search online for '*Antony and Cleopatra*, Act 1 Scene 1, Royal Shakespeare Company' for a Royal Shakespeare Company production of *Antony and Cleopatra*.

Self-assessment checklist

Reflect on what you've learnt in this unit and indicate your confidence level between 1 and 5. If you score below 3, revisit that section. Come back to this list later in your course. Has your confidence grown?

	Confidence level	Revisited?
I can analyse characterisation in words and action		
I am alert to stage directions and how they contribute		
I can discriminate character types including chorus figures		
I identify and discuss conflict and persuasion		
I can appreciate and discuss parallels and contrasts		
I acknowledge the importance of audience sympathy and identification		

Unit 17
The language of drama

Learning objectives

In this unit you will:

- explore poetry and prose in Shakespeare and other dramatists
- review the use of dialogue
- consider realistic speech patterns
- clarify soliloquies, wit combats and songs
- discover characteristic idiom.

Language, form, structure, genres, context, style, interpretation.

Before you start

- Identify a play you know well and choose a short extract from it.
- With a friend, try re-writing the dialogue in another form. If your play was written before 1900, put it into your own words with the kind of language you might use. If it's a more contemporary piece, try making it more formal, even using verse if you can.
- Read the original and the new version out loud.
- What do you learn about the original from trying to modify it?

Plays are written in dialogue that is expressed in poetry or prose (or both), so the analytical skills you have been developing will prove useful. This unit will look at dramatic dialogue and give special emphasis to the language of Shakespeare. Shakespeare was a poet and a man of the theatre, so his plays are both dramatic and poetic in language and structure. However, even a modern playwright like Caryl Churchill will on occasion use a poetic form, for example in *Serious Money*. T.S. Eliot, probably better known for his poetry, wrote some verse dramas, the most well-known of which is *Murder in the Cathedral*.

Shakespeare the poet

Shakespeare's plays are verse dramas with some sections written in prose. The use of poetry does not mean the characters are poets – it means that the playwright is using the power, descriptiveness and flexibility of poetry to express the thoughts and feelings of many of his characters. The basic metrical scheme of each line of the poetic speeches is blank verse. (Remember that blank verse or the iambic pentameter has ten syllables arranged in five feet, or repeated units of unstressed followed by stressed syllables. See Unit 4 for more on blank verse) Here are two examples of regular lines of iambic pentameter:

I will not be afraid of death and bane,
Till Birnam Forest come to Dunsinane.

Macbeth in *Macbeth* Act 5 Scene 3

I looked upon her with a soldier's eye,

That liked, but had a rougher task in hand, …

Claudio in *Much Ado About Nothing* Act 1 Scene 1

Although iambic pentameter is the basic structure, it is not always easy to find perfectly regular examples of it because the conversational impact of the lines may require some irregularities, however minor.

The verse is also dramatic and needs to be spoken out loud by actors to make sense, not just to scan perfectly. A good actor can make dramatic verse sound very natural. A recent play, *King Charles III* (2014) by Mike Bartlett, was written entirely in blank verse and it was so skilfully spoken that many of the audience didn't realise the verse structure of the dialogue. The playwright chose it because it was a play about kingship and power, great Shakespearean themes, but it was set in the present day.

ACTIVITY 17.1

Find the stressed syllables in the following lines from *Romeo and Juliet* and show how they contribute to the dramatic effect of the speech. Romeo is about to commit suicide, thinking that Juliet is dead. Speak the words out loud so that you can hear the effect.

O, here

Will I set up my everlasting rest,

And shake the yoke of inauspicious stars

From this world-wearied flesh. Eyes, look your last.

COMMENT

The verse in Activity 17.1 is fairly regular iambic pentameter until the final line, where Romeo's determination to die, and powerful emotion, are made more emphatic by the extra stresses, which make the line irregular. I think *world*, *wearied* and *flesh* should be emphasised, as well as *eyes*, *look* and *last*. Which syllables did you stress?

Reflection: Do you find it more difficult to read plays from a book? Compare it with reading a novel. Consider why this is.

In his earlier plays, Shakespeare uses rhyme quite extensively, but as his style matures, rhyme disappears apart from the occasional rhyming couplet, often to end a scene emphatically, or to make a really memorable point. Here is an example where Hamlet has been told by his father's ghost to avenge his murder:

The time is out of joint. O cursèd spite,

That ever I was born to set it right!

The word *cursèd* has two syllables because the *-ed* is pronounced; if it were one syllable it would be spelt *curs'd* or even *curs't*.

Here is a 20th-century example from Wole Soyinka's play *Death and the King's Horseman*. The Praise-singer and the women are chorus figures who speak in unrhymed verse, although the play is largely in the prose of ordinary conversation:

ACTIVITY 17.2

Look closely at the verse for the irregularities, which give emphasis to the emotional or dramatic qualities of the speech you are analysing.

Praise: The gourd you bear is not for shirking.
Singer: The gourd is not for setting down
At the first crossroad or wayside grove.
Only one river may know its contents
Women: We shall all meet at the great market
We shall all meet at the great market
He who goes early takes the best bargains
But we shall meet and resume our banter.

Wole Soyinka *Death and the King's Horseman* (1975)

There is a great deal of repetition of phrases and lines. Some lines (for example, 2, 4 and 7) have the tone of traditional sayings and the whole effect is of a chant or ritual, which contrasts strongly with the conversations of the European administrators – one of the key effects of the play. (You will find an exercise on the dialogue of this play in Unit 28.)

Contemporary playwrights use poetic techniques too. Look at these two examples of rhyming couplets used by Caryl Churchill in *Serious Money:*

Jacinta: I tell you I've caught a Big cocoa importer,
Your deal goes without a hitch. His school was at Eton
Where children are beaten,
He's a prince and exceedingly rich.
Zac: The last couple of years in the United States it's been takeover
mania
And I guess the deals there have gotten somewhat zanier.
Junk bonds are a quick way of raising cash, but it's kind of a hit _n'
run method, which doesn't go down too well in Britain.

Caryl Churchill *Serious Money* (1987)

Churchill's use of rhyming couplets in this play can be very witty and amusing: it is difficult not to be amused by a speech which rhymes *hit 'n'* with *Britain*, and *zanier* with *mania*. The first example has a comic effect because it has some of the rhythms of a limerick. The clever rhyme scheme makes these money-obsessed characters sound very shallow, and lends a fast pace to the action, which is highly appropriate for this play.

Shakespeare's prose

Shakespeare uses prose in his plays as well as verse, more often in comedies than tragedies. However, be careful not to make simplistic assertions about this. Prose *is* used for lower-class characters, true. But it is also used for the nobility, both in tragedies and comedies. Sometimes the scene moves from prose into verse even when the same characters are speaking. This is usually to indicate that the emotional quality of the action is becoming more intimate or intense. However, there are also examples of longer prose speeches that are forcefully emotional. You do need to look closely at each instance, rather than rushing into a generalising comment about the use of prose.

ACTIVITY 17.3

Try to find examples from several plays, especially your set play, to indicate the varied use of verse and prose. Look particularly for scenes where both are used.

Many students claim wrongly that prose is only used by Shakespeare for the lower classes: servants and peasants. This is not so. Beware of making this false claim yourself.

KEY TERMS

Stichomythia: single lines of verse uttered by alternate speakers as in the example from *The Comedy of Errors*.

Hemistichomythia: this device is where half-lines of verse are uttered by alternate speakers, as in the example from *The Tempest*. If you don't remember the word, discuss the effect!

Dialogue

When characters speak to each other, the interplay of the contributions to the scene is known as *dialogue*. Sometimes when the scene is in verse, such as in Shakespeare, the characters speak alternate lines, often showing that they are evenly matched or sparring with each other.

Luciana: What, are you mad, that you do reason so?
Antipholus: Not mad, but mated, how I do not know.
Luciana: It is a fault that springeth from your eye.
Antipholus: For gazing on your beams, fair sun, being by.

Shakespeare *The Comedy of Errors* Act 3 Scene 2

Characters sometimes even share the lines with each other, and this suggests a particularly close interaction between them.

Prospero: What is't thou canst demand?
Ariel: My liberty.
Prospero: Before the time be out? No more.
Ariel: I prithee,
Remember I have done thee worthy service, …

Shakespeare *The Tempest* Act 1 Scene 2

Reflection: Think about the effects that the playwright has created by this.

In this dialogue between Prospero and Ariel, the first two speeches form one line and the second two speeches form one line, showing their intimacy even though they are disagreeing.

In *Romeo and Juliet*, Shakespeare reveals the immediate affinity of the two lovers by having them share a sonnet:

Romeo: If I profane with my unworthiest hand
This holy shrine, the gentle fine is this:
My lips, two blushing pilgrims, ready stand
To smooth that rough touch with a tender kiss.

Juliet: Good pilgrim, you do wrong your hand too much,
Which mannerly devotion shows in this;
For saints have hands that pilgrims' hands do touch,
And palm to palm is holy palmers' kiss.

Romeo: Have not saints lips, and holy palmers too?

Juliet: Ay, pilgrim, lips that they must use in pray'r.

Romeo: O, then, dear saint, let lips do what hands do!
They pray; grant thou, lest faith turn to despair.

Juliet: Saints do not move, though grant for prayers' sake.

Romeo: Then move not while my prayer's effect I take.

Shakespeare *Romeo and Juliet* Act 1 Scene 5

ACTIVITY 17.4

Find some more examples of these dialogue variations in the play you are studying and try to work out the relationships of the characters involved and the dramatic effect of the scene.

Realistic speech patterns

In contemporary drama, some playwrights have striven to create the effect of real-life speech, with all its repetitions, interruptions and unfinished sentences. Churchill uses a method in *Top Girls* to capture the way people interrupt each other, using a slash (/) in the text to show the point of interruption. Here is an example from Act 1:

Joan: The day after they made me cardinal I fell ill and lay two weeks without speaking, full of terror and regret. / But then I got up

Marlene: Yes, success is very …

Joan: determined to go on. I was seized again / with a desperate longing for the absolute.

Isabella: Yes, yes, to go on …

Caryl Churchill *Top Girls* (1982)

Churchill also shows characters continuing to speak right through another's speech (typical of real life) or responding to an earlier speech than the one immediately preceding.

This method is also used in Amy Herzog's *4000 Miles*. In the following dialogue, incomplete sentences and questions add to the effect of natural conversation with all its repetitions and omissions:

Vera: You what, came over the GW?

Leo: The –?

Vera: The George Washington Bridge?

Leo: I guess, yeah.

Vera: Was it pretty? At night?

Leo: … yeah, actually. Yeah. I'm not much of a city guy, but. It was all right.

Vera: I'm – I must say I'm surprised, and this is not a complaint, that you came here instead of your – I've lost track whether she's your girlfriend or not, the chubby one, isn't she up at / whaddayacallit –

Leo: She's not chubby.

Vera: She's – well, she's not thin.

Leo: She's healthy, she's / strong.

Vera: I don't see what that has to do with it.

Amy Herzog *4000 miles* (2011)

KEY TERM

Soliloquy: a dramatic convention in which characters are alone on the stage and speak their thoughts aloud to the audience.

Soliloquy

Some plays have very few such long speeches; others, like *Hamlet*, have many. Often the character is confronting some truth about himself or his life as in Richard III's **soliloquy** *I am determined to prove a villain ….*

ACTIVITY 17.5

Read and consider the following examples of soliloquies.

Example 1

The first is from South African playwright Athol Fugard's *My Children! My Africa!*, a play with only three characters but each has a soliloquy – here Thami, the teenage student who becomes caught up in violence.

> I'm sorry to say, but I can't do it any more. I have tried very hard, believe me, but it's not as simple as it used to be to sit behind that desk and listen to the teacher. That little world of the classroom where they used to pat me on the head and say 'Little Thami, you'll go far!' … that little room of wonderful promises where I used to feel so safe has become a place that I don't trust any more. Now I sit at my desk like an animal that

has smelt danger, heard something moving in the bushes and knows it must be very, very careful.

Athol Fugard *My Children! My Africa!* (1989)

Example 2

Macbeth speaks his soliloquy reflecting on the meaninglessness of life when he hears of his wife's death:

Tomorrow, and tomorrow, and tomorrow
Creeps in this petty pace from day to day
To the last syllable of recorded time;
And all our yesterdays have lighted fools
The way to dusty death. Out, out, brief candle
Life's but a walking shadow, a poor player
That struts and frets his hour upon the stage
And then is heard no more. It is a tale
Told by an idiot, full of sound and fury
Signifying nothing.

Shakespeare *Macbeth* Act 5 Scene 5

Example 3

In *Death of a Salesman*, Linda, Willy's wife, speaks out loud to the audience at the end of the play, ironically addressed to her dead husband. This is part of the final speech of the play:

Forgive me, dear. I can't cry. I don't know what it is but I can't cry. I don't understand it. Why did you ever do that? Help me, Willy, I can't cry. It seems to me that you're on another trip. I keep expecting you. Willy, dear, I can't cry. Why did you do it? I search and search and I search, and I can't understand it, Willy. I made the last payment on the house today.

Arthur Miller *Death of a Salesman* (1949)

TIP

The word *soliloquy*, like the word *tragedy*, is often misspelled by students in their exam essays. Try to make sure that you can spell words such as these, which are central to the study of literature.

Reflection: What kinds of characters are given soliloquies by the playwright? Does it automatically make the audience more sympathetic to that character, or not necessarily?

ACTIVITY 17.6

Find a soliloquy in the play you have studied and consider what sort of effect it has on the audience at that point of the play.

Wit combats

In comedies, in particular, there are many examples of scenes in which characters are shown having witty dialogues with each other.

Lady Bracknell: … Is this Miss Prism a female of repellent aspect, remotely connected with education?

Canon Chasuble: [*somewhat indignantly*] She is the most cultivated of ladies, and the very picture of respectability.

Lady Bracknell: It is obviously the same person. May I ask what position she holds in your household?

Canon Chasuble: [*severely*] I am a celibate, madam.

Oscar Wilde *The Importance of Being Earnest* (1895)

This wordplay, revealing opposite values, is delightful for the audience, who are by now familiar with the two speakers and Miss Prism. In Shakespeare's comedies, characters try to score points by outdoing each other's puns. These are not so much funny scenes as admirably clever, and an audience would have to be very quick to catch every nuance of the witty interchange between the characters. Here is a short sequence from *As You Like It*:

had as lief = would rather

buy you = be with you

mar = make marks on

Jacques: I thank you for your company, but, have good faith,
I had as lief been myself alone.

Orlando: And so had I. But yet, for fashion sake, I thank you too for your society.

Jacques: God buy you. Let's meet as little as we can.

Orlando: I do desire we may be better strangers.

Jacques: I pray you mar no more trees with writing love-songs in their barks.

Orlando: I pray you mar no more of my verses with reading them ill-favouredly.

Jacques: 'Rosalind' is your love's name?

Orlando: Yes, just.

Jacques: I do not like her name.

Orlando: There was no thought of pleasing you when she was christened.

Jacques: What stature is she of?

Orlando: Just as high as my heart.

Jacques: You are full of pretty answers: have you not been acquainted with goldsmiths' wives, and conned them out of rings?

Orlando: Not so; but I answer you right painted cloth, from whence you have studied your questions.

Jacques: You have a nimble wit …

Shakespeare *As You Like It* Act 3 Scene 3

In the play, Orlando, the lover, has carved Rosalind's name on the trees in the forest; Jaques, the cynic, is against love but enjoys talk and philosophising. Here, at the beginning, each professes to dislike each other's company and says he is only being polite because it is fashionable to do so. Jaques has already shown he is witty in the play, but Orlando holds his own: his quick-witted retorts impress Jaques, as he admits at the end rather grudgingly. Notice that both accuse the other of getting their jokes from another source – carved on a ring or out of a cloth book. Shakespeare's audiences loved originality in wit, if not plots.

KEY TERM

Comedy of manners: concerned with social conventions and what lies behind them.

Verbal wit also runs throughout Restoration comedies and **comedies of manners** such as *The Rivals* but it is not only a feature of comedy. Hamlet is savagely witty and his pun on the word 'kind' in *a little more than kin and less than kind* sums up one of the great paradoxes of the play: that your kin – your family – are not always kind – well-disposed – towards you, a point already noted.

Songs

Songs, set to music, are used by playwrights to enhance the atmosphere of a scene, especially in comedies. Such verses are rhymed, and they often have a refrain or a repeated line, as songs usually do.

- Caryl Churchill ends each of the two acts of *Serious Money* with rousing, raucous, scurrilous songs that encapsulate the supremely confident and careless atmosphere of those whose greed makes them masses of money in the City of London.
- In Edward Bond's political drama *Restoration*, songs are used to point the satire of the plot and show its contemporary relevance.
- Lady Fidget's song in *The Country Wife* (1675) by William Wycherley, although lively and witty, has a serious point to make about men's treatment of women.

In each case, the words of the song point to a theme of the scene or play as a whole. Sometimes they are jolly and cheerful, but not always. In *Twelfth Night*, for example, the song sung by Feste the Clown in Orsino's court dwells on the tragic potential of unrequited love. Here is the first verse:

William Wycherley (1641–1716).

Come away, come away, death;
And in sad cypress let me be laid;
Fly away, fly away, breath,
I am slain by a fair, cruel maid.
My shroud of white, stuck all with yew,
 O prepare it!
My part of death no one so true
 Did share it.

Even in a comedy, love can be explored as an experience that causes terrible suffering. You have already seen that it can be shown as a kind of madness too.

Characteristic idiom

Plays such as Herzog's *After the Revolution* and *4000 Miles*, with their naturalism of dialogue, express American idiom throughout.

Vera: Well will somebody come taste my eggplant?

Leo: Your eggplant is perfect, take a load off, join us.

The following example of idiom is from *Fugitives* by the Singaporean playwright Alfian Sa'at:

Scene 7 Ruler/Ruled:

[*Son and Zainal are at Raffles Place MRT after midnight. They are sitting at a parapet and Zainal's foot is idly playing on a skateboard.*]

Son: So you guys always hang around this late on Saturdays?

Zainal: Yah. [*Looks up at one of his 'friends' doing a stunt*] Alamak! Lagi sikit lagi![1] Did you see that?

Son: What?

Zainal: That stunt lah! It's called a Kickflip. It's more difficult than the Ollie

Son:: Your friends are very good.

Zainal: This is our hangout every Saturday. You, when are you going to get your own skateboard? Cannot just borrow mine all the time you know.

Son: It's so new to me, this subculture.

Zainal: Subculture your backside lah. We need another line of space here, between the extract and the gloss

1 Just a bit more (Malay)

Alfian Sa'at *Fugitives* (2001)

The places referred to are in Singapore and the MRT or Mass Rapid Transport is their underground rail system. However, note that there is also the idiom of the skateboarding community in the words *Kickflip* and *Ollie*.

TIP

It is much easier to understand and appreciate a play if you can see a production of it. You would grasp that the situations and minor language difficulties, such as those in the final example, become unimportant.

FURTHER STUDY

Search online for '*The Tempest:* Ariel and spirits' for a short video showing the magic spirits in *The Tempest* sing to Ferdinand.

Self-assessment checklist

Reflect on what you've learnt in this unit and indicate your confidence level between 1 and 5. If you score below 3, revisit that section. Come back to this list later in your course. Has your confidence grown?

	Confidence level	Revisited?
I am alert to the different uses of poetry and prose in Shakespeare		
I realise and can discuss how dialogue works to produce effects		
I acknowledge the contribution of realistic speech		
I can analyse and understand wit combats and their function		
I note the significance of songs, where they occur		
I am attentive to characteristic idiom		

Drama unseens

Learning objectives

In this unit you will:

- clarify how you can prepare to approach unseen drama questions with confidence
- study the drama unseen checklist
- develop critical ideas by annotating passages
- compare the work of students and the assessments of it, adding your own thoughts.

KEY CONCEPTS

Language, form, structure, genres, context, style, interpretation.

Before you start

- The advice given here is very similar to the advice given in the poetry and prose sections. If you are going to have a choice of material to respond to in an unseen assessment (you will have a choice in the Cambridge examination), it's always sensible to make your decision on the day, not to go into examination thinking 'I always like the poem best', or 'I much prefer to write on drama'. Each piece is different and has a different appeal. It's important to read and choose very carefully and not to rush into it. In preparation for examination, and before using the material here, discuss with a partner how you feel about having to write on a drama unseen and the challenges you face. This unit should help you!

If you are taking the 9695 AS Level course, you will now have a compulsory unseen paper, which could have a drama passage in it. In this unit, you have some guidelines to help you to frame your responses so that you feel confident about answering on a passage of drama you haven't seen before. First you have to read and appreciate it as a piece of drama, then to write on it, so there are two different kinds of activity here: considering the elements of the printed scene and how they fit together; and writing a successful essay incorporating these ideas.

It's natural to feel apprehensive. You may be thinking 'There's a lot of reading in this passage' or 'Can I visualize this on the stage?', but remember, what has been set will be just right for you at your level, and all the other students are in exactly the same situation. If there are any unusual words the meanings will be given to you. Examiners are not trying to catch you out: they want to give you the best opportunity to show what you can do. You won't be expected to know about the historical context or the writer's life – what is being tested is the effect of drama in the words and actions created by the writer. All the work you've done on your plays and all your previous reading will help you too.

In this unit, you will have reminders of the different aspects of a drama passage that should be considered in any critical appreciation and examples of students' essays on unseen extracts at different levels.

Take an active approach to analysis

An unseen exercise tests close reading, so you need to annotate your passage: underlining, highlighting, linking, commenting in the margin. It becomes a working document and will be the basis of your answer.

Use a highlighter and coloured pens to pick out and underline different aspects of the piece; for example, significant stage directions that show what characters are doing, language choices to indicate characterisation and climactic moments.

Every passage is different, so you need to be flexible

Figure 18.1 reminds you of what you need to think about, but each passage is part of a play which creates its own world. The exam passage that has been picked for you to comment on will be complete in itself, but it will be very suggestive of the work as a whole, which you haven't got in front of you.

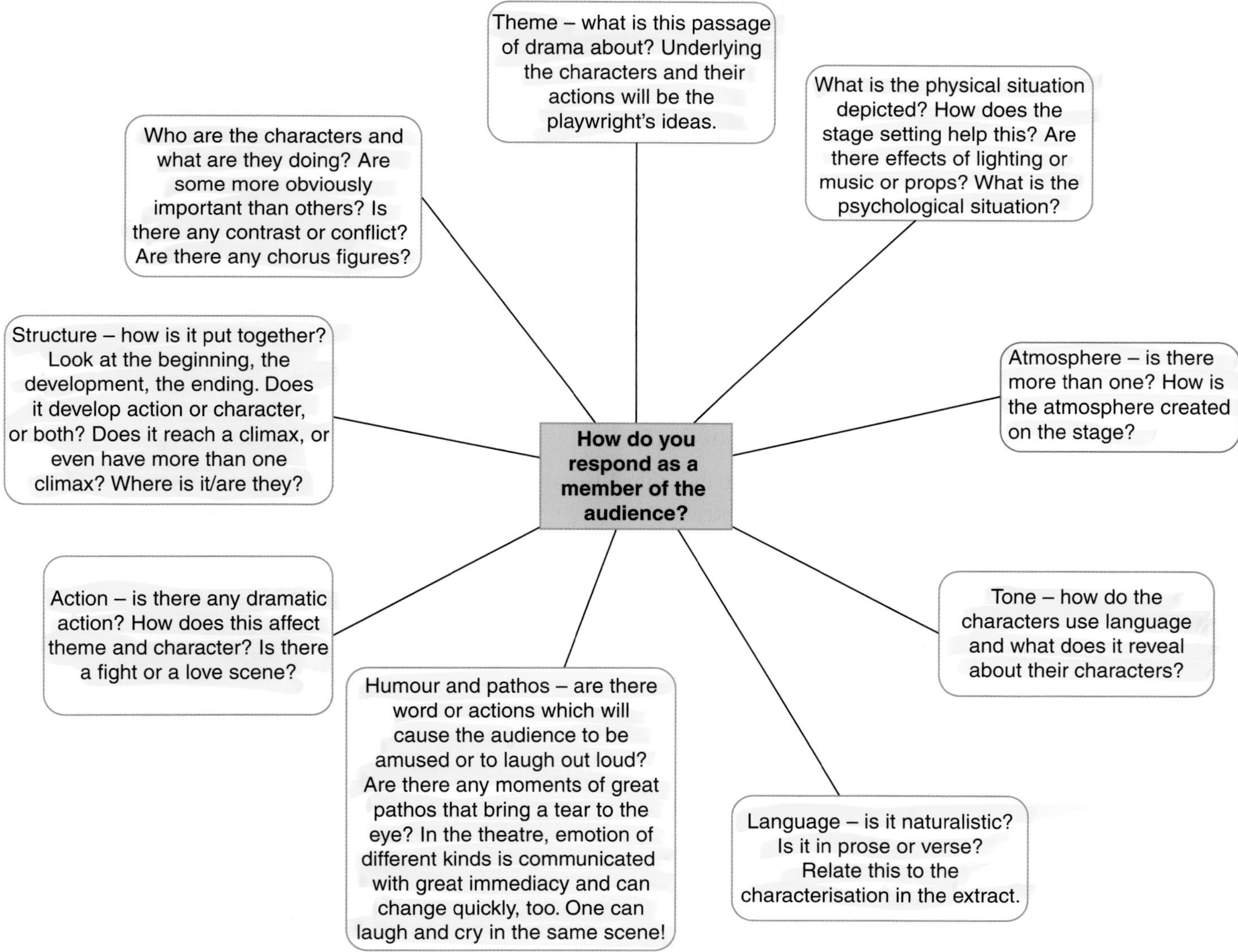

Figure 18.1: Checklist for analysing drama.

ACTIVITY 18.1

A passage of drama, an extract from a full-length play, written by Australian dramatist David Williamson in 1977, is printed here, with a sample response. Read the passage carefully and, using your highlighters, underline and colour the different elements such as changes of mood, contrasts of character and use of persuasive language. Do this before you read the response to the passage. Then look at the sample essay, noting the comments made by the marker in the margin.

If you have the opportunity, work with a classmate to act out this dialogue, so that you have two voices. Williamson writes very naturalistic dialogue so you won't find this difficult. Afterwards, try swapping the roles so that you both have a chance to act both parts – you will find this helpful. Then look at the essay question.

This is from a play about a football club which was once successful but that hasn't had a premiership win in 19 years. Ted is the President of the club and a businessman who has never played football himself but now throws his weight around, interferes with the selection committee and is trying to get rid of the coach, Laurie, a loyal and longstanding member of the team. Laurie has just told the press that he has resigned and Ted has intervened and persuaded him to stay on. (His reason for this is not respect for Laurie, but that he fears the team will go on strike as they are devoted to the coach.)

Essay: *Write a critical appreciation of the following extract from the play, with close reference to the playwright's methods and effects.*

Ted:	What are we going to say to the press?
Laurie:	Just that we're prepared to keep working with each other and that I've withdrawn my resignation.
Ted:	I'd like a bit more than that Laurie. You called me autocratic in the press this morning. Don't you think that calls for some sort of retraction?
Laurie:	The fact that I've said we can still work together will be more or less a retraction.
Ted:	No it won't. All that means is that you still think I'm autocratic but you've decided to grit your teeth and sit it out.
Laurie:	That's not too wide of the mark.
Ted:	Yes, well, I want a bit more. I've got my pride. I want to say that we've had discussions, that several misunderstandings have been ironed out, and that we're sure we can re-establish a fruitful and harmonious working relationship.
Laurie:	Is it true?
Ted:	No but it sounds good.
Laurie:	I'll say that we've talked with each other and found that we can still work together. That's all.
Ted:	We shouldn't be fighting like this Laurie. It's all so ironic. I've always been one of your greatest admirers. Do you remember the day you played your first game?

▶

Laurie: Of course.

Ted: You've just turned seventeen three days before. Or was it eighteen?

Laurie: Seventeen.

Ted: There was a real sense of occasion and anticipation right around the ground. We all knew already that you weren't just another recruit. We all knew we were going to see the first game of a great new champion and I don't think anyone was disappointed. Do you remember your first kick?

Laurie: Not that well. I know I booted a goal, but there was so much adrenalin pumping through me in the first half that when I came off the field I could hardly remember a thing.

Ted: It was magic Laurie. It really was. I was only fourteen at the time but I can still see it as clearly as if it was a video replay. You read the play and started sprinting for the goal, picked up a long, low pass from Wally Baker, steadied, did a beautiful blind turn around Stan Jackson, and slammed it through the centre. I've seen every game we've played since I was six and I remember that one better than most.

Laurie: Yes it was a good game. I settled down in the second half and everyone seemed pretty pleased when I ran off the ground.

Ted: Pleased? They went bloody wild. Do you know that right up to the time I was twelve I used to cry every time we lost. If we won, I went home and booted a football around our back yard in the dark trying to remember every kick of the match and pretending I was in the side. Ha! By the time I was sixteen I could barely hold my place in the school thirds.

Laurie: We've all got different talents.

Ted: I would like to put *harmonious* somewhere in that press statement Laurie.

Laurie: You're a trier aren't you?

Ted: It would make me feel a lot better.

Laurie: Say we've had a long talk and have resolved our differences. That's as far as I'll go.

Jock comes in at the left door.

Jock: I got onto Geoff and he's on his way in.

Ted: You're a hard man, Laurie. I'll write it out and give it to Gerry.

Laurie: I want to check it before it's released.

Ted: Don't worry. I won't slip anything in.

From *The Club* (1978)

SAMPLE RESPONSE

This passage is set in a room at the club and there is very little action in it, although ironically the action of a football game is described in detail by one of the characters. There are two contrasting characters, Ted the club's president and Laurie the coach of the team, and their dialogue is tense. The audience is aware that their relationship is not a particularly friendly one: we have been told that before this scene takes place, Laurie had given a press statement which was critical of Ted and Ted is trying to get him to take it back and be more supportive of him in the press. It is a scene of words and persuasions, with conflict never far from the surface. The more dramatically active character is Ted, as he is the man doing the persuading while Laurie remains steady and firm, and on the stage would have to respond and react constantly to what is being said to him, even if he has few words.

A clear introduction with clear sense of audience response to the basically tense tone of the scene and awareness that this is not an action scene but one of words and persuasions, both between the characters and in connection with the wording of a press statement. The contrast of characters is made clear.

The structure of the extract is in three parts: the first section involves the wording of the press statement and the two different approaches to it; the second part is Ted's persuasion of Laurie by talking about his admiration for him which dates from a long time ago when Laurie was first a player; and the final section returns to the press statement. We see that Laurie hasn't changed his mind at the end of the sequence in spite of Ted's words, leading to Ted saying *You're a hard man Laurie*.

Confident sense of structure shows close reading and attention to tone.

In the first section the audience is made aware of the different characters of the men by what, and how much, they say. Laurie wants to stick to the truth – he even asks *Is it true?* whereas Ted says *No but it sounds good*, so we see that Laurie is a much more straightforward and honest person, who sticks to his simpler version of events, *we've talked with each other and found that we can still work together* whereas Ted wants to elaborate on the story and make it sound better – more of a public relations response which will make him seem superior in the pages of the sports press. The language he uses, for example:

We've had discussions

Several misunderstandings have been ironed out

We can re-establish a fruitful and harmonious working relationship

is very smooth and glib and he comes out with it so easily that we expect he has said these things before. The audience is familiar with this kind of language in the press and on television when people like politicians and other public figures are being interviewed. This is not factual language, but it is typical of the rather vague and euphemistic register used in the newspapers on occasions such as this. Ted has also been irritated by being called *autocratic* by Laurie and admits that he wants *a bit more* because *I've got my pride*. He wants a new press statement that paints him in a better light. On the other hand, Laurie's responses are brief and to the point. It's not surprising that Ted moves into a different strategy with Laurie as he hasn't been particularly successful so far in getting him to be a little more generous in his intended press statement.

The contrast between Laurie's laconic style and Ted's journalese is well-illustrated here. The kind of language used is related to a wider context than a football club disagreement.

Ted decides in the next section to try to persuade Laurie by telling him he has always been one of Laurie's greatest admirers. He gives an account of a game in which Laurie played for the first time with the club, which Ted saw himself when he was 14. First of all, his overarching method is flattery – Laurie was so young and gifted: *I've always been one of your greatest admirers*, but he stresses that everyone felt the same: *There was a real sense of occasion and anticipation right around the ground*. He exaggerates to make his point – *a great new champion. … Pleased? They went bloody wild*, swearing for effect. He describes the kick, using footballing jargon and the names of players to make Laurie feel at home: *You read the play and started sprinting for the goal, picked up a long, low pass from Wally Baker, steadied, did a beautiful blind turn around Stan Jackson, and slammed it through the centre.* And he uses the word *magic* – who would be immune to such praise? Ironically, Laurie hardly remembers the occasion in such detail and describes it in a much more moderate way. *It was a good game….everyone seemed pretty pleased.* Ted goes on to recount personal anecdotes as further persuasion, casting himself (perhaps with false modesty) as the useless player who loved the game and never missed a match, even that he *cried.* Laurie's comment *We've all got different talents* is very ironic and its bathetic tone contrasts strongly with the rather sentimental climax Ted has been building up to. It seems clear that straightforward Laurie is not convinced by this flattery and his stance has not shifted. He can see what Ted was doing ('You're a trier'.) He doesn't trust Ted not to slip something into the press statement as we see from the final lines of the scene. No wonder Ted calls him *hard,* but the audience sees him as determined and firm.

Although this is a sequence of words and persuasions, the tense atmosphere engages the audience. Ted's description of the football match, although intended to persuade Laurie by flattering him, also has the effect of taking the audience imaginatively onto the pitch where they can envisage the match being played – a very effective strategy by the playwright to create action in a static scene. The strong contrast between the two characters and their distinctive use of language makes this a vividly dramatic scene.

The whole play is one of argument and persuasion, manoeuvre and manipulation. Although it's about a football club, it is also symbolic of public life and politics, and the way that men react to each other and try to gain control and prestige.

The point about the playwright's use of the reported match to create action in the minds of the audience in a static scene is an insightful one. However, the actor playing the part of Ted could also express some of the actions physically to give action to the scene and this would be an opportunity to consider different interpretations. The contrast between the characters is again emphasised.

A fitting conclusion to the essay, widening its relevance by relation to political drama. In fact?

This is an interesting section of the dialogue and the essay uses the text well to support points made. Ted goes all out to persuade Laurie using various methods such as flattery, personal anecdote and exaggeration of Laurie's skills when he was a footballer in the team. Another interpretation might be more sympathetic to Ted, whose speeches about the early match and his boyhood are quite imaginative, even lyrical. There is an opportunity for the actor playing Ted to act out the football match physically on the stage and for Laurie to respond – perhaps with cynicism or possibly with some sympathy, which the audience might share.

Reflection: This is a dramatic piece with apparently very little physical action. What strategies has the playwright used to keep the audience interested even though it's basically two men talking to each other? Discuss with a friend and try to make a list. Thinking in this way will take you into the core of how dramatists work, in contrast with poetry and prose writers.

ACTIVITY 18.2

The following passage has two student responses after it. Read and annotate it yourself with the help of a friend, then read the student responses and the marker comments that go with them.

Essay: *Write a critical appreciation of the following passage, showing how the playwright depicts the relationship between the two women.*

The play is set in a rural South African village at the time of apartheid. Miss Helen is an Afrikaner, a white South African. Katrina (the maid who is mentioned but does not appear) is a black South African.

The set shows the lounge and bedroom alcove in the house of Miss Helen, a frail woman in her late sixties. She is fussing around an old-fashioned washstand. She moves an overnight bag and briefcase into the alcove before Elsa enters. She is a young woman in her twenties wearing a tracksuit.

Elsa:	Not cold enough yet for the car to freeze up, is it?
Helen:	No. No danger of that. We haven't had any frost yet.
Elsa:	I'm too exhausted to put it away. *(Collapses on the bed)* Whew! Thank God that's over. Another hour and I would have been wiped out. The road gets longer and longer every time.
Helen:	Your hot water is nearly ready.
Elsa:	Good *(Starts to unpack her overnight bag)*
Helen:	Nice clean towels…and I've opened that box of scented soaps you brought me last time.
Elsa:	What? Oh, those. Haven't you used them yet?
Helen:	Of course not! I was keeping them for a special occasion.
Elsa:	And this is it?
Helen:	Yes. An unexpected visit from you is a very special occasion. Is that all your luggage?
Elsa:	When I said a short visit I really meant it.
Helen:	Such a long way to drive for just one night.
Elsa:	I know.
Helen:	You don't think you could…?
Elsa:	Stay longer?
Helen:	Even just two nights?
Elsa:	Impossible. We're right in the middle of exams. I've got to be in that classroom at eight thirty on Monday morning. As it is I should be sitting at home right now and marking papers. I've even brought a pile of them with me just in case I get a chance up here. *(Starts to undress…tracksuit top, sneakers and socks)*
Helen:	Put anything you want washed on one side and I'll get a message to Katrina first thing in the morning.
Elsa:	Don't bother her with that. I can do it myself.
Helen:	You can't leave without seeing Katrina! She'll never forgive me if I don't let her know you're here, Please…even if it's only for a few minutes.

▶

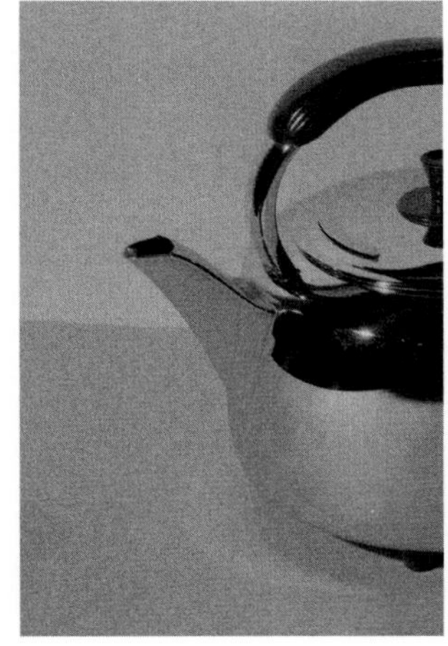

Elsa:	I won't leave without seeing Katrina, Miss Helen! But I don't need her to wash a pair of pants and a bra for me. I do my own washing.
Helen:	I'm sorry... I just thought you might...There's an empty drawer here if you want to pack anything away.
Elsa:	*(an edge to her voice)* Please stop fussing Miss Helen. I know my way around by now.
Helen:	It's just that if I'd known you were coming, I would have had everything ready for you.
Elsa:	Everything is fine just the way it is.
Helen:	No, it isn't! I don't even know that I've got enough in the kitchen for a decent supper tonight. I did buy bread yesterday, but for the rest...
Elsa:	Please, Miss Helen! If we need anything, I'll get old Retief to open his shop for us. In any case I'm not hungry. All I need at this moment is a good wash and a chance to unwind so that I can forget I've been sitting in a motorcar for twelve hours.
Elsa:	Be patient with me, Elsie. Remember the little saying: 'Patience is a virtue, virtue is a grace, and...'
Elsa:	*(Unexpectedly sharp)* For God's sake Helen! Just leave me alone for a few minutes!

Pause

Helen:	*(timidly)* I'll get your hot water.

Miss Helen exits. Elsa slumps down on the bed, her head in her hands. Miss Helen returns a few seconds later with a large kettle of hot water. She handles it with difficulty.

Elsa:	Let me do that!

She jumps up and takes the kettle away from Miss Helen. The two women stand staring at each other for a few seconds. Elsa puts down the kettle and then puts her hands on Miss Helen's shoulders.

Helen	I've got the small one on for tea.
Elsa:	My turn to say sorry.
Helen:	You don't need to do that.
Elsa:	Please! It will help. Sorry Miss Helen. I also need to hear you say you forgive me. ▶

Helen: To tell you the truth, I was getting on my own nerves.

Elsa: *(now smiling)* Come on.

Helen: Oh, all right…But it isn't necessary. You're forgiven.

Elsa: Now sit down and stop worrying about me. We're both going to close our eyes, take a deep breath and start again. Ready?

Helen: Ready.

Elsa: One, two, three…*(closed eyes and deep breaths)*And now?

Helen: *(with the sly, tongue-in-cheek humour we will come to recognise as characteristic of the relaxed Miss Helen)* Well, if you really mean it, I think the best thing is for you to get back into your car, drive around the block and arrive again. And this time I want you, please, to hoot three times the way you usually do, so that I don't think a ghost has walked in through the front door when you appear.

Elsa: *(calling Miss Helen's bluff)* Right. Where are the car keys? *(Finds them and heads for the front door)*

Helen: Where are you going?

Elsa: To do what you said. Drive around the block and arrive again.

Helen: Like that?

Elsa: Why? What's wrong?

Helen: Elsie! Stirling Retief will have a heart attack if he sees you like that.

Elsa: But I wear less than this when I go to the beach. Oh, all right then, you old spoilsport, let's pretend.

Elsa runs into the other room, revs up her motorcar, grinds through all its gears and 'arrives'. Three blasts on the horn. The two women play the 'arrival game' (specifics to be determined in rehearsal) At the end of it they come together in a good laugh.

If my friends in Cape Town were to have seen that!

From *The Road to Mecca* by Athol Fugard (1985)

STUDENT RESPONSE A

The two women are of different ages and have a different attitude to life. Miss Helen is a typical old fusspot, worrying about the supper and the washing. Elsa is young and has a job in Cape Town and isn't bothered about wearing something revealing when she goes to the shops. She also does her own washing and isn't used to having a maid.

It isn't surprising when Elsa snaps at Helen who is being a bit preachy. Nobody want to be told that patience is a virtue so we sympathise with Elsa here. There is a bit of a stand-off between them and then they both say sorry. You get the impression that they have known each other for quite a while and you wonder why Elsa only comes there occasionally and is only going to stay one night. The audience would be thinking this. Did she once live in that village? If so, Cape Town is a long way away (12 hours drive is a long way) and it's a major city whereas this feels like a village with rather conventional attitudes.

I like the part where they decide to start again and they pretend that she's arriving in the car. I think it shows another side to Miss Helen and this is also in the playwright's stage direction about her sense of humour 'sly, tongue-in-cheek humour') The audience would definitely enjoy the actor making the sound of three blasts on the horn and the car's gear changes.

At the end, though, I am still wondering what's so important that Elsa has bothered to turn up for one night only.

A clear start which identifies some important contrasts between the two women and shows that the passage has been read closely.

Again, the student is responding to the scene, but not being quite analytical enough of what evokes the responses they feel.

A good sense of audience response, although it needs to be linked more directly to the portrayal of the relationship between the women.

The build-up of tension is noted and the audience response to the situation. However, these valid points need support from the text. What words and actions create the impression that they have known each other for a long time? Also, this student uses rather casual phraseology ('a bit of a stand-off', for example), which isn't suitable for an exam essay.

This response has some good features. It's obvious that the sequence has been read and responded to in a lively fashion, but the writer needs to use much more text to support the points made. A little more reflection on the implication of words and actions would be useful. A more formal essay style would help, too.

What's missing is a sense of how the dialogue between the two women suggests wider themes. There is no reference to the political situation, imaged so clearly in the attitudes to the maid, or to the strong sense of contrast between old and young, or urban/rural values and conventions. Thinking a little more deeply about the implications of the passage would make this a stronger answer.

STUDENT RESPONSE B

This passage from the beginning of the play is part of the exposition: it establishes the situation, the characters and the relationship of the two women effectively for the audience. The younger woman Elsa has arrived unexpectedly for a visit after driving a long way into the country to see her old friend Miss Helen, a much older woman. The sequence begins with tension and awkwardness between the two women and ends with their warm relationship being re-established. Themes of youth and age as well as political insights are suggested through the scene with very naturalistic dialogue and action. The stage directions helpfully indicate to a reader what an audience would see on the stage ▶

in performance. The playwright skilfully uses domestic props and situations to suggest underlying themes and relationships.

> An introduction which draws together comment on the two women and their relationship and the wider themes of the passage such as the political and the generation gap. Audience response is highlighted from the outset.

The scene moves from rather conventional talk about the weather to begin with ('we haven't had any frost yet'), through some awkward domestic interactions about the length of the visit, the washing and the supper to a climax of bad temper in line 20 ('For God's sake Helen! Just leave me alone') after which the whole tone of the scene changes, developing to a climax of amusing action at the end which confirms the intimacy of the two women.

> Strong sense of the structural development of the sequence and the climax, with awareness of tone and the way it changes. It might be useful to mention that domestic interactions often symbolise underlying tensions (think of any festive celebration in the home!).

Elsa has to drive a long way ('*twelve hours*' from Cape Town) and she is very tired after this, perhaps making her irritable, especially as she is evidently a teacher with a lot of exam marking to do. However, she is determined that she can only stay one night, to the disappointment of Helen. The audience wonders why she won't stay longer. It's clear that they know each other well because Elsa has visited before and brought a present – the soaps. She finds Helen's fussing about very annoying: the stage directions say she has *an 'edge to her voice'* and she says '*Please stop fussing*' and she reacts strongly to Helen's little saying about patience, bringing this section of the extract to a climax.

> Close reading, supported by textual reference. The audience is kept in mind constantly.

Helen meanwhile seems a lonely person – she has kept her soaps for '*a special occasion*' and there hasn't been any other visitor to use them, evidently. She is trying to be the good hostess even though she has been caught without food in the house suitable for supper or a chance to organise things. When Elsa is sharp with her, she reacts '*timidly*'. These expectations of her character (fussy old woman, typical attitudes) are gradually eroded as the scene progresses, however.

> This is a sympathetic view of the character, based on close reading.

The interchange about the dirty washing has a more serious implication than just domestic arrangements. This is apartheid South Africa and Katrina is obviously Miss Helen's domestic, who does the washing and cleaning around the house. Helen knows that Elsa gets on well with Katrina: '*You can't leave without seeing Katrina*', but misunderstands Elsa's attitude. Elsa doesn't want the maid to do her washing as she does it herself. She just wants to say hello to Katrina in a friendly way. Attitudes to black servants are suggested clearly here as well as the difference between the generations; and perhaps urban more liberal attitudes and a village in the country with old-fashioned views. This is suggested economically and naturally in Fugard's dialogue.

> This major theme, handled subtly by the playwright, is well-discussed here.

After the climax of tension and irritation, apologies are expressed and the two women act more naturally to each other. The suggestion that they '*start again*' is a good one, proposed by Elsa, but it is Helen who shows herself to be open-minded and imaginative suggesting that Elsa '*arrive again*' and '*hoot three times the way you usually do*'. Their close collusion is then revealed when Elsa picks up the keys as well as the idea and instead of actually going out and coming back with the car, pretends to do so, going into the other room and making car noises and horn noises. The playwright calls this the '*arrival game*' and suggests that it can be developed between the two actors in rehearsal, reminding us of the important ways in which plays differ from film and depend on actors' interpretations. This is very amusing for the audience and brings the scene to a lively climax, reinforcing the close relationship of the two women; they have '*a good laugh*'.

> The way in which each woman contributes to the arrival game and the gradual easing of tension in the scene is well-documented.

The structure of the scene allows contrasting tones and atmosphere, from the stilted conversation at the beginning to the warm interchanges of the two old friends at the end. We are aware of the difference between the generations too: the way young people don't care about convention and custom and the more careful conventional attitudes of the old.

> Sums up aptly but the final point is one which could be developed further, for example by reference to the clothing issue.

This is a very good essay, with an emphasis on the dramatic structure and tone as well as the relationship of the characters. Another answer might have made more of the 'generation gap', but this is suggested here, if not developed fully.

Reflection: Consider if there are ways in which you could add to or improve these essays. Do you agree with the marker's comments? What have you learnt from looking closely at other students' work?

FURTHER STUDY

1. Going to the theatre and watching plays is the best preparation for dramatic work. However, if you find filmed versions of plays on the internet, try to find theatrical performances, not feature films.
2. One-act plays are a good preparation for reading plays and there are many anthologies of one-acters which you would enjoy.
3. Alan Ayckbourn's one-act plays, which include Ernie's Incredible Illucinations, are delightful.
4. The website www.thoughtco.com has a series of amusing plays for acting which are accessible to read, too.

Self-assessment checklist

Reflect on what you've learnt in this unit and indicate your confidence level between 1 and 5. If you score below 3, revisit that section. Come back to this list later in your course. Has your confidence grown?

	Confidence level	Revisited?
I can understand the requirements of the new drama unseen question		
I have assimilated the checklist of important elements for discussion		
I have assessed the work on the Williamson passage and discussed the marker comments		
I have considered critically the two essays on Fugard and can discriminate between them, using the marker's notes		

Unit 19

Timed drama essays, critical and passage type

Learning objectives

In this unit you will:

- recognise how you can be prepared to answer questions on your drama set texts under timed conditions
- clarify the differences between the a) essay question and the b) passage question
- analyse what aspects of a passage need to be considered
- engage with sample and students' answers in both forms a) and b)
- account for the marginal comments made and reflect on the essays and the comments.

KEY CONCEPTS

Language, form, structure, genres, context, style, interpretation.

Before you start

- Look carefully at Unit 29 and remind yourself of the importance of writing a well-structured essay.
- Review your checklists of elements in the units on poetry and drama (Figures 5.1 and 18.1). Do you know what to look for in a passage? You will have seen any extract before because you have studied the play, but this will be a small extract so all your skills of observing, noting and thinking will be required!
- So that you can appreciate the essays on *Hamlet*, read a summary of the play so that you know the basics of the story and the characters. You will then be in a good position to judge the two essays on family relationships in the play. Similarly, review the plot of *Macbeth* for the plot concerning Macbeth and the witches.

In this unit, as well as studying some student essays on plays with marker comments, you'll also apply a method for close analysis of a scene or extract to help you to answer passage questions on plays.

Essay questions

ACTIVITY 19.1

Read the following two sample essays and consider how effective they are as answers to the question, which is a typical exam essay topic. Study the marker's comments and note what is thought to be important in tackling such a question topic.

SAMPLE ESSAY 1

Essay: Discuss Shakespeare's presentation of family relationships in the play Hamlet.

Shakespeare's *Hamlet* tells the story of a tragic hero, Hamlet, who is driven by his father's murder to avenge his death. However, Hamlet turns mad and his plan is foiled. Throughout the play, the audience sees the relationship between Hamlet and his father and how they differ.

The introduction to the essay emphasises the father/son relationship, which is certainly an important one, but it doesn't suggest any others. The idea that Hamlet 'turns mad' is arguable and is not entirely relevant to this essay topic.

Hamlet's relationship with his late father is based on admiration for him. He is frequently seen comparing his father to strong and confident men and gods, shown when he compares his father to Mars. Mars was the God of War, which shows how good a soldier Hamlet's father was, but also shows his strength and courage, which is why the way he died was very unnatural; Claudius his brother poisoned him through his ear. Furthermore, comparing him to a god show how much Hamlet aspires to be like him as well as how superior he is. God has connotations of worthiness, holiness and power which further emphasises Hamlet senior's might and strength but could also show that he was a kind and generous man. Gods are shown as omnipotent and omnipresent, which is evident in this play as the ghost is always there and still has an effect on the happenings in Denmark. Hamlet displays his love for his father by trying and nearly succeeding in avenging his father's death.

This is a lengthy paragraph on Hamlet's admiration and hero-worship of his father, which could be expressed and illustrated more concisely.

Throughout the play, Hamlet pays tribute to his father by wearing black, while other people in the play like Claudius wear more colourful and bold clothes, showing that Hamlet is in constant mourning for his father, further demonstrating how omnipresent the ghost is. Also, Hamlet is the only one that can talk to the ghost, which suggests their love for each other.

The question of costume is a matter for the director of the play and not as important as the fact that Hamlet can talk to the Ghost, a point which could have been included in the last paragraph.

However, Hamlet's relationship with his uncle Claudius is based on hatred and distrust asboth of the characters know what the other one can and will do. Claudius tries to getrid of Hamlet many times in the play. Evidence of this is when he sends him to England,and then the sword fight with Laertes. Hamlet was given an unbated sword whileLaertes had a sharper sword with poison at the tip, showing that Claudius is desperate to kill Hamlet. Hamlet had earlier arranged a ***play within a play*** to try to catch out Claudius, ***wherein I'll catch the conscience of the king***. These all show the distrust between the two.

Verges on telling the story – always to be avoided!

When speaking to Gertrude about Hamlet, Claudius refers to Hamlet as ***your son***, showing that he wants nothing to do with him and that he is Gertrude's son. Hamlet also calls Claudius a ***smiling villain*** showing that he has a split personality, appearing to be pleasant and kind but actually a devil, playing on the theme of appearance and reality.

Appearance and reality is a worthwhile theme, although the paragraph begins with Gertrude, then moves to Claudius.

Gertrude and Hamlet's relationship is seen as fractured because of the death of his father and her quickly moving on to Claudius, Hamlet senior's brother. Hamlet calls this incestuous, showing disgust and scorn. However, they do love each other, evident when Gertrude saves Hamlet twice – once when he kills Polonius and later when she drinks the poison, showing her motherly love. Hamlet says ***I must be cruel to be kind*** showing that he does care about his mother and he only calls her actions foul because he is warning her away from Claudius. Gertrude shows hurt and pain as she thinks Hamlet has deserted her as she says ***Hamlet thou hast cleft my heart in twain***, suggesting she has been broken by Hamlet's actions.

Some worthwhile comments here on the Hamlet/Gertrude relationship, with illustration.

▶

Ophelia is introduced, which is good, but the comments on her relationship with her father are rather superficial and sadly there is no conclusion to the essay.

Another family relationship in the play is Polonius and Ophelia. Ophelia in the play is demonstrated as a weak and stereotypical lady of the Renaissance period and her relationship with her father Polonius is purely one of obedience. This is evident in the quote ***I shall obey, my lord***. This shows Ophelia's submissive nature and that she will do her utmost to obey her father. This is also a microcosm of society at the time as women were viewed as inferior and men had all the authority.

As a whole, the essay's structure doesn't help the student to group ideas together very well, and more forward planning might have helped. There is too much on Hamlet and his father and not enough on other key relationships. There is no mention of Laertes, for example, and the points about Ophelia are rushed. The section on Gertrude shows understanding. Knowledge of the text is obvious but shouldn't be used to tell the story. A conclusion would have helped.

SAMPLE ESSAY 2

Essay: Discuss Shakespeare's presentation of family relationships in the play Hamlet.

Family relationships, particularly the one between father and son are fundamental to understanding Hamlet's motives in the play, which drive him to ponder over the course of seven soliloquies and five acts the very roots of his existence. This is a revenge tragedy based on what his father's ghost commands him to do, but more than that – it is a very philosophical one.

A relevant introduction which shows a thoughtful approach to the play.

The Ghost's demand that Hamlet avenges his *foul and most unnatural murder* will lead inevitably to Hamlet's demise, but it was set in motion before that. Hamlet's father was a glorious man who killed old Fortinbras of Norway in battle and so symbolises the epitome of masculine glory. It is this shadow of *Hyperion* that Hamlet has to try to live up to and admits to himself when he remarks that Claudius is no more like his brother than Hamlet is to Hercules, so he is doomed from the beginning to feel inferior before he even hears about the murder. This relationship is therefore the basis of the play's plot.

The relationship of Hamlet and his father is contextualised by reference to Fortinbras and to Claudius.

Hazlitt said that Hamlet's passion is to *think and not to act* and herein lies the cause of all his hesitation. The Ghost demands revenge, which Hamlet finds very difficult to undertake. Claudius had claimed his grief for his father is *unmanly* and this is contrasted to the drive and readiness for action of Claudius who is prepared to murder a brother, like Cain and Abel. This highlights Hamlet's weakness in the shadow of his uncle as well as his father, unable to act and only able to think about it and try to spur himself on to *dull revenge*.

Wider reading, not essential at AS, but showing engagement with the subject.

The issue of Hamlet's relationship with his mother and the complexities of it can be understood when one considers what he says: *I will speak daggers to her but use none.* This mirrors his earlier despairing question *Must I like a whore unpack my heart with words?* Hamlet is disgusted with his own cowardice, reminding us of Macbeth, whose wife calls his masculinity in question with *Are you a man?* Hamlet asks himself *Am I a coward?* This emerges in his treatment of Ophelia when he tells her to go to a nunnery *why would'st thou be a breeder of sinners*, suggesting that he sees himself as a sinner.

An apt comparison, thoughtfully discussed.

It is significant also that Gertrude is the one to whom he reveals that his antic disposition is in fact a fake, when he says he is only *mad in craft* in the closet scene. Hamlet's obsession with his mother's and uncle's sexual behaviour, revealed in the language of this scene, has led some critics to see his relationship with his mother as incestuous itself. But what is important is that she recognises how she has behaved towards his father and comes to recognise that marrying Claudius was *o'erhasty*. The end of the play shows her genuine affection for Hamlet, symbolised in her drinking the cup with poison intended for him.

The complex relationships with his mother and uncle are well-discussed in these paragraphs.

The father–son relationship is vital to the play, mirrored also in the relationships between Laertes and Polonius as well as young Fortinbras and his father. Laertes is Hamlet's foil, saying that he would be happy to take revenge and cut his throat i' the church, very unlike Hamlet's delaying and dithering. This directly contrast Hamlet's inability to kill Claudius while he is praying. It is very ironic that Laertes is also trying to avenge his father's murder and that Hamlet is the murderer in this situation.

Laertes's position in the play in relation to Hamlet is appreciated and the irony understood.

In conclusion, family relationships and particularly that of father and son are integral to the play. The exploration of the relationship provides a fascinating examination of masculinity, without which there would be no play at all and as Hamlet says *The rest* [would be] *silence*.

A thoughtful conclusion.

This essay shows a thoughtful approach and an awareness of the play's themes. The student uses references to wider reading which are apt, but more importantly discusses a number of key family relationships within the play. It would have been helpful to incorporate some discussion of Ophelia, but what is here is relevant and illustrated.

ACTIVITY 19.2

Read the following student essay on *Macbeth*. You do not need to have studied this play to appreciate its clear structure. If you have studied it, you will have other ideas about the topic that this particular essay did not include. For example, you may want to have said more about Banquo's ghost. However, this is an important reminder of the multiple possibilities for selecting material from complex texts to create an argument in answer to a question. As long as you can support your points with close textual reference, your opinion is valid.

STUDENT ESSAY

Essay: *In what ways does the supernatural contribute to the effect of the play Macbeth?*

Macbeth is a play filled with supernatural events and references, and the supernatural is clearly a very important aspect of the dramatic effect of the play on the audience. At the time that Shakespeare was writing, the audience would have been more superstitious than we are today, but a modern audience is still fascinated by the supernatural aspects of the play, which emphasise its themes and characterisation.

Clearly focused introduction, with a sense of context and audience.

▶

Clear structural phrase begins topic idea.

Point supported with clear textual evidence.

The first important feature of the supernatural is the way in which the disorder in the kingdom is mirrored in the stormy weather and strange behaviour of animals on the night when Duncan is murdered. *Strange screams of death* were heard, and the earth was *feverous and did shake*. The sky became unnaturally black: *dark night strangles the travelling lamp* and Duncan's horses *turned wild in nature ... as they would make war with mankind* and began to eat each other. These completely unnatural and alarming events are symbolic of the way in which the murder of the king will affect the kingdom. It was believed that a king had a sacred right to rule and his death would have major repercussions on society, symbolised by the supernatural events in nature and the cosmos.

Useful linking word.

Well-supported discussion of Macbeth's character in relation to the topic.

But the supernatural is also used to show that Macbeth himself is not just a murderer, but a man with a vivid imagination. Just before doing the terrible deed of murdering the king, he sees a dagger floating in the air in front of him, drawing him onward to do the murder. It is possible that this is not a ghostly dagger but *a dagger of the mind, a false creation, / Proceeding from the heat- oppressed brain*, a weapon which has gouts of blood on its handle. Whether supernatural or not, what it does remind us is that Macbeth does not find it easy at this point to be the hard, unfeeling man, murdering to advance his career. He seems genuinely stressed and emotional and has, in the scene before, even had second thoughts about committing the murder at all, which Lady Macbeth soon overturns by her powerful persuasions.

Links paragraph clearly with previous one, and introduces the witches. NB the essay is not chronological, but thematic in approach.

Good sense of audience response.

Lady Macbeth is very persuasive, but she is a human woman of apparently strong character, not a supernatural agent. Possibly the most memorable examples of the supernatural in the play are the three witches, who also persuade Macbeth, but they use mysterious, ambiguous statements to do this. Their scene opens the play, immediately arousing a sense of curiosity in the audience as to why they have singled Macbeth out, especially when in the next scene he is praised for his valour, loyalty and nobility. They represent evil and overturn the values of goodness; they make this clear when they say *Fair is foul and foul is fair*. The audience gets a shock when the first words of Macbeth seem to echo this statement: *So foul and fair a day I have not seen* – a verbal echo which seems to link him mysteriously with the witches and prepares us for the effect they will have on his stability.

Thoughtful discussion of the role of the witches and their great importance.

The witches' meeting with Macbeth influences him profoundly. Because they promise him that he will be Thane of Cawdor and King *thereafter* and he is immediately and unexpectedly given the first title, his mind starts to churn, imagining the possibility of becoming king. Although he does have some misgivings at different points, he starts to plan to murder Duncan and make the witches' prophecy happen. He describes their words as *supernatural soliciting*, but who actually suggested the deed of murder? They did not tell him to make it happen, they just said he would be king, and fate might give him the throne without him lifting a finger. But his own ambition and his wife's strong persuasions lead him along the fateful path that will end eventually with his own death. The witches may represent supernaturally those events in life which unexpectedly knock us off course and lead us to making the wrong decisions. On the stage, they are terrifyingly evil and influential.

▶

Another very dramatic example of the supernatural is the apparitions conjured up when Macbeth visits them later, having murdered Banquo to prevent his children becoming king as the witches had also promised. But the apparitions only confirm that the issue of Banquo will be kings and his children will not. Moreover, they give him prophecies that are true but so ambiguous that he misunderstands them (that Birnam Wood will move to Dunsinane before he will be caught; that he will die at the hand of one not born of woman). This ambiguity suggests the way in which we make assumptions about the future on the basis of misunderstandings.

Good discourse marker helps the development of the argument.

Ultimately, the presence of the supernatural in the play is part of the framework of good and evil on which it is structured, and which is reflected in the language, with mentions of angels, darkness and light. There is supernatural goodness at work too, in the English king who has the gifts of healing and prophecy. The ghost we see – Banquo attending the feast – was a good man whose spirit is haunting the guilty Macbeth, one of the most exciting moments in the play. But the real interest of the play lies in the character of Macbeth himself, who is not just an ambitious butcher, as he is described at the end, but an imaginative and intelligent man who could perhaps have chosen good, but is persuaded into evil by his wife and the three weird sisters.

The conclusion links the essay topic with the play's image patterns as well as the characterisation of Macbeth.

An interesting aspect of the essay's structure is that it doesn't go through the play chronologically – in other words, starting with the witches at the beginning. The witches are the main point in the essay and are left to the climax, just before the conclusion. In Part 2 of this book, you will find different ways of handling the same question, all of which are equally valid, as there is no such thing as a model answer in this subject. This essay reveals a sense of theatre too, which is very important in a drama essay. Audience response must always be considered.

Reflection: Discuss with your friend or classmate the qualities of the essays you have just read and the marker's comments. In what ways could this help your own essay work?

Passage questions

In this part of the unit, you are going to work further on the skills of drama analysis so that you feel confident about tackling the passage questions on your play and any other dramatic work that you study in the future. Many of the lessons learnt in poetry and prose passage questions are just as useful here, and Figure 19.1 provides a checklist for how to respond. You will find further reminders in Section 3 of this book.

How do you respond? think about this all the time.

- Audience response – what are their thoughts and feelings as the scene progresses? Be constantly aware of this!
- Themes – what major concerns of the work as a whole are developed here?
- Dramatic action – is there any exciting physical action? Does anyone have a soliloquy? Does action build up then a change of tempo occurs and alters the mood of the scene? Try to envisage the scene on the stage.
- Highlight useful brief quotations – never more than two lines.
- Is the passage from a comedy? Are there any 'wit combats' or exaggerated action providing humour?
- Features of language – what unusual words, imagery or descriptive language are used and what do they mean?
- For Shakespeare – poetry or prose? And for which characters? What effect does it have?
- Characters – who is here, who speaks, who is silent? Is there a character we've never seen before? What are our impressions? Do we learn more of a character we already know? How do they interact?
- Where does this extract come in the context of the play? Be aware but don't tell the story!

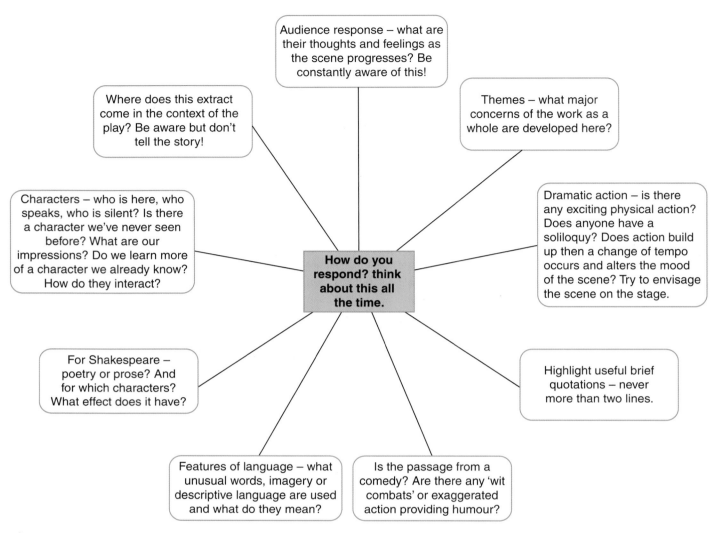

Figure 19.1: Responding to a passage question: checklist.

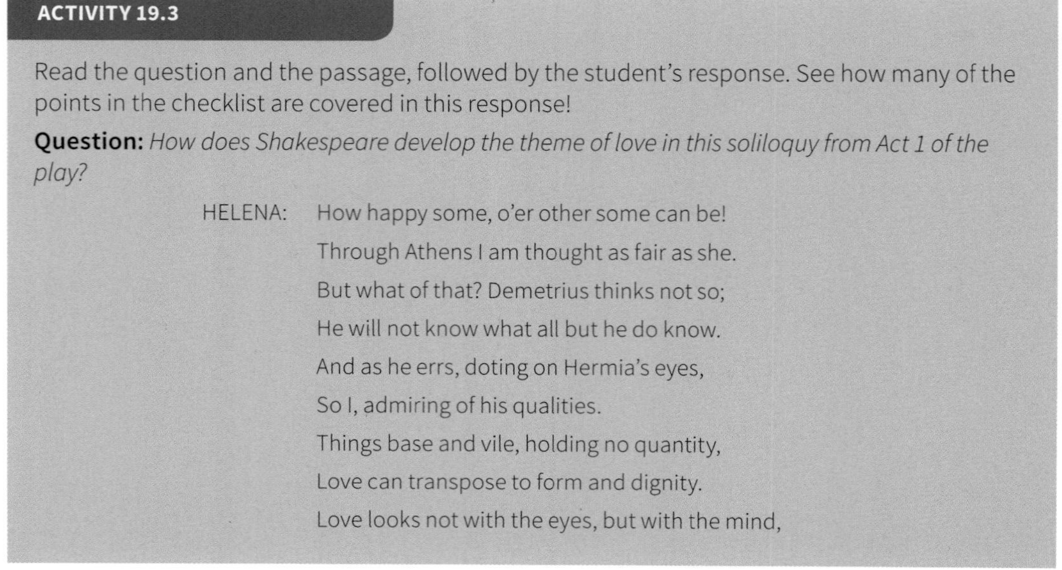

ACTIVITY 19.3

Read the question and the passage, followed by the student's response. See how many of the points in the checklist are covered in this response!

Question: *How does Shakespeare develop the theme of love in this soliloquy from Act 1 of the play?*

HELENA: How happy some, o'er other some can be!
Through Athens I am thought as fair as she.
But what of that? Demetrius thinks not so;
He will not know what all but he do know.
And as he errs, doting on Hermia's eyes,
So I, admiring of his qualities.
Things base and vile, holding no quantity,
Love can transpose to form and dignity.
Love looks not with the eyes, but with the mind,

And therefore is winged Cupid painted blind.
Nor hath love's mind of any judgement taste;
Wings, and no eyes, figure unheedy haste;
And therefore is love said to be a child
Because in choice he is oft beguiled.
As waggish boys in game themselves forswear,
So the boy Love is perjured every where;
For, ere Demetrius looked on Hermia's eyne,
He hailed down oaths that he was only mine,
And when this hail some heat from Hermia felt,
So he dissolved, and showers of oaths did melt.
I will go tell him of fair Hermia's flight:
Then to the wood will he tomorrow night,
Pursue her; and for this intelligence,
If I have thankes, it is a dear expense;
But herein mean I to enrich my pain,
To have his sight thither, and back again.

Shakespeare *A Midsummer Night's Dream* Act 1 Scene 1

STUDENT RESPONSE

Helena has decided to tell Demetrius that Hermia and Lysander are intending to run away together. She thinks that this perhaps might make him love her again. Her soliloquy reflects on the main theme of the play: Love. Helena is thought by others as beautiful as Hermia, but Demetrius doesn't love her anymore, leading to Helena's ten-line reflection on Cupid, the god of Love, and his attributes. He is blind, so her beauty makes no difference; he is hasty, lacks any rationality and is fickle, changing his mind at a moment's notice. All these ideas will be followed through in the action of the play, when the lovers get to the forest. *Things base and vile* being transformed through love into *form and dignity* foreshadows Titania falling in love with the ass. This relatively long speech on Love is appropriate here as a prelude to the farcical to-ings and fro-ings of the lovers in the forest. The audience is also reminded that romantic passion supersedes friendship. Helena may have been Hermia's friend from childhood, but her passion for Demetrius is more important than loyalty to her friend! Helena is clearly overwhelmed by her love for Demetrius if she is prepared to betray her friend's trust. Thinking he will love her for telling him is somewhat unrealistic, but she shows all the hopefulness of an unrequited lover. Her reflections on Love lift this part of her speech into a mode which is more like a chorus – what she says is general truth, the sort of thing a chorus would say, rather than an individual. But as an individual, it shows her to be thoughtful and intelligent, as well as full of feeling. But, the central part of the speech is a ten-line reflection on Love and its qualities, using the classical figure of blind Cupid, the boy god of love, whose image can still be found on Valentine cards even in the 21st century. The language emphasises his immature nature: *and therefore is Love said to be a child*. He is just a boy; his blindness and haste remind us how quickly one can fall in love with someone, and often someone quite unsuitable. The whole speech is in rhyming couplets (aabb throughout), which suits well the chorus-like comments made by Helena here (*As waggish boys in game themselves forswear, / So the boy Love is perjur'd every where*).

▶

A vivid weather metaphor is used by Helena to describe what happened when Demetrius's affections shifted from her to Hermia. First he *hail'd down oaths* to Helena, but the *heat* from Hermia melted the hail, so *he dissolved* and changed his affections.

The audience could feel that Helena is being really selfish here, but more likely they will feel sorry for her and understand that she is driven by passion. This soliloquy also prepares us for dramatic action, since what Helena intends to do will clearly advance the drama in the forest later, made worse by the actions of Oberon and Puck. The lovers will shortly be completely confused and their love antics are very funny for the audience.

ACTIVITY 19.4

Read the following short scene which comes from *A Man for All Seasons* by Robert Bolt. Find some friends and read it together, trying to bring out the character's personalities and the tone of their words.

More: Where are they?

Enter Margaret *and* Roper

Margaret: Here, Father.

More: [*regarding them, resignedly*] Good morning, William. It's a little early for breakfast.

Roper: [*solidly*] I haven't come for breakfast, sir. *More looks at him and sighs.*

Margaret: Will wants to marry me, Father.

More: Well, he can't marry you.

Roper: Sir Thomas, I'm to be called to the Bar.

More: [*warmly*] Oh, congratulations, Roper!

Roper: My family may not be at the Palace, sir, but in the City –

More: The Ropers were advocates when the Mores were selling pewter; there's nothing wrong with your family. There's nothing wrong with your fortune – there's nothing wrong with you – [*sourly*] except you need a clock –

Roper: I can buy a clock, sir.

More: Roper, the answer's 'no'. [*Firmly*] And will be 'no' as long as you're a heretic.

Roper: [*firing*] That's a word I don't like, Sir Thomas!

More: It's not a likeable word. [*Coming to life*] It's not a likeable thing! [*Margaret is alarmed and from behind More tries to silence Roper*]

Roper: The church is heretical! Doctor Luther's proved that to my satisfaction!

More: Luther's an excommunicate.

Roper: From a heretic Church! Church? It's a shop – Forgiveness by the florin! Joblots now in Germany! … Mmm, and divorces.

More: [*expressionless*] Divorces?

Roper: Oh half England's buzzing with that …

……………………………………………

More: Listen, Roper. Two years ago you were a passionate Churchman; now you're a passionate – Lutheran. We must just pray, that when your head's finished turning your face is to the front again.

Robert Bolt *A Man for All Seasons* (1960)

STUDENT RESPONSE

Essay: In what ways, and how effectively, does the playwright develop the characters in this short sequence?

This sequence comes from relatively early in the play and adds little to the plot. It is a scene of family life, with Roper asking for Margaret's hand in marriage – they have evidently been out very late, as we hear the clock chiming three just before this dialogue starts. Thomas greets him kindly, if wearily, and does not scold Margaret for being with him so late. More refuses to grant Margaret's hand to Roper because he is a '*heretic*' and at this point influenced by Luther's ideas. The audience is aware of tensions from the start because More is so firm and uncompromising. ('*and will be 'no' as long as you're a heretic*') Although apparently a domestic scene with no importance to the main action of the play, More's clear-cut opposition to the marriage because of Roper's religious position is a foreshadowing of his firm refusal to countenance King Henry's divorce. He knows his mind and he will not be swayed. Roper's wavering – he changes his mind easily on religious matters – '*Two years ago you were a passionate Churchman; now you're a passionate – Lutheran*' suggests the turmoil the church will shortly be subjected to.

Roper is eager to show that he has prospects as far as his work is concerned and that his family is respectable. He becomes passionate when he speaks of Luther and his criticisms of the Church. Mentioning *divorces* is provocative. More is resolute and firm, as he will be throughout the play. He speaks warmly of Roper's work prospects and his family, but is adamant when it comes to religious matters. His uncompromising nature is made clear in this sequence. Margaret is conciliatory. The stage direction gives us the clue to this [*Margaret is alarmed and from behind More tries to silence Roper*]

Roper's increasing excitement when he speaks of religious matters will be reflected in his action and gesture. Margaret is trying to hold him back physically, meanwhile, so that he does not anger her father – he is, after all, supposed to be asking for her hand in marriage. All the passion in the world will not sway More, however. The actor playing the part should seem firm, resolute and unbending here: kindly in personal matters but entirely unbending in religious ones. Margaret says little but her actions show that she knows both of them well.

The language of the passage supports the characterisation: More uses a **tricolon** to speak out his support of Roper: *there's nothing wrong with your family. There's nothing wrong with your fortune – there's nothing wrong with you*, followed by the humorous anti-climax – *except you need a clock*. Roper is suitable except for one, to More, extremely important thing.

Roper's passionate language in speaking about the Catholic Church becomes more poetic, using alliteration: *forgiveness by the florin; Joblots now in Germany*.

The tone of the dialogue becomes more impassioned with Roper's exclamations, but More remains relatively calm, and he refuses to be drawn when Roper mentions *divorce*. The stage direction *expressionless* gives the hint to the actor.

Reflection: At this point in the play the audience could be amused by More's words to Roper, and the physical action of Roper and Margaret trying to restrain him. Consider ways in which the scene suggest future conflict and serious consequences.

KEY TERM

Tricolon: a series of three parallel words, phrases, or clauses, which can be very persuasive in both speech and writing.

Here is another example of a dramatic scene, from the play *A View from the* Bridge by Arthur Miller. Eddie Carbone, with his wife Beatrice, is waiting for his niece Catherine to come home after being out at the cinema with one of the illegal immigrants they are giving a home to.

Eddie:	It's after eight.
Beatrice:	Well, it's a long show at the Paramount.
Eddie:	They must've seen every picture in Brooklyn by now. He's supposed to stay in the house when he ain't working. He ain't supposed to go advertising himself.
Beatrice:	Well, that's his trouble, what do you care? If they pick him up they pick him up, that's all. Come in the house.
Eddie:	What happened to the stenography? I don't see her practise no more.
Beatrice:	She'll get back to it. She's excited, Eddie.
Eddie:	She tell you anything?
Beatrice:	*[Comes to him, now the subject is opened]* What's the matter with you? He's a nice kid, what do you want from him?
Eddie:	That's a nice kid? He gives me the heeby-jeebies.
Beatrice:	*[smiling]* Ah, go on, you're just jealous.
Eddie:	Of *him*? Boy, you don't think much of me.
Beatrice:	I don't understand you. What's so terrible about him?
Eddie:	You mean it's all right with you? That's gonna be her husband?
Beatrice:	Why? He's a nice fella, hard workin', he's a good-lookin' fella.

Arthur Miller *A View from the Bridge* (1955)

STUDENT RESPONSE

Essay: *Show how the dialogue develops the relationship between Eddie and Beatrice and exposes the tensions between them.*

The pattern of the dialogue here is one of aggression (Eddie) followed by peacemaking justifications of Catherine's behaviour (Beatrice). '*It's after eight*.' '*Well, it's a long show*.' This creates tension since the couple are in disagreement and there is an underlying sense that there is more to the disagreement than at first appears. Eddie keeps changing the ground for his objections: first, it is just that they are late, so late they could have seen every film that was on; second, he takes issue with the fact that Rodolpho, the immigrant, is out at all – he should be hiding at home, in Eddie's opinion. Then it is Catherine's lack of study – she is not practising her shorthand skills any more. Gradually the objections begin to focus in on the boy she is spending time with – Eddie does not like him, he does not think he is good enough for his beloved niece, and by the time the end of this extract is reached he is coming directly to the point: That's gonna be her husband? The position of Beatrice is interesting: she knows what Eddie is getting at but tries to keep the peace at first and make justifications for Catherine's behaviour, which she sees as natural. When she says affectionately: '*She's excited*,' Eddie, his immediate response is suspicion: '*She tell you anything?*' And her response to her husband is also affectionate. When she says: '*go on, you're just jealous*,' Miller makes it clear that she is smiling. But this lack of agreement or connection between them is part of a wider pattern of distrust and suspicion in the play, which will end tragically. Here, suspense is created as the audience waits to see what will happen when Catherine does finally come home from the movies. We expect trouble of some kind.

Reflection: All of the passages you've looked at include some sort of 'foreshadowing'. What effect does it have on the audience to feel that situations are going to develop, either comically or tragically? Discuss with a friend any further examples of foreshadowing you have come across, in either drama or the novel.

FURTHER STUDY

Search online for '*A Midsummer Night's Dream*, Act 3 Scene 1, Shakespeare's Globe' to watch a short video of the scene from *A Midsummer Night's Dream* where the queen of the fairies falls in love with Bottom the weaver (who has been transformed into having a donkey's head). You can hear the audience responding to the play, as this was filmed at The Globe Playhouse in London.

Self-assessment checklist

Reflect on what you've learnt in this unit and indicate your confidence level between 1 and 5. If you score below 3, revisit that section. Come back to this list later in your course. Has your confidence grown?

	Confidence level	Revisited?
I understand what I have to do in the exam in relation to my set texts		
I can describe clearly the difference between the a) question and the b) question requirements		
I am fully aware of the different elements of a passage which need to be considered and can describe them		
I have studied and learnt from the student responses		
I have read the marker comments carefully and appreciate what I can gain from them		

Part 2
A Level

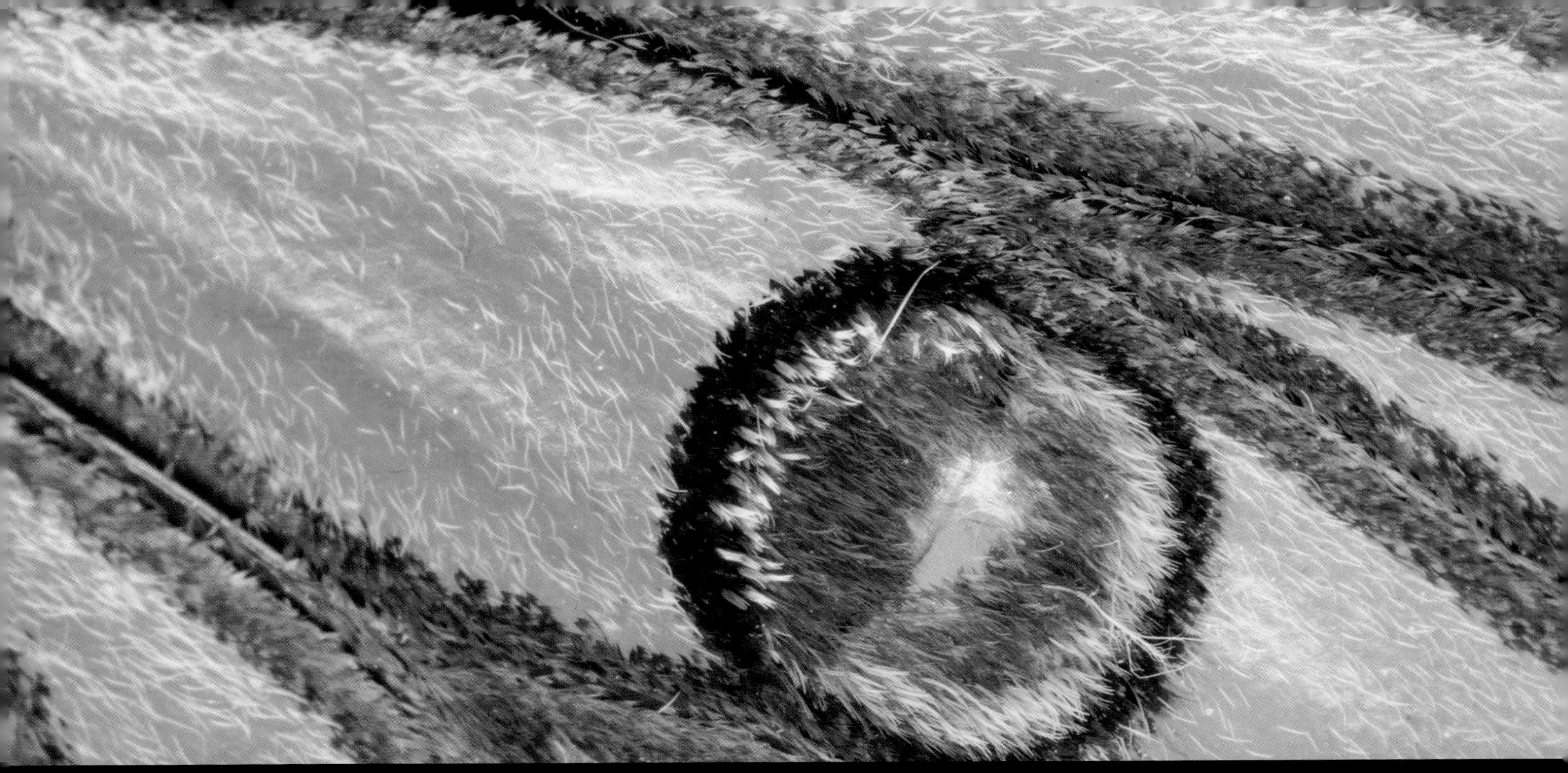

Section 4
Poetry 2

Poetry – critical essays

Learning objectives

In this unit you will:

- recognise and understand the ways in which the same essay title can generate different, but equally valid, responses
- apply basic essay construction principles acquired from a case study of Keats to your own work on a set poet
- appraise and compare your work and that of a friend for the purpose of analysis
- examine two essays on Eliot and the marker's comments for the purpose of extending your understanding
- evaluate the use of contextual material in a student essay on Wordsworth.

KEY CONCEPTS

Language, form, structure, genres, context, style, interpretation, critical reading.

Before you start

- Review Units 1–4 of the AS section of the book.
- Remind yourself of your AS Level poetry set text and what you enjoyed about it.
- If you are beginning A Level poetry work, discuss with a friend what you see as the challenges facing your poetry study at A Level.
- When you are further on in the course and have both written an essay on the same topic, you will be able to analyse them using the advice in the Keats Case Study (Activity 20.2).
- Refer to the advice given on essay writing in Unit 29 in Part 3 of this book.

This unit focuses on the Advanced Level critical essay on poetry. The poet you are studying in detail may not feature here, but you will learn how to write better essays from all the examples given. I hope you'll also be inspired to read more of the featured poets, whose work is readily available on the internet.

Your set texts

Poetry set texts in the second year of an advanced course tend to be a selection of the work of individual poets, rather than anthologies. The anthology is a useful way of introducing lots of different poetic voices and a wide variety of themes and styles.

ACTIVITY 20.1

What do you think are the advantages of studying the work of one poet in depth rather than an anthology? Discuss this with a friend.

You might have come up with some of the following:

- recurring themes or concerns
- coherence of vision
- common features of style.

You are given a selection of perhaps 20 or 30 poems (or fewer if the poems are more substantial, such as those of Keats). You are asked in any exam to write on three (or sometimes two or three) or in some syllabuses, if you wish, to 'range more widely'.

Are there any difficulties to overcome? If your test or exam is a 'closed book' one, where no textbooks can be referred to, then you've got to remember all the poems clearly to choose ones that are appropriate for your essay title, and you must be able to quote reasonably accurately from memory to support your ideas.

Critical essays

These are essays that pose a question or ask you to discuss a proposition or idea, sometimes using a critical prompt for you to respond to. (You will look at poetry passage questions in the next unit.) In Part 3 of this book, you will find examples of typical exam question-style wording, with the common command words that are used, and what they mean. Every essay topic in this book is the kind of question you can expect to see in your exam paper and after each essay topic, there will be further titles for you to explore.

TIP

Don't limit the number of poems you study and hope you can always use your favourites in any essay question. You will see in the 'Troubleshooting' advice in Unit 36 that this can be very unhelpful. A moment or two spent thinking carefully about your best options for the particular question will bring clear benefits to your essay. You need to have studied most of the poems, if not all, to be sure of having the best possible choice.

Detailed case study: Keats

ACTIVITY 20.2

If you are not studying Keats, use the general principles here to guide your own poetry work. Read the following answers to the essay question. You'll see that the examples given show the varied possibilities for answering relevantly, but with a different approach.

Essay: *'The atmosphere of Keats's poetry is always a melancholy one.' How far do you agree with this view? You should use three poems in your answer.*

Away! away! for I will fly to thee,
    Not charioted by Bacchus and his pards,
But on the viewless wings of Poesy,
    Though the dull brain perplexes and retards:
Already with thee! tender is the night,
    And haply the Queen-Moon is on her throne,
    Cluster'd around by all her starry Fays;

▶

But here there is no light,
Save what from heaven is with the breezes blown
Through verdurous glooms and winding mossy ways.

I cannot see what flowers are at my feet,
Nor what soft incense hangs upon the boughs,
But, in embalmed darkness, guess each sweet
Wherewith the seasonable month endows
The grass, the thicket, and the fruit-tree wild;
White hawthorn, and the pastoral eglantine;
Fast fading violets cover'd up in leaves;
And mid-May's eldest child,
The coming musk-rose, full of dewy wine,
The murmurous haunt of flies on summer eves.

Two stanzas from Keats's *Ode to a Nightingale* (1819)

She dwells with Beauty—Beauty that must die;
And Joy, whose hand is ever at his lips
Bidding adieu; and aching Pleasure nigh,
Turning to Poison while the bee-mouth sips:
Ay, in the very temple of Delight
Veiled Melancholy has her sov'reign shrine,
Though seen of none save him whose strenuous tongue
Can burst Joy's grape against his palate fine;
His soul shalt taste the sadness of her might,
And be among her cloudy trophies hung.

One stanza from Keats's *Ode on Melancholy* (1819)

St Agnes' Eve—Ah, bitter chill it was!
The owl, for all his feathers, was a-cold;
The hare limped trembling through the frozen grass,

►

And silent was the flock in woolly fold:
Numb were the Beadsman's fingers, while he told
His rosary, and while his frosted breath,
Like pious incense from a censer old,
Seemed taking flight for heaven, without a death,
Past the sweet Virgin's picture, while his prayer he saith.

One stanza from Keats's *The Eve of St Agnes* (1819)

All of Keats's poems are available on the internet and I advise you to read the rest of the poems used by students here, of which you have a selection printed in this book.

SAMPLE ESSAY 1

Introduction

It cannot be denied that Keats's poems have a strong sense of sadness running through them. Illness, death, the impermanence of happiness and, especially, beauty: these are themes which underlie everything that Keats wrote. He even wrote an ode *on Melancholy.* The poems that I have chosen to explore, *The Eve of St Agnes*, *Ode to a Nightingale* and the *Ode on Melancholy* itself, all illustrate the statement in the question perfectly.

Main body 1

Keats was a devotee of beauty and his poetry often delights in it: *A thing of Beauty is a joy forever,* for example. His work is filled with images of the senses: fruit, flowers, stars, birds singing, and he uses rich images to explore this beauty. However, this is merely superficial. I hope to show that below all this surface beauty is a profound sense of the tragic nature of life with a corresponding feeling of melancholy that lies under all that he wrote.

Main body 2

My first example, *The Eve of St Agnes*, is a romantic poem about two lovers running away together, so you would expect this to be a happy poem. However, the beginning sets the scene in the atmosphere of a miserably cold winter: *The hare limp'd trembling through the frozen grass* and in the chapel, *The sculptur'd dead, on each side, seem to freeze,* and the living *ache in icy hoods and mails.* The warmth inside Madeleine's bedroom is a strong contrast, but the opening does remind the reader of the cold world outside it. The framework structure of the poem stresses the impermanence of all love: at the end, *they glide like phantoms; and they are gone: aye, ages long ago / These lovers fled away into the storm.* The story was over

▶

long ago, and even before the end of the story they were like ghosts – *phantoms*. The atmosphere of melancholy is enhanced with the death of the old Beadsman and the ancient deformed Angela (who in themselves remind us that youth becomes age). The young lovers' passion, warmth and happiness are all too brief.

A nightingale.

Main body 3

Ode to a Nightingale is similarly focused on life's miseries. The song of the nightingale may be beautiful but it doesn't stay very long: *Adieu! Adieu! Thy plaintive anthem fades ... Fled is that music.* The nightingale has not known the realities of life for human beings: *the weariness, the fever and the fret / Here, where men sit and hear each other groan ... Where youth grows pale, and spectre-thin and dies.* Even as the poet listens to the bird's song, he is reminded of death: *I have been half in love with easeful Death,* wishing he could *cease upon the midnight with no pain.* The whole poem is suffused with a melancholy atmosphere and the beauty of the song finally leaves him: *Fled is that music,* so much so that he wonders if the vision was a kind of dream: *Do I wake or sleep?*

Main body 4

The Ode on Melancholy shares most of the concerns and melancholic atmosphere of the other two poems. It begins with suicidal thoughts (a little like the beginning of the *Nightingale ode*), the temptations to suicide creating a sinister atmosphere of gloom: *Wolf's-bane, tight-rooted, for its poisonous wine;* a *rosary of yew-berries.* However, these are rejected because they will take away the intensity of experience: *shade to shade will come too drowsily.* He speaks of the *wakeful anguish of the soul* and suggests that the lover should enjoy Beauty while he can: *feast* on his mistress's beauty – *feed deep, deep upon her peerless eyes,* because they won't last: *She dwells with Beauty—Beauty that must die.* Any pleasure that you feel will be brief and fleeting: *aching Pleasure nigh / turning to Poison while the bee-mouth sips.* The phrase *Turning to Poison* expresses very powerfully the idea that pleasure is not only transient, but can actually become poisonous – in other words, make you very ill or even kill you. The paradox that pleasure and suffering co-exist is central to the poem's language and form, creating images with a strikingly gloomy atmosphere.

Conclusion

It is clear that the statement in the essay title is true to a very large extent. All three poems I have chosen have powerfully melancholic atmospheres. Perhaps the most convincing argument of all is expressed in the lines: *in the very temple of delight / Veil'd Melancholy has her sovran shrine.* At the very heart of the temple of happiness is the shadowy figure of Melancholy: she is in her own dedicated holy place and can be worshipped there.

KEY CONCEPTS

Keats was dying when he wrote these poems and one cannot help feeling that his own impending death made a difference to his outlook on life and sharpened his perceptions of the world.

Much have I travelled in the realms of gold,
And many goodly states and kingdoms seen;
Round many western islands have I been
Which bards in fealty to Apollo hold.
Oft of one wide expanse had I been told
That deep-browed Homer ruled as his demesne;
Yet did I never breathe its pure serene
Till I heard Chapman speak out loud and bold:
Then felt I like some watcher of the skies
When a new planet swims into his ken;
Or like stout Cortez when with eagle eyes
He stared at the Pacific—and all his men
Looked at each other with a wild surmise—
Silent, upon a peak in Darien.

Keats's *On First Looking into Chapman's Homer* (1816)

Season of mists and mellow fruitfulness,
Close bosom-friend of the maturing sun;
Conspiring with him how to load and bless
With fruit the vines that round the thatch-eaves run;
To bend with apples the mossed cottage-trees,
And fill all fruit with ripeness to the core;
To swell the gourd, and plump the hazel shells
With a sweet kernel; to set budding more,
And still more, later flowers for the bees,
Until they think warm days will never cease,
For Summer has o'er-brimmed their clammy cells.

One stanza from Keats's *Ode to Autumn* (1819)

Here is the second sample essay, with its different approach to the same title.

SAMPLE ESSAY 2

Introduction
Although Keats felt the sadness of life: *the weariness, the fever and the fret*, his poems are filled with the powerful beauty of the natural world, and this means that the overwhelming impression of the atmosphere of his poems is not melancholy, but intense with sense impressions. I have chosen the odes to *Autumn* and *the Nightingale* to illustrate this. He is also very aware of other pleasures such as reading, so the sonnet *On First Looking into Chapman's Homer* is the first poem I intend to consider.

Main body 1
Keats died very young and wrote some of his best poetry when ill with tuberculosis (which his brother died of too). He was therefore particularly aware of the sadness which life could bring and sensitive to the way that Beauty does not last. Inevitably there is some melancholy in his work – he even wrote an *Ode on Melancholy*, which is very Gothic and dramatic. However, this is not the overwhelming mood of his poems.

Main Body 2
The sonnet *On First Looking into Chapman's Homer* is warm in its appreciation of a particular book. Keats has read a great deal and been affected positively by what he has read. He considers these books to be *realms of gold . . . with goodly states and kingdoms,* a metaphor that gives a sense of the breadth and magnificence of what is described. Only now that he reads the ancient poet Homer in Chapman's translation does he realise the excitement: he imagines himself as an astronomer finding a *new planet,* or like the explorer Cortez staring at the Pacific, with his men, *with a wild surmise – silent, upon a peak in Darien*. All the thrill of discovering something new is imaged here in this sonnet. There is nothing 'melancholy' about it: the very reverse in fact. The poem's imagery is on a vast scale: the seas, the skies, the golden kingdoms, all from one small book that he is looking at. The sonnet form allows the sestet to focus on the excitement of his discovery, with the two similes expanding his thought almost limitlessly.

Main body 3
Another poem whose imagery is very evocative is *Ode to a Nightingale*, although here the poet is in a garden listening to the bird's song. From the very first stanza, he speaks of his 'happiness' – *being too happy in thine happiness*, and the atmosphere of the bird singing in the trees is positive, all of summer: *In some melodious plot / Of beechen green, and shadows numberless, / Singest of summer in full-throated ease.* From the darkening garden, he looks up to the sky and sees the moon and stars, beautifully described as *the Queen-Moon . . . on her throne*, surrounded by her fairies. He is in the darkness, imagining the beauty of the flowers that surround him, their sweet scent: *The coming musk-rose, full of dewy wine, / The murmurous haunt of flies on summer eves.* Again, he moves from something small – here a nightingale – to a much wider canvas: the early summer evening, the sky, and later in the poem, Ruth, a character from the Bible. His *vision* transcends the bird and the garden in an atmosphere of sensuous beauty: *Half in love with easeful Death* is often quoted to show his desire to *cease upon the midnight with no pain,* but obviously he must ▶

be half in love with life as well, and it is the sensory images of life which dominate in this poem.

Main body 4

The final poem, which creates an almost unbroken atmosphere of warm beauty and calm fulfilment, is *Ode to Autumn,* with its harvest images of plenty: *fill all fruit with ripeness to the core*, the maturing of the year into a season of *mellow fruitfulness*: sunshine, fruit, flowers and all the musical sounds of autumn. The poet imagines the spirit of the season as a woman, sometimes in the granary doing the harvesting, or making cider, or asleep among the poppies *Drows'd with the fume of poppies*. The diction used creates an atmosphere of relaxed calm: *sitting careless; sound asleep; steady; patient*. The reader is overwhelmed with the atmosphere of warmth, beauty and calm in this poem.

Conclusion

It would be wrong to assume that Keats, ill as he was, thought only gloomy thoughts of the short-lived nature of happiness and death. His poetry is filled with the beauty of nature and the intensity of sensory pleasure, so I cannot agree with the statement in the essay title. When I think of his poetry, I remember the beauty, not the sadness.

ACTIVITY 20.3

Look at the different approaches made to the same question in these two essays. You don't need to have studied Keats to appreciate this. Write down any other ideas you have for approaching this topic differently. See what your partner has said and compare notes.

These are some of the ideas you might have decided on:

- a different essay structure
- different poem choices
- a different argument

Different essay structure

Although each of these essays presents a different line of argument, their structures are similar: introduction and conclusion, as you would expect, and the main body of the essay organised in four paragraphs – the first paragraph to quickly acknowledge the opposite point of view to the one being argued, then one paragraph for each of the chosen poems to illustrate the argument. Having a brief paragraph to show you can see the other point of view always shows you are thinking! To have a poem in each paragraph is a perfectly logical way to approach a task like this, and it is the most popular method for students writing under exam conditions to structure their essays on poetry. However, the essay writer could have decided to make the topic of each paragraph an idea, and then illustrated the idea from all three chosen poems. It's not easy to do this and if you think you'll become muddled, stick to the 'one poem per paragraph' method. However, look at the following lists to see how you could do it!

What ideas can you find in the first essay to shape the structure of your essay?

a Nothing lasts; everything is transient + examples from each poem. (There are many words to express impermanence: *transient, transitory, fleeting, ephemeral, momentary* – all rather beautiful, melancholy words, I feel. Can you find any others?)

b Human life is full of suffering and ends with death + examples from each poem.

c You may experience intense pleasure but there will be pain at the very heart of it + examples from each poem.

a + b + c = the main body of the essay

This structure would make it easy to show that the poet uses *contrast* very effectively as one of his main methods: between intense pleasure and pain or loss; between beauty and illness; dark and light, warmth and cold, and so on. This readily suggests the concept of *paradox*, which is so important in Keats's work.

What ideas can you find in the second essay?

a The pleasure of discovering something new and thought-provoking + examples from each poem. (You might have to look closely to find examples of this from the two poems other than *On First Looking into Chapman's Homer,* but of course, there are other poems by Keats that could provide evidence.)

b The intensity of sensory experiences + examples from each poem.

c The beauty of the natural world + examples from each poem.

a + b + c = the main body of the essay

This structure would also make it clear that contrast is used effectively again: here, for example, between small, self-contained images and expansive wide-ranging ones; and between the present and the past.

Keat's grave in Rome. Note the inscription 'Here lies one whose name was writ in water'.

Different poem choices

There are many other possible examples in this selection of poems by Keats that would illustrate both of these arguments. And there are other poems whose diction and imagery could be used selectively to prove opposite points, just as *Ode to a Nightingale* does with these two essays. Keats's poetry is paradoxical in nature and this allows a broad range of responses and interpretations.

KEY CONCEPTS

At the Advanced Level, you need to show you have briefly considered different interpretations.

KEY TERMS

Paradox: often an important feature of more demanding texts. The writer is aware that nothing is as simple as it seems. Keats is a good example of a writer who works constantly with paradox. Life is short, beauty may be fleeting, but this makes the pleasure in them more intense.

Synaesthesia: a device often associated with Keats but widely used by other poets. It means describing one sense in terms usually used for another; for example, melodious plot (auditory and visual), *Tender is the night* (tactile and visual). In ordinary language, we use this as well, for example *a loud shirt* (auditory and visual) or *glowing comments* (visual and auditory).

Transferred epithet: *Melodious plot* in *Ode to a Nightingale* is a transferred epithet, a descriptive word which is shifted from one thing to another – it's the bird which is melodious, not the plot of trees.

A different argument

Both of the sample essays answer the question, they have chosen very suitable poems, both are clearly structured and they use examples to support their arguments. Interestingly, there is evidence in *Ode to a Nightingale* to support two opposing views, so it appears in both essays.

Perhaps a more sophisticated essay would take elements from both arguments and discuss the relative merits of each in more depth. The first paragraph of the main body in each essay is rather sketchy and the ideas could be given more weight. The question does ask 'how far?' and this gives scope for some discrimination. A new idea in such an essay could be that art has permanence even though individual human lives do not, and *Ode on a Grecian Urn* could be cited in evidence. You could also use critic Kenneth Muir's comment that *the cold pastoral, though perfect, is lacking in the warmth of reality.*

KEY CONCEPTS

Quoting a critical comment shows your wider reading as well as acknowledging the possibility of more than one interpretation of a work. This also provides a useful means of showing your evaluation skills - an important new assessment objective. Discuss the critical comment and perhaps introduce another critic's ideas, for example those of Helen Vendler.

Reflection: This exercise is connected with the work of a poet who is very famous, but he is not necessarily the poet you are studying for your exam. Think carefully about how you can transfer what you are learning here to the poet you ARE studying in detail.

What you have also learnt from these sample essays is that there is no limit to the different ideas generated by works of literature; there is no limit to the ways of doing things creatively **provided that your ideas are rooted in the text**. This applies equally to works of prose and drama.

FURTHER ESSAY QUESTIONS

1 *Discuss some of the ways in which Elizabeth Jennings uses language and imagery to illuminate her presentation of human relationships.* (Style focus)

2 *How far do you agree that Elizabeth Jennings is 'above all, a Nature poet'?* (Topic focus)

ACTIVITY 20.4

Take a poetry essay title you and your friend have been given. If you haven't started work yet, try to think of as many ways as possible of answering it and as many relevant poems as you can. Decide finally which you would use to represent your personal view of the topic.

If you have already completed your assignment, work together on the two essays, identifying differences and thinking of other ways you could handle your basic material: different essay structure, different poem choices, different argument.

ACTIVITY 20.5

You have looked at the work of an important Romantic poet and his creation of atmosphere. Now read carefully the two student essays that follow. They are on the Modernist poet T.S. Eliot, whose work you came across first in the AS Level section of the book. As you've been exploring melancholy moods, I've chosen an essay title which is very similar to the one on Keats you analysed earlier. At A Level, titles often have more emphasis on the poets' methods and effects, not just on their main themes. The creation of a distinctive mood or atmosphere is one such focus. Read the essays with a pencil in your hand, assessing them as you go, and then read them again with the marginal notes. How far were your points the same as the marker's?

Essay: *How far do you agree that the dominant mood of Eliot's Selected Poems is one of melancholy? You should use at least two poems in your answer.*

KEY CONCEPTS

Modernism began to develop in the late 19th and early 20th centuries. Writers consciously tried to break with traditional ways of writing, in both poetry and in fiction such as the novels of Virginia Woolf and James Joyce.

The street lamp said, 'Regard that woman
Who hesitates towards you in the light of the door
Which opens on her like a grin…'

The street lamp said,
'Remark the cat which flattens itself in the gutter,
Slips out its tongue
And devours a morsel of rancid butter.'

▶

So the hand of a child, automatic,

Slipped out and pocketed a toy that was running along the quay.

I could see nothing behind that child's eye. …

'The bed is open; the tooth-brush hangs on
the wall,

Put your shoes at the door, sleep, prepare for life.'

The last twist of the knife.

T.S. Eliot, from *Rhapsody on a Windy Night* (1920)

We are the hollow men
We are the stuffed men
Leaning together
Headpiece filled with straw. Alas!
Our dried voices, when
We whisper together
Are quiet and meaningless
As wind in dry grass
Or rats' feet over broken glass
In our dry cellar

T.S. Eliot, from *The Hollow Men* (1925)

What are the roots that clutch, what branches grow

Out of this stony rubbish?…

…you know only

A heap of broken images, where the sun beats,

And the dead tree gives no shelter…

Unreal City,

Under the brown fog of a winter dawn,

A crowd flowed over London Bridge, so many,

I had not thought death had undone so many.

T.S. Eliot, from *The Waste Land* (1922)

> I grow old…I grow old…
> I shall wear the bottoms of my trousers rolled.
> Shall I part my hair behind? Do I dare to eat a peach?
> I shall wear white flannel trousers and walk upon the beach,
> I have heard the mermaids, singing each to each.
>
> I do not think that they will sing to me.
>
> T.S. Eliot, from *The Love Song of J. Alfred Prufrock* (1915)

STUDENT RESPONSE A

Eliot's pessimistic and melancholic outlook on life echoes through these poems, with little that is optimistic to relieve the reader. Whether his depiction of the world as '*withered stumps of time*' ('A Game of Chess') or of the lack of meaning in our lives, Eliot's poetry is dominated by melancholic concepts and language.

The best examples of this can be found in '*The Waste Land*,' specifically the section 'Burial of the Dead' and in '*the Hollow Men*'. When he describes the crowds flowing over London Bridge, he says '*I had not thought death had undone so many*'. He implies that the working classes are no longer living or that they are not really alive when they are part of the crowd. This concept of the unlived life can be found throughout the *Selected Poems*, whether it be Prufrock who is looking back on his life with regret, questioning its lack of meaning, or the hollow men, '*Headpieces filled with straw. Alas / Our dried voices, when / We whisper together / Are quiet and meaningless*'. The representation of individuals as scarecrow figures shows clearly the emptiness Eliot is alluding to. This is also echoed in 'A Game of Chess' where the questions '*Are you alive or not?*' '*Is there nothing in your head?*' appear once again to question our existence and its meaning.

Some of Eliot's pessimism, which creates the melancholy mood, has been attributed to his feelings about industrialisation and its impact on society. Often he compares humans to inanimate objects or unindividualized in crowds doing pointless things: '*I see crowds of people walking round in a ring*'. This all detracts from the worth of the individual, which in turn creates a depressing tone.

He also examines the setting of post-industrial society – the city. '*What branches grow / Out of this stony rubbish*' reveals a barren wasteland for a fragmented society to live in. '*A heap of broken images, where the sun beats / And the dead tree gives no shelter*'. This pessimism comes from his depiction of the modern world, even if he does try to use the fragments in his work: '*These fragments I have shored against my ruin*'.

This is a good introduction, referring clearly to the essay topic and even including a brief, apt quotation.

A lengthy paragraph with a number of good points which could perhaps have been discussed more fully and divided into separate paragraphs or certainly separate sections of the paragraph. The writer refers to *The Waste Land, The Hollow Men* and *The Love Song of J Alfred Prufrock*, Comments on *The Waste Land* should be kept together and *Prufrock* should be discussed more fully.

There are really two separate points here – the one about the crowds and the individual should be with the similar subject matter in paragraph 2; the point about industrialisation deserves fuller discussion and some proper illustration.

And now we have the paragraph about industrialisation, with some apt quotation as illustration! Paragraphs 3 and 4 need re-structuring.

Eliot's exploration of loneliness also contributes to the melancholy mood of his poetry. As he puts it in '*The Hollow Men*', '*It is like this / In death's other kingdom / Waking alone*', suggesting that life here is like being the living dead. We may not exist, or certainly don't matter. Prufrock can hear the mermaids singing but they are not singing to him.

To conclude, Eliot's poetry is predominantly sad. This is because of his constant questioning of life and death and whether there is any meaning at all in either. His pessimistic view is revealed in the images he uses of barrenness. Although he finishes '*The Waste Land*' with a hopeful Buddhist prayer, it is the hopeless and melancholic world that he has created in the poem that stays with the reader.

Loneliness is a very important point in the discussion and could be illustrated more fully, particularly regarding *Prufrock*, a poem which deserves much more than the throwaway line about the mermaids!

A sound summing up with a personal response to the poetry.

COMMENT

The essay has a great deal of potential. The introduction and conclusion are good, but the main body needs to be more carefully structured, so that the good ideas about the essay topic are grouped together more logically and, in some cases, illustrated more fully. The student hasn't used the 'one paragraph for each chosen poem' method but tried to have one idea for each paragraph illustrated from the poems chosen. However, this hasn't worked very well, and more practice is needed.

T.S. Eliot (1888 – 1965)

STUDENT RESPONSE B

Eliot's selected poems feature themes such as the loss of individuality, the pressure of society, urbanisation and a yearning of the ideal world. Poems such as *Prufrock*, *Rhapsody on a Windy Night* and *preludes* make the reader question the values of society, and in Eliot's opinion we have lost our important values, making us pessimistic.

'Rhapsody on a Windy Night' from the title suggests a lively jubilant mood; however, it is not so. We are presented with a solitary person contemplating his isolation which heightens the melancholy mood of the poem.

On his journey the persona witnesses a cat eating rancid butter from a gutter. This sinister scene is far from happy. Another tragic image is of the woman who hesitates in the light of the door that opens like a '*grin*' behind her. The persona sees a child stealing a toy, but instead of play evoking happiness, it seems a criminal and evil child, like the world around him.

The hesitant persona in Prufrock evokes sympathy because he is so fearful of society and life itself, not daring to do anything. His inability to eat a peach shows he is unable to lead a life of his own. To act as a foil to him, Eliot describes society, confident and pretentious, but it unsettles the unconfident Prufrock who worries about his physical appearance. Eliot creates sympathy for him and this creates a mood of melancholy in the reader. ▶

In the introduction, the writer makes a list of themes that could be examined when answering this question. If you do this, it's important that your essay follows through with some consideration of these themes, which doesn't entirely happen here. The writer also mentions the poems *making us pessimistic* which needs to be developed by saying *Eliot's use of language creates a melancholy mood which makes us pessimistic.*

There are a few comments on *Rhapsody on a Windy Night* but they are not entirely connected, starting with loneliness and going on to some unhappy images from the poem. There is also a misunderstanding of the word 'rhapsody' which leads to the assertion that the title creates a lively jubilant mood – surely not!

This is a good paragraph on *Prufrock* and its effects, but could be illustrated more closely from the text to support the points made.

This is a much more detailed discussion of *Rhapsody*, but it should have been part of the second paragraph. The student has chosen the 'one poem per paragraph' method, but if you do this, you must stick to it!

At the end of '*Rhapsody on a Windy Night*', the poet exclaims '*Memory! / You have the key*'. However, although the persona is happy to have found his home, the reader is able to see what sadness is brought upon him when he arrives home; '*The bed is open, the toothbrush hangs on the wall / Put your shoes by the door, Sleep. Prepare for life*'. The home is oppressive. He has to conform to society and this is '*The last twist of the knife*'. The reader can relate to this. We are all forced to conform to things we don't necessarily agree with and this evokes empathy, emphasising the mood of melancholy.

There is plenty of personal response to *The Hollow Men*, but further illustration and analysis of the ways in which a melancholy mood is created by Eliot's language would enhance the essay.

In *The Hollow Men*, the protagonists are stuck in a world between heaven and hell. He evokes their melancholy in the first lines '*We are the hollow men / We are the stuffed men*'. All they can say is '*Alas!*' They live an existence of regret and they must bear it for eternity. It makes the reader feel are we doing enough to not become like the hollow men ourselves? It is difficult to tell, and it may lead to depression. Eliot's poetry is a stark reminder of the perils of not making the most of life and this may evoke despair from the reader.

The interesting point about religion is one which could have been developed in the main body of the essay. However, the essay is concluded neatly and related once again to the reader's response.

Although the main mood of the poems is one of melancholy, it ends with a sentiment of hope in religion. The end of *The Waste Land* and *Ash Wednesday* can redeem and make life more rewarding. I do not know if Eliot intended to have religion as an escape from the possible evils of existence, but it comes as a suitable solution and allows some optimism in the selection of poems as a whole.

COMMENT

This essay has a strong personal response to the poetry and one feels that the student has become engaged by the texts chosen. Greater clarity of essay structure would have helped, as Paragraph 2 is not very cohesive and comment on *Rhapsody* divided and separated. Further illustration throughout would help to sharpen the points made. This is an essay title which demands focus on the effects of language.

Reflection: Look critically at an essay you have written. Have you always structured carefully and illustrated fully?

FURTHER ESSAY QUESTIONS

1. *In what ways, and with what effects, does T.S. Eliot present images of city life in his poetry?* (Style focus)
2. *'Loneliness is at the heart of T.S. Eliot's poetry.' To what extent do you agree with this view?* (Topic focus)

ACTIVITY 20.6

Read the following essay on the topic of childhood from another well-known Romantic poet. I've included it to show how contextual points can overwhelm literary considerations and make an essay rather shallow. The Keats essays did have some biographical context, mentioning his illness and the fact that he liked reading, for example, but these facts were always relevant to the literary considerations being thought through. The Eliot essays incorporated references to the city and to industrial society, but these references were equally appropriate.

Essay: *Discuss Wordsworth's presentation of childhood in the selection of poems. You should use two or three poems in your answer.*

Then up I rose,
And dragged to earth both branch and bough, with crash
And merciless ravage….
I felt a sense of pain when I beheld
The silent trees and the intruding sky.

William Wordsworth, from *Nutting* (1850)

One evening (surely I was led by her)
I went alone into a Shepherd's Boat,
A Skiff that to a Willow tree was tied
Within a rocky Cave, its usual home.
'Twas by the shores of Patterdale, a Vale
Wherein I was a Stranger, thither come
A School-boy Traveller, at the Holidays.
Forth rambled from the Village Inn alone
No sooner had I sight of this small Skiff,
Discover'd thus by unexpected chance,
Than I unloos'd her tether and embark'd.

In thought and wish
That time, my shoulder all with springes hung,
I was a fell destroyer. On the heights
Scudding away from snare to snare, I plied
My anxious visitation, hurrying on,
Still hurrying, hurrying onward…

William Wordsworth, from *The Prelude* (1805)

> Dear child! Dear girl! That walkest with me here,
> If thou appear'st untouched by solemn thought,
> Thy nature is not therefore less divine...
>
> From *It is a beauteous evening, calm and free by* William Wordsworth (1802)

STUDENT RESPONSE

William Wordsworth, who was born in THE Lake District in 1770, presents childhood in his poetry in a multitude of different ways. As a poet of the ~~Romantic~~ era it was his agenda to record the life of rural men and because of the migration of people from the countryside into towns at the time, this meant bringing them back to their childhood and reminding them of childhood experiences such as Wordsworth had in the Lake District. Wordsworth's poetry evolved naturally over time and changes from his happy childhood memories surrounded by Nature such as in '*Nutting*' and '*The Prelude*' to less conventional tales of childhood such as 'It is a beauteous evening calm and free' written in 1802.

Although the writer mentions childhood being presented in a multitude of different ways in the first sentence, the second sentence doesn't quite follow. Why does the migration of people into towns mean bringing them back to their childhood and reminding them of childhood experience? It would have been more helpful to say that his agenda was to remind people of childhood, whether they are rural people or people who have moved into towns. The essay could have started with the last sentence of the paragraph, which is relevant and suggests the poems that will be discussed.

Wordsworth wrote '*The Prelude*' while he was writing Lyrical Ballads with his friend Coleridge in 1798. Coleridge wrote well-known poems such as *Kubla Khan* and *The Ancient Mariner*, but they are not about childhood. In Books 1 and 2, Wordsworth reflects on happy childhood memories in the Lake District. '*We ran a boisterous race*' reflects the boundless energy and freedom of childhood, something which is also reflected in the poet's use of blank verse. The lack of rhyme helps to show the freedom and lack of boundaries in childhood. In childhood there is equality and acceptance of others that comes naturally. This idea is typical of the Romantic poet. Wordsworth rejects the Enlightenment ideal of celebrating intellectuals and the upper classes and shows that equality between people is what is important, and it comes naturally to children.

Again, the most relevant section of the paragraph is at the end, although the claim that equality comes naturally to children needs support from the text.

Wordsworth also presents in '*Nutting*' and '*The Prelude*' a destructive aspect to childhood. There is a story in '*The Prelude*' where he steals a shepherd's boat, and in '*Nutting*' he recalls beating the trees with a '*nutting crook*'. Considering that this poem shows a child close to nature and all its beauty with '*fairy water breaks*' and '*sparkling foam*', it still reveals that he is actively destroying it, emphasised in the onomatopoeia of '*crash*' as the branches fall to the ground. He could be showing us the childish behaviour of youth or perhaps symbolising industrialisation, where Man is destroying Nature. In this way, his presentation of childhood is ambiguous but always connected with nature.

There are some useful details from poems here, but the final comment about his destructiveness symbolising industrialisation needs more discussion. As it stands, it's rather a throwaway line. *Ambiguous* needs discussion.

In the poem '*It is a beauteous evening, calm and free*', ~~Wordsworth~~ writes about his illegitimate daughter Caroline who he visits in France. He shows his love for her although she is illegitimate which would have been frowned upon in England at the time. He hasn't spent much time with her before. They are walking together on this lovely evening and he is overwhelmed by the beauty and holiness of the scene but she seems to be '*unmoved by the solemn scene*'. In spite of this, Wordsworth shows that during childhood you are under the protection of God, so childhood is the time when you are closest to nature.

Too much biography here, and not enough discussion of the poem, which deserves much more exploration.

In conclusion, Wordsworth presents childhood in a plethora of ways. He shows how children are connected to nature and to God, yet they are also capable of destruction and could even represent the destruction of industrialisation at the time of writing.

COMMENT

The conclusion sums up an argument that hasn't been developed in the main body of the essay. Too much time has been wasted on context of a biographical nature, and there is not nearly enough on the poems. This is a frustrating piece of work because some valid points are suggested and they are not developed thoughtfully or illustrated. The essay is weak.

Reflection: Consider how helpful the biographical and social details are. Do we need to know where Wordsworth was born, or that he was composing *Lyrical Ballads* with his friend Coleridge? Does it help the argument to know that Wordsworth's daughter was illegitimate, for example? Is the point about symbolising industrialisation explored and illustrated fully?

ACTIVITY 20.7

Take two different coloured highlighters and use your photocopy. With one colour, highlight those parts of the essay that make points about Wordsworth's life, the Romantic poets generally and the social situation. With your other colour, highlight those parts of the essay that discuss and illustrate literary points such as form, structure and language.

FURTHER ESSAY QUESTIONS

1. *Consider the significance of remembered experience in the poems of William Wordsworth.* (Topic focus)
2. *In what ways and how effectively does William Wordsworth use imagery of destruction in his work?* (Language focus)

FURTHER READING

The poetry of Keats and Wordsworth is readily available on the Internet. You might find Keats's letters fascinating, too. Eliot's work is all published by Faber, with selected poems available on websites.

TIP

Contextual material should always enhance literary discussion, never just be a substitute for it.

Reflection: Have you used extraneous contextual material in your poetry essays? You may be wasting time and space that you could be using for analysis.

Self-assessment checklist

Reflect on what you've learnt in this unit and indicate your confidence level between 1 and 5. If you score below 3, revisit that section. Come back to this list later in your course. Has your confidence grown?

	Confidence level	Revisited?
I acknowledge the way that different responses can emerge from the same essay title and still be relevant		
I can apply principles of essay construction from Keats to my own set poet		
I gain insight from comparing my and my friend's essays on the same subject		
I appreciate the validity of the marker comments on the two Eliot essays		
I am alert to the issues involved in using contextual material in the Wordsworth essay		

Poetry – passage questions

Learning objectives

In this unit you will:

- understand the distinguishing characteristics of a passage question compared with a critical essay question
- analyse the example essay on Wright
- use the notes on Rossetti to develop an essay
- study the Larkin essay and what makes it an excellent piece of work
- explore the notes on Chaucer, working with a friend.

KEY CONCEPTS

Language, form, structure, genres, context, style, interpretation, critical reading.

Before you start

- Refer to the advice given on essay writing in Unit 29 in Part 3 of this book.
- Read again the relevant units from the AS Level section of the book (Part 1), considering what differences you notice in level and style.
- Prepare for the exercises by studying the printed poems carefully. You may like to research the poets before starting.

This unit will help you to develop your close reading skills and apply them to your poetry set text. An A Level passage question on poetry involves a close critical analysis of a complete poem from one of your poetry set texts, or an extract of some 30 lines if it is from a longer poem (such as Milton's *Paradise Lost*). These lines are printed in your examination paper. You'll need to do the analysis and relate what you say to some other poems from the same set text, two being a useful number to show your wider reading. In this Unit there are sample responses to help you to see how it's done.

Reflection: Refer to the different methods of approaching passage questions in Unit 30 of this book.

ACTIVITY 21.1

The first exercise is on a poet whose work you met right at the beginning of the course – the Australian poet Judith Wright. Read the poems and the essay, noting the way in which the printed poem is analysed and other poems are introduced in support. The wording of the essay title is exactly the same type that you would be given in an examination, but afterwards you will see an example of another possible wording for this exercise.

Essay: *Paying close attention to language and imagery, write a critical appreciation of the following poem and consider ways in which it is characteristic of Wright's methods and concerns.*

Naked all night the field
breathed its dew until
the great gold ball of day
sprang up from the dark hill.

Now as the children come
the field and they are met.
Their day is measured and marked,
its lanes and tapes are set;

and the children gilt by the sun
shoulder one another;
crouch at the marks to run,
and spring, and run together –

the children pledged and matched,
and built to win or lose,
who grow, while no one watches,
The selves in their sidelong eyes.

The watchers love them in vain.
What's real here is the field,
the starter's gun, the lane
the ball dropped or held;

and set toward the future
they run like running water,
for only the pride of winning,
the pain the losers suffer,

till the day's great golden ball,
that no one ever catches,
drops; and at its fall
runners and watchers

▶

pick up their pride and pain
won out of the measured field
and turn away again
while the star-dewed night comes cold.

So pride and pain are fastened
into the heart's future,
while naked and perilous
the night and the field glitter.

Judith Wright *The Sports Field* (1994)

SAMPLE RESPONSE

In this poem, Wright compares the advancement of a person on the sports field in a game with the progression of a day moving from sunrise to night and a life moving from birth to death. It is typical of Wright's work to use physical symbols to express complex concepts such as life and death, particularly the way in which human beings move through life struggling and striving until its inevitable end.

A sports field is an effective extended metaphor for a person's efforts in life, from their early years: *as the children come / the field and they are met*. From the beginning they are competitive, they *shoulder one another* and *spring, and run together* and watch each other's progress with *sidelong eyes*. They may be supported by their families who are like *the watchers* at the edge of the field, but the children are on their own and will suffer if they lose, and feel proud if they win. Wright extends the metaphor very effectively by comparing the sun to a great golden ball which *no one ever catches* because we can never stop the passage of time and its inevitable end. This is enhanced by the simile of the children being *like running water*, which flows away and is never seen again.

Just as on a running track, we are measured and marked and *lanes and tapes are set* in life. Society fixes us into its patterns and restrictions, and we will suffer *pride and pain* both in childhood and in *the heart's future*. The final lines give a bleak impression of the field of life: *naked and perilous / the night and the field glitter. Naked* is a **transferred epithet**, since it applies to us having no defences against time passing. *Glitter* perhaps suggests that life seems beautiful but is full of danger.

Wright uses a similar metaphor for life in her poem *The Diver*, which imagines our progress through life as like a diver making a dive from a high board and then resurfacing in the pool. He takes a breath and then launches himself out in a curve in his dive: *the crest of time, the pride, the hour / that answers death*, suggesting that our efforts demand courage and daring in the face of time passing and the threat of life ending eventually – *the step to take / from birth to death*. What differs in this poem is that the physical effort is not imagined as one race or one game on the field, but a continuous, cyclical set of actions which we repeat through life. The diver has to come

▶

KEY TERM

transferred epithet: a descriptive word that qualifies something other than the thing it is describing.

up and climb up the steps and dive off again and again. Unlike *Sports Field*, the poem introduces a sympathetic persona in the final stanza, who identifies themselves with the diver and empathises with his situation: *with you I draw that breath, and dare, / time's worst being known.*

In contrast with both these poems is Wright's early poem *The Surfer.* She uses very vivid physical details of action, once again using the images of golden sun and water, but the surfer is strong and joyful like the gulls (although both he and they are described as *mortal, masterful, frail*. In the later poems, she explores the idea of *mortality* more fully). In this poem, the danger comes from the sea, whose waves are described metaphorically as like a *wolf* with teeth, which snatches broken toys on the beach.

In addition to extended metaphors, Wright uses rhymes, verse forms and sounds very effectively and this is typical of her methods. Alliteration and assonance in *Sports Field* underline the poem's themes: The alliteration of *met, measured* and *marked* emphasise the guidelines that are already established when children enter the race of life, and the linking through assonance of *children, gilt* and *built* underlines the link in meaning as well as sound. The poem is in quite regular four-line stanzas rhyming or half-rhyming abab throughout. Enjambment in some lines suggests the way in which the children could break free if given the chance, but like the lines of the poem, they are fixed in a pre-determined shape. *The Diver also* uses enjambment, with the lines flowing aptly into one another throughout in a pattern of longer and shorter bursts but maintaining the rhyme and half-rhyme throughout in abab like *Sports Field*. The stanza length goes from ten lines to eight to four, imaging the shortening of life, but also emphasising the final sympathetic stanza.

Sports Field is typical of Wright's concerns and methods, combining quite philosophical reflections on life with vivid physical imagery and effectively controlled verse forms. In much of her poetry, we are very aware that she is Australian, using history, geography and imagery from that country, but the three poems I've used could have been written anywhere.

The diver pausing on the tower
draws in one breath –
the crest of time, the pride, the hour
that answers death
and down to where the long pool lies
marks out his curve;
descending light that star-like flies
from air to wave
as auturmn falls from trees and eyes,
and youth, and love.

▶

Then from the rocking depths' release,
naked and new
the headfirst man springs up, and sees
all still to do –
the tower to climb, the pause to make,
the fill of breath
to gather in – the step to take
from birth to death.

Then you, who turn and climb the stair
and stand alone –
with you I draw that breath, and dare,
time's worst being known.

Judith Wright *The Diver* (1994)

He thrust his joy against the weight of the sea;
climbed through, slid under those long banks of foam—
(hawthorn hedges in spring, thorns in the face stinging).
How his brown strength drove through the hollow and coil
of green-through weirs of water!
Muscle of arm thrust down long muscle of water;
and swimming so, went out of sight
where mortal, masterful, frail, the gulls went wheeling
in air as he in water, with delight.

Turn home, the sun goes down; swimmer, turn home.
Last leaf of gold vanishes from the sea-curve.
Take the big roller's shoulder, speed and serve;
come to the long beach home like a gull diving.

For on the sand the grey-wolf sea lies, snarling,
cold twilight wind splits the waves' hair and shows
the bones they worry in their wolf-teeth. O,
wind blows
and sea crouches on sand, fawning and mouthing;
drops there and snatches again, drops and
again snatches
its broken toys, its whitened pebbles and shells.

Judith Wright *The Surfer* (1994)

FURTHER ESSAY QUESTION

Because passage questions always demand a close analysis of the printed poem first, the range of essay wording is more limited. However, it could involve a theme, not the general *methods and concerns* formula. See the following example.

Write a critical appreciation of the following poem, relating it to the presentation of sports and physical activity in Wright's verse.

ACTIVITY 21.2

The next exercise is focused on another female writer – Christina Rossetti.

Essay: *Write a critical appreciation of the following poem, relating it to two other poems by Rossetti in your selection.*

Does the road wind up-hill all the way?
    Yes, to the very end.
Will the day's journey take the whole long day?
    From morn to night, my friend.
But is there for the night a resting-place?
    A roof for when the slow dark hours begin.
May not the darkness hide it from my face?
    You cannot miss that inn.
Shall I meet other wayfarers at night?
    Those who have gone before.
Then must I knock, or call when just in sight?
    They will not keep you standing at that door.
Shall I find comfort, travel-sore and weak?
    Of labour you shall find the sum.
Will there be beds for me and all who seek?
    Yea, beds for all who come.

Christina Rossetti *Up-hill* (1858)

Reflection: Looking closely at the sample response, reflect on the way in which the critical appreciation is extended by reference to the other poems. Of course, if the essay title was different (such as an exploration of her animal poems) then the prompt poem would be a different one and the two supporting poems would be quite different from this. Remember how important it is to choose the right poems when writing at this level. Don't just choose your favourites and hope for the best!

SAMPLE ESSAY 1

Introduction

In *Up-hill*, Rossetti does not directly discuss Christ and his life as she does in many of her other religious poems. The poem is, rather, based on the extended metaphor of life as a spiritual journey, which takes all day and ends with rest at an inn at night. Perhaps the most striking aspect of the poem is its use of question and answer form, with the questioner asking for reassurance about the end of the journey. Readers may, however, respond differently to the tone of the poem, some finding it encouraging, but

Introduction has emphasis on the printed poem but relates to all three poems.

others less so. The two other poems I have selected to discuss, *A Christmas Carol* and *Good Friday*, are directly about Christ – his birth and his crucifixion.

Main body 1: *Up-hill*

- Spiritual journey + examples
- **Dialectical** question and answer form + tone: could be ambiguous?
- Effect of regular patterns, rhythm and rhyme
- Comment on some diction, for example *yea*
- Effect on reader – is it reassuring, or rather sinister and mysterious?

Main body 2: *A Christmas Carol*

- Very different from *Up-hill* – more imaginative imagery, stronger confidence, no ambiguity
- Winter – sense images of sound and sight
- Repetition of words for emphasis
- Contrast between the heavenly and cosmic importance of Christ / very humble and domestic image of the baby in the manger
- The poet's personal contribution: the 'I' enters the poem
- The regular metrical scheme in eight-line stanzas and rhyme abcbdefe and the emphatic short last lines – strong, calm and confident tone
- Contrast is used, as in *Up-hill*, but it is not between two different speakers, rather the baby Christ with his mother/his eternal significance

Main body 3: *Good Friday*

- Another strong contrast – poet's anguished questions and exclamations, but questioning herself – not like *Up-hill* with its dialogue form
- Metaphor of herself as *stone* – hard and apparently unfeeling
- Uses parallelism: *Not so* used four times emphasises her difference
- Regular stanza form with its shorter first and fourth lines and more expansive second and third lines, rhyming abba, different effect
- Biblical reference (as in previous poem): she wants Christ, greater than Moses, to look at her and crack her stone-like exterior.
- In this, as in *A Christmas Carol*, the speaker is shown as inadequate

Conclusion

These three poems all reveal Rossetti's profound faith and trust in God. The events in the life of Jesus are evidently important to her and her response is a strongly personal one, often passionate, although not in *Up-hill*. She uses a variety of verse forms – usually regular but in distinctive forms, such as the dialogue, giving clear emphasis in the verse to the important lines in the poems' thought. Her doubts are usually answered, her inadequacies all compensated by Christ's love, and the poems reach a confident conclusion which affirms her faith. However, the indirect and slightly evasive tone of *Up-hill* gives it an ambiguous quality that some readers may find the opposite of reassuring.

KEY TERM

Dialectical: a format of question and answer, or opposing voices, to present ideas. This form was favoured by the Metaphysical poet Andrew Marvell.

Details of language and effects of printed poem.

Clear movement in argument as next poem is discussed.

Finds a point of comparison, neatly linked.

Next shift in the argument as the third poem is introduced, relating back to the printed text.

Compares poems 2 and 3.

Sums up in a conclusion which relates to all the poems but with particular emphasis on *Up-hill*. This illustrates the way in which different critical readings of a text (a key concept at A Level) can be incorporated. Try to find a critical view of Rossetti's religious poetry which you can **evaluate** as part of your essay.

ACTIVITY 21.3

Look closely at the poems to support and develop the points made in note form. You'll need to make the notes into sentences and expand each textual reference into a suitable brief quotation from the poem.

Am I a stone and not a sheep,
That I can stand, O Christ, beneath Thy Cross,
To number drop by drop Thy Blood's slow loss,
And yet not weep?

Not so those women loved
Who with exceeding grief lamented Thee;
Not so fallen Peter weeping bitterly;
Not so the thief was moved;
Not so the Sun and Moon
Which hid their faces in a starless sky,
A horror of great darkness at broad noon—
I, only I.

Yet give not o'er,
But seek Thy sheep, true Shepherd of the flock;
Greater than Moses, turn and look once more
And smite a rock.

Christina Rossetti *Good Friday* (1896)

In the bleak mid-winter
Frosty wind made moan,
Earth stood hard as iron, Water like a stone;
Snow had fallen, snow on snow, Snow on snow,
In the bleak mid-winter
Long ago.

Our God, Heaven cannot hold Him,
Nor earth sustain;

▶

Reflection: Look at the critical essays in the previous unit and try to distinguish between the possible approaches you could use for a critical essay and the approaches to the passage question that you've observed in the Wright and Rossetti exercises.

Heaven and earth shall flee away
When He comes to reign:
In the bleak mid-winter
A stable-place sufficed
The Lord God Almighty
Jesus Christ

Two stanzas from Christina Rossetti *A Christmas Carol* (1872)

FURTHER ESSAY QUESTION

Write a critical appreciation of the following poem, relating it to Rossetti's concern with religious themes.

Now it's time for another 20th-century poet – Philip Larkin.

ACTIVITY 21.4

Read the poems by Philip Larkin and the student response to the essay title, together with the marker's marginal and summative comments. (It is printed in full, so if you are not studying Larkin, you can appreciate the exercise anyway.)

Essay: *Write a critical appreciation of the following poem, relating it to two other poems by Larkin in your selection.*

Home is so sad. It stays as it was left,
Shaped to the comfort of the last to go
As if to win them back. Instead, bereft
Of anyone to please, it withers so,
Having no heart to put aside the theft
And turn again to what it started as,
A joyous shot at how things ought to be,
Long fallen wide. You can see how it was:
Look at the pictures and the cutlery.
The music in the piano stool. That vase.

Philip Larkin *Home is so Sad* (1958)

TIP
It is always useful to practice different essay types so that you can remain flexible in your approach and thinking.

STUDENT RESPONSE

The poem begins with a very surprising, indeed paradoxical, statement: *Home is so Sad*, seemingly the reverse of what most people may feel. But the poem goes on to express the pathos of the home environment, emphasising how the passage of time has left it sterile and unchanged. Time has passed and stolen the family away so that home has no *heart to put aside the theft* and go back to being a more vibrant place. The objects in the house seem pathetic, mere relics of a past time that was better: *You can see how it was.*

> The essay goes straight into a comment on the printed poem.

Although the language used is relatively simple, it is very effective. The poet uses a kind of personification for the house, or at least makes it seem alive, with its persuasions to the family to return *as if to win them back*, but it has now *wither[ed]* in its abandonment. There is a strong contrast between the diction used in stanza 1 (*sad, bereft, withers*) and the powerful adjective *joyous* to describe how things used to be. The objects in the house are isolated images – *pictures, cutlery, music in the piano stool* – all suggesting a previous life that had more vitality: perhaps photos of the family, shared meals, music being played – now tucked away. *Look at* is an imperative that tells the reader to examine the objects closely, as if to say: don't miss any of the evidence I'm presenting to prove my point. The final phrase of the poem – *That vase* – suggests an object that once had some history, a story to it, now abandoned and meaningless.

> Close attention to the detail of the language and imagery, with perceptive comments.

The two stanzas with their short lines are regular, with the first stanza rhyming fully (ababa) but in the second the rhyme breaks down into half-rhymes – *as, was, vase*, and *be* and *cutlery*, as if to mirror the withering of the home into the final bathos of the last line.

> An example of the apt critical vocabulary used throughout.

Considering that the home is the centre of the family, the poem suggests that the passage of time renders it a failure. Family members leave and the place they once madealive with their presence is now filled with meaningless objects, unchanged and lifeless.objects, unchanged and lifeless.

> Sums up the theme of the poem succinctly.

Another poem in which objects appear to symbolise a sad life deadened with routine and failure is *Mr Bleaney*. It also has a domestic setting but here it is a rented room, one which Mr Bleaney used to stay in but which now the persona of the poem is renting. All the objects in the room have a tired secondhand feeling about them: *Flowered curtains, thin and frayed; Bed, upright chair, sixty-watt bulb*. There is nothing comfortable or luxurious here and the speaker is constantly reminded of the previous inhabitant, when he stubs his cigarette out on the same *saucer-souvenir*, and is forced to listen stubs his cigarette out on same saucer-souvenir, and is forced to listen to the same jabbering television set that Bleaney persuaded the landlady to buy. The room is also defined by what it doesn't have – no hook, no room for books or bags. Critic J.D. McClatchy's definition of Larkin's poetry as *about stunted lives and spoiled desires* seems apt here. Unlike the previous poem, stunted lives and spoiled desires seems apt here. Unlike the previous poem, the objects that are there are not meaningless: theirdrab, impersonal, utilitarian nature causes the persona to wonder how this environment reflects on him; he begins to question his own identity. This shift to a morephilosophical questioning of his life takes place in the final stanza: the speaker museson whether *how we live measures our own nature*. Did Bleaney with his unchanging habits and boring life warrant *no better*, and is he, by extension, in the same situation? The poem is therefore similar to *Home is so Sad* in its use of everyday objects to symbolise domesticlife, but differs in its final development, beyond the observation of thehome andits contents into questioning one's life and how one leads it.

> The topic sentence clearly links to the previous discussion and moves us on to the next poem.

> The answer refers helpfully to apt sections of the text to support the point made.

> A useful critical comment here

> The differences between the poems are now being developed.

> Makes the relationship between the points of comparison and the points of contrast clear.

▶

STUDENT RESPONSE

These poems are sombre in tone, undermining domestic life and the family, questioning their value and their contribution to a sense of personal identity. Larkin did not always write such gloomy verse and the last poem I have chosen, *Water*, is about an everyday commodity but one which assumes a special importance in the way it is described here. The poem begins with a speculation: *If I were called in to construct a religion*. Not a very likely occurrence, as Larkin was an atheist, and not in fact very likely in anyone's life. This sets the poem, from the very outset, as an imaginative flight of fancy. If the poet were called in, then he would use water as the centre of his religion. Going to church would mean walking through water and needing dry clothes afterwards, the change suggesting a transformative experience. Instead of the customary words of the church service, the *liturgy*, he would use images of being completely soaked: *a furious devout drench*, with the alliteration of *devout* and *drench* linking the words fully. And finally, he uses imagery from the Bible to make his point: he would *raise in the east* not a star as the wise men followed, but a simple *glass of water*, so that all the rays of light would be attracted: *any-angled light*. Instead of a congregation of people, as in a church, the rays of light would *congregate endlessly*. The use of diction connected with religion suits his theme, and this surprising little poem even ends with a suggestion of eternity: endlessly.

Clear discourse marking and a new direction to the argument.

These poems all use simple objects – a piano stool, a vase, an ashtray, a glass of water – to express more complex ideas. In *Home is so Sad*, the reader is faced with the paradox that home is not supportive and enabling; in *Mr Bleaney*, ordinary things are seen as possibly giving an indication of our own personal identity and worth; but in *Water*, the humble glass of water creates an image of beauty and endlessness in which time and personal concerns all fall away and become irrelevant.

Sums up clearly, using appropriate vocabulary and relating to all three poems.

COMMENT

This student essay has an effective essay structure because it clearly responds to the question asked, both by writing the critical appreciation and by referring relevantly to other related poems. Close reference to the texts is also evident in this essay, with interpretations supported throughout. The writer has a well-developed and sophisticated style and has written a strong essay.

'This was Mr Bleaney's room. He stayed
The whole time he was at the Bodies, till
They moved him.' Flowered curtains, thin and frayed,
Fall to within five inches of the sill,
Whose window shows a strip of building land,
Tussocky, littered. 'Mr Bleaney took
My bit of garden properly in hand.'
Bed, upright chair, sixty-watt bulb, no hook
Behind the door, no room for books or bags –

▶

'I'll take it.' So it happens that I lie
Where Mr Bleaney lay, and stub my fags
On the same saucer-souvenir, and try
Stuffing my ears with cotton-wool, to drown
The jabbering set he egged her on to buy.
I know his habits – what time he came down,
His preference for sauce to gravy, why
He kept on plugging at the four aways* –
Likewise their yearly frame: the Frinton folk
Who put him up for summer holidays,
And Christmas at his sister's house in Stoke.
But if he stood and watched the frigid wind
Tousling the clouds, lay on the fusty bed
Telling himself that this was home, and grinned,
And shivered, without shaking off the dread
That how we live measures our own nature,
And at his age having no more to show
Than one hired box should make him pretty sure
He warranted no better, I don't know.

Philip Larkin *Mr Bleaney* (1964)

(*doing the football pools where you hope to win a fortune by predicting the results.)

If I were called in
To construct a religion
I should make use of water.

Going to church
Would entail a fording
To dry, different clothes;

My liturgy would employ
Images of sousing,
A furious devout drench,

▶

And I should raise in the east
A glass of water
Where any-angled light
Would congregate endlessly.

Philip Larkin *Water* (1964)

Reflection: Consider a passage question you have answered yourself. How effectively have you analysed the printed poem? How effectively have you brought in other relevant poems?

KEY CONCEPTS

The domestic environment is an important context to our lives, revealing much about our concerns and aspirations. Although these poems were written about 50 years ago, homes still have pictures and cutlery; cheap rented accommodation can still be very drab. 'Context' isn't just about wars and politics.

FURTHER ESSAY QUESTION

With close reference to the language and tone of this poem, consider Larkin's use of everyday objects in his poetry.

Answering passage questions on poetry

Answering poetry passage questions may invite a different method from prose and drama. When you write a passage question essay which begins with a critical appreciation of a passage of prose or drama, you may wish to use a different structure, writing your appreciation and incorporating wider reference as you go. This is possible because you are writing about the same text: the passage is from the novel or play you are studying. The exception to this may be Chaucer because his works *are* poetry but in the form of one longer poem. If you have studied *The Rape of the Lock* by Alexander Pope or some works by John Milton, the same applies.

In the three examples given, the essays are on separate poems – they may be by the same writer, but they are separate little texts, so it makes more sense to do it in the way illustrated (main body paragraphs 1st poem + 2nd poem + 3rd poem).

Passage questions: Chaucer

Here are two examples of an essay title on Chaucer where you could write your critical appreciation first and then bring in wider reference, or you could incorporate wider reference as you go.

ACTIVITY 21.5

Essay: *Write a critical appreciation of the following passage, relating it to Chaucer's methods and effects in the 'Prologue' and 'Tale' as a whole.*

You should always consider carefully the character who is speaking in *The Canterbury Tales*, through either their *Prologue* or their *Tale*. Chaucer creates characters in order to offer insight into human behaviour, so often what they say is both confessional (telling all about themselves) as well as thematic (showing Chaucer's wider concerns). If you are studying *The Wife of Bath*, the fact that she seems to make a great many allusions to the Bible, as well as other authorities, may seem unrealistic if you are judging from a purely characterisation point of view. 'How can she know all these things?' you may ask yourself. Remember that Chaucer is always the author behind her character, shaping the narrative to produce a recognisable woman, as well as a way of discussing wider issues. This tension means that his tales are always ironic, with the limited perspective of an individual and a wider perspective behind it. Or, in the case of the Pardoner, his confessions seem to be too honest about revealing his character and thus self-defeating. If he tells his audience all his tricks, they won't buy from him, so why does he do it? To ask this question is to treat the Pardoner too much like a real person. He is a creation of Chaucer, who again is shaping the *Prologue* and *Tale* to create a vivid character as well as to raise wider issues. *The Knight's Tale* is a story of knights and ladies and battle told by a superior, upper-class fellow – the Knight – with much experience of 'noble' deeds. But there are many poignant and even tragic elements of the story which the Knight is not sensitive enough to grasp. Through his narrative, Chaucer allows us, the readers, to see them even though the Knight is not aware of them.

Students often forget that *The Canterbury Tales* are all written in verse. The following is typical of Chaucer passage questions, this one on *The Wife of Bath's Prologue*.

Illustration of the Wife of Bath.

TIP

Chaucer's language may seem challenging, but it is an older version of modern English, with many words the same, just spelt differently. Become familiar with it and you will enjoy his perceptions and delightful ironic humour.

And whan I saugh he wolde nevere fine
To reden on this cursed book al night,
Al sodeynly thre leves have I plight
Out of his book, right as he radde, and eke
I with my fest so took him on the cheke,
That in oure fyr he fil bakward adoun.
And he up stirte as dooth a wood leoun,
And with his fest he smoot me on the heed,
That in the floor I lay as I were deed.
And whan he saugh how stille that I lay
He was agast, and wolde han fled his way,
Till atte laste out of my swogh I breyde,
'O, hastow slain me false theef?' I seyde,
'And for my land thus hastow mordred me?
Er I be deed, yet wol I kisse thee.'
And neer he cam, and kneled faire adoun,
And seyde, 'Deere suster Alisoun,
As help me God! I shal thee nevere smite.

fine = finish

plight = pulled out

wood = mad

my swogh I breyde = awoke out of my swoon

▶

wite = blame

eftsoones = immediately after

wreke = revenged

We fille acorded by us selven two = we were reconciled

yaf = gave

of his tonge, and of his hond = what he said and did

brenne = burn

maistrie = victory

soverainetee = supremacy

lust = want

estaat = rank

That I have doon, it is thyself to wite.
Foryeve it me, and that I thee biseke!'
And yet eftsoones I hitte him on the cheke,
And seyde, 'Theef, thus muchel am I wreke;
Now wol I die, I may no lenger speke.'
But atte laste, with muchel care and wo,
We fille acorded by us selven two.
He yaf me al the bridel in myn hond.
To han the governance of hous and lond,
And of his tonge, and of his hond also;
And made him brenne his book anon right tho.
And whan that I hadde geten unto me,
By maistrie, all the soverainetee,
And that he seyde, 'Myn owene trewe wyf,
Do as thee lust the terme of al thy lyf;
Keep thyn honour, and keep eek myn estaat' –
After that day we hadden never debaat.

An extract from Geoffrey Chaucer (born *c.*1343) *The Wife of Bath's Prologue* from *The Canterbury Tales*

TIP

The language of the passage is all-important and the starting-point for your analysis.

ACTIVITY 21.6

Working with a friend from your class, consider the following points, which take you to a detailed consideration of the language, which is all-important in any passage question.

COMMENT

Theme

This passage follows a 70-line or so summary of the book of *wikked wyves* that her husband is reading, which she says has given her *wo* and *pine*. It is the Wife's account of her final argument with Jankin, which results in her achieving dominance over him, so the themes of *maistrie* and *soverainitee* are the climax of the passage. Not long after this, she tells her Tale.

Presentation of events and tone

- The wife is here recounting an incident full of action. How would you describe her tone of voice as she describes the incident? Is there a change when she comes to line 24?
- How is direct speech used to develop the story?

▶

- Do you find any irony in the Wife's account of herself lying on the floor *as I were deed*? (How did she know about Jankin's reaction, for example?)
- Is there any other obvious irony in the passage? (Look at line 35.)
- Can you see any elements of knockabout farce in this account? If so, how are they achieved?

Figures of speech and diction

- Can you find any metaphorical language? What do you conclude from this? (I found one simile and one metaphor. Here's a tip for the metaphor: *He yaf me al the bridel.* What is being compared to what?)
- Are there any descriptive words?
- What do you notice about the diction connected with the action? (e.g. *fest, cheke, stirte, smote*)
- What little word is used repeatedly to advance the action and to introduce parallelism? Consider some of the effects of this.
- Do you find antithesis used for effect in the passage?
- Do you find hyperbole (exaggeration) used for effect in the passage?
- What kind of words are these: *governance, maistrie, soverainetee, honour, estaat*? What effect do these abstract concepts have at the climax of a story of action?

Effects of the verse form and sound effects

- Rhythmically, the extract has a very regular rhythm and rhyme. Consider the effect of this overall, finding some examples to support your point. What can you say about the pace?
- Can you see any examples of alliteration and assonance which link and emphasise particular words and phrases? Are there any onomatopoeic words?

Relating to the Tale as a whole

There are a number of points you could make here:

- The wife has earlier informed the pilgrims *for half so boldely kan ther no man / Swere and lyen, as a woman kan*. We see her here being very devious and manipulative (but on the other hand, Jankin's behaviour is extremely provocative!), accusing Jankin when it was she who started the fight, and then claiming to be on the point of death.
- The total submission at the end of this passage sums up the Wife's desire for dominance and, for that matter, the theme of the Tale which follows. Her comments on *maistrie* and *soverainetee* lead directly into the Tale, which is also linked with this passage by violent action (the rape of the girl).
- The style is lively, bold and amusing, with action and direct speech. There are no examples here of the Wife's quoting of authorities such as the Bible, nor of her descriptions of her previous marriages, which we have seen elsewhere in the *Prologue and Tale*.

TIP

In answering passage questions on Chaucer that involve lengthy *Prologues* as well as Tales, you should always make sure that you refer to both. If the passage is taken from the *Prologue*, don't neglect the *Tale* in your wider comments, and vice versa.

KEY CONCEPTS

The Wife of Bath is an example of imperfect or unreliable narrators, such as we have seen in later prose fiction. There will always be irony in the presentation of such different points of view. If you are studying one of the *Canterbury Tales*, you should try to read the *General Prologue* as well as some other Tales. You will gain a clear sense of Chaucer's concerns and methods. Reading a good modern version can give you a feel for this before you study the original, but remember – it is the original you are studying! Other favourite tales often set as examination texts are *The Franklin's Prologue* and *Tale, The Merchant's Prologue* and *Tale* and *The Nun's Priest's Tale*. *The Knight's Tale* is apparently told by a very upright and noble narrator, but his view of life is a limited one even so.

FURTHER ESSAY QUESTIONS

1. *Write a critical appreciation of the following passage, showing how Chaucer helps to create the Wife's characterisation.*
2. *Looking closely at the effect of the language and tone in the following passage, show how Chaucer makes the Nun's Priest's speech lively and dramatic.*

Writing – two methods

ACTIVITY 21.7

Look closely at the following alternative methods of writing a passage-based answer.

Reflection: The examples here may be on Chaucer texts that you have not studied. Or perhaps you are not studying Chaucer at all! You can still learn from this. The basic principles of essay construction are valid for any poetry text from a longer poem and can be applied.

Essay Plan 1: Use your answers to the bullet point questions in both examples given to make three or four main body paragraphs. Then add another paragraph with further examples of similar features from the *Prologue and Tale* afterwards. Write a suitable introduction and conclusion.

Essay Plan 2: Use your answers to the bullet point questions given to make three or four main paragraphs. Find further examples of your points by ranging more widely in the *Prologue and Tale* and include them at the end of the relevant paragraphs. You have, in this way, shaped the main body of an essay which has both useful textual detail and wider reference. Then write a suitable introduction and conclusion.

FURTHER READING

Collected Poems by Judith Wright are available, published by 4th Estate (2016), but a useful range are on poetry websites. Rossetti's poems are also all available on the internet. Larkin's work is published by Faber and available at www.poetryfoundation.org. You would enjoy a modern English version of *The Canterbury Tales*, such as the one by David Wright (Oxford Paperbacks, 2008).

Self-assessment checklist

Reflect on what you've learnt in this unit and indicate your confidence level between 1 and 5. If you score below 3, revisit that section. Come back to this list later in your course. Has your confidence grown?

	Confidence level	Revisited?
I can quickly identify the characteristics of a passage-based answer		
I am able to analyse and discuss Wright's poems		
I know how to develop an essay from notes		
I have read and can fully appreciate the quality of the essay on Larkin		
I can engage positively with Chaucer's language		

Unit 22
Poetry – close analysis and comparison

Learning objectives

In this unit you will:

- consider the form, tone and meaning of a poem by Andrew Marvell
- research and analyse the extract from Milton's *Paradise Lost*
- engage with the lines by Pope and the commentary on them
- develop and synthesise ideas about three modern poems – Lo, Plath and Senior
- explore poetry comparisons to help refine your close reading skills
- enhance appreciation by contrast.

KEY CONCEPTS

Language, form, structure, genres, context, style, interpretation, critical reading.

Before you start

- Revise the unseen poetry unit (Unit 5) in the first section of the book.
- Review Unit 32 in the third section of this book (Essay Skills and Techniques), entitled unseen comparisons.
- Prepare for the exercises by studying the printed poems carefully. You may like to research the poets before starting.

You have been developing writing skills throughout your course, and you are well-equipped to analyse any poem you have not come across before. If you write it as an essay, what you write should be thoughtful, well-structured and well-illustrated. Don't be so carried away with technical details that you forget to say briefly what the poem is about!

TIP

Each poem creates its own world, which you are visiting and responding to. The focus of all the units in Section 1, also summed up in Unit 20, represent possible areas for you to discuss, but they do not exist equally in every poem. Some poems have many figures of speech, others hardly any. Some are structured around an anecdote (or little story), others are reflective from the beginning. Some build to a climax and have an increasingly fast pace, others are steady throughout, and so on. The more poetry you read and discuss, the more confident you become at analysis.

FURTHER ESSAY QUESTION

Your teacher might give you this wording:

Write a critical appreciation of (or Write a critical commentary on) the following poem, commenting on (or discussing) the poet's methods and concerns.

SECTION A: Older poetry

The Definition of Love by Andrew Marvell

KEY TERM

The Metaphysical poets: this term groups together certain 17th-century poets; Andrew Marvell, John Donne and George Herbert are usually included in the list and often set for examination study. Their work is characterised by intelligence and an energetic style, often using witty, unusual comparisons known as conceits. Their subject matter was often religious, although Donne and Marvell also wrote passionate love poems.

ACTIVITY 22.1

Read the following poem and consider the questions that follow it, which help you to respond to the language in detail.

My love is of a birth as rare
As 'tis for object strange and high;
It was begotten by Despair
Upon Impossibility.

Magnanimous Despair alone
Could show me so divine a thing
Where feeble Hope could ne'er have flown,
But vainly flapp'd its tinsel wing.

And yet I quickly might arrive
Where my extended soul is fixt,
But Fate does iron wedges drive,
And always crowds itself betwixt.

For Fate with jealous eye does see
Two perfect loves, nor lets them close;
Their union would her ruin be,
And her tyrannic pow'r depose.

And therefore her decrees of steel
Us as the distant poles have plac'd,
(Though love's whole world on us doth wheel)
Not by themselves to be embrac'd;

Unless the giddy heaven fall,
And earth some new convulsion tear;
And, us to join, the world should all
Be cramp'd into a planisphere.*

As lines, so loves oblique may well
Themselves in every angle greet;
But ours so truly parallel,
Though infinite, can never meet.
Therefore the love which us doth bind,
But Fate so enviously debars,
Is the conjunction of the mind,
And opposition of the stars.

Andrew Marvell *The Definition of Love* (1621–1678)

*__Planisphere__ = projection of a round object (here the globe) onto a flat surface

Andrew Marvell (1621–1678).

> **Reflection:** Answering these questions will help you to appreciate the way that Marvell's mind works. Look back at all the metaphors used and see what area of life they come from. Many of them take in Fate, the globe, the stars, the abstractions of mathematics. Do you gain any impression of the lover or of his feelings? Have you ever read a love poem with similar patterns of images? Discuss with a classmate.

This is a love poem, but it's a most unusual one that defines love by concentrating on its elevated, even cosmic qualities and the impossibility of reaching any kind of happy physical conclusion to it. The poet idealises his love, using elaborate **conceits** rather similar to those of other **Metaphysical poets** such as John Donne. He emphasises the spiritual qualities of his feelings by using language associated with the globe, the stars and the planets. The abstractions of maths such as parallel lines and angles are also part of the pattern of images. Equally, the love of his lover is also perfect in itself and they are in a kind of opposition of perfection, but unable to meet. *Conjunction* means that they are joined in time and space, but *opposition* means they are facing each other in the heavens. These two words are from astronomy, but they create a kind of paradox.

ACTIVITY 22.2

1. Looking at the first two lines, pick out any individual descriptive words which seem to praise his love highly. Are they physical words or conceptual ones?
2. If something or someone is *begotten* it means 'procreated from'. Who are the two parents?
3. In the second stanza, despair and hope are described. In what way can despair be *Magnanimous* (generous)? This is the opposite of what we normally associate with despair, so what figure of speech is being used and what does it imply? When you are thinking about this, remember that he sees his love as *divine* and *perfect*, and that hope is *feeble* by comparison.
4. What is *tinsel* and where do we usually see it? In what ways is this an appropriate metaphor for hope? What does it imply about the situation of his relationship?
5. He imagines that he could *quickly* [...] *arrive* at where his soul is *extended* towards the object of his love, but Fate makes this impossible. The next three stanzas deal with Fate and its opposition to the union of the lovers.

   What figure of speech is used for Fate? What effect does this have? Find some examples of what Fate does to keep them apart.
6. *Iron wedges, decrees of steel*. What effect do these metallic images have in the poem?
7. What would have to happen for the two lovers to be able to meet in a physical union? Think on a global scale!
8. Now think back to mathematics and parallel lines. What does the metaphor of parallel lines for the lovers say about their relationship? Compare this with another kind of relationship where the lines meet in corners. You could try drawing some parallel lines and some angles to see what they imply visually.
9. *Object, despair, impossibility, hope, soul, Fate, union, decree*... What kind of nouns are these? Do we normally associate them with a love affair?
10. What physical life situation could give rise to such a poem? Discuss the possibilities with a friend.

KEY TERM

Conceit: an extended metaphor, which is often ingenious and sophisticated. A persona is a role adopted by the poet for effect.

KEY CONCEPTS

You can see that some knowledge of basic mathematics as well as simple astronomy would be helpful here. The Metaphysical poets are always very knowledgeable, often using imagery from science and geography to illuminate their work.

Working with longer poems

At Advanced Level, poets are sometimes set for study whose work includes longer poems. Alexander Pope's *Rape of the Lock* is an example. If you had studied Keats, you would know that in your selection there are longer works such as *The Eve of St Agnes* or *Lamia*. If you are now studying Milton, you will be aware that *Paradise Lost* is a very long poem in 12 books, only two of which are ever set for examination study. Sometimes longer poems are narratives: that is, they tell a story, and you can consider the structure and development of such a poem as if it were a short story in verse. However, you should not neglect poetic effects such as figures of speech and poetic form, which are just as important as in shorter poems. A longer work will allow the poet to develop approaches to her/his material for which more space is required, such as satire or more developed characterisation.

Paradise Lost by John Milton

ACTIVITY 22.3

Read the following lines and be prepared to do some research! John Milton (1608–1674) is one of the great poetic figures of his age.

Of Man's first disobedience, and the fruit
Of that forbidden tree whose mortal taste
Brought death into the World, and all our woe,
With loss of Eden, till one greater Man
Restore us, and regain the blissful seat,
Sing, Heavenly Muse, that, on the secret top
Of Oreb, or of Sinai, didst inspire
That shepherd who first taught the chosen seed
In the beginning how the heavens and earth
Rose out of Chaos: or, if Sion hill
Delight thee more, and Siloa's brook that flowed
Fast by the oracle of God, I thence
Invoke thy aid to my adventurous song,
That with no middle flight intends to soar
Above th' Aonian mount, while it pursues
Things unattempted yet in prose or rhyme.
And chiefly thou, O Spirit, that dost prefer
Before all temples th' upright heart and pure,
Instruct me, for thou know'st; thou from the first
Wast present, and, with mighty wings outspread,
Dove-like sat'st brooding on the vast Abyss,
And mad'st it pregnant: what in me is dark
Illumine, what is low raise and support;
That, to the height of this great argument,
I may assert Eternal Providence,
And justify the ways of God to men.

John Milton, *Paradise Lost* (Lines 1–26) (1667)

John Milton (1608–1674).

These lines are the first 26 lines of Book 1 of Milton's great epic poem *Paradise Lost*, parts of which are often set for study at the Advanced Level. It is typical of Milton's distinctive concerns and methods in various ways. Studying Milton does involve having a sense of the context in which he planned and wrote his great work.

First of all, Milton wanted to write an epic poem in the classical style, following the example of the Greek poet Homer who wrote the *Iliad* and the *Odyssey* in about 800 BCE and Vergil, the Roman poet who wrote the *Aeneid* in the 1st century CE. Other writers had done this, for example Italian Dante's *Divine Comedy* (written in the 14th century) and Englishman Spenser's *The Faerie Queen* in 1590. However, the Italian poet Ariosto, with his *Orlando Furioso* of 1532, was probably the most influential for Milton. He wrote a long narrative poem which copied classical style and language, and Milton tried to do the same.

However, Milton's work was also to be like the Bible: using the myths of Adam and Eve and Satan and the loss of Paradise (thus the title of the poem). Using classical style, language and references, he Christianises the characters so that the whole is a complex mingling of myth, epic and religious faith. You will have to look up classical references to make sense of the poem if you are studying it.

Additionally, because he wants the poem to feel classical, he tries to make his English like Latin, changing the order of words (deviation – a feature we looked at in Unit 2), and creating long and complex sentences. We have to subdivide these sentences into manageable parts or clauses to understand what he is saying. However, once you are used to it, it becomes easier!

ACTIVITY 22.4

Look closely at the poem and answer the following questions as far as you can, working with your classmate. You will need to look up all the references such as Siloa and Sinai (some are biblical and others classical).

1. How long is the first sentence?
2. Can you see where the first six lines are leading from a grammatical point of view? (Beginning with 'of' seems unusual).
3. Who is the *one greater man*? If you don't know the Bible story of the Garden of Eden and how Christianity relates to it, you will need to look it up.
4. What is a Muse? Why is she important? What does it imply that she is called *Heavenly*?
5. Find as many inversions as you can and turn them into natural speech order. Remember this is for effective poetic emphasis; *that with no middle flight intends to soar* would be 'intends to soar with no middle flight'. This also incorporates a litotes ('no middle flight' actually means a really high flight).

SAMPLE RESPONSE

1 16 lines long! A good introduction to a Miltonic sentence.

2 This is an inversion with the main clause as 'Sing heavenly muse' in line 6 – an instruction which would read 'O Heavenly Muse, sing of Man's disobedience…' in normal word order. It is an imitation of the opening of Homer's classical poem the *Iliad*.

3 This is a reference to Jesus Christ, whose death on the cross was supposed to cancel out the sin committed by Adam and Eve in the Garden of Eden.

4 A Muse was, in Greek mythology, a goddess who inspired humans in artistic ventures. Milton wants to make it clear that she is *Heavenly*; in other words, inspiring him like the Bible's writing was inspired, so he is combining the Christian and the Classical.

5 Apart from the example and the very first sentence, you might have found: *if Sion hill / Delight thee more; upright heart and pure; with mighty wings outspread, Dove-like sat'st brooding* (there are two here); *what in me is dark / Illumine, what is low raise and support*.

Reflection: What do you think of Milton's aim here – *to justify the ways of God to men?* Do you think it's admirable, or somewhat arrogant? Don't forget, he is calling on the Muse to help him (this is known as the 'invocation'), so he is aware of what a great undertaking it's going to be.

These questions on this relatively short passage from the poem give you a sense of Milton's style and concerns, leaving aside his use of very regular iambic pentameter.

Epistle to Mrs Teresa Blount by Alexander Pope

ACTIVITY 22.5

Read the following extract from *Epistle to Mrs Teresa Blount* by Alexander Pope and analyse it by discussing it with your friend. The language is not as difficult as Milton's and you won't need to look up any classical or biblical references! Then read the sample response for some other ideas on the poem.

Note: Mrs Teresa Blount was a friend of Alexander Pope's who was returning to the country after being in London for the funeral of George I in 1714.

She went to plain-work, and to purling brooks,
Old-fashion'd halls, dull aunts, and croaking rooks:
She went from op'ra, park, assembly, play,
To morning walks, and pray'rs three hours a day:
To part her time 'twixt reading and bohea,[1]
To muse, and spill her solitary tea;
Or o'er cold coffee trifle with the spoon,
Count the slow clock, and dine exact at noon;
Divert her eyes with pictures in the fire,
Hum half a tune, tell stories to the 'squire;
Up to her godly garret after sev'n,
There starve and pray, for that's the way to heav'n.

Alexander Pope (1688–1744).

(buss = kiss)

Some 'squire, perhaps, you take delight to rack;
Whose game is whisk, whose treat a toast in sack;
Who visits with a gun, presents you birds,
Then gives a smacking buss, and cries – 'No words';
Or with his hounds comes hallooing from the stable,
Makes love with nods, and knees beneath a table;
Whose laughs are hearty, though his jests are coarse,
And loves you best of all things – but his horse.

An extract from *Epistle to Mrs Teresa Blount* by Alexander Pope (1688–1744)

[1] **Bohea** is a kind of strong tea. Both it and *tea* were pronounced with an 'ay' sound: 'bohay' and 'tay' in Pope's day.

SAMPLE RESPONSE

Pope evidently feels his friend is going to be very bored now that she has left London, and throughout the poem, he offers the contrasts of town and country in an amusing way. He doesn't appear in the poem himself; these are his observations. The first part of the extract is in the third person 'she', but he moves to 'you' a little later on when he comes to matters of relationships.

Although there are some words which have a specific 18th-century meaning, the diction is not difficult to understand. *Plain-work* means ordinary sewing rather than fancy embroidery, and the only *purling*, a word associated in a pun with knitting (plain and purl), is in the little rivers of the countryside, 'flowing' being the other meaning of the word. Immediately the plainness and lack of sophistication of the countryside is established. The places and people are *old-fashioned* and *dull*. Birds are *croaking* in the countryside, but this implies by association that the people speak rather harshly too (an implied transferred epithet). This transference is seen elsewhere too: her tea is *solitary*, her coffee *cold*, just as she is in the country – without good company to cheer her and warm her up. The clock seems to be *slow* because the time moves so boringly, and she has her meals earlier than they would be in fashionable London.

Pope uses lists very effectively to paint both the fun of London life: *op'ra, park, assembly, play*, and its antithesis, the sheer boredom of the country: *morning walks, and pray'rs three hours a day*. Later on, it will be: *Up to her godly garret after sev'n / There starve and pray, for that's the way to heav'n*. When Pope progresses to the subject of her love life, moving into the second person, he paints a picture of the country squire, coarse and loud: *Who visits with a gun, presents you birds* (nothing like flowers or delicate gifts, but dead birds that he's just shot!), plays cards (*whisk*) for a treat and actually prefers *his horse* to *you*.

▶

You can't have a conversation with such a man: *No words*. Country life is thus satirised by Pope, making fun of its dull routines, its little events, its boring and uncultured characters.

The light and amusing tone of the poem is promoted by its lines having a very regular metrical scheme of iambic pentameter and an aabb rhyme that creates a complete idea in each couplet, neatly rounded off (heroic couplets, a favourite form of Pope's). In addition to this, the lines are often balanced with a central caesura, giving balance and symmetry. The pace is steady throughout. The antithesis of town and country is thus offered in a manner reasonable and witty, polished and elegant, with rhymes that clinch each point aptly and reinforce the humour (such as *coarse* and *horse*). In a sense, the elegant, balanced form represents perfectly the civilised, cultured city life which Pope evidently prefers.

KEY TERMS

Augustan: the name given to a style of literature written in the period between around 1690 and 1744 (the year Alexander Pope died). Writers imitated classical models and emphasised order and rationality. It is sometimes referred to as the Neo-classical Age.

Satire: a genre in which the follies, vices and shortcomings of humankind are held up to ridicule. Satire criticises society and individuals, using wit and irony to point the criticism. It can vary from vicious attack to gentle, humorous disapproval.

KEY CONCEPTS

If you wanted to comment on the literary context of the poem, you would be able to point to 18th-century **Augustanism** very readily from the evidence of this poem. There are no Romantic flights of fancy or passionate loves and hates. The lady *diverts her eyes with pictures in the fire*, but they are not too stirring, just pictures rather than thoughts or feelings, and her religion seems more a matter of going through the motions than any kind of passionate commitment. All is orderly and under control, just like the verse.

If you have read T.S. Eliot's poem *The Love Song of J. Alfred Prufrock*, you might have remembered *I have measured out my life with coffee spoons*. Perhaps Eliot had these lines of Pope in mind, although the poem is a very different one in theme and tone!

Reflection: At this point in the book, you've looked at works by Chaucer, by Shakespeare, by Donne, Milton and Pope, Keats and Wordsworth and by the Victorian poet Rossetti. Do you find these older works particularly difficult? Which poets are you studying in detail? Discuss with a friend whether you prefer the older poets or more modern and contemporary works (which are not always simple in any case!) Examples of these follow in the next section.

SECTION B: Modern poetry

This section concentrates on more modern poems. Because all the older works are by British men, I have chosen three poems written by women: one Chinese/Malaysian, one American and one Caribbean. The forms used are less regular in each case.

The Letter by Miriam Lo

How it sits in his hands.
'Who's it from?'
Her son looks away.
'Susan.'

▶

Su-san. A girl's name.
An Australian girl is writing to her son.
The coffeeshop patrons grow quiet.
Fat sizzles in the restaurant's woks, upstairs.
Traffic roars round the corner.

Questions,
as if he is suddenly a stranger,
as if he has come from a far-away place,
sat down in strange clothes, demanding a coffee.

Someone strange *has* come in and sat down in their coffeeshop.
There! Her breath in the words of the letter.
A glimpse of the handwriting—
round, neat letters.
A faint outline of a person is starting to form.

His mother thinks of how words
flow out of a body and carry the ghost
of fingers, a face, a heart.
She thinks of the words that have etched themselves
on the walls of her life: *I surrender,*
We are at war; the words that weigh heavily
on her tongue as she stands and watches
the face of her son: *I love you, Come home.*
Come Home.

But she cannot hold him, how quickly he slips from her gaze
to those words on the page
that are taking him away,
to a place she has no name for.

Miriam Lo *The Letter* (2004)

KEY CONCEPTS

This is a poem about family love and close relationships, a context that many of us share. Poems do not have to be about historical events to have a context, although here a past war is implied, as part of the mother's experience.

KEY TERM

Free verse: does not have a regular metrical or rhyme scheme, but linking devices such as repetition, parallelism and the careful use of very short lines, enjambments, direct speech and sound effects make it as careful a construct as a rhymed iambic pentameter. Make sure that you don't muddle 'free verse' with 'blank verse', which is regular iambic pentameter unrhymed.

At first sight, this is a very different poem from those by Donne, Milton and Pope. It is written in **free verse** (see the Key Terms box for a reminder of what to look out for).

ACTIVITY 22.6

Read the poem carefully several times. Refer to the checklist for poetry in Unit 5, Figure 5.1, or Unit 31 and then make notes for your response to the poem, using the following table to help you. (Revise all the poetry units in Part 1 of this book if you need to!) You could work on this with a classmate.

	Points to consider	Your response
Subject and situation It is always useful to ask yourself these basic questions to help you to enter the little world created in the poem.	• Who is the voice of the poem and what is she doing? • What other characters are there? What are they doing? Are they named? • Where is the poem set? Are there any other settings and, if so, where are they? • Look at the time frame – is it all contemporary? (Remember that memory can be very important.)	Start to think of the *effect* of these elements of the poem as you pick out your examples.
Structure Because this is free verse, considering the structure from the very beginning will give you the framework of the poem.	• How many stanzas? What are the different stages of the poem, represented in these stanzas? • Find examples of short lines, enjambments, repetitions or parallelism, direct speech.	It's worth being meticulous about this – how many times is the word *strange* used, for example, or the word *name*, and with what effect?
Imagery and figures of speech	• There are not many metaphors in the poem, although there is a significant one in stanza 5. • *Her breath in the words of the letter* – do you remember what figure of speech this is (one thing compared with another closely connected with it)? • Irony – in what ways is the poem ironic? • Sense images: find examples of sight, sound, touch – how do they help to create the setting?	

(*Continued*)

(*Continued*)

	Points to consider	Your response
Diction	• Look at simple pronouns – is it a first-person or third-person poem? Is it entirely focalized on the speaker? • Is it in the past or the present tense? • How many words can you find that are 'body' words (e.g. *face*, *hands*?) • Consider the effect of some of the repeated words: *away*, *far away*, *strange*, *stranger*, *words*. • What is the effect of some of the other words (e.g. *demanding* a coffee?)	Remember the *effects* of all your observations.
Versification: rhythm, rhyme, sound effects	Don't neglect these because it is free verse. There is some extremely effective use of alliteration and assonance in this poem, which links words in meaning as well as sound. • Look closely at the last nine lines of the poem. Find one example of alliteration and one of assonance. • Can you find other instances of these effects in the poem? Is there any onomatopoeia? • Find some examples of particular emphasis in the rhythm of the words.	
Tone and atmosphere	• The poem is not in the first person, but it is focalized on the mother's thoughts and feelings. What words could you use to describe the tone of the poem? • Atmosphere? How would you characterise this?	
Theme	This is a poem about a mother whose grown-up son is in a relationship with a woman from another culture, another country. She knows that she cannot keep him, and that the words of the letter in his hands are drawing him away from her. It is also a poem about the power of words and their effects in our lives – they are what we use to think and to talk.	
Where do your sympathies lie?	How does the poet help you to empathise with the mother in this poem? What aspects of the poem do you find particularly effective in evoking your sympathies?	You might consider her own past life which has been very hard, with experience of war (emphasised by alliteration of the 'w' sound); her sense of loss (emphasised by the final pattern of assonance of *gaze*, *page*, *taking away*, *place*, *name*), her imaginative recreation of the girl from the shape of her words on the page.

Bringing it all together: The detailed points you've found, expressed in the table, can be combined in any order and referred to briefly. However, you need a general introduction before you plunge into the detail.

- You could comment on the central figure of the mother and how sensitively her feelings are expressed and evoked – very delicately, it seems to me.
- You could pick out the obvious theme of loss, of grown-up children leaving home and making their own way with their chosen partners, who may be from other cultures and other countries.
- An interesting structural approach would be to focus on the way the poem begins and ends on a similar but contrasting note: with the name *Susan* (or *Su-san* – neatly encapsulating another culture) and ends with *no name*; equally, it also begins with what the son holds in his hands and ends with what the mother cannot hold – him. This makes the poem's structure cohesive.
- The theme of **words** and the way they make things and people real is very imaginative, especially in the lines which suggest the shape of the letters gradually forming the person who wrote them: *words / flow out of a body and carry the ghost / of fingers, a face, a heart.* These are particularly rhythmical lines, too.

Reflection: This poem is written in the third person, as if the poet is telling an intimate story about two people well-known to her. Consider whether it would be more effective if written in the first person, with the 'I' of the poem as the mother; or, conversely, the son. Discuss with your friend the different effects that might develop in each case. You might even try writing the new poem!

Private Ground by Sylvia Plath

ACTIVITY 22.7

Read and analyse the following poem. Using the guidelines suggested in the left-hand column of the table in Activity 22.6, see what you can make of this poem, which follows the actions of the persona as she walks around the large estate of the person to whom the poem is partly addressed at the beginning, the 'you' of the poem.

First frost, and I walk among the rose-fruit, the marble toes
Of the Greek beauties you brought
Off Europe's relic heap
To sweeten your neck of the New York woods.
Soon each white lady will be boarded up
Against the cracking climate.
All morning, with smoking breath, the handyman
Has been draining the goldfish ponds.
They collapse like lungs, the escaped water
Threading back, filament by filament, to the pure
Platonic table where it lives. The baby carp
Litter the mud like orangepeel.
Eleven weeks, and I know your estate so well
I need hardly go out at all.
A superhighway seals me off.

Platonic: (second stanza) perfect, ideal.

Trading their poisons, the north and south bound cars
Flatten the doped snakes to ribbon. In here, the grasses
Unload their griefs on my shoes,

The woods creak and ache, and the day forgets itself.
I bend over this drained basin where the small fish
Flex as the mud freezes.
They glitter like eyes, and I collect them all.
Morgue of old logs and old images, the lake
Opens and shuts, accepting them among
its reflections.

Sylvia Plath *Private Ground* (1959)

SAMPLE RESPONSE

The situation of the persona seems to be that she is alone on a grand estate owned by someone who is not there, or if he is, is not around in a meaningful way. She knows the estate well and has been there for 11 weeks, apparently without leaving it: *I know your estate so well / I need hardly go out at all* (rather an odd comment – do we take walks in order to get to know the details of our surroundings, or to enjoy being out in the fresh air?), but evidently she has taken a lot of walks and knows the whole estate well. She is *seal*[ed] *off* from the outside by a *superhighway*. The estate seems to be being shut up for the winter – the marble statues are being boarded up so that they are not spoilt by frost, and the goldfish ponds are being drained for the same reason. (The water escapes down into some 'perfect' place below the surface.) The handyman doesn't seem bothered about the death of the goldfish and the persona picks them up and puts them into the lake. The action of the walk seems to cover a whole day, as the handyman is working *all morning* and by the time she gets to the lake, *the day forgets itself*, suggesting evening drawing in. Her attitude to the owner/s of the estate is negative: they are rich if they can buy marble statues *Off Europe's relic heap/To sweeten* [their] *neck of the New York woods. Neck of the woods* is an informal expression meaning 'your neighbourhood', but it also implies the size of the estate, with its lake and ponds, its statues and woodland. It gives a sardonic tone to the first stanza, implying criticism. They haven't given instructions to the handyman to save the lives of the fish – the latter are expendable, not being worth a lot of money like the *Greek beauties*. The persona's action may save them, but perhaps they are already dead, as the lake is compared metaphorically with a morgue, a place for dead bodies. ▶

How do the images in this poem relate to the persona and the little anecdote we have been given? The poem is called *Private Ground*, which suggests a place which is not public, an estate which belongs to someone. However, by implication, it also suggests one's own mind, a private place where no-one else comes. This may be about the persona's own *private ground*. There is no-one else mentioned in the poem other than the *handyman*, an anonymous worker, and indirectly the *you*, the owner of the estate, or owners. But all the other objects in the poem could have relevance to the persona: the *Greek beauties* – the *white ladies* who are there to enhance the environment; the fish – pretty ornaments for the summer but now finished, now *litter … like orangepeel*; the doped snakes killed on the roads outside the estate. These are disturbing images, suggesting by implication her own suppression, her own expendability. The imagery and diction in the poem contain many images of smothering or stifling: the statues (personified as animate) are *boarded up*; the ponds *collapse like lungs* (a horrible image of breathing being stifled – healthy lungs are not supposed to collapse); she is *seal*[ed] *off*; the lake is a *morgue*, opening and shutting to accept bodies. (It is contrasted with the pond water, which escapes back into the *pure* realm below the ground.) The day *forgets itself,* like an old person with dementia, its clarity and rationality smothered. She is part of this environment, no longer a going concern, but all being shut up and suffocated. Critic Anne Stevenson speaks of *the surreal landscape of the imprisoned psyche* and this observation is borne out in the poem. The fish, which *glitter like eyes*, perhaps suggests a fear of being watched. From this we can deduce that this stay of 11 weeks has not been a positive experience for her, although she shows us this rather than tells us.

The mood of the poem is sombre because of these images and the calm reflective tone of the persona. There are moments of colour – the orange of the fish, for example – but the evocative sound effects of the alliteration *cracking climate*, the *grasses unload their griefs on my shoes*, the *woods creak and ache* all add to a disturbingly negative poem. Her action with the fish could be seen as an attempt to do something positive, or it could be her confirming the death of the fish and laying them to rest in a suitable place, the lake which has seen everything, *morgue of old logs and old images*, the ambiguity of *reflections* meaning 'thoughts' as well as 'light'.

I find this poem very memorable: the imagery is so precise and evocative, the mood so subtly negative. If you didn't know who the poet was, you could gain all of this from the words and images used.

KEY CONCEPTS

If you know some of the biography of the poet, Sylvia Plath, then you might also see suicidal images here in the sense of entrapment, loss of life and the suppression of beauty and warmth. However, biographical contexts must be used very sparingly or they become merely speculative. Plath wrote this while she was staying at a writers' retreat named Yaddo in the USA, which wealthy benefactors had endowed; there were also plenty of other people around. Your contextual 'knowledge' here could be very misleading – her poetic imagination creates a quite different effect from what she actually knew and saw around her.

Another way of looking at the poem – environmental concerns

With its images of the *superhighway*, the *doped snakes*, the careless destruction of the fish, the *griefs* of the grass, you could see this as an environmentally concerned poem.

ACTIVITY 22.8

Try to develop an essay on this poem with an emphasis on the destructiveness of human activity. Do you find it as convincing as the former interpretation? Could you incorporate a paragraph on it into the previous essay?

TIP

Beginning with an anecdote and then moving outward into more philosophical speculation is a common poetic strategy. Philip Larkin is a case in point, with *The Whitsun Weddings* and *Dockery and Son*, for example. Elizabeth Bishop writes similarly. Plath does not draw specific conclusions: she allows the poem to close around itself like the lake, reflecting and suggesting, remaining in our minds.

ACTIVITY 22.9

Read the following poem by Caribbean poet Olive Senior in which she reflects on her ancestry in the country. She has left home and gone to live in an urban environment, but she still feels the pull of her past.

I

My ancestors are nearer
than albums of pictures
I tread on heels thrust
into broken-down slippers

II

My mother's womb impulsed
harvests perpetually. She
deeply breathed country air
when she laboured me.

III

The pattern woven by my
father's hands lulled me
to sleep. Certain actions
moved me so: my father
planting.

▶

When my father planted
his thoughts took flight.
He did not need to think.
The ritual was ingrained
in the bold, embedded
in the centuries of dirt
beneath his fingernails
encased in the memories
of his race.

(Yet the whiplash of my
father's wrath rever-
berated days in my
mind with the inten-
sity of tuning forks.
He did not think.
My mother stunned wept
and prayed Father
Forgive Them knowing not
what she prayed for.)
One day I did not pray.
A gloss of sunlight through
the leaves betrayed me so
abstracted me from rituals.
And discarded prayers and
disproven myths
confirmed me freedom.

IV
Now against the rhythms
of subway trains my
heartbeats still drum
worksongs. Some wheels

▶

sing freedom, the others:
home.

Still, if I could balance
water on my head I can
juggle worlds
on my shoulders.

Olive Senior *Ancestral Poem* (1986)

ACTIVITY 22.10

Using what you have learnt about working with unseen poems, make notes on this poem ready to transform them into an essay response. Some hints for you to discuss with a partner:

- Look at the contrast between the past and present.
- What does she have to say about her parents?
- Why is a section of the poem in brackets? Think about the effect of this.
- How does the last stanza sum up her conflicted feelings?
- What can you say about the effect of the arrangement of lines, enjambments and words split across lines?

SECTION C: Comparison of two unseen poems

Exercises which ask you to compare two unseen poems seem demanding. However, the big advantage for you is that each poem helps you to understand the other, and in looking for points of comparison and contrast, you discover elements in both poems that you perhaps would not have noticed. Pairing two poems suggests that they have something in common – the subject matter, the theme, perhaps some language elements. When you're planning your essay, you'll be looking for these. You may not have any comparison exercises in your exam. But even so, these exercises are very good for sharpening your critical skills.

FURTHER ESSAY QUESTION

Typical essay wording is as follows:

Compare and contrast the two following poems, with occasionally a clue as to subject matter (such as 'and their presentation of lost love') *or style* ('paying particular attention to their use of imagery').

Read each poem carefully several times. Note any interesting words or phrases and underline any obvious figures of speech as you go. Before considering how to structure an essay of this kind, let's look at a couple of poems and see how they relate to each other.

Remember, you are looking for connections: do the poets use the same word or image? Do they have any similarities in their structure? Don't forget you are also looking for contrast. Are they pursuing the same sort of idea but expressing it differently? Is the speaker's tone completely different? Do the words in the poems create distinctive atmospheres which are entirely unlike each other? What effects do these have?

Poem comparison 1

ACTIVITY 22.11

Read and analyse. Have a look at the following pair of poems.

Essay: *Compare the two following poems, Poem A, Villanelle, by William Empson (1906–1984) and Poem B, Grief, by Carol Ann Duffy (1955–).*

Poem A

It is the pain, it is the pain endures.
Your chemic beauty burned my muscles through.
Poise of my hands reminded me of yours.

What later purge from this deep toxin cures?
What kindness now could the old salve renew?
It is the pain, it is the pain endures.
The infection slept (custom or change inures)
And when pain's secondary phase was due
Poise of my hands reminded me of yours.

How safe I felt, whom memory assures,
Rich that your grace safely by heart I knew.
It is the pain, it is the pain endures.

My stare drank deep beauty that still allures.
My heart pumps yet the poison draught of you.
Poise of my hands reminded me of yours.

You are still kind whom the same shape immures.
Kind and beyond adieu. We miss our cue.
It is the pain, it is the pain endures.
Poise of my hands reminded me of yours.

William Empson *Villanelle* (1935)

poise = balance, stability

inures = becomes accustomed to pain

immures = shuts in

Poem B

Grief, your gift, unwrapped,
my empty hands made heavy,

▶

holding when they held you
like an ache; unlooked for,
though my eyes stare inward now
at where you were, my star, my star;
and undeserved, the perfect choice
for one with everything, humbling
my heart; unwanted, too, my small voice
lost for words to thank you with; unusual,
how it, given, grows to fill a day, a night,
a week, a month, teaching its text,
love's spinster twin, my head bowed,
learning, learning; understood.

Carol Ann Duffy *Grief* (2005)

SAMPLE RESPONSE

Poem A

The speaker in this poem is speaking of his painful feelings of loss at the end of a relationship. The poem is addressed to 'you', the ex-lover, who is still beautiful, but now distant, *kind* but no longer loving. The relationship hasn't lasted but the pain has. He uses an extended metaphor of his love for her as like an *infection* – an illness which is in his blood and cannot be cured. In fact, so powerful is it that it is like a *poison draught*, a *toxin*. Every time his heart beats it is sending the poison around his body. Coupled with this extended metaphor is the poet's use of the villanelle form, which involves a great deal of repetition.

Here the villanelle's repetitions are insistent and inescapable. They convey well the obsessive mental suffering, the heartache and the tyranny of memories, the ache of loss. But the poem also stresses the physical throughout: the balance or positioning of his own hands which remind him of hers all the time, because they were so physically close; his muscles, burnt by her poisonous beauty, his heart beating, her physical appearance which is just the same on the outside – but she is no longer the same inside. The circular form suggests the confinement of his situation.

Any more tricky aspects here are probably ones of vocabulary, although you could guess from the context what a word like *immures* means.

Poem B

Poem B is also a poem about loss and 'grief', as we see from its title. The poem is also addressed to 'you' the ex-lover, and also has an extended metaphor running through, signalled in the first line: *Grief, your gift*. We expect a gift to be a delightful present, which gives pleasure on a special occasion – here it is an unwanted, wretched thing: the poet wanted the relationship to continue and all she has left is the pain of parting. The poem deserves close, careful reading, particularly in its

▶

sentence structure, which is probably the most demanding aspect of the poem's meaning. You'll see that it's all one sentence, separated by semi-colons. Semi-colons are almost full stops, but not quite, giving the sense of a relationship which is almost over, but not quite for the voice of the poem. Running through the lines like a refrain is the prefix *un*: *unwrapped*, *unlooked for*, *undeserved*, *unwanted*, *unusual*; all negatives, the opposite of all those positive feelings – wanted, deserved, usual – which we would like in our relationships. Once the grief is *unwrapped* and faced in the open, all the negative aspects of the situation crowd in – it was unexpected, *unlooked for*, *undeserved* (the poet worshipped the lover); *unwanted* certainly. But it is *unusual* too, not like a normal gift because it keeps growing and fills the days and weeks, teaching the persona left behind the terrible lessons of loss, which are finally *understood*. The final line with its *understood* links with all the other negatives now – 'to understand' is to realise the relationship is over, it's now an 'un-relationship'. The gift has become a lesson to be learnt, a grim metaphor, where grief has to be learnt again and again (like one's mathematical tables or spellings list). The fact that it is all in one sentence of 14 lines (but nothing like a love sonnet) makes the loss seem inescapable, the negatives cannot be avoided – they crowd in at regular intervals leaving the persona with *head bowed*. The persona's physical self runs through the poem too: *my hands*, *my eyes*, *my heart*, *my small voice*, culminating in *my head*.

The challenge here is reading the poem really carefully and noticing the structural links which bind the lines together.

Bringing the ideas together

If you were to jot down some similarities and differences between the poems using the headings for the rows in the table in Activity 22.6, you would come up with the following:

The voice is first person ('I') addressing a former lover ('you') in both poems. A sense of loss and grief runs through both poems, constantly thinking of the loved one. Both poems are about a lover rejected and the pain they feel.

Both poems use extended metaphor – infection and poison in Poem A, a gift and a lesson in Poem B. Both refer to parts of the body and are very physical, focused more on the speaker than the lover, although not exclusively. Both poems focus on the hands, which are more significant in Poem A, as the speaker's hands, so well-known to him, remind him constantly of her hands which used to be with his and are now gone. In Poem B, the hands are now empty of the lover, but heavy with the grief of 'the gift'.

Poem A is in the highly structured old form of the **villanelle**, following its strict rules to create a sense of inescapable obsession. Poem B seems an unstructured paragraph, but looked at more closely has the *un* prefix, the negative running through the poem, as well as the repetition of the speaker's physical parts: *my hands*, *my voice*, and so on.

The tone of each poem is one of a kind of obsessive sadness, a continuous reflection of innermost feelings of hurt and loss with an atmosphere of grief. You may feel that the voice of Poem B is more focused on herself, although she does call her lover *my star*. Poem A's voice is still much affected by the *beauty* and *grace* of his lover and is generous enough to say she is still *kind* to him.

KEY TERMS

Villanelle: an old medieval form, with five stanzas of three lines followed by a quatrain. The rhymes are interwoven and there are only two of them throughout. The first and third lines of the first stanza are repeated as refrains at the end of each of the following stanzas alternately and then together in the final quatrain. If you don't know the name for this form, it doesn't matter, as long as you identify the repetition and the limited rhyme scheme and the effects they have.

Incremental repetition: the name given to an effect of repeated lines recurring again and again, as here. Ballads often have repeated lines of this kind. *Incremental* means 'adding' and 'adding to the effect'.

Reflection: Do you see any evidence that the personae of the poems are of different genders? Discuss with your partner or group, paying particular attention to details of language which could lead you to this conclusion.

ACTIVITY 22.12

Now go to Part 3, Units 31 and 32, of this book and look at the two possible methods for structuring and then writing your comparison. Try writing the comparison as an essay.

FURTHER READING

Here is another poem about lost love by Liz Lochhead, with a different tone. She uses the image of a bottle of shampoo, bought on a Spanish holiday, now finished, to symbolise the loss of her lover.

Today saw the last of my Spanish shampoo.
Lasted an age now that sharing with you,
such a thing of the past is.
Giant size. The brand
was always a compromise.
My new one's tailored exactly to my needs.
Nonspill. Protein-rich.
Feeds body, promises to solve my problem hair.
Sweetheart, these days it's hard to care,
But oh oh insomniac moonlight
how unhoneyed is my middle of the night.
I could see you
far enough. Beyond me
how we'll get back together.
Campsites in Spain, moonlight,
heavy weather.
Today saw the end of my Spanish shampoo,
the end of my third month without you.

Liz Lochhead *The Empty Song* (2011)

COMMENT

The tone here is an attempt at first to be light-hearted. A giant-sized bottle was always a sign of hope that it would be shared, but it hasn't worked out. She tries to console herself with the new bottle: no more compromise; it's perfect for her alone, *tailored exactly to my needs*; *promises to solve my problem hair*. But her bravado breaks down half way: *Sweetheart, these days it's hard to care* about the state of her appearance, now that he's gone. She misses him in the middle of the night and imagines getting back together: *campsites in Spain, moonlight*. But the *heavy weather* was an ominous sign, and now he's gone. The form of the poem is apparently free, but there are rhymes and half-rhymes, and the poem begins and ends with

COMMENT

a near-exact repetitive couplet. Writing about the tone of this poem is, in some ways, more complicated than either of the previous ones, as her attempts to be jokey are undercut by her sadness coming in. The language here is also complex in another way, typical of much contemporary poetry in its **inter-textuality**.

Lochhead, first of all, employs the language of advertising when she describes the effects of the shampoo: *Giant size*; *nonspill*; *protein-rich*; *feeds body*; *solve … problem hair.* These are use ironically to suggest the advantages she will now enjoy that she is on her own without the compromise of a partner. *How unhoneyed is my middle of the night* is a reference to the poem by John Keats, *The Eve of St Agnes*, where the *honey'd middle of the night* is the time for the lovers Porphyro and Madeleine to meet, before they run away. I can see some phrases which have an atmosphere of song lyrics too: *heavy weather*; *back together.* These references are enriching, linking the experience of the poem to those suffered by other people, although there is irony in them. Was her affair really like the classical lovers in *The Eve of St Agnes*? Well, it does feel like it to you if you're the one suffering.

KEY TERM

Inter-textuality: is the shaping of a text meaning by another text. The older word for a similar language effect is allusion.

Poem comparison 2

ACTIVITY 22.13

Read and analyse. Have a look at the following pair of poems, on a completely different subject.

Essay: *Compare and contrast the two following poems: Poem A The Shell by James Stephens (1882–1950) and Poem B Relic by Ted Hughes (1930–1988).*

Poem A

And then I pressed the shell
Close to my ear
And listened well,
And straightaway like a bell
Came low and clear
The slow, sad murmur of the far distant seas,
Whipped by an icy breeze
Upon a shore
Wind-swept and desolate.
It was a sunless strand that never bore
The footprint of a man,
Nor felt the weight
Since time began
Of any human quality or stir
Save what the dreary winds and waves incur.
And in the hush of waters was the sound

▶

Of pebbles rolling round,
For ever rolling with a hollow sound.
And bubbling sea-weeds as the waters go
Swish to and fro
Their long, cold tentacles of slimy grey.
There was no day,
Nor ever came a night
Setting the stars alight
To wonder at the moon:
Was twilight only and the frightened croon,
Smitten to whimpers, of the dreary wind
And waves that journeyed blind—
And then I loosed my ear … O, it was sweet
To hear a cart go jolting down the street.

James Stephens *The Shell* (1909)

Poem B

I found this jawbone at the sea's edge:
There, crabs, dogfish, broken by the breakers or tossed
To flap for half an hour and turn to a crust
Continue the beginning. The deeps are cold:
In that darkness camaraderie does not hold:
Nothing touches but, clutching, devours. And the jaws,
Before they are satisfied or their stretched purpose
Slacken, go down jaws; go gnawn bare. Jaws
Eat and are finished and the jawbone comes to the beach:
This is the sea's achievement; with shells,
Vertebrae, claws, carapaces, skulls.

Time in the sea eats its tail, thrives, casts these
Indigestibles, the spars of purposes
That failed far from the surface. None grow rich
In the sea. This curved jawbone did not laugh
But gripped, gripped and is now a cenotaph.

Ted Hughes *Relic* (1960)

SAMPLE RESPONSE

Comment on Poem A

The poem is written in the first person ('I') and begins with his action of putting a seashell close to his ear. (If you have never done this, it makes a strange hollow sound, much as he describes in the poem.) He imagines the sound of the sea, the wind-swept *desolate* shore and the complete absence of human life, now or ever *since time began*. The only life is that of the slimy seaweed (the *tentacles* suggest hostile life) and the pebbles rolling round, the *dreary wind* blowing all the while. When he takes the shell away from his ear, he hears a completely different sound: the jolting of a cart going down the street, with all that that implies of human beings and their busy, normal lives. Normal, busy, everyday life filled with people is greatly preferable to the desolate waves of the sea and the dreary wind blowing on the beach, as it has done since the beginning of time.

The poem has a very insistent form, rhyming throughout in a pattern which interweaves until the final lines when it rhymes aabb. It has a regular iambic rhythm for the most part, but in lines of varying lengths, which can be dramatically short, or build to an iambic pentameter: the following example illustrates the pattern, which has an almost chant-like rhythm and is very sinister in its inevitability. The fact that the lines are of different lengths is quite disturbing and unpredictable, perhaps mimicking the action of the waves on the beach going up and down.

It was a sunless strand that never bore

The footprint of a man,

Nor felt the weight

Since time began

Of any human quality or stir

Save what the dreary winds and waves incur.

Together with this is a consistent use of alliteration and assonance throughout, for example: *Smitten to whimpers*, *of the dreary wind*. At the end of the poem, the reader is reminded with a *jolt* that this is all in the poet's imagination. After all, it's only a shell making a sound in his ear, which reminds him of eternal desolate shores and seas.

Comment on Poem B

The poem begins in the first person with the poet walking on the beach and finding a jawbone: *I found this jawbone at the sea's edge*. But he does not mention himself directly after this line, reflecting instead on the life under the sea. The only other mentions of human life are indirect ones at the end of the poem, where the poet claims: *None grow rich / In the sea*. Human life may be aggressive, but some humans manage to thrive at the expense of others. And the curve of the jawbone makes him think of laughter, but this jawbone *did not laugh*: it was used for gripping other creatures, and the word *gripped* is repeated to emphasise it. The sea is rough and cold, and the creatures in it are only focused on eating: *Nothing touches but, clutching, devours*, and then the bigger jaws eat the smaller ones in an endless cycle of 'eat and be eaten'. The sea's *achievement* is that it casts the bone up on the beach with all the other relics of life below the surface. The poet personifies Time, imagining it as *eating its tail* and growing and thriving: a contrast with the creatures who do not thrive or grow rich, or even survive. The bones and relics are the *indigestibles* which are thrown

▶

up, *the spars of purposes / That failed far from the surface*. There are two words used in the poem which suggest human strife: one is *camaraderie*; the other *cenotaph*. Humans fight, but they often band together in a spirit of camaraderie against a common enemy – unlike under the sea where it's each creature for itself. A cenotaph is a monument to the fallen, engraved with lots of names, but the monument here is the jawbone, the single relic of a dead creature which immortalises the laws of nature – implacable and harsh, favouring no individuals at all.

The poem is written in three stanzas of five, six and five lines, rhyming in the last couplet of each and with ten syllables in each line. There are also some significant half-rhymes, alliteration and assonance. This regularity with reflective long lines emphasises the continuous regular action of the sea and its inhabitants.

ACTIVITY 22.14

Bringing the ideas together.

When preparing to make a comparison, many students find a table helpful. First, revise the Poetry checklist in Unit 31 of this book. Now try to find similarities and differences preparatory to writing an essay. You can use the table to help you.

Poem A	Poem B
1 The poet holds the shell to his ear and goes on an imaginative flight of fancy about the desolate sound of the sea, and his pleasure at finding his own ordinary life is peopled by others with busy lives. There are no sea creatures mentioned. It is entirely in the first person and the past tense.	**1** The poet is walking on the beach and finds a jawbone which causes him to reflect on the life under the sea and its alienness compared with human life in general. He only speaks of himself in the poem's first line.
2 The poet contrasts everyday life and human company with the eternal desolateness of the world imaged in the sea.	**2** The poet reflects on the harsh violence of the sea and the creatures that live in it, each for itself, focused on eating and being eaten.
3 A few personifications, many sound images, which fits a poem that begins with sound. Language – day and night mentioned but no differentiation. The shell is an image for sound, not the empty husk of a once live creature, as it is in poem B.	**3** Images of eating, Time personified; many images of touch, grasping, clutching. A list of the body parts thrown onto the beach by the sea: *shells / Vertebrae, claws, carapaces, skulls*.
4 Structure – goes from the first action to the imagined world created, then back to the real world.	**4** Goes from the sea shore and its relics cast up on the beach to the deeps of the sea, then to thoughts on time and the pointlessness of animal life.
5 One long stanza, rhyming, with varied lines giving uncertain feeling, assonance and alliteration.	**5** Regular, three stanzas, reflective ten-syllable lines, some half-rhyme, some rhyme, assonance, alliteration.
6 Rather dramatic, considering that it is an imagined scene created by an imaginary sound.	**6** Thoughtful, reflective, uncompromising in his vision of the harshness of nature and Time.

(Continued)

(Continued)

Poem A	Poem B
7 This is a very atmospheric poem; a kind of exercise in atmosphere, but not particularly profound.	**7** This is a harsh poem, far from the pleasure of a day at the beach. It creates a serious atmosphere, reflecting on the harsh natural world: even the world of 'the jungle' seems a friendlier place than the undersea world with its jaws gripping each other.

This is an exercise where you may be tempted to say which poem you prefer. They are very different: the first one all about feeling and atmosphere, the second one very grim and thought-provoking.

ACTIVITY 22.15

Try writing an essay about the two poems using these points, following the guidelines in Part 3 of this book.

FURTHER READING

Follow through the poets you have enjoyed here. Poems by Marvell, Milton, Pope and Plath are easily found on websites. You may find it more difficult to research Lo, although the poem here is on the international poetry website www.poetryinternationalweb.net. Senior's work can be found on websites, although this particular poem is in the *Penguin Book of Caribbean Verse* (edited by Paula Burnett, 2005). The work of Empson, Duffy, Hughes and Stephens is also readily available. William Empson is an eminent literary critic, although his work is difficult, as you can tell by the title *Seven Types of Ambiguity* (Pimlico, 2004)!

Self-assessment checklist

Reflect on what you've learnt in this unit and indicate your confidence level between 1 and 5. If you score below 3, revisit that section. Come back to this list later in your course. Has your confidence grown?

	Confidence level	Revisited?
I can analyse the Marvell poem and discuss it		
I can analyse the Milton extract and acknowledge the value of research		
I can appreciate both the Pope commentary and the comments on it		
I know how to use my skills in tackling more modern poems		
I acknowledge the value of comparative work		
I can discuss both theme and form through contrast and with discrimination		

Section 5
Prose 2

Unit 23
Prose – critical essays

Learning objectives

In this unit you will:

- recognise and understand the ways in which an essay on a typical novel topic can be constructed successfully
- apply basic essay principles acquired from scrutinising student work to your own work on a set novel
- evaluate essays and explore the marker's comments to learn more about your own work
- appraise and compare your work with that of a friend for the purpose of analysis.

KEY CONCEPTS

Language, form, structure, genres, context, style, interpretation, critical reading.

Before you start

- Review the units on the novel in the AS Level section of the book
- Remind yourself of your AS Level prose set text/s and what you enjoyed about it/them
- If you are beginning A Level prose work, discuss with a friend what you see as the challenges facing your prose study at A Level
- When you have both written an essay on the same topic, you will be able to analyse them
- Refer to the advice given on essay writing in Unit 33 in Part 3 of this book

This section on prose follows the same pattern as A Level poetry in Section 4, with units on critical essays, passage questions, close analysis and comparisons.

Critical essays on novels focus on key elements such as particular themes or features of style. In the unit, you will look closely at a range of topics which are common in discussion of novels, such as the place of the individual within a community or in society as a whole; the development of characterisation and its place in the novel's structure; and more abstract themes such as the presentation of time or memory. Further essay questions will be suggested at the end of each section to help to develop your sense of what areas of a novel can be explored.

The first essay title covers an area that is very significant in almost all novels: the relationship between an individual and the community, or society in general. If you have not studied a Thomas Hardy novel, keep this in mind as you read the essay, because its insights will help you to evaluate the novels you are studying. Additionally, Hardy uses the great natural force of Egdon Heath. The relationship between people and their natural environment is another common theme of the novel. If you are studying *Tess of the D'Urbervilles* or *Far From the Madding Crowd* you will find these themes, too.

ACTIVITY 23.1

Read and consider the following essay on *The Return of the Native* (1878) by Thomas Hardy.

This is a question which could be asked of many novels, so even if you are not making a particular study of this one, you will gain valuable ideas for working.

Essay: *Discuss the way in which the novel explores the relationship between the community and the individual characters in the novel.*

STUDENT RESPONSE

Like many of Hardy's novels, *The Return of the Native* is influenced by Greek tragedy. As in the work of the Greek tragedians that Hardy was familiar with, the relationship between the individual and his community is inevitably one of conflict. D.H. Lawrence called the novel a *study of the way communities control their misfits* which is a harsh but apt judgement. The individual must sacrifice any kind of independence in order to be accepted into the community, or be labelled a 'misfit', and acting against the 'rules' of the community will unavoidably mean a tragic end.

The essay begins relevantly and shows understanding of the influence of Greek tragedy on Hardy's writing as well as using a critical view.

Clym and Eustacia are both characterised as out of the ordinary. Clym Yeobright, the native who returns, has *the typical countenance of the future.* He has a social conscience and aspirations which set him apart from the rustic community who inhabit Egdon Heath. He wants to return to bring progress, but it is more focused on himself than the Heath folk and their desires. Eustacia Vye is perhaps even more unconventional. Her evident sexuality, the hints of witchcraft (she is accused by Susan Nonsuch of allegedly bewitching her children and is constantly associated with darkness): these illustrate her individualistic nature. Hardy uses language to associate her with the mythic rather than the naturalistic, too. She is *Queen of the night* and a *model goddess.* These are all indications of a woman quite unlike the meek and conventional Victorian ideal: she is contrasted with Thomasin, who is a well-integrated character, throughout. It is inevitable that these two characters will come into conflict with the community represented by the chorus of rustics, the community of those who live on Egdon Heath, *colossal and mysterious in its swarthy monotony.*

Aware of contrast of characters being used by Hardy as a structural or symbolic device in the novel.

Relates the two main characters to the community, who are then discussed in the next paragraph.

The rustics who breathe the air of Egdon Heath are entirely in tune with it: it is part of them as they are part of it. They are superstitious; their lives are governed by customs and traditions which have existed for many years. The Mummers'[1] play is a case in point, and Eustacia's involvement with it is not because she is blending into rustic values, but because Wildeve was going to be there. She hates the Heath, it is *her Hades, it is a jail to her;* and her death in the boiling cauldron of Shadwater Weir is inevitable. Her attempts to escape with Wildeve, another outsider to the Heath, are doomed to failure.

Contrast of community and personal values.

Good discourse marking as the essay considers others who are not in conflict.

However, there are other characters who survive and still remain part of the community. Thomasin may be a colourless character compared with Eustacia, but she is satisfied with life on the Heath's *impersonal open ground* as she calls it, as is the man she eventually marries, Diggory Venn, 'the *reddleman*'[2]. D.H. Lawrence said of them that they had *nothing in them to put them out of the bounds of convention.* They embrace the life of the Heath and are committed to it and its values. Their wedding symbolises the survival of the community, just as Eustacia's death shows the ruthless destruction of the individual who doesn't fit in.

Development of more complex interpretations of main characters, with useful textual illustrations.

Although Clym is an outsider, his situation is more complex than that of the other characters. His dreams of altruistic philanthropy lead to tragedy as he refuses to see the true needs and desires of the Heath folk. While he wants to seek some rational occupation and do good, Hardy makes it evident that these desires will be thwarted: *the rural world was not ripe for him and a man should be only partially ahead of his time.* The refusal to see the reality around him is represented metaphorically in his physical blindness. He becomes a furze-cutter[3] eventually, drawing closer to the Heath,

Clym, the 'native' of the book's title, is discussed.

►

thereby appearing as a mere parasite on its vast surface. His is the greatest tragedy in a sense: he wanted to be a great social educator, taking the Heath folk away from superstition, paganism and witchcraft, but ends up merely giving *morally unimpeachable* lessons to the inhabitants about commonplace things.

Those who wish to change or escape the Heath and its community and their customs are not successful in the novel; their lives will end tragically or reductively. But those who are prepared to involve themselves in conventional community life and accept the Heath ways will prosper. Society will always be stronger than the individualist.

A neat summing up and clear answer to the question.

[1] Mummer an actor in a folk play.

[2] reddleman a rural worker who deals in red dye for marking livestock.

[3] furze a prickly heath plant.

SUMMATIVE COMMENT

The essay is well-organised and always well-expressed. It reveals a strong knowledge of the text and insight into its main concerns and is always relevant.

KEY CONCEPTS

Comments about Greek tragedy or about Victorian society can clearly be linked to the points made in this essay. There are also similarities with Hardy's other tragic novels, such as *The Mayor of Casterbridge* and *Jude the Obscure.*

ACTIVITY 23.2

With your classmate, look at the main body of the essay and expand the range of illustrations and references used.

When you have finished, see whether your research in the text has raised further points to augment the argument. Is there enough in this essay about the activities of the *rustic chorus*, for example? Would you like to see a paragraph about Clym's mother and how she fits into the community? If you are not studying this novel, consider the ways in which characters other than the main ones help to enhance the main themes of a novel. Of course, you can't say everything about a particular topic on a novel in one hour, but in preparation, it's always useful to think of as many relevant points and illustrations as you can. Under timed conditions, you will need to de-select the least important, concentrate on the most important and write a well-structured argument.

FURTHER ESSAY QUESTIONS

1. *In what ways does Maxine Hong Kingston present the experiences of immigrants in a foreign society in The Woman Warrior?*
2. *'A study of loneliness in the community.' How far do you see this as the main theme of George Eliot's Silas Marner?*

Essays on characterisation

At Advanced Level, there are no simple 'character sketch' sorts of question and those that focus in any way on character tend to be comparative, or link character to the novel's structure or language in some way.

The following essay is on the topic of characterisation. At Advanced Level, you are never asked a question which is simply a 'character sketch' of one of the main characters. That doesn't mean you shouldn't prepare notes and quotations on character beforehand, but you must be ready to use them skilfully to answer the particular question asked.

ACTIVITY 23.3

Read the essay on the character of Bertha Mason in *Jane Eyre*. This is a popular text at AS and A Level, and even at IGCSE, so I hope you have come across it!

Essay: *What does Brontë's presentation of Bertha Mason contribute to the novel as a whole?*

SAMPLE RESPONSE

Although Bertha's physical appearance in the novel is fairly brief, her character is still omnipresent throughout the novel. She comes to represent the passionate aspect of Jane's nature, set in contrast to the austerity of Helen Burns, also contrasted with Jane. Both of them must die so that Jane can acquire a balanced temperament, reconciling passion with judgement. It becomes clear that with Bertha's death, Jane loses the passion that has so often defined her, becoming compressed into a so-called 'equal' marriage and the respectable world of Victorian female conformity. Bertha is a kind of 'double', an 'alter ego' of Jane throughout the novel.

> This is an ambitious opening paragraph, suggesting that the character has various functions in the novel: as a representation of one aspect of the main character; as a point of contrast in a novel which has a number of contrasts of character; and as a kind of 'double' to Jane within an exploration of Victorian society.

Bertha's explosive appearance is foreshadowed by the novelist's use of Gothic settings. The third story of Thornfield Hall is highly Gothic with its *narrow staircase* and *dark low ceilings*, prompting Jane's reflection *If a ghost were to live here, this would be its haunt*. Most significantly however, she likens the corridor to one in *Bluebeard's Castle*. This allusion to the fairy tale where Bluebeard allows his young wife the key to every room except the one in which she discovers all his previous wives lie dead is highly significant, anticipating the discovery of Bertha's own entrapment and resonating with Jane's own life: *forever condemned* at Gateshead, incarceration in the *convent-like garden* of Lowood, and potentially trapped as a *mistress* in an ill-fated marriage with Rochester. Thus, through Bertha's obvious connection with the Gothic settings, Brontë presents the idea of female entrapment.

> Another paragraph bursting with ideas: Bertha's link with Gothic settings and Bertha's incarceration mirroring Jane's own entrapments in the novel, which are typical Gothic themes.

The Red Room at Gateshead is a further foreshadowing of Bertha, giving greater clarity to what is entrapped. Jane is sent to be punished and shut into the Red Room for being *too passionate* after lashing out at John Reed. The red furnishings are symbolic of this excess of feeling. Just as Jane is shut into the Red Room, so is Bertha shut in at Thornfield, coming to symbolise the madness of passionate feeling that Victorian women were told to suppress in the metaphorical attics of their minds. Sending Jane off to the cold, bleak Lowood School after the Red Room incident is intended to calm her down.

▶

Yet as well as symbolising repressed passion, Bertha also comes to signify the oppressed female in the Victorian patriarchy. She is shut up for seemingly being *mad*, a state which is associated with her 'otherness'. When she eventually appears, she is tied to a chair, described as a *clothed hyena* with a *mane*, dehumanising her and strengthening the idea that she has been oppressed by Rochester. This scene also recalls the scene at Gateshead when Bessie says to Jane: *If you won't sit still you must be tied down*. Interestingly, it is Bessie who threatens to tie Jane down and Grace Poole who takes care of Bertha, creating the impression that women seem to be colluding in the restraint of other women.

Bertha's otherness is also because she is a Creole, the daughter of a white European settler in the West Indies. Brontë's references to her *dark* hair and *discoloured*, *black* face suggest her racial identity, and Brontë portrays her as unstable, dangerous and threatening. This gives us an indication of another aspect of Bertha's role in the novel – the colonial oppressed figure who is feared because she is different. The harsh treatment of mad people at the time of writing of the novel is also an insight into Victorian society, shutting away what is different and threatening.

The many comparisons of Bertha with Jane present the former as the Gothic 'double' of the latter. This is often achieved through the use of mirrors – in the Red Room, Jane sees *half fairy, half imp*, paralleling with the sinister moment at Thornfield where she is expecting to see herself but sees instead Bertha, something like the *foul German spectre – the vampire* take her wedding veil. The first example shows Jane about to enter adolescence and trying to reconcile the fairy with the imp (or her inner angel with her devil) The 'alter ego' figure of Bertha will die and Jane will be able to find her own identity as a balanced personality.

Bertha represents passion, a key element of Jane's nature, and the oppressed female in the Victorian patriarchy. She is only directly in the novel for a short time, yet her presence seems constant. Just as she is incarcerated in the attic and her passionate nature repressed, Jane is incarcerated in the repressive society of the Victorian age, but she survives. The reader finds Bertha fearful, but is also sympathetic to her, as Jane herself is. She is one of the most powerful and memorable characters in the novel.

A paragraph discussing the symbolism of repressed passion represented by Bertha, linking Jane's experience in the Red Room at Gateshead with Bertha at Thornfield, using the useful critical term 'foreshadowing' once again. The idea that a character can represent a link before she has even appeared is a sophisticated structural point. (You would not notice this at first reading of course, but subsequent readings enhance your appreciation of techniques such as this.)

Bertha's description and her 'otherness', together with her status in the novel as a symbol of repressed Victorian women.

Racial 'otherness' considered usefully and the treatment of madness briefly referred to.

A return to the idea of the Gothic and Bertha as Jane's 'alter ego' or other self.

A summing up of the main ideas of the essay in this conclusion.

COMMENT

From the point of view of ideas about a character, this is an excellent essay, showing appreciation of social and colonial themes; the Gothic genre; narrative structure and doubling; contrasts of characters and symbolism. It uses critical terminology with confidence.

However, the essay as a composition could be organised more coherently. The ideas about passion could be grouped together, as could the 'Gothic' ones. We don't get a strong sense of the impact of Bertha on the reader and the idea that Jane is sympathetic to her is not explored. Bertha's contrast with Helen Burns could also be more clearly articulated. There is a slight feeling that this student wanted to write about Victorian society rather than the character of Bertha that we respond to – more quotations about her would have helped.

Nonetheless, this essay shows you how to introduce ideas beyond the character sketch! There are many excellent critical analyses of this novel for you to evaluate. *The Madwoman in the Attic* by Gilbert and Gubar is one of the most significant.

Reflection: Think about the novel you are studying. What characters in it are used symbolically? Do they act as doubles or foils to the main character?

KEY CONCEPTS

Gothic fiction refers to a style of writing that is characterised by elements of fear, horror, death and gloom, as well as romantic elements. Gothic heroines are usually young, passive females who are imprisoned in remote and gloomy castles.

FURTHER ESSAY QUESTIONS

1 *Discuss the role and characterisation of Mr Ashok in The White Tiger by Indian writer Aravind Adiga.*
2 *To what extent do you see Orlick as Pip's alter ego in Great Expectations?*

Essays on more abstract topics

At times, the essay title you are given to work on will involve a more abstract topic such as memory or time, particularly if you are dealing with a more modern work where the narrative is discontinuous or non-chronological.

Some novelists, particularly Modernist or post-modernist ones, in other words in the 20th or 21st century, are fascinated by the theme of time and its effects. Here are two essay outlines on this subject from Virginia Woolf's great novel *To the Lighthouse*.

ACTIVITY 23.4

Read and consider the following essay title on *To the Lighthouse* (1927) by Virginia Woolf, and comment on the two essay outlines.

Essay: *Discuss some of the ways in which Woolf explores the concept of time in To the Lighthouse.*

SAMPLE RESPONSE

ESSAY 1

Introduction

Time in the novel has a complex nature and it is used in many different ways. Woolf struggled with depression and this made her aware of the relentless nature of time passing.

Main body 1

First, it is used to create a sense of realism. The slow pace of the dinner party takes place in real time and the reader can appreciate that the passage of time is a never-changing aspect of human existence. Social situations such as the dinner party are the same for us now as they were then.

Main body 2

The reader forgets the passage of time because we are immersed in the characters' lives, which are evoked in detail in the first and last sections of the novel.

Main body 3

However, the section of the novel *Time Passes* covers ten years, in spite of being the shortest chapter. No emotion is shown for the deaths that we are told about and this is shocking. We are reminded of the rhythmical nature of time passing that affects all living people and ends in death.

▶

Conclusion
Time is the 'big idea' of the novel because Woolf's mother and sister died in childbirth and she is exorcising her demons by writing the book.

ESSAY 2

Introduction
Time is necessary to human existence and part of our everyday lives. However, it is also destructive because it brings death.

Main body 1
This action is most clearly seen in the second section of the novel, *Time Passes*, where the whole of society undergoes change, so time is destructive to society too. Although this has some good effects such as the destruction of typical Victorian gender roles, it may bring war (such as the First World War) with its overwhelming losses.

Main body 2
But to the individual it brings suffering with ageing and death, so we perceive its effects as emotionally dangerous and even tragic.

Main body 3
There are moments of joy and beauty, but they are ephemeral. The dinner is a symbol of warmth and fellowship which must be appreciated for what it is at the time, even if it doesn't last. The stroke of the lighthouse is also a symbol used by Woolf to remind us of the brief moments: constant but individually brief.

Main body 4
Works of art such as Lily's painting have permanence which transcends time.

Conclusion
The change which is brought by time is at the heart of the novel. As long as the characters accept this they can enjoy the brief ephemeral moments; Art may be more lasting.

COMMENT

Both essays have sound points and engage with the topic closely. However, the first essay makes two biographical statements about Woolf, which detract from the critical essay tone: the first that she struggled with depression and that this made her more alert to the passage of time, and the second that her mother and sister died in childbirth and she was somehow 'exercising her demons' by writing the book. These are entirely arguable assertions. Woolf was a genius; if everyone with depression could write as well as this we would have many more great novels. Everyone suffers deaths in their families – this is the human condition, and it does not lead to prowess in composition. Such statements must be avoided: they suggest an unwillingness to analyse the work, preferring to find 'explanations' in the life of the writer. However, leaving aside these two comments, some useful analysis takes place in this essay. The paragraph summary about the dinner party shows insight. The second essay also refers to the dinner party scene, but uses it as part of a more developed argument which shows that brief moments of beauty and pleasure must be savoured against the generally destructive nature of time. The paragraph which deals with art as a source of greater permanence within the flux and change of time is very apt. This essay also takes a wider view, drawing in comments about change in society and the First World War. Using opportunities for critical evaluation would enhance both essays.

Virginia Woolf (1882–1941).

KEY CONCEPTS

The effects of the First World War and of the patriarchal society are elements that could validly be developed as a contextual background.

FURTHER ESSAY QUESTIONS

1 *Compare and contrast the presentation of Rosamund Vincy and Dorothea Brook in George Eliot's Middlemarch.*

2 *In what ways, and with what effects, is Lucille's character developed in relation to Ruth's in Housekeeping by US writer Marilynne Robinson?*

3 *'In the society of Wuthering Heights, Catherine Earnshaw has no choice but to marry Edgar Linton.' Discuss Emily Brontë's portrayal of social pressures on female characters in the light of this statement.*

Cat's Eye (published 1988) by Canadian writer Margaret Atwood is another novel which has a strong concern with time and memory.

Margaret Atwood's best-known work is *The Handmaid's Tale*, a work of speculative fiction set in a **Dystopian** society.

KEY TERM

Dystopian fiction: (the opposite of 'Utopian', which deals with ideal societies) focuses on societies which are frightening and oppressive. The main characters of such works are often shown in opposition to their society, or at least deeply affected by its restrictions. Typical examples are George Orwell's *Nineteen Eighty-Four*, Aldous Huxley's *Brave New World*, Margaret Atwood's *The Handmaid's Tale* and Kazuo Ishiguro's *Never Let Me Go*. These works are often used to comment critically on aspects of present society.

ACTIVITY 23.5

Read the following essay title and discuss its implications with your classmate. (You could consider, for example, the fact that different characters, like real people, are shown remembering different aspects of the past and are convinced their view is the right one). Then read the essay that follows, considering it critically and noting the marker's comments on it.

Essay: *Discuss the importance in the novel Cat's Eye of remembering the past.*

SAMPLE RESPONSE

Within Margaret Atwood's *Cat's Eye*, the past is hugely important within the actions of the book and the events that unfold because of the past. As Elaine grows up and reaches her peak adulthood in the book, she is able to look back on her life and the choices she made, as well as the people she has encountered.

> A clear and straightforward introduction.

The structure of the book sees Elaine switch between childhood and adulthood in the book. The structure of the novel is fractured and disfigured, meaning the book intertwines between the past and present, even the future sometimes as Elaine looks to escape from her past and enter the future to see what lies ahead for her.

> A useful point about the book's structure, but there are no examples given, so it seems rather vague. The word 'disfigured' is not appropriate for a carefully wrought work of art.

The very first line of the book states that *Time is not a line but a dimension*. Seeing as this is the very first line of the entire book, it leaves an important reminder to the reader to see throughout the rest of the novel. This quote also has huge importance as it allows Elaine to remember her conversations with Stephen in the past. Her brother Stephen is a renowned physicist and this quote shows a recurring idea in the book as it reminds Elaine of the conversations she had with Stephen as he spoke the same way about time due to his involvement with Physics.

An apt quotation. The references to Stephen are written rather repetitively.

Contextually, *Cat's Eye* as a whole book had been written in 1964 but wasn't published for another 20 years in the early 1980s. The reason for this was unknown; however, it did give Atwood time to see the world change around her before finalising the book. Critic Taylor agrees with this idea of the past reminding Elaine of Stephen by saying 'Time as a dimension offers Elaine the chance to rekindle former past memories, most notably her happiness with Stephen.' This shows the importance of the past in Elaine's life.

This paragraph doesn't add anything to the argument. Whether the book was started earlier and published later is not relevant to the exploration of remembering the past. Yet again Stephen the brother is mentioned, as if he were the most important aspect of the book. The critic's words do not enhance the ideas and could usefully be disputed as part of critical evaluation.

Due to the fragmented double narrative of the novel, the past is just as relevant as the present in regard to the fact that the events that have moulded Elaine's persona have been created in her childhood, such as the impact of psychological torment that Cordelia has given her throughout her difficult childhood. This is notably the physical as well as the psychological and she continues to suffer from it into adulthood. For example, Elaine says: *My fingers begin to bleed, I've been biting them again* in the present which provides the reader with the clear suffering she suffers from due to Cordelia's actions. Elaine in the past says *I sit in the dark, attacking my fingers*. This key theme of self-mutilation is a recurring prospect.

This paragraph has much more to say and uses quotations helpfully too, although it needs more precise linking to the essay topic of remembering the past. 'Fragmented double negative' could be developed usefully.

Contextually, although Atwood denies any sort of relation between herself and Elaine, there are clear autobiographical elements. As Atwood's father was an entomologist, the same profession as Elaine's father. It is important to see from a reader's perspective the similarities between Atwood and Elaine, showing the importance of the past for Elaine and Atwood.

This piece of biographical information is not relevant. Why is it important for the reader to see autobiographical elements in the novel and how could this possibly reveal the importance of the past for a created character? Elaine is not Margaret Atwood. Margaret Atwood is a writer of great talent who uses her imagination to create works of art in prose.

Finally, as the past is a result of time moving forwards, it is important to see how the past is triggered through parts of Elaine's present, such as her paintings, the cat's eye marble and the ravine and bridge. However, as well as being able to remember Stephen and Cordelia, the past allows us as the reader to see what happened in her past and childhood that has broken her so badly. A quote from Elaine reads *I do not look back along time, but through it like water.* This links with the very first line of the book *time is not a line but a dimension.* And shows us Elaine's notable skills and interest into observation and perspective. Atwood's language here creates interesting connotations such as 'but through me like water.' This creates a simile regarding observation and perspective, as water is clear and transparent but also reminds the reader of Elaine's disturbance and revelation during the ravine incident.

Another more effective paragraph with useful instances, although little quotation in support.

In contextual terms, during the 20 years between the completed book and publishing date, Atwood watched her daughter grow up from a child to a teen and then into an adult. This allowed Atwood to observe the changing nature of girls growing up. This concludes the importance of the past in the novel.

Again, this is reductive of Atwood's achievement. You don't have to have a daughter or even to be female to be able to observe girls (or boys) growing up.

To conclude, remembering the past allows the reader to see how although Elaine has suffered many traumatic event in her life, she is still able to remember everything that has happened to her. Although the book's narrative comes in the first-person form of Elaine, her account of actions can't be seen as 100% trustworthy, but can provide the reader with sufficient information into her past within childhood.

The conclusion contains a valid observation of Elaine as an unreliable narrator which would have been useful to explore in the main body of the essay. However, Elaine does not, at the beginning of the narrative 'remember everything that has happened to her' so this is not accurate.

In all, this is not a very successful account of the importance of remembering the past in the novel. What you can learn from this is that biographical 'information' or speculation about a writer's life is not worth mentioning. What matters is the handling of the material chosen by the writer and an analysis of this in detail.

Reflection: Discuss with a friend how this essay could be improved. What would happen if you removed all the contextual paragraphs? Highlight the places where you could add supporting quotation.

ACTIVITY 23.6

Compare an essay of yours with one on the same topic written by your friend. Work together to list the strengths and weaknesses of each one.

FURTHER ESSAY QUESTIONS

1. *In what ways, and with what effects, does George Eliot present time passing in Silas Marner?*
2. *Discuss the significance of religious faith in the novel The Tenant of Wildfell Hall by Anne Brontë.*

FURTHER READING

Any novel by Thomas Hardy; *Silas Marner* by George Eliot; *The Handmaid's Tale* by Margaret Atwood (recently made into a very successful TV series with the involvement of the author); *To the Lighthouse* and *Mrs Dalloway* by Virginia Woolf. I enjoy many works of speculative fiction: try *Children of Men* by P.D. James and of course *Never Let Me Go* by Kazuo Ishiguro.

Self-assessment checklist

Reflect on what you've learnt in this unit and indicate your confidence level between 1 and 5. If you score below 3, revisit that section. Come back to this list later in your course. Has your confidence grown?

	Confidence level	Revisited?
I am alert to this common novelistic theme (the individual and society) and can discuss it		
I perceive the importance of handling characterisation at advanced level		
I take note of and incorporate the insight gained from studying an essay with more abstract themes (Woolf)		
I actively involve my skills in improving an Atwood essay		
I know how to evaluate and compare my essay with my friend's, learning valuable insights from this		

Unit 24

Prose – passage questions

Learning objectives

In this unit you will:

- appreciate the elements that you need to consider when analysing an extract from your set prose text
- apply basic essay principles acquired from scrutinising student work to your own work on a passage from a set novel or short-story collection
- evaluate essays and explore the marker's comments to learn more about your own work
- create a passage question working with a friend.

KEY CONCEPTS

Language, form, structure, genres, context, style, interpretation, critical reading.

Before you start

- Review the advice given in the checklist on prose analysis in Unit 11
- Refer to the advice given on passage question writing in Unit 30 (in Part 3 of this book)

Close reading of prose is vital for appreciating a writer's methods in detail. The focus here is on the kinds of effects you can spot and discuss in a small section and these exercises will help you to develop your skills. If you are not studying the particular prose works mentioned here, you can use them as unseens. But you'll learn from these exercises how to judge and analyse your own set texts. You will need to be able to relate your close analysis of a short extract to the methods and concerns of the whole: either the novel or group of short stories (for example, those of Katherine Mansfield or James Joyce).

Working with a whole novel – especially a long 19th-century one by Hardy, Dickens, Eliot or the Brontës for example, or a 21st-century one with similar characteristics, such as the novels by Adichie – seems very different from writing on two or three poems. Yet many areas for analysis are the same: structure, use of language and imagery, tone, atmosphere, and so on.

Emma by Jane Austen

ACTIVITY 24.1

Read closely the passage from *Emma* (1815) by Jane Austen and prepare to analyse it.

Note: In the following passage, Emma is making a drawing of Harriet Smith. She has convinced herself that Mr Elton is in love with Harriet. Mr Elton is reading to them while Harriet sits and Emma draws.

I've chosen this passage as it has a wealth of characters who are clearly presented by Austen in a very amusing way for you to enjoy. You could read it aloud with a friend – this always helps in understanding. It's a little longer than the normal passage you'd be given in an exam, but the sort of question you'd have would be:

Paying close attention to language and dialogue, write a critical appreciation of the following passage, showing what it contributes to your understanding of Austen's methods and concerns.

or possibly

Paying close attention to language and dialogue, write a critical appreciation of the following passage, showing what it contributes to your understanding of Austen's characterisation.

Mr Elton was only too happy. Harriet listened, and Emma drew in peace. She must allow him to be still frequently coming to look; any thing less would certainly have been too little in a lover; and he was ready at the smallest intermission of the pencil, to jump up and see the progress, and be charmed.— There was no being displeased with such an encourager, for his admiration made him discern a likeness almost before it was possible. She could not respect his eye, but his love and his complaisance were unexceptionable.

The sitting was altogether very satisfactory; she was quite enough pleased with the first day's sketch to wish to go on. There was no want of likeness, she had been fortunate in the attitude, and as she meant to throw in a little improvement to the figure, to give a little more height, and considerably more elegance, she had great confidence of its being in every way a pretty drawing at last, and of its filling its destined place with credit to them both—a standing memorial of the beauty of one, the skill of the other, and the friendship of both; with as many other agreeable associations as Mr Elton's very promising attachment was likely to add.

Harriet was to sit again the next day; and Mr Elton, just as he ought, entreated for the permission of attending and reading to them again.

'By all means. We shall be most happy to consider you as one of the party.'

The same civilities and courtesies, the same success and satisfaction, took place on the morrow, and accompanied the whole progress of the picture, which was rapid and happy. Every body who saw it was pleased, but Mr Elton was in continual raptures, and defended it through every criticism.

'Miss Woodhouse has given her friend the only beauty she wanted,'—observed Mrs Weston to him—not in the least suspecting that she was addressing a lover.— 'The expression of the eye is most correct, but Miss Smith has not those eyebrows and eyelashes. It is the fault of her face that she has them not.'

'Do you think so?' replied he. 'I cannot agree with you. It appears to me a most perfect resemblance in every feature. I never saw such a likeness in my life. We must allow for the effect of shade, you know.'

'You have made her too tall, Emma,' said Mr Knightley.

Emma knew that she had, but would not own it; and Mr Elton warmly added,

'Oh no! certainly not too tall; not in the least too tall. Consider, she is sitting down—which naturally presents a different—which in short gives exactly the idea—and the proportions must be preserved, you know. Proportions, fore-shortening.—Oh no! it gives one exactly the idea of such a height as Miss Smith's. Exactly so indeed!'

'It is very pretty,' said Mr Woodhouse. 'So prettily done! Just as your drawings always are, my dear. I do not know any body who draws so well as you do. The only thing I do not thoroughly like is, that she seems to be sitting out of doors, with only a little shawl over her shoulders—and it makes one think she must catch cold.'

▶

'But, my dear papa, it is supposed to be summer; a warm day in summer. Look at the tree.'

'But it is never safe to sit out of doors, my dear.'

'You, sir, may say any thing,' cried Mr Elton, 'but I must confess that I regard it as a most happy thought, the placing of Miss Smith out of doors; and the tree is touched with such inimitable spirit! Any other situation would have been much less in character. The naiveté of Miss Smith's manners—and altogether—Oh, it is most admirable! I cannot keep my eyes from it. I never saw such a likeness.'

The next thing wanted was to get the picture framed; and here were a few difficulties. It must be done directly; it must be done in London; the order must go through the hands of some intelligent person whose taste could be depended on; and Isabella, the usual doer of all commissions, must not be applied to, because it was December, and Mr Woodhouse could not bear the idea of her stirring out of her house in the fogs of December. But no sooner was the distress known to Mr Elton, than it was removed. His gallantry was always on the alert. 'Might he be trusted with the commission, what infinite pleasure should he have in executing it! he could ride to London at any time. It was impossible to say how much he should be gratified by being employed on such an errand.'

Jane Austen *Emma* (1815)

COMMENT

Jane Austen's prose is always worthy of close critical analysis. You can pick any section of any of her novels and find much to comment on. It is not particularly rich in imagery, so you won't find complex metaphors. Nonetheless, every sentence structure is worth analysing and her slyly ironic tone underlies almost every paragraph, offering indirect criticism and a great deal of humour. Dialogue is also used to great effect: every character's utterances are individualised with vocabulary and phrasing entirely suitable to them.

As with a poem, it is helpful to consider the situation presented in any extract from a novel or short story and the characters involved in it. Emma is doing a portrait of Harriet, watched by Mr Elton. *The party* additionally contains Mrs Weston (Emma's former governess), Emma's father Mr Woodhouse and Mr Knightley, the man whom Emma will eventually marry. There is also reference to Isabella, Emma's sister who has married Mr Knightley's brother. Not all passages from novels have such an array of characters and so much dialogue, so this is a very good place to start.

The passage is focalized (see Unit 7, mixed narrative) from Emma's point of view, with her thoughts and feelings, but the novelist is able to suggest the characters economically through their dialogue, as well as hinting at Emma's misunderstanding of the situation. Taking the characters in turn:

Harriet is the subject of the picture and here says nothing, although her looks are discussed. (She is not a lively conversationalist and is, in fact, almost illiterate.) She is evidently a pretty girl, but the *beauty* that is referred to in the second paragraph is very much Emma's view and linked with her own *skill* and their *friendship*. Mrs Weston is more dispassionate in her appraisal: *Miss Woodhouse has given her friend the only beauty she wanted* ('wanted' here meaning 'lacked'). ▶

Mrs Weston is only mentioned in one paragraph and, as suggested, has judgement and is able to criticise Emma's drawing, while justifying Emma's embellishment by reference to the relationship between Emma and Harriet.

Mr Knightley has only one sentence, but it is in a paragraph of its own, so particularly emphasised: *You have made her too tall, Emma*. As well as suggesting that he is the only person who criticises Emma when she deserves it, rather than lavishing praise on her, it could be seen as a symbolic remark too: Emma is in the process of making Harriet too tall, trying to arrange a marriage 'above her station' with someone inappropriate. Mr Knightley's laconic one-liner is juxtaposed (see Unit 14) with the effusions of Elton, but linked with Emma's own realisation of what she has done to the picture, suggesting their essential closeness.

Mr Woodhouse, Emma's father, praises her highly, without reservation: *I do not know any body who draws so well as you do*. But he is also shown as a valetudinarian (someone who pessimistically focuses on matters of health all the time), constantly worrying whether he or someone else will catch cold or some other illness. His characterisation is humorous: *it is never safe to sit out of doors, my dear* as it shows Austen's use of exaggeration for effect (hyperbole) or even caricature. However, his cautious approach to life, which later in the passage prevents his other daughter Isabella from going to London to get the picture framed (because it is winter and therefore foggy), suggests a deadening, frustrating attitude that does not afford Emma any healthy challenge or stimulation. In the novel generally, he hates change and he hates marriage because it means change, and this moves him beyond an amusing caricature into something more sinister. If you have read the novel, you will know that it is Mr Knightley, rather than her father, who provides Emma with the challenges she needs to grow as a personality – but you might guess it from reading this extract carefully.

Mr Elton has a great deal to say here, which is presented both in direct and indirect speech. He *was only too happy*, for example, which opens the extract is indirect; *Mr Elton, just as he ought, entreated for the permission of attending and reading to them again* is also indirect, and the *just as he ought* shows clearly Emma's point of view, because she thinks a lover should want to be in the same room as the beloved. If you look at his direct speech, you will see that it is often expressed in disjointed sentences with ideas joined by dashes: *Consider, she is sitting down—which naturally presents a different—which in short gives exactly the idea—and the proportions must be preserved, you know; The naiveté of Miss Smith's manners—and altogether—Oh, it is most admirable!* This captures very successfully his breathless gush and exaggerated enthusiasm. He also has a formal vocabulary which he uses when he wishes to appear gallant – *entreated for the permission* has already been noted, but the free indirect of *Might he be trusted with the commission, what infinite pleasure should he have in executing it ... it was impossible to say how much he should be gratified by being employed on such an errand*. If you have a look at his later proposal to Emma in the carriage, it is characterised in just the same **register**.

KEY TERM

Register: the language used for a particular purpose or in a particular social setting.

His comments to Mr Woodhouse are exaggerated and grovelling: *You, sir, may say anything*, and he flows on effusively *but I must confess that I regard it as a most happy thought, the placing of Miss Smith out of doors; and the tree is touched with such inimitable spirit!* The later moment where Emma has to face his pompous proposal and the realisation of her misunderstanding is one of the jewels of this wonderful novel!

The narrative is focused on Emma herself and any criticism of her is suggested in the novelist's irony. *There was no want of likeness* is not exactly a ringing endorsement of the picture, but she is always very sure of herself: *she had great confidence of its being in every way a pretty drawing*. The words *great* and *in every way* suggest the novelist's ironic eye. Although Emma enjoys being praised, she is at least aware of some of her own faults, although she doesn't enjoy others commenting on them. She knows Mr Elton lacks ►

judgement in his appraisal of the picture but she's enjoying it: *She could not respect his eye, but his love and his complaisance were unexceptionable*. She knows that her picture has made Harriet too tall, indeed she has deliberately tried to do this, but she doesn't want to admit it when criticised by Mr Knightley: *Emma knew that she had, but would not own it*. She likes to be praised: *There was no being displeased with such an encourager*, and of course believes that she is securing an attachment between Mr Elton and Harriet. However, there are hints throughout that she has misread the situation. The references to *love* (above) and *a lover* in the passage are all ambiguous. For example, *any thing less would certainly have been too little in a lover* in Emma's mind means the lover of Harriet, but we are beginning to suspect that she is the object of his affections. In the paragraph dealing with Mrs Weston's response, we see *not in the least suspecting that she was addressing a lover*, and again we are aware of the ambiguity of the word, which runs ironically through the passage, drawing attention to the ambiguity.

One of the key features of Austen's style is balance: she constantly uses balanced sentences, and these can give an effect of order and logic. They may be antithetical: *She could not respect his eye, but his love and his complaisance were unexceptionable*, or they may incorporate antithesis leading to a climax: *a standing memorial of the beauty of one, the skill of the other, and the friendship of both*. However, because these examples both relate to Emma's confidence that she is always right, they are being used ironically. Emma will create disorder before balance is restored at the end of the novel.

Other aspects of Austen's style, not seen here, are the presence of direct authorial comment and the use of letters. Here is an example from *Persuasion*, her last novel, to illustrate direct authorial intrusion:

Who can be in doubt of what followed? When any two young people take it into their heads to marry, they are pretty sure by perseverance to carry their point, be they ever so poor, or ever so imprudent, or ever so little likely to be necessary to each other's ultimate comfort.

Jane Austen *Persuasion* (1816)

I have chosen this quotation because it also illustrates the use of tricolon well (*ever so* ...). I think too that the use of the alliteration of the 'p' sound: *pretty* ... *perseverance* ... *point* ... *poor* ... (im)*prudent* builds-up to and emphasises the tricolon effectively.

In order to relate this further to the rest of the novel in answering a passage question, you would need to give further examples of characteristic behaviour and further evidence of the narrative irony created by Austen to enhance the main theme of Emma's education into self-awareness and greater humility. You will be able to find critical views on the subject to enhance your evaluation, too.

KEY CONCEPTS

Austen's novels are very popular and well-known, not least because of the number of films and TV series which have been based on them, often using Austen's own dialogue. However, no filmed version can capture the sharp wit and ironic ambiguity of Austen's prose style which is such a delight.

REMINDER

A **tricolon** is a series of three words, phrases or clauses arranged for rhetorical effect.

Reflection: Consider the novel you are studying in detail. Have you seen a filmed version of it? Discuss with a friend what the good points of the filmed adaptation were. Then try to list what you think was omitted, or distorted. You may find that a first-person novel is more difficult to film.

Eveline by James Joyce

ACTIVITY 24.2

The next exercise is on Irish writer James Joyce's *Dubliners* (first published in 1914). Although this work is composed of short stories, they are linked in theme and style and more like a novel. Read the passage carefully and then study the student essay which follows it. Look closely at the marker's comments on the essay. The essay title is typical of those set on prose passage questions. Joyce is often considered one of the most influential writers of the 20th century and in the avant-garde of Modernism.

Essay: *Paying close attention to language and characterisation, discuss the following passage from the story Eveline, commenting on what it contributes to Joyce's methods and concerns in Dubliners.* [Eveline has met a man and agreed to run away with him to Buenos Aires in Argentina]

She sat at the window watching the evening invade the avenue. Her head was leaned against the window curtains and in her nostrils was the odour of dusty cretonne. She was tired.

Few people passed. The man out of the last house passed on his way home; she heard his footsteps clacking along the concrete pavement and afterwards crunching on the cinder path before the new red houses. One time there used to be a field there in which they used to play every evening with other people's children. Then a man from Belfast bought the field and built houses in it—not like their little brown houses but bright brick houses with shining roofs. The children of the avenue used to play together in that field—the Devines, the Waters, the Dunns, little Keogh the cripple, she and her brothers and sisters. Ernest, however, never played: he was too grown up. Her father used often to hunt them in out of the field with his blackthorn stick; but usually little Keogh used to keep nix and call out when he saw her father coming. Still they seemed to have been rather happy then. Her father was not so bad then; and besides, her mother was alive. That was a long time ago; she and her brothers and sisters were all grown up her mother was dead. Tizzie Dunn was dead, too, and the Waters had gone back to England. Everything changes. Now she was going to go away like the others, to leave her home.

Home! She looked round the room, reviewing all its familiar objects which she had dusted once a week for so many years, wondering where on earth all the dust came from. Perhaps she would never see again those familiar objects from which she had never dreamed of being divided. And yet during all those years she had never found out the name of the priest whose yellowing photograph hung on the wall above the broken harmonium beside the coloured print of the promises made to Blessed Margaret Mary Alacoque. He had been a school friend of her father. Whenever he showed the photograph to a visitor her father used to pass it with a casual word:

- He is in Melbourne now.

She had consented to go away, to leave her home. Was that wise? She tried to weigh each side of the question. In her home anyway she had shelter and food; she had those whom she had known all her life about her. Of course she had to work hard, both in the house and at business. What would they say of her in the Stores when they found out that she had run away with a fellow? Say she was a fool, perhaps; and her place would be filled up by advertisement. Miss Gavan would be glad. She had always had an edge* on her, especially whenever there were people listening.

- Miss Hill, don't you see these ladies are waiting?

- Look lively, Miss Hill, please.

She would not cry many tears at leaving the Stores.

But in her new home, in a distant unknown country, it would not be like that. Then she would be married—she, Eveline. People would treat her with respect then.

*had an edge = enjoyed being superior

James Joyce 'Eveline' from *Dubliners* (1914)

SAMPLE RESPONSE

In the short-story collection *Dubliners*, and especially in this one, there is a dominant theme of characters feeling trapped in their lives and unable to escape. Joyce explores the hope of escape from the paralysis of Dublin life but also the disappointment when hopes are crushed. The characters' deadening lives and habitual ways of thinking and acting make it impossible for them to move on.

In this passage, the opening of the story, Joyce begins with the physical situation of Eveline, sitting by the window and looking out. He creates vivid sense impressions that engage the reader immediately – of smell, of sight and of hearing. This is a typical feature of his writing throughout the collection of stories. Eveline feels 'tired' and the smell of the dusty curtains she is leaning against is *in her nostrils*, suggesting her own and the house's weariness. Joyce uses the word 'invade' for the evening coming into the avenue – an unusual word for something that happens every day but one that suggests from the very opening of the story a sense that change is dangerous. She notices the sound of a man coming home – his footsteps are described in a vivid onomatopoeic way 'clacking' and 'crunching'. Joyce uses both realistic physical details and symbolism – the window is a motif that runs throughout the collection of stories to represent the barrier between escape and freedom and the reality of life trapped on the inside of houses, with their often difficult domestic situations.

Joyce establishes the strong ties that Eveline has to her life: she reflects on the past as she looks out of the window, remembering the details of her childhood, people and changes to the place itself. Where they played was once *a field*, for example. Her mother is dead now and her father, still alive, is shown to be a violent man. Yet she still relates to him and to an old friend of his whose picture hangs on the wall (ironically now in Australia). The house's dusty, shabby atmosphere is evoked economically by Joyce, and there is a brief but telling reference to a religious picture suggesting the dominance of religion in the lives of the Dubliners.

Joyce shows Eveline moving from thoughts of the past to thoughts of the future, trying to weigh up both sides of the situation – should she go or should she stay? In this paragraph, he is entirely focalized on Eveline, using free indirect speech to come close to her thinking, questioning herself: *Was that wise? What would they say of her in the Stores..?* She doesn't particularly enjoy her job or her immediate boss Miss Gavan, who ▶

The opening paragraph confidently relates this story to one of the main themes of the story collection. The literary context of the story – its place in the whole collection – is well-appreciated.

Very good detailed analysis of language and symbolism, with close examples from the text.

Further discussion of Eveline, here her vivid memories of the past, her childhood and her ties to the house and her family.

Joyce's narrative method and concern with a speculative future as well as the past, is highlighted here.

Joyce brings to life through dialogue. Eveline speculates and imagines a future where she would be a married woman, worthy of respect.

Clear understanding of the reasons for Eveline's unwillingness to commit herself to dramatic change, with very apt use of quotation to support the idea that her failure is 'tragic'.

But the way in which Joyce has begun the story, with the weight of domestic detail and memory (including, later in the story, her promises to her mother to look after the family) never gives the reader confidence that Eveline will be able to be decisive and to move away. When she goes to the docks to board the ship with her lover Frank, we are not surprised when she pulls back, desperately praying for guidance and filled with *distress*. Her thoughts are tragic ones, symbolised in the image of her drowning in *the seas of the world* if she leaves her home: *All the seas of the world tumbled about her heart. He was drawing her into them: he would drown her.* Her hopes are crushed and he leaves without her. She has been trapped by the past, by tradition and fear of the unknown. The sea image is particularly appropriate because Frank is a sailor, but it is also a powerful natural force, one to be afraid of.

A useful comment on Joyce's narrative methods. These points could perhaps have been incorporated into the commentary.

Joyce's prose style is always very effective. His use of third-person narrative is flexible, with passages of focalization and free indirect to bring the reader close to the thoughts of the characters. He uses very short sentences at times to point an idea, such as *she was tired; everything changes* and *was that wise?*

Another story with a similar theme is discussed, showing knowledge of the text and understanding of the writer's concerns.

A Painful Case is another story that develops the themes of entrapment and escape. This story also explores the chance of an escape, not from Dublin itself, but from a life of unchanging routine. Mr Duffy is a bachelor of fixed and rigid habits who begins a very friendly relationship with a married woman (whose husband is usually away), and Joyce's language reveals that this affects him profoundly: *this union exalted him, emotionalized his mental life,* However, when she becomes more physical in her affections, his inability to respond physically makes him reject her in a cold manner and he returns to his old dry ways, to the *orderliness of his mind*. Joyce makes him an unsympathetic character at this point. When he reads in the newspaper four years later that she has died after being struck by a train, apparently under the influence of drink, this event causes him to reassess his rejection of her and the likely pain it must have caused her. He sees clearly the limitations of his life, like the protagonist of *The Dead*, the last story in the collection, and we are drawn into sympathy for him: *He gnawed the rectitude of his life; he felt that he had been outcast from life's feast*. The *painful case* of the essay title is not just the woman – it is Mr Duffy as well. The final line of the story *He felt that he was alone* is a tragic conclusion, just as the conclusion of Eveline as *passive, like a helpless animal* is.

The conclusion makes apt reference to the readers' likely response to the characters and makes a valid distinction between them. The essay ends by reinforcing one of the main themes of *Dubliners*, together with its overwhelmingly poignant tone. In all, a very thoughtful and detailed response to the passage and to Joyce's methods and concerns.

Eveline is a character we can sympathise with more readily, stuck in her situation looking after the home with her aggressive father and with no prospects. But Mr Duffy is not so likeable and it is a tribute to Joyce's skill and empathy that we can see him re-thinking his behaviour and habits and coming to the painful conclusion that he has missed out on life. Many of the stories have a conclusion which can only be described as tragic – wasted lives and wasted opportunities, with tragic realisation of the limitations of the lives depicted.

KEY CONCEPTS

Literary context means the place of a passage within its text (here, one of 15 thematically linked stories in *Dubliners*). It can also mean where a whole text belongs within the writer's work as a whole, or its place within a literary genre such as tragedy.

FURTHER ESSAY QUESTION

Paying close attention to language and tone, consider Joyce's presentation of Eveline in the following passage, considering it in relation to at least one other story in the collection.

Her First Ball by Katherine Mansfield

ACTIVITY 24.3

Read the extract from the story *Her First Ball* and study the passage and the pointers for working that follow it. This is the essay question:

Essay: *Write a critical appreciation of the following passage from the story Her First Ball by New Zealand writer Katherine Mansfield, relating its concerns and methods to two other stories by Mansfield in your selection.*

When you have done this exercise and looked at the points made to help your working, you will use a passage from your own set text.

Note: For those who have not studied Mansfield's stories, Leila is a country girl who is coming to a ball for the first time, with her more experienced cousins. She feels shy and a little out of place as her cousins are so used to this sort of thing.

'Floor's not bad,' said the new voice. Did one always begin with the floor? And then, 'Were you at the Neaves' on Tuesday?' And again Leila explained. Perhaps it was a little strange that her partners were not more interested. For it was thrilling. Her first ball! She was only at the beginning of everything. It seemed to her that she had never known what the night was like before. Up till now it had been dark, silent, beautiful very often—oh yes—but mournful somehow. Solemn. And now it would never be like that again—it had opened dazzling bright.

'Care for an ice?' said her partner. And they went through the swing doors, down the passage, to the supper-room. Her cheeks burned, she was fearfully thirsty. How sweet the ices looked on little glass plates and how cold the frosted spoon was, iced too! And when they came back to the hall there was the fat man waiting for her by the door. It gave her quite a shock again to see how old he was; he ought to have been on the stage with the fathers and mothers. And when Leila compared him with her other partners he looked shabby. His waistcoat was creased, there was a button off his glove, his coat looked as if it was dusty with French chalk.

'Come along, little lady,' said the fat man. He scarcely troubled to clasp her, and they moved away so gently, it was more like walking than dancing. But he said not a word about the floor. 'Your first dance, isn't it?' he murmured.

'How *did* you know?'

'Ah,' said the fat man, 'that's what it is to be old!' He wheezed faintly as he steered her past an awkward couple. 'You see, I've been doing this kind of thing for the last thirty years.'

'Thirty years?' cried Leila. Twelve years before she was born!

'It hardly bears thinking about, does it?' said the fat man gloomily. Leila looked at his bald head, and she felt quite sorry for him.

▶

'I think it's marvellous to be still going on,' she said kindly.

'Kind little lady,' said the fat man, and he pressed her a little closer, and hummed a bar of the waltz. 'Of course,' he said, 'you can't hope to last anything like as long as that. No-o,' said the fat man, 'long before that you'll be sitting up there on the stage, looking on, in your nice black velvet. And these pretty arms will have turned into little short fat ones, and you'll beat time with such a different kind of fan—a black ebony one.' The fat man seemed to shudder. 'And you'll smile away like the poor old dears up there, and point to your daughter, and tell the elderly lady next to you how some dreadful man tried to kiss her at the club ball. And your heart will ache, ache'—the fat man squeezed her closer still, as if he really was sorry for that poor heart—'because no one wants to kiss you now. And you'll say how unpleasant these polished floors are to walk on, how dangerous they are. Eh, Mademoiselle Twinkletoes?' said the fat man softly.

Leila gave a light little laugh, but she did not feel like laughing. Was it—could it all be true? It sounded terribly true. Was this first ball only the beginning of her last ball, after all? At that the music seemed to change; it sounded sad, sad; it rose upon a great sigh. Oh, how quickly things changed! Why didn't happiness last for ever? For ever wasn't a bit too long.

Katherine Mansfield *Her First Ball* (1921)

COMMENT

Study the following method of approach: Situation

What is the situation here? Leila is dancing in turn with the men who have claimed a dance at the beginning of the evening by writing on her programme. She is elated and overwhelmed by the intensity of the experience, taking in all the sensory images around her. One of the partners is a *fat man* who, as they dance, punctures her happiness by imagining her future as an older woman, no longer attractive or able to dance. (The story ends with her recovering her spirits somewhat as she again dances with a *young man with curly hair*.) Much of the passage is their dialogue, interspersed with description.

Begin by looking at the characterisation

Starting with the *fat man*, how many times is this phrase used for him in the passage, and what does it suggest? (I found eight.) How else is he described (*old, shabby, wheezed faintly, gloomily*)? What is it that makes him seem *to shudder* (the thought of her arms turning into short fat ones, perhaps)? What is your response to *he pressed her a little closer* and *he squeezed her closer still*? Do you feel any sympathy for him? Does the writer give him any symbolic function, do you think? (Your consideration of the writer's concerns may help you to answer this.) He has a long passage of direct speech. Consider the use of repetition of words in the passage, and the opening of sentences. What effect does this have?

Clearly the story is focalized on Leila. She is excited and responsive to everything around her. Find evidence from the language to support this. You could consider:

- sensory description
- exclamations
- rhetorical questions
- repetition of sentence structure (look at the use of 'And' and 'How' at the beginning of sentences)

▶

The novelist's concerns

What are the novelist's concerns here? Consider the following points, see if you can add to them, and find examples from the passage to support them all:

- the intensity of sensory experience
- the contrast of youth and age
- the acquisition of experience
- the impermanence of happiness, youth, life itself
- women's position in society as merely decorative objects

The narrator's position

What is the narrator's position? The narrator's focalized attention on Leila and her use of free indirect speech suggest much greater sympathy for her. Do you detect any criticism of Leila? Do you think the *fat man*, so unsympathetically imagined and described, is a representative or even symbolic figure? If so, what does he represent?

Mansfield's stories often end with an **epiphany**, a word also applied to James Joyce's work.

Relating the passage to the novel as a whole – two methods

First, you need to select two stories that relate closely to the issues here. If this is an exam situation, think carefully about relevance before plunging in. Remember that you have two options here as far as your essay structure is concerned:

1 You could write a few further paragraphs relating your points to what you see in two other stories: for example, the presentation of the young and their view of the world; the contrast between this view and that of their elders; moments of intense experience of different kinds; the position of women in society; the narrator's use of description and dialogue; her point of view and apparent sympathies. If you are studying Mansfield's stories, go through each of the stories in your selection and decide how far they meet the criteria.

2 You could relate the points to the other stories as you go, so that, for example, at the end of your paragraph on the contrast between youth and age you could add some comment on *The Garden-Party*; at the end of your paragraph on women's restricted expectations, you could incorporate your comment on *The Daughters of the Late Colonel*. The stories are not of course exactly the same as each other – it is Laura's family, not a *fat man*, who provide a contrast to her impulses in *The Garden-Party*; and the daughters of the late colonel are two middle-aged ladies who have never experienced much of life owing to their domineering father.

TIP

Remember, considering the situation is to help you get your bearings. You do not need to write this in any final essay!

KEY TERM

Epiphany: a moment of sudden realisation or illumination. These often happen at the climax of a short story or novel.

ACTIVITY 24.4

Put into practice what you've learnt in this unit. Together with your classmate, make a short list of possible passages you could use from the novel or short-story selection you are studying as a set text. You could each try to find two different ones, so that you'll have four to choose from. You need approximately four paragraphs. Now select the best one for practising a passage question. These are some of the elements you will need, depending on your text:

- Strong character interest
- Obvious major concerns of the novelist being suggested
- Vivid description may be a feature
- Be careful about storytelling. You don't want a passage where a lot happens that tempts you into just narrating the events
- A variety of style (for example, some dialogue, some short sentences for emphasis, some longer description)

Now create your question. Remember that passage questions tend to follow the same format, as you've already seen. Refer to the following further essay questions.

Reflection: Now, together with your friend, think about your question and how you might answer it. Did you choose a passage with lots to say? Why not suggest it as an exercise for your class?

FURTHER ESSAY QUESTION

Paying close attention to language and tone, consider Katherine Mansfield's presentation of the fat man in the passage, showing its significance to the novel as a whole.

FURTHER READING

Any novel by Jane Austen is fun to read. If you are new to her work, you could try *Pride and Prejudice* or her satire of the Gothic, *Northanger Abbey*. When you've read a couple of the novels, try watching filmed versions, of which there are many.

Read the other stories in *Dubliners*. Joyce's most famous work is *Ulysses* but I'm not going to suggest it, as it's very difficult. Look out for it at University, though!

Katherine Mansfield's short stories are very accessible, on the other hand, as are the stories of US writer Raymond Carver who shows how to suggest a great deal in only a few words!

Self-assessment checklist

Reflect on what you've learnt in this unit and indicate your confidence level between 1 and 5. If you score below 3, revisit that section. Come back to this list later in your course. Has your confidence grown?

	Confidence level	Revisited?
I appreciate the elements of prose analysis		
I can apply basic principles from looking at specific texts		
I am able to evaluate student essays and learn from marker comments		
I enjoy creating a suitable passage question from my set text and working on it with a friend		

Prose – close analysis and comparison

Learning objectives

In this unit you will:

- focus on detail and answer directed questions
- complete text boxes and a table linked with a passage
- explore unseen prose comparisons.

KEY CONCEPTS

Language, form, structure, genres, context, style, interpretation, critical reading.

Before you start

- Revise the unseen prose unit (Unit 11) in the first section of the book.
- Prepare for the exercises by studying the printed passages carefully. You may like to research the writers before starting.

Every time you read a prose passage for the first time, it is, like a new poem, 'unseen' to you. This unit helps you by giving advice and practice on approaching close reading of prose whether you have an unseen component in your examinations or not.

Here you've got a variety of examples of individual passages with some suggested responses, and further ideas for different ways of handling the same issues for discussion. The examples chosen have very different styles and range from a Victorian novel to more contemporary works, but you can learn something from all of them.

Individual passages

The following activities may be done as unseens, or you can answer the questions at the end of each one as help towards developing your skills of close analysis.

ACTIVITY 25.1

Essay: *Write a critical appreciation of the following passage from the beginning of The Mill on the Floss by George Eliot.*

Passage 1

The rush of the water and the booming of the mill bring a dreamy deafness, which seems to heighten the peacefulness of the scene. They are like a great curtain of sound, shutting one out from the world beyond. And now there is the thunder of the huge covered wagon coming home with sacks of grain. That honest waggoner is thinking of his dinner, getting sadly dry in the oven at this late hour; but he will not touch it till he has fed his horses, – the strong, submissive, meek-eyed beasts, who, I fancy, are looking mild reproach at him

▶

from between their blinkers, that he should crack his whip at them in that awful manner as if they needed that hint! See how they stretch their shoulders up the slope toward the bridge, with all the more energy because they are so near home. Look at their grand shaggy feet that seem to grasp the firm earth, at the patient strength of their necks, bowed under the heavy collar, at the mighty muscles of their struggling haunches! I should like well to hear them neigh over their hardly earned feed of corn, and see them, with their moist necks freed from the harness, dipping their eager nostrils into the muddy pond. Now they are on the bridge, and down they go again at a swifter pace, and the arch of the covered wagon disappears at the turning behind the trees.

Now I can turn my eyes towards the mill again, and watch the unresting wheel sending out its diamond jets of water. That little girl is watching it too; she has been standing on just the same spot at the edge of the water ever since I paused on the bridge. And that queer white cur with the brown ear seems to be leaping and barking in ineffectual remonstrance with the wheel; perhaps he is jealous because his playfellow in the beaver bonnet is so rapt in its movement. It is time the little playfellow went in, I think; and there is a very bright fire to tempt her: the red light shines out under the deepening grey of the sky. It is time, too, for me to leave off resting my arms on the cold stone of this bridge …

Ah, my arms are really benumbed. I have been pressing my elbows on the arms of my chair, and dreaming that I was standing on the bridge in front of Dorlcote Mill, as it looked one February afternoon many years ago. Before I dozed off, I was going to tell you what Mr and Mrs Tulliver were talking about, as they sat by the bright fire in the left-hand parlour, on that very afternoon I have been dreaming of.

George Eliot *The Mill on the Floss* (1860)

Unseen alert! If you are doing this as an unseen, do not read on. You can answer the questions later when you have tried it for yourself.

ACTIVITY 25.2

Work through the sections with your classmate.

First thoughts on Passage 1:

1. Very descriptive of the water and the horses
2. Focus on a little girl and her dog
3. Seems to be part of the scene herself
4. Speaks directly to the reader
5. Focuses at the end on what is going to happen next (the conversation between Mr and Mrs Tulliver)

Find examples to illustrate these points and comment on them.

SAMPLE RESPONSE

1. Water and mill – metaphor: *curtain, thunder, unresting wheel*; onomatopoeia: *rush, booming*. Suggests power, constant movement, exclusion of world beyond. The horses are also powerful: *grand...feet, patient strength, mighty muscles*. They are powerful but meek and submissive. This could suggest that it is possible to tame them, to use them. The environment is evidently an agricultural one – they are carrying grain sacks; however, they are perhaps also contrasted with the water, which is more powerful but also tamed to an extent, and, if you know the novel, the girl, whose powers are constantly suppressed to try to make her meek (but you could not know this from this passage so early in the novel).
2. The child is, however, very focused: *so rapt in its movement*; juxtaposed with the dog which is *leaping and barking*, she is capable of quiet attention and absorption in the scene before her, suggesting what sort of character she may turn out to be.
3. The novelist imagines herself at the scene, watching: *Now I can turn my eyes towards the mill again*; *I paused on the bridge* – this has the effect of a narrator who is telling a true story, because she was there at the scene. She is not afraid to intrude on the narrative, and seems to empathise with the characters' feelings: not only the girl and the waggoner, but the horses and dog as well.
4. She makes a number of direct addresses to the reader: *See*; *Look*; *I think*; *Before I dozed off, I was going to tell you*. This should be taken together with the previous point. We are always aware of her presence telling the story. And although she speaks of *dreaming*, we do not find the narrative at all dreamlike – it has a very naturalistic feel. Try not to use the words *reality* or *realism* when you are talking about the world of a novel. The 19th-century novelists, of whom Eliot is one, did try to create worlds which seem close to 'real life', but of course, it is not real life: the novelist shapes the material **(verisimilitude)**.
5. She looks ahead to what happens next: the narrative proceeds clearly; we know what has happened and will see her comments on the significance of it. She guides the reader throughout.

This passage is very descriptive. In addition to the metaphors and similes, used for the water and the horses, the use of the verbs is worth noting. The passage is written in the present tense (perhaps you thought this was a modern idea!) In the second paragraph, the *-ing* form is used a great deal, either descriptively, as in ▶

KEY TERM

Verisimilitude: a useful word meaning the 'likeness of a narrative to real life'.

unresting and *deepening*, or as the present continuous form of the verb: *watching*, *standing*, *leaping*, *barking*, *resting*. These give an active immediacy to the situation and to the description, setting the scene of the girl and the water, which will remain with us until the end of the novel.

KEY CONCEPTS

If you are studying Eliot, compare her writing with Jane Austen's. There is no dialogue, no humour, no irony; it is more descriptive, its narrator is more intrusive. There is more direct address to the reader. However, both are written in the third person – they are not first-person narratives, although the 'I' in this passage is so dominant, it is like a first-person narrative! If we were to read both novels, we would be struck by the wealth of wider social comment made by Eliot, but Austen's close scrutiny of a small group in a community, while less broad, is very intensive.

ACTIVITY 25.3

Write a critical appreciation of the following passage.

Note: Pip has come into a fortune from an unknown benefactor and is about to leave the Forge where he has lived his life up to this point, cared for by Joe and Biddy.

Passage 2

'Saturday night,' said I, when we sat at our supper of bread and cheese and beer. 'Five more days, and then the day before the day! They'll soon go.'

'Yes, Pip,' observed Joe, whose voice sounded hollow in his beer-mug. 'They'll soon go.'

'Soon, soon go,' said Biddy.

'I have been thinking, Joe, that when I go down town on Monday, and order my new clothes, I shall tell the tailor that I'll come and put them on there, or that I'll have them sent to Mr Pumblechook's. It would be very disagreeable to be stared at by all the people here.'

'Mr and Mrs Hubble might like to see you in your new genteel figure too, Pip,' said Joe, industriously cutting his bread, with his cheese on it, in the palm of his left hand, and glancing at my untasted supper as if he thought of the time when we used to compare slices. 'So might Wopsle. And the Jolly Bargemen might take it as a compliment.'

'That's just what I don't want, Joe. They would make such a business of it,—such a coarse and common business,—that I couldn't bear myself.'

'Ah, that indeed, Pip!' said Joe. 'If you couldn't abear yourself—'

Biddy asked me here, as she sat holding my sister's plate, 'Have you thought about when you'll show yourself to Mr Gargery, and your sister and me? You will show yourself to us; won't you?'

'Biddy,' I returned with some resentment, 'you are so exceedingly quick that it's difficult to keep up with you.'

('She always were quick,' observed Joe.)

'If you had waited another moment, Biddy, you would have heard me say that I shall bring my clothes here in a bundle one evening,—most likely on the evening before I go away.'

▶

Biddy said no more. Handsomely forgiving her, I soon exchanged an affectionate good night with her and Joe, and went up to bed. When I got into my little room, I sat down and took a long look at it, as a mean little room that I should soon be parted from and raised above, for ever. It was furnished with fresh young remembrances too, and even at the same moment I fell into much the same confused division of mind between it and the better rooms to which I was going, as I had been in so often between the forge and Miss Havisham's, and Biddy and Estella.

The sun had been shining brightly all day on the roof of my attic, and the room was warm. As I put the window open and stood looking out, I saw Joe come slowly forth at the dark door, below, and take a turn or two in the air; and then I saw Biddy come, and bring him a pipe and light it for him. He never smoked so late, and it seemed to hint to me that he wanted comforting, for some reason or other.

He presently stood at the door immediately beneath me, smoking his pipe, and Biddy stood there too, quietly talking to him, and I knew that they talked of me, for I heard my name mentioned in an endearing tone by both of them more than once. I would not have listened for more, if I could have heard more; so I drew away from the window, and sat down in my one chair by the bedside, feeling it very sorrowful and strange that this first night of my bright fortunes should be the loneliest I had ever known.

Charles Dickens *Great Expectations* (1860)

KEY CONCEPTS

Striving to better oneself is an important theme of the Victorian novel, but it is often conceived in purely materialistic terms. It will take the whole novel for Pip to appreciate moral betterment and the enormous misapprehensions that have accompanied his journey through the novel.

Unseen alert! If you are doing this as an unseen do not read on.

ACTIVITY 25.4

Consider the following questions in relation to Passage 2:

1. There are three characters involved directly here: Joe and Biddy, and Pip the narrator – with some mention of others. Look at the phrase *soon go* at the beginning of the passage. What is the tone of each of these phrases? In other words, how does each character say the same words?
2. What does the little interchange between Pip and Biddy in the middle of the passage suggest about Biddy? You should include Joe's comment about her.
3. Find examples which show how Pip is now thinking of himself as above those around him, both at home and in his immediate environment.
4. There are also hints that beneath his growing snobbery is an awareness of what he is losing and a sympathy for those he is leaving behind who have always loved and cared for him. Find examples in the language which support this.
5. *'Ah, that indeed, Pip!' said Joe. 'If you couldn't abear yourself—'* What does this draw attention to? Think about what Pip thinks of himself now, and what Joe's unfinished comment suggests about different ways of looking at a person's sense of identity, by other people.
6. What impression do you gain about Joe from reading this passage? Find brief examples to support your points.
7. Consider the interplay of dialogue with description in this passage and the effect of this.
8. In what ways does the final sentence of the passage sum up its themes?

Reflection: Your answers to these questions should help to show that a first-person narrator can be very limited in her/his thoughts, focused on their own self-importance. The novelist must offer other possible interpretations of words and actions for the reader to notice, in order to point the irony. How does Dickens achieve this in Passage 2?

ACTIVITY 25.5

Read the following passage from a short story *The Courthouse* by Bangladeshi British writer Tahmima Anam and find examples for the text boxes that follow.

Note: Following the death of Iqbal, Rehana's husband, Iqbal's brother has been successful in a legal bid to adopt the children of Iqbal and Rehana. They have just left.

Passage 3

In the morning the children were gone. Rehana had packed their things in a hurry, crying into the comb, the ragged copy of *Treasure Island*, forgetting to fold, jamming shoes into the corners of the trunk. Sandwiched between their clothes was a photograph of Iqbal in his three-piece suit, one thumb hooked into his waistband, another on the dial of his pocketwatch. She packed a copy of the Holy Book, then took it out. She had tried to write them a letter, but she had no words. Finally she settled for a few mooris[1] and a bar of chocolate.

Afterwards, when the door was shut behind them, Rehana turned to find their little things strewn over the bedroom, the corridors. A sock, a sliver of ribbon. A page from Sohail's notebook. The stray things rattled around the bungalow like a cough.

They still called it the bungalow, because it was a modest house on a vast, empty plot – a one-storey building with just two bedrooms, a drawing room, a kitchen, a wrap-around veranda. The bedrooms faced the garden and the empty land beyond; the living room and kitchen faced the street. There were plans for a grander house at the back of the property. The bungalow would be for visitors, perhaps an office. But Iqbal hadn't stayed to build the big house.

It was Iqbal's idea to buy the plot in Dhanmondi. Less than a year after they were married, he had insisted they move out of their flat on Aga Masih Lane in the old part of town. Rehana was reluctant to go; she loved the narrow streets, the smell of the Buriganga river, the shuttered buildings built by the first pioneers into the city: the river-boat owners, the traders, the Bible-wielding Jesuits. It had a sense of its own history. Dhanmondi, on the other hand, was a new residential area, just a few dirt roads carved out from the paddy. It's the future, Iqbal had said. Soon this will be the best neighbourhood in Dhaka.

And so it was. Sprawling, flat-roofed buildings set back from the road, speaking of prosperity and new money.

Rehana looked out at her tract of empty land. She had created a border with rose bushes and red hibiscus and a pair of banana trees. Inside the border was the bungalow, the small vegetable patch, and the sagging mango tree that had come with the plot. Beyond it the land was wild, the earth soft and yielding, the kind of earth that swallowed sandals and sprouted thick tufts of moss even on the coldest days.

Rehana unlatched the veranda gate and stepped into the garden. She took off her sandals and felt the grass prickling her feet, and then, a few seconds later, the cool embrace of silt between her toes. She made her way to the back of the

▶

garden, and found the small garden tap she'd used to water her roses – pink – all through the dry season. Their tired blooms surrounded her, staring as she kneeled in front of the tap and pressed her forehead against it. The metal felt cool and indifferent; once she twisted the knob, inviting her to squat underneath the stream, which she did, bending her neck to make it fit. She had been here before; she knew what to do.

She sat under the tap until she was fully soaked. She was not sure if she was cold. She closed her eyes and felt the poisonous sting behind them. Then she lay down beneath the tap and fell asleep.

Tahmima Anam *The Courthouse* (2006)

[1] **mooris (L.11):** rice snacks

ACTIVITY 25.6

Copy and complete the following text boxes following the instructions at the foot of each box for writing about the passage. After you've done this, you'll be looking closely at the different sentence structures used in the passage. The 'Themes' box is left until last, but you may want to look at that box first to help you.

Subject and situation

One character's thoughts and actions following the taking away of her children; domestic setting – her home and garden, with her memories of her previous house. However, her husband's words and ideas are reported.

Give brief textual support for these points from Passage 3.

Diction and figures of speech

Words and images relating to the children and their activities.

Personifications in the penultimate paragraph – what effect does this have?

Give examples of these points from Passage 3.

Symbolism

Are any aspects of the house and garden used symbolically to represent the writer's concerns, or Rehana's situation and state of mind? You could consider objects in the house too.

Give your response to these questions about Passage 3, with examples.

Narrative position

Third-person omniscient narrator focused on one character; past tense, no dialogue.

Give brief textual support for these points from Passage 3.

Structure

Does the passage tell a straightforward story of Rehana's actions? How do the third and fourth paragraphs contribute, for example?

Give your response to these questions about Passage 3, with examples.

Tone and atmosphere

Does the third-person narrator of the story betray any direct sympathy for Rehana? How does the writing show this rather than telling it to us?

How would you describe the atmosphere of the passage?

Give your response to these questions about Passage 3, and find examples to support your point of view.

Themes

- Loss – personal and environmental
- Contrast of past and present
- Memory
- Contrast of built environment and natural world
- Multicultural references suggest a post-colonial setting.

Find examples of these themes in Passage 3.

Close study – sentence structure

All good prose writers use a variety of sentence structures to express their work in the most effective way. If you look closely at Passage 3, you will see that Anam is no exception.

ACTIVITY 25.7

Look at this table on *The Courthouse*, by Tahmima Anam. Find further examples from the passage and note the effects they create.

Feature	Example	Effect
Simple short sentence	*And so it was.* (line 43)	Emphasis of Iqbal's point of view.
Longer descriptive sentence with a number of clauses	*Beyond it the land was wild, the earth soft and yielding, the kind of earth that swallowed sandals and sprouted thick tufts of moss even on the coldest days.* (lines 51–54)	Develops the atmosphere of the garden, incorporates a transferred epithet for Rehana herself, *soft and yielding*, relates to life with the children (lost sandals), implies the richness of nature even in a suburb.
Repeated present participles (*-ing* parts of the verb)	*crying … forgetting … jamming* (lines 2 and 4)	Continuous action words to show what Rehana is doing at the beginning.
Sentence fragments	*A sock, a sliver of ribbon.* (lines 15 and 16)	Physical images of the disconnected suggest what life has become as well as symbolising the children's concerns.
Use of lists	*… the river-boat owners, the traders, the Bible-wielding Jesuits.* (lines 36 and 37)	Emphasises the rich diversity of the area and its history.
Reported speech	*It's the future, Iqbal had said. Soon this will be the best neighbourhood in Dhaka.* (lines 40–42)	Although the passage is all about Rehana and her thoughts and feelings, the presence of her husband is felt through the passage. This scrap of reported speech is part of the effect.

ACTIVITY 25.8

Essay: *Write a critical appreciation of the following passage from Disgrace by South African novelist J.M. Coetzee (1999).*

Note: David Lurie is a middle-aged university professor of literature who is attracted by Melanie, one of his students. Meeting her by accident, he has invited her in and cooked supper for them. He has just given her a drink.

Passage 4

As she sips, he leans over and touches her cheek. 'You're very lovely,' he says. 'I'm going to invite you to do something reckless.' He touches her again. 'Stay. Spend the night with me.'

Across the rim of the cup she regards him steadily. 'Why?'

'Because you ought to.'

'Why ought I to?'

'Why? Because a woman's beauty does not belong to her alone. It is part of the bounty she brings into the world. She has a duty to share it.'

His hand still rests against her cheek. She does not withdraw, but does not yield either.

▶

'And what if I already share it?' In her voice there is a hint of breathlessness. Exciting, always to be courted: exciting, pleasureable.

'Then you should share it more widely.'

Smooth words, as old as seduction itself. Yet at this moment he believes in them. She does not own herself. Beauty does not own itself.

'From fairest creatures we desire increase,' he says, 'that thereby beauty's rose might never die.'*

Not a good move. Her smile loses its playful, mobile quality. The pentameter, whose cadence once served so well to oil the serpent's words, now only estranges. He has become a teacher again, man of the book, guardian of the culture-hoard. She puts down her cup. 'I must leave. I'm expected.'

The clouds have cleared, the stars are shining. 'A lovely night,' he says, unlocking the garden gate. She does not look up. 'Shall I walk you home?'

'No.'

J.M. Coetzee *Disgrace* (1999)

**From fairest creatures we desire increase / That thereby beauty's rose might never die:* from Shakespeare's first Sonnet.

Unseen alert! If you are doing this as an unseen do not read on.

ACTIVITY 25.9

Analyse the text and ask yourself the following questions:

1. What tense and person are the passage written in? What effect does this have? (Hint: past or present? 'I' or 'He/she'?) When you've finished all the questions, you could return to this question and think about it again, exploring Coetzee's use of focalization and its effects.
2. How does the language show that the focus is on the 'he' of the passage – find some examples. These can include moments where he makes assumptions about her responses. (Hint: consider the word breathlessness, for example.)
3. Find some examples of words or phrases which describe Melanie's responses and feelings. What effect do they have? They may help you to answer Q6.
4. Find an example to show that he sees life in literary terms. What effect might this have on his behaviour?
5. Using the evidence from this passage, how would you describe the attitudes David seems to hold about women?
6. Consider the possible response of readers to the two characters. Where do your sympathies lie? Find detailed examples in the language to support your response.
7. If you answered question 6 by saying you were more sympathetic to Melanie, see if you can find any places where you have some sympathy for David. Justify your response.
8. Consider the image of 'the serpent's words' and the final description of the night sky – what effects do these have in the passage?
9. Some of the 'sentences' used are not complete sentences. Find examples and discuss their effects.
10. How would you describe the tone of this passage? In what ways does Coetzee create irony, for example?

ACTIVITY 25.10

Read the following passage carefully and then look at the sample response if you aren't trying this as an unseen. If you are doing it unseen, then only look at the sample response afterwards, to see if there are points you have missed; or you may have thought of something not covered in the sample response.

The following passage is from the novel *The Lives of Others* (2014) by Indian writer Neel Mukarjee. Sandhya is part of a large family who share a house in Calcutta. Her 21-year-old son Supratik has left the family home without warning and joined a dissident group who are planning radical violence, but she does not know this. He has sent her two postcards.

Essay: *Read the following passage from the novel The Lives of Others (2014) by Indian writer Neel Mukarjee and write a critical appreciation of it.*

Reflection: Look again at Unit 7: mixed narrative, where focalization is discussed. It is possible for the main character of a novel, or indeed a play, to be unlikeable (Macbeth is a murderer, for example; so is Balram in *The White Tiger*). Yet, because we have access to their innermost thoughts and feelings, we cannot be indifferent to them.

Passage 5

Her thinning and now greying hair spread out in a pitiful swathe across the bank of stale pillows on which her head rests, Sandhya runs the indelible film of her son's two postcards in her head. She had taken to her bed ever since Supratik left a year ago, only very occasionally leaving it to perform the bare minimum of tasks that would keep her from puncturing a vital divisive membrane and slipping form the world of humans to something less-than-human. Overnight she had dropped out of her life and become a spectre, giving up on all her duties and privileges as the eldest daughter-in-law at the helm of the family ship and letting it drift, keelless and rudderless; she didn't care any more about anything. The images of the two postcards burn through her: six inches by four inches (yes, she had measured them with a ruler) of light-beige ordinariness, the imprint of the head of the Royal Bengal Tiger, along with the denomination, fifteen paisa, on the top right-hand corner, just above the ruled space for the address...she knows every atom of those two postcards now.

She has stared at them so hard, willing them to release the imprisoned meanings from behind the cursive cage of the words, the *real* meanings that would communicate something special to her beyond what its surface said. She has handled them, stroked them, slept with them under her pillow, all with the wish to touch what he had touched, a kind of communion of distance, of air. And she had done it so often that even she was prepared to admit, had she been faced with such a requirement, that she had erased all traces of his touch from the postcards by now. There were times when she had wanted to ingest them, chew them into a bolus, swallow them and assimilate their essence into her blood. That would have been a way of holding on to his presence.

Two postcards in a year. That was all a firstborn owed his mother.

The first one, dated 19th April 1968 – it was her mother-in-law who had pointed out, over the weeks spent dissecting and anatomising it to its very elementary particles, that the date was the New Year – that first postcard, addressed to her, contained only five sentences:

▶

Respected Ma, I am well, don't worry about me. I hope all of you are too. The postal services where I am are a bit erratic and infrequent, so I'm getting someone to post it to you from Calcutta. I will be in touch again. Give everyone my love. Supratik

It was his hand, confident, elegant, neat, there was no doubt about that; Sandhya would have been able to identify it as her sons with her eyes shut. The second one, sent five months after the first, was even more parsimonious and ungiving:

Respected Ma, Hope all your news is well. I am in good health and spirit. Truly. Don't worry about me. Again, this postcard is being mailed to you from Calcutta. My love to everyone. Supratik.

The arrival of the first one had created such a huge jag in expectations that for the ensuing month or two Sandhya had left her bed and taken up an almost immoveable position in an armchair on the verandah in the daylight hours, willing the postman to arrive with another letter from her son. That hope had turned to ashes slowly and Sandhya had taken to her bed again.

Neel Mukarjee *The Lives of Others* (2015)
*Paisa = a unit of currency in India
*Bolus = ball of chewed food

SAMPLE RESPONSE

This passage is a third-person account of a mother whose son has left home and whose only communication with her has been a couple of postcards. She is deeply upset and has taken to her bed. The narrator focuses on her thoughts and actions, but the wording on the postcards does also create a sense of the character of her son and provides a contrast to the descriptions in the structure of the main passage, which are very detailed and often metaphorical. The writer's use of symbolism is striking.

The narrator makes it clear that the mother's behaviour is obsessive and he stresses this through his use of metaphorical and symbolic language, often using the present tense for immediacy. She does nothing except grieve in bed all day and only leaves her bed to do a minimum of tasks that keep her *human* rather than *less-than-human*, apart from a brief period when she waited in a chair on the verandah for the post to arrive. She is a *spectre* – a ghost, not a real being anymore. This is shocking and effective for the reader. She has studied the postcards so hard that they are an *indelible film in her brain* that cannot be rubbed out. Her actions with the postcards are given in a tricolon: *she has handled them, stroked them, slept with them under her pillow* as if they had feelings. They seem to have become symbols of her son and she wants to keep him close. As well as measuring the postcards and memorising their appearance, she even wanted at times to eat them so that she could hold *on to his presence*. The reader is constantly reminded of their physical properties, *every atom*; their *very elementary particles*. Sandhya is living in a large family group but has given up all her responsibilities. She and the large extended family are imaged metaphorically as the captain and the family ship, but she is now letting it *drift, keelless and rudderless*. She is described as *pitiful*, with her *thinning … greying hair*

▶

in the first sentence of the extract, lying on her *stale pillows*, but her behaviour is so extreme that it is hard for the reader to feel complete sympathy for her.

The language of the postcards is a complete contrast, giving variety to the passage and suggesting the youth and vitality of her son. They are written in simple typical postcard language, with brief reassurances and advice not to worry about him. Sandhya's attitude to them as symbolic of Supratik is reinforced here in another tricolon: his handwriting is *confident, elegant, neat* like him. The narrator suggests (with some humour in the exaggeration) that she would have recognised his writing *with her eyes shut*. The metaphor of the words on the postcard being like a *cage* for the meaning is very striking. The second postcard is personified as a miserly person *even more parsimonious and ungiving*, although in fact it says more about his health than the first: *I am in good health and spirit. Truly.* The use of the postcards effectively contrasts the boy and his mother through the very different language used.

The contrast between youth and age is suggested here: the boy is thoughtlessly pursuing his own agenda, as young people do, and his mother is an extreme example of a doting mother. He has taken care to tell her that the postcard was posted in Calcutta even though he is not there, perhaps to stop her from searching for him, as he is involved in illegal activity. The passage is also a close study of obsessive behaviour – which cannot have a good outcome, the reader feels. Even if he returns home, her obsession with him would make both of their lives very difficult. This is an unusually physical passage, which takes us close to the life of a person and their physical preoccupations.

Reflection: How did you respond to this passage from the novel? Were you sympathetic to the mother, or did you feel some distance from her because her behaviour is so extreme? Sometimes one's response to literature is coloured by one's own situation. If your mother is very possessive, for example, you might have instinctive sympathy for Supratik. Were there other points on language that you wanted to make? Discuss some of the descriptive words and phrases with a friend.

ACTIVITY 25.11

The following passage is the very end of the novel *The Remains of the Day (1989)*) by British-Japanese writer Kazuo Ishiguro. During the 1930s, Stevens, the first-person narrator of the novel, serves as a very dignified and proper English butler to Lord Darlington in a great country house (now owned by a wealthy American, Mr Faraday, whom Stevens still works for). Stevens is so dedicated to his role as butler to a great house that he doesn't even go to his father on his deathbed so that he can continue to serve his master and the important guests. He overlooks Darlington's Nazi sympathies and anti-Semitism and suppresses his warm feelings towards Miss Kenton, the Head Housekeeper at the time. Twenty years after his employer's death, Stevens tries to reconnect with Miss Kenton, and begins to question his devotion to his former master. Here, he has just spoken to a man on the pier who tells him to enjoy his final years and not to look back with regret.

This is not an easy passage, since Stevens is the kind of narrator who reveals his character in spite of himself and it is our job to probe the language closely. Ishiguro is masterly in his creation of imperfect or unreliable narrators. (He once said in an interview that his main narrators were always the same as each other – repressed and unable to express their feelings.)

If you are doing this as an unseen, your question would be:

Essay: *Write a critical appreciation of the following passage, paying particular attention to the narrator's tone and use of language.*

If you prefer, you can read the passage and answer the questions in Activity 25.12.

Passage 6

It is now some twenty minutes since the man left, but I have remained here on this bench to await the event that has just taken place – namely the switching on of the pier light. As I say, the happiness with which the pleasure-seekers gathering on this pier greeted this small event would tend to vouch for the correctness of my companion's words; for a great many people the evening is the most enjoyable part of the day. Perhaps, then, there is something to his advice that I should cease looking back so much, that I should adopt a more positive outlook and try to make the best of what remains of my day. After all, what can we ever gain in forever looking back and blaming ourselves if our lives have not turned out quite as we might have wished? The hard reality is, surely, that for the likes of you and I, there is little choice other than to leave our fate, ultimately, in the hands of those great gentlemen at the hub of this world who employ our services. What is the point in worrying oneself too much about what one could or could not have done to control the course one's life took? Surely it is enough that the likes of you and I at least *try* to make our contribution count for something true and worthy. And if some of us are prepared to sacrifice much in life in order to pursue such aspirations, surely that is in itself, whatever the outcome, cause for pride and contentment.

A few minutes ago, incidentally, shortly after the lights came on, I did turn on my bench a moment to study more closely those throngs of people laughing and chatting behind me. There are people of all ages strolling around this pier: families with children; couples, young and elderly, walking arm in arm. There is a group of six or seven people gathered just a little way behind me who have aroused my curiosity a little. I naturally assumed at first that they were a group of friends out together for the evening. But as I listened to their exchanges it became apparent they were strangers who just happened upon one another here on this spot behind me. Evidently, they had all paused a moment for the lights coming on, and then proceeded to fall into conversation with one another. As I watch them now they are laughing together merrily. It is curious how people can build such warmth among themselves so swiftly. It is possible these particular persons are simply united by the anticipation of the evening ahead. But, then, I fancy it has more to do with this skill of bantering. Listening to them now, I can hear them exchanging one bantering remark after another. It is, I would suppose, the way many people like to proceed. In fact it is possible my bench companion of a while ago expected me to banter with him – in which case, I suppose I was something of a sorry disappointment. Perhaps it is indeed time I began to look at this whole matter of bantering more enthusiastically. After all, when one thinks about it, it is not such a foolish thing to indulge in – particularly if it is the case that in bantering lies the key to human warmth.

It occurs to me, furthermore, that bantering is hardly an unreasonable duty for an employer to expect a professional to perform. I have of course already devoted much time to developing my bantering skills, but it is possible I have never previously approached the task with the commitment I might have done. Perhaps, then, when I return to Darlington Hall tomorrow – Mr Faraday will not himself

▶

be back for a further week – I will begin practising with renewed effort. I should hope, then, that by the time of my employer's return, I shall be in a position to pleasantly surprise him.

Kazuo Ishiguro *The Remains of The Day* (1989)

*Banter = to exchange remarks in a playful, friendly and teasing way.

ACTIVITY 25.12

Closely analyse the language in Passage 6 by considering the following:

1 Can you find any metaphors, similes or descriptive language in this passage? What does your answer suggest about the character of the narrator?

2 Stevens speaks in a very formal way and his sentences are not the casual ones of ordinary speech. Find some examples of this formality – there are many! I've given you one to start:

> the happiness with which the pleasure-seekers gathering on this pier greeted this small event would tend to vouch for the correctness of my companion's words;

When you have found several examples, look closely at the way these sentences are constructed. What makes them so stiff and formal? Try making them into more casual utterance. Consider what this tells us about Stevens's character and background.

3 The understatement (litotes) is sometimes considered typically British in its reticence, using phrases such as 'not bad' when you mean 'good', for example. Find an example here.

4 He repeats the phrase *the likes of you and I*. What assumptions is he making about the reader? (This construction is not entirely grammatical – it should be 'the likes of you and me', but putting 'I' instead of 'me' is a common mistake made by people trying to show they can use the language well. It shows Ishiguro's ability to 'get inside the head' of a man like Stevens)

Look through the passage and find some examples of Stevens's concern with his duty – what he did in the past and ought to do in the future.

5 ...*those great gentlemen at the hub of the world*: what does this expression suggest about Stevens's attitude to his previous employer and the kind of guests he had at the house? What does it suggest about his own self-image, by implication?

6 Can you find any examples that suggest a sense of loss in Stevens's life? Is he entirely happy with what he has done?

7 How do you react to the idea that Stevens can teach himself to 'banter'? Do you think there is any chance of this? Say why you have answered as you have.

8 Based on Ishiguro's use of language and tone, what impression overall do you gain of the character of Stevens? Discuss this with your classmate.

9 Do you find his limitations tragic or comic? You may need to read this novel (which is recommended) in order to answer this question fully. It is a novel with very humorous moments, but it is also very poignant.

Prose comparisons

Comparing two passages of prose is, like comparing two poems, a very effective way of appreciating the individual qualities of both of them. These exercises will develop your skills of close reading. As with poetry comparisons, you need to be systematic in your approach. Look again at method 1 and method 2 for structuring a poetry comparison in Unit 21, Activity 21.7. If you want to do these entirely unseen, avoid the guidance questions.

ACTIVITY 25.13

Read closely and consider carefully the two passages that follow. Then compare and contrast the two passages, working with your classmate if you like.

Note: Passage A is by Tim Winton, an Australian writer, Passage B by Annie Proulx, an American. In Passage A, the narrator is going to seek out his father who left his wife and family 20 years before and has gone to live on his own in the Outback (the remote bush country in Australia). His son has brought a message from his mother, who is dying of cancer.

In Passage B, the main character has given up city life for the country, left his wife for another woman (Catherine) and has ideas about making money out of playing music. Both passages contain references to Australian or American trees and shrubs whose names may be unfamiliar to you. Tim Winton's short-story collection *The Turning* resembles *Dubliners* in that the stories are a coherent whole, like a novel.

Passage A

I drove on up the thin black road awhile until I found the dirt turnoff indicated by the pencil map. The track was broad but muddy from the recent rains and when I turned into it the car felt sluggish and skittish by turns. I really had to concentrate to keep from sliding off into the scrub. Out here the earth was red, almost purple. Set against it, the flesh-coloured eucalypts and the grey-blue saltbush seemed so high-keyed they looked artificial. I had expected a desert vista, something rocky and open with distant horizons, but this woodland, with its quartzy mullock heaps and small trees, was almost claustrophobic. Mud clapped against the chassis and wheel arches. When I hit puddles, great red sheets of water sluiced the windscreen. Wrestling the wheel, I drove for half an hour until I came to a junction marked with a doorless fridge. It corresponded to my pencil map; I turned north. Five minutes later I turned off onto a slippery rutted track that ended in a four-way fork. After some hesitation I took the most northerly trail and drove slowly through old diggings and the pale blocks of fallen walls. The car wallowed through shimmering puddles and the track narrowed until saltbush glissed against the doors.

I'd begun to sweat and curse and look for some way of turning back when I saw the dull tin roof and the rusted stub of a windmill amongst the salmon gums. A dog began to bark. I eased into the clearing where a jumble of makeshift buildings and car bodies was scattered, and the moment I saw the man striding from the trees beyond, I knew it was him. I stalled the car and did not start it again. I was dimly aware of the dog crashing against the door, pressing itself against the glass at my shoulder. It really was the old man. He was taller than I remembered and I was startled by the way he carried himself, the unexpected dignity of him. All my manly determination deserted me.

Tim Winton *Commission* from *The Turning* (2005)

Passage B

He came out of the hemlocks into brushy tangled land and missed the narrow track hidden in weeds at the left. He had to back up to make the turn at the rusted mailbox leaning out of the cheatgrass like a lonesome dog yearning for a pat on the head. The guitar sounded in its case as Catherine's car strained up the grade, alder and willow whipping the cream-colored finish. The potholes deepened into washouts and shifting heaps of round, tan stones. He passed an old pick-up truck abandoned in a ditch, its windshield starred with bullet holes, thick burdocks thrusting up through the floor. Snipe felt a dirty excitement, as though he were looking through the train window again. When the Peugeot stalled on the steep grade he left it standing in the track, although it meant he would have to back down the hill in the dark.

He felt the gravel through the thin soles of his worn snakeskin boots; the guitar bumped against his leg, sounded a muffled chord. A quarter of a mile on he stopped and again took out the creased letter.

Dear Sir, I seen your ad you wanted to play with a Group. I got a Group mostly my family we play contry music. We play Wed nites 7 pm if you want to come by. – Eno Twilight

A map drawn with thick pencil lines showed only one turn off the gravel road. He folded it along the original creases and put it back in his shirt pocket so it lay flat and smooth.

He'd come this far, he might as well go all the way.

The grade leveled off and cornfields opened up on each side of the track. A mountaintop farm. Godawful place to live, thought Snipe, panting and grinning. He could smell cow manure and hot green growth. Pale dust sprayed up at every step. He felt it in his teeth, and when his fingers picked at his face, fine motes whirled in the thick orange light of the setting sun. A hard, glinting line of metal roof showed beyond the cornfield, and far away a wood thrush hurled cold glissandos into the stillness.

The house was old and broken, the splintery grey clapboards hanging loosely on the post-and-beam frame, the wavery glass in the windows mended with tape and cardboard. A hand-painted sign over the door said GOD FORGIVES. He could see a child's face in the window, see fleering mouth and squinting eyes before it turned away. *Arook*, *arook*, came a ferocious baying and barking from the dogs chained to narrow lean-tos beside the house. They stood straining at the edges of their dirt circles and clamored at his strangeness. Snipe stood on the broken millstone that served as a doorstep. Threads of corn silk lay on the granite. He was let into the stifling kitchen by the child whose uncontrolled face he had seen.

Annie Proulx *Heartsongs* (1994)

Unseen alert! If you are doing this as an unseen, do not read on.

ACTIVITY 25.14

With your classmate, work together on answering the following questions.

What similarities did you note between these two passages? You should look at the situation, the characters and what they are doing and any other language details.

COMMENT

Similarities

At first sight, the passages seem very similar, having much in common. You could have noted:

- Both have one main, male character, seeking something.
- Both involve journeys by car into the deepest countryside; both involve pencil-drawn maps, difficult narrow roads.
- The cars struggle and stall.
- The ways are punctuated by abandoned items: *a doorless fridge, an old pick-up*.
- Their destinations are tin huts, makeshift buildings, an air of neglect.
- There are characters at their destination: the father, and the child at the window as well as the members of the band Snipe has come to meet.
- At the level of language details, the idea of airlessness is mentioned – claustrophobia in the first and the *stifling kitchen* in the second; both use the word *glissando* (a musical term for a sliding effect) or its abbreviation *gliss*.
- Structurally, the passages both reach the destination being sought. Both stories are told in the past tense.

ACTIVITY 25.15

What differences are there between the two passages? Find brief quotations to support these points.

COMMENT

Differences

Setting

Writers often use setting symbolically or metonymically to enhance our appreciation of what is happening in a character's life. The description of the car in Passage A is almost personification: it is *sluggish and skittish by turns*. When the wet road attacks it, *mud clapped against the chassis*; *red sheets of water sluiced the windscreen*, the vigorous description transfers itself to the narrator's turbulent feelings, which are barely evident in the passage directly. The *old diggings and the pale blocks of fallen walls* symbolise the crumbled relationship he has with his father, the broken family. In Passage B, there are many more sensory descriptions of sight, sound, touch and smell. The guitar's sound is evoked on two occasions, almost personifying it, reminding us of the reasons for Snipe's visit. The word *glissando* used for a thrush in Passage B also reminds us of the importance of music; in Passage A it is just the sound of grasses against the car. The two indicators on the road – the fridge without a door and the abandoned vehicle full of bullet holes – symbolise lives at the edge of 'civilised' life: the broken family and the rough life riddled with violence.

Narrative position

Passage A is narrated in the first person and B in the third person. Given that the aim of both characters is to reach a particular destination with a specific purpose, it is important to consider how the choice of narrative position affects the presentation of their state of mind. Look closely at all evidence that suggests state of mind. The following comparative table may be helpful.

Passage A	Passage B
I really had to concentrate ... I had expected ... *After some hesitation ... I'd begun to sweat and curse and look for some way of turning back ... I knew it was him.*	*Snipe felt a dirty excitement ... He'd come this far, he might as well go all the way.* *Godawful place to live, thought Snipe, panting and grinning.*
I was startled ... I was dimly aware [of the dog] ... All my manly determination deserted me.	*He felt the gravel ... He could smell cow manure ... He felt it in his teeth ...*

You can see that the first-person narrator tells us what he is doing, and to some extent thinking, in more detail than Snipe does. If you had to choose only two of the examples in column A, which would you choose? And which would you take as contrast from column B?

I would choose from column A *I'd begun to sweat and curse and look for some way of turning back* with *He'd come this far, he might as well go all the way* from column B; and *All my manly determination deserted me* from A with *Godawful place to live, thought Snipe, panting and grinning* from B. The account suggests Snipe's state of mind is much less fraught, with *might as well* and *Godawful place*. You can't imagine our first narrator *panting and grinning*. Snipe is open-minded and hopeful of the future. There is something grimly determined about the narrator of Passage A.

You may also have noticed that the first narrator tells us in detail what he did with simple verbs: *I drove*, *I turned*, *I took*. He appears to be very controlled and only occasionally do his emotions escape, as we see here. When they do, they are profound: Winton builds to the climax here of the grown-up man meeting his father after 20 years. His journey is one into the past.

Other characters

The father in Passage A is the purpose of the narrator's visit and the emotional investment of the passage is focused on him, not surprisingly. In Passage B, the child's face at the window is part of the strange atmosphere that Snipe has come into, of poor hill farmers whose literacy is limited. Catherine is mentioned: a reader might have wondered why Snipe was driving Catherine's car, not his own.

If you read the whole story, you will discover that it is Catherine who has money and a job, and Snipe depends on this while he dreams of making money from being in a band. The character of Eno Twilight is implied in his letter, its spelling and grammar poor, as is the environment of his house when we see it.

Atmosphere

These are atmospheric pieces, creating a clear image of an alien rural environment, a place far from the 'normal' routine; this is where the events of the story will happen. These are poor environments for people, although Snipe enjoys the 'excitement' of slumming it.

KEY CONCEPTS

These are stories of the country, the Outback, in places which still have wild places. Life may be closer to the natural environment, but human interactions – of family, of shared interests, of conflicts – may be as raw as the land that surrounds them.

ACTIVITY 25.16

Passage A is from a short story by Vietnamese writer Nam Le; Passage B from a novel by Indian writer Anita Desai. The narrator in A is Vietnamese, but now living in the United States; he has just picked up his father, who is visiting for the first time, from the airport. In B, the main character, Deven, arrives home to find his wife has returned from a visit to her parents. Manu is their son.

Essay: *Compare and contrast the following passages of prose.*

Passage A

'You'll sleep in my room, Ba.' I watched him warily as he surveyed our surroundings, messy with books, papers, dirty plates, teacups, clothes – I'd intended to tidy up before going to the airport. 'I work in this room anyway, and I work at night.' As he moved into the kitchen, I grabbed the three-quarters-full bottle of Johnnie Walker from the second shelf of my bookcase and stashed it under the desk. I looked around. The desktop was gritty with cigarette ash. I threw some magazines over the roughest spots, then flipped one of them over because its cover bore a picture of Chairman Mao. I quickly gathered up the cigarette packs and sleeping pills and incense burners and dumped them all on a high shelf, behind my Kafka Vintage Classics.

At the kitchen swing door I remembered the photo of Linda beside the printer. Her glamour shot, I called it: hair windswept and eyes squinty, smiling at something out of frame. One of her ex-boyfriends had taken it at Lake MacBride. She looked happy. I snatched it and turned it facedown, covering it with scrap paper.

As I walked into the kitchen, I thought, for a moment, that I'd left the fire escape open. I could hear rainwater gushing along gutters, down through the pipes. Then I saw my father at the sink, sleeves rolled up, sponge in hand, washing the month-old crusted mound of dishes. The smell was awful. 'Ba', I frowned, 'you don't need to do that.'

His hands, hard and leathery, moved deftly in the sink.

'Ba' I said, halfheartedly.

'I'm almost finished.' He looked up and smiled. 'Have you eaten? Do you want me to make some lunch?'

'*Thoi*,' I said, suddenly irritated. 'You're exhausted. I'll go out and get us something.'

I went back through the living room into my bedroom, picking up clothes and rubbish along the way.

'You don't have to worry about me,' he called out. 'You just do what you always do.'

Nam Le *The Boat* (2008)

Passage B

He stood very still, though he was immensely agitated, and immensely worn out by a sleepless night spent at the bus depot. 'Why didn't you tell me you were returning today? I would have come to the station to meet you.'

'I did write,' she snapped, and pointed at an unopened letter that lay on the small table next to his chair. 'You never opened it,' she accused him, and started sweeping again.

He did not move out of her way but stood watching her crawl about the floor, sweeping the dust into little hills before her. He found he was no longer irritated by the sight of her labour, or disgusted by the shabbiness of her limp, worn clothes, or her hunched, twisted posture, her untidy hair or sullen expression. It was all a part of his own humiliation. He considered touching her, putting an arm round her stooped shoulders and drawing her to him. How else could he tell her he shared all her disappointment and woe?

But he could not make that move: it would have permanently undermined his position of power over her, a position that was as important to her as to him: if she ceased to believe in it, what would there be for her to do, where would she go? Such desolation could not be admitted. So he turned aside, asking, 'Where is Manu? I don't see him. Manu!'

'He has gone to the neighbours to show them his new clothes,' Sarla said, not looking up. 'My parents have given him new clothes. And shoes.'

He nodded, entirely accepting this slap to his pride and dignity as the breadwinner. He deserved their insults. They were perfectly right to insult him. When had he last bought his son anything? And now of course he never would – he was ruined.

He sat down on the cane chair and stared out of the open door at the garden gate, waiting for Manu. At least, that was what Sarla thought he was doing. She felt moved to ask, 'Tired? Shall I make you tea?' Contrary to appearances, she was actually quite pleased to be back in her own domain, to assume all its responsibilities, her indispensable presence in it; in her parents' home she had missed the sense of her own capability and position.

Deven only shook his head, saying nothing. She began to get irritated by his inaction. She wanted to get on with the cleaning of the house. She got up and went to fetch a duster, shouting from the kitchen,

'How could you let the house get so filthy? Why didn't you call for the sweeper to come and clean?'

Anita Desai *In Custody* (1984)

Unseen alert! If you are doing this as an unseen do not read on.

ACTIVITY 25.17

Answer the following question, working with your friend to find similarities between them. In the next activity, you'll look for the differences.

Essay: *What similarities did you note between these two passages? You should look at the situation, the characters and what they are doing and any other language details.*

COMMENT

Similarities

You could have said:

- Domestic situation – one person cleaning up after the other's mess: a father and son, a wife and husband. The one cleaning is the one who has arrived after a journey and found housework needing to be done.
- Guilt, tiredness and irritation are present in both.
- Theme of family pressures is present in both.
- Both refer to other close people important but not present – the photo of the girlfriend, Linda; the son Manu.

ACTIVITY 25.18

What differences are there between the two passages? Find brief quotations to support these points.

COMMENT

Differences

Setting

Both passages are set in the main character's home. Passage A is much more descriptive of the environment than Passage B.

- In Passage A, what impression do you get of the room and the occupant from the narrator's descriptions in paragraph 1? Consider some of the cultural associations of the objects mentioned – what effect does this have?
- Which objects are mentioned in Passage B? What effect does this difference have?

Narrative position

Passage A	Passage B
First person Focus on actions (find examples of these actions) Are there any examples of the first person's thoughts and feelings? You will need to look closely here to find anything obvious.	Third person, focused mostly on Deven, but there is a change later in the passage. (Can you identify where exactly?) Focus on thoughts and feelings (find examples of these, firstly related to Deven and then to Sarla). You have a great many examples to choose from.

Characterisation

What impression do you gain of the characters in each of these passages? Give examples to support your points. For which of the characters have you gathered more evidence? What effect does this have on your response to the character? Does Deven's self-criticism and self-questioning make you sympathetic to him?

Use of dialogue

There is not much dialogue in either passage. However, in Passage A the son tells his father what to do and his father is conciliatory. Any tension is below the surface. In Passage B,

▶

KEY CONCEPTS

The Vietnamese man who has made his home in the United States is surrounded with the paraphernalia of the (relatively) wealthy and culturally complex first world. Deven and his wife live quite simply and are not well-off. Their relationship is a traditional one, based on respect for different responsibilities.

there is more open hostility between husband and wife. The questions are aggressive ones. (Find examples of this.)

Language features

Both writers use lists – find some examples and consider what effect they have as well as how they differ from each other. What is the effect of rhetorical questions in Passage B?

Tone

Who is dominant in each situation and how is this conveyed in the tone of each passage? In any domestic situation, there may be a power struggle and these extracts illustrate this struggle clearly. Find some examples of this.

Do you find any humour or satire in the presentation of the first-person narrator's way of life in Passage A?

Reflection: Think of stories or novels you have studied where married couples or family groups are shown quarrelling (or disagreeing with each other more indirectly.) Why do you think writers favour this subject?

FURTHER READING

George Eliot's work is a great experience, although you need staying power for *Middlemarch.* (Ask your teacher why this is every English teacher's favourite novel!) *The Remains of the Day* is one of Ishiguro's most well-known works. The film of *Never Let Me Go* is heart-rending, by the way. *The Lives of Others* contains many graphic scenes of sex and torture, so avoid it if these topics upset you. Anita Desai's *Fasting, Feasting* is an excellent novel about young people growing up.

Self-assessment checklist

Reflect on what you've learnt in this unit and indicate your confidence level between 1 and 5. If you score below 3, revisit that section. Come back to this list later in your course. Has your confidence grown?

	Confidence level	Revisited?
I can analyse a passage with a third-person, intrusive narrator (Eliot)		
I can analyse closely and complete the text boxes (Anam)		
I can read with close attention, answer questions and note narrative features such as focalization (Coetzee)		
I can read with close attention and appreciate the essay (Mukarjee)		
I can read with close attention and identify the presentation of the unreliable narrator (Ishiguro)		
I can read with close attention and learn from the prose comparison exercises		

Section 6
Drama 2

Unit 26
Drama – critical essays

Learning objectives

In this unit you will:

- explore the meaning of the word 'dramatic' in essay questions
- read an essay on characterisation and evaluate its references to audience response
- consider and work on an essay on the drama-based theme of disguise
- consider and work on an essay on the dramatic theme of tragic-comedy.

KEY CONCEPTS

Language, form, structure, genres, context, style, interpretation, critical reading.

Before you start

- Revise the drama units in the first section of the book.
- Prepare for the exercises by studying the essays carefully. You may like to research the writers and the works before starting.
- Refer to the advice given on essay writing in Unit 29 in Part 3 of this book.

Writing an essay on plays

- When you write a critical or passage-based essay on poetry or the novel, you consider all the elements of language as words on the page and their effects on the reader. When you discuss plays, another dimension becomes very important and it's a dimension frequently highlighted in exam essay questions – the fact that the work you are analysing is a play, or an extract from a play *written for performance.*

- What this means is that in addition to discussing the language of the play – poetry or prose – you need to consider its effects in the theatre. In your mind, you become a member of the audience, so you need to visualise and use your imagination to create the scene mentally.
- When I say 'theatre' it doesn't necessarily mean a grand building with a stage and velvet curtains and hundreds of seats arranged in an auditorium. It could be a room with a space for the actors and seats around the edge for a small audience, or no seats at all! The actors could even be on the street.
- It's the thoughts and feelings of an audience as they watch the drama that are important. They could be shocked, fascinated, amused, disturbed, surprised, moved or just further informed by what they see, and you need to keep this in mind at all times. Unlike in a novel or short story, the characters of drama are directly in front of the audience, interpreted by actors who act their parts and unfold the personalities of their characters in real time.

In this unit you are going to look at three student essays on topics that are like those you will come across in your course or examination: one on a complex character from Shakespeare and the effect he has on an audience, one on a typical dramatic theme – disguise – from a play written by a woman in the Restoration Drama period and a modern play, which has been described as a 'tragi-comedy' – a genre word linked to drama. In all of them, the effect on an audience needs to be incorporated into the comments on the play. However, you will also notice important themes in all three, such as colonialism, the position of women in society and the purposelessness of modern life.

KEY CONCEPTS

Nature/Nurture debates have raged throughout the centuries. Is a person's development and personality a result of the genes they were born with (their DNA) or is it mostly influenced by life experiences, education and environment? Alternatively, is it a complicated mixture of both?

The Tempest by William Shakespeare

ACTIVITY 26.1

Caliban from *The Tempest* is one of Shakespeare's most fascinating characters. He and the spirit Ariel were the only inhabitants of the enchanted island where the exiled Duke of Milan, Prospero, was shipwrecked with his baby daughter Miranda 15 years ago, and Prospero has tried to educate him and teach him language. The play starts with a further shipwreck on the island of a group of courtiers from Milan, some of whom who had a hand in Prospero's banishment. Now they are in his power.

Read the essay on Caliban and then take your coloured marker pen and highlight all the points in the essay where the idea of dramatic effect on an audience is considered. Read the marker's comments on the essay.

Essay: *Prospero says of Caliban that he is 'a devil, a born devil, on whose nature / Nurture can never stick'. (Prospero's comment means that the character that Caliban was born with – his nature – can never be changed by attempts to educate and civilise him – his nurture). Discuss the dramatic presentation of Caliban in the light of this comment.*

STUDENT RESPONSE

In *The Tempest*, Shakespeare explores the relationship between human nature and civilisation and Caliban is a central character used to explore this theme. Shakespeare's sources suggest that Caliban is a natural man and some post-colonial modern critics consider that he is ill-treated by the coloniser Prospero who has failed to nurture him properly and acknowledge that he was on the island first. Other interpretations see him as the baser side of human nature who lacks all social graces and skills in contrast with the spirit Ariel and is thus incapable of nurture. But, however much we know about Shakespeare's sources and philosophical interpretations of his plays, Caliban is a very memorable character on the stage who audiences love as his dramatic presentation is so lively and engaging. He is directly contrasted with both Ferdinand and Ariel, which adds to the audience's appreciation of all three characters, enabling their understanding of complex and quite abstract themes.

The stock from which Caliban comes implies that he is not destined to be of good nature. Caliban's mother is Sycorax, a deformed hag '*grown into a hoop*' who worships the god Setebos and who was banished from society. Prospero says that Caliban's father was '*the devil himself*' and whether we can believe this or not, there is a great deal of dehumanising vocabulary attached to Caliban in the play – he is a '*fish*,' a '*monster*,' a '*mooncalf*' and a '*tortoise*,' mostly animal images rather than supernatural, but they all allow the director of the play free rein for his costumes on the stage and the nature of the food he eats!

One of Shakespeare's most important sources in writing the play was an essay by Montaigne: 'Of the cannibals', suggesting that that the creation of Caliban was inspired by the essay, as his name is an anagram of Canibal. He has been seen as a representative of the noble savage, the natural man, an idea which we can see in other literature up to the present day. But Caliban is much more than this, a far more complex character than the simply exploited native who is basically good by nature and corrupted by civilised man's arrival in his world. He is not what Prospero says he is in the prompt quotation, but he is not the noble savage either.

If 'nature' is all -important, then his parentage doesn't give Caliban a very good start. But 'Nature' means something more powerful in '*The Tempest*.' nature is the island itself and its beauties are expressed most expressively by Caliban and appreciated by the audience:

'*Be not afear'd; this isle is full of noises,*

Sounds and sweet airs which give delight and hurt not.'

When he is discussing the skills that come naturally to him by his association with the island, '*I with my long nails will dig thee pignuts*' or '*snare the nimble marmoset*,' his language is filled with imagery and expressed in blank verse. Yet in Prospero's company he declares that his use of language (that Prospero has taught him) is '*to curse*'. This aspect of his nurturing has enhanced his relationship with his own nature but it has not civilised him.

Another feature of civilisation brought to the island is alcohol. Stephano's 'book' of drink does not help to 'nurture' Caliban, though the drunken exploits of himself, Stephano and Trinculo are very amusing for the audience and provide striking contrast with the 'court party' many of whom are politicians and schemers, without sincerity or respect for the king. Thinking Stephano is a god, or at least a king, Caliban is an innocent, a little like Miranda who sees the court party and exclaims '*O brave new world, that has such people in it*'. Neither of them has been nurtured in the ways of the world but Caliban learns his lesson by the end of the play, seeing that Prospero is in fact vastly superior to Stephano: '*How fine my master is*'. In this sense he has been educated by his experiences and Prospero is wrong to say he is not educable.

The contrast with the courtly Ferdinand adds to the dramatic effect of the play's characterisation. The sexual chivalry displayed by Ferdinand and encouraged by Prospero is completely different from Caliban's approach to Miranda, whom he has attempted to rape before the action of the play starts and the image of the isle '*peopled...with Calibans*' is grotesque. Ferdinand is also willing to work for Prospero

▶

The introduction makes it clear that Caliban is a complex character who has been interpreted in different ways but that in performance he is always a favourite with audiences.

Clear knowledge of Caliban's parentage and the language that is used about him, giving hints for the director of the play.

Useful discussion of Shakespeare's sources and the way in which some interpretations have seen him as the 'noble savage'. This paragraph clearly suggests that Caliban is more complex.

An interesting and quite sophisticated point about Nature in the play, showing that it is not just human nature, and emphasising Caliban's appreciation of beauty, which is at odds with the idea of him as simply savage. The final point could be explored.

Caliban's relationship with Stephano and Trinculo, very amusing for the audience, shows him to be naïve, but the important point is made that by the end of the play he has learnt some discrimination, reinforcing the argument.

The contrasts with other characters add a dimension to this essay that enhances its argument clearly.

The central contrast between Caliban and Ariel is illustrated by an important structural example of the way in which the scenes are arranged by the playwright for both thematic and dramatic effect.

A clear summing up of the argument, ending with a personal reaction to the character and emphasising once again the audience response.

to show his worthiness, whereas Caliban complains all the time about his duties. You could argue that this is because Ferdinand's nature is a good one and he has been well-brought-up (both his nature and his nurture being superior), whereas Caliban's nature is base. But there are others on the island in the court party who are barbarous who supposedly have been nurtured into being 'civilised' – yet Antonio and Sebastian are evil and potential murderers. Even Prospero himself is sadistic at times, resorting to physical punishment '*cramps / side-stitches*' and using the animal goblins who chase Caliban, Stephano and Trinculo. All these characters compare and contrast with Caliban and allow the audience to see him as a complex character.

Most importantly, Caliban is also contrasted with Prospero's other servant Ariel, a spirit of the air, whilst Caliban is connected to the 'earth'. Physically the two are entirely different and it has been suggested that they represent the extremes of human nature – the spirit and the flesh. The contrast between them gives directors of the play great opportunities for costume, lighting and stage business. Ariel and Caliban can both be viewed as the "*colonized subjects*" of Prospero, and the differing attitudes of these subjects towards their master is indicative of the differing ways in which human nature responds to modern civilization. Both Ariel and Caliban are controlled by Prospero, yet they behave quite differently towards him, Ariel being respectful and willing and Caliban sullen and aggressive. The scenes of *The Tempest* are structured so as to emphasize this. As the play progresses, dialogues between Ariel and Prospero come directly before or directly after those between Caliban and Prospero. The contrasting nature of these interactions occurring dramatically portrays the contrast between the attitudes of these central characters, allowing the audience to see clearly the contrast between them and the language they use, and to enjoy the great variety of scenes in the play.

However this interpretation does not explain the beauty of the lines given to Caliban about the island, and his potential for development. These factors make it impossible to agree with what Prospero says about him in the prompt quotation. In spite of his unappealing habits and attitudes, the audience cannot help feeling sorry for Caliban and fascinated by him. The play's 'happy ending', restoring Prospero to his dukedom in Milan and the lovers to their noble marriage, does also allow Ariel his freedom and the return of the island to Caliban.

Reflection: Take any essay you have written on drama previously and go through it with your highlighter. Have you said enough to show that you are always keeping audience response in mind?

COMMENT

This is a very good essay that touches on many aspects of this complex play but is always in touch with audience response. Ideally a few more textual illustrations would be a bonus, but there is evidently a very good knowledge and appreciation of the play's structure, themes and characterisation, nonetheless. There is also room for evaluation of critical comment.

FURTHER STUDY

Search online for 'Shakespeare animated tales The Tempest' for an animated version of the whole play which you would enjoy. Discuss with your friend the depiction of Caliban. The Globe Theatre has excerpts on YouTube, but they don't include him.

Search online for 'The Tempest Act 1 Scene 2 Shakespeare's Globe' for some good sequences between Prospero and Ariel that show Prospero's commanding nature.

The Rover by Aphra Behn

ACTIVITY 26.2

The next essay for you to look at is on *The Rover* (1677), a play by the female dramatist Aphra Behn who was a British playwright from the Restoration era. She was one of the first English women to earn her living by her writing and she creates lively scenes as well as being frank about sexual roles and relationships.

Essay: *Consider the presentation and dramatic significance of disguise in The Rover.*

Read the essay and highlight all the points where audience response is indicated. Using a different colour, show where useful contextual points are made. With a third colour, highlight all the discourse markers, which are particularly well used in this essay.

KEY CONCEPTS

Restoration drama: The revival of drama in England after the restoration of the monarchy in 1660. Theatres were opened after 20 years of closure by the Puritans. New acting companies were formed and women appeared on the stage for the first time. Many of the plays were comedies of manners. In Unit 28 there is an unseen passage from one of these comedies.

STUDENT RESPONSE

The idea of disguise within *The Rover* is deeply embedded within the key themes of mistaken identity and appearance in contrast to reality. Behn uses it to create a subtle social commentary around contemporary issues of gender roles and the patriarchy. The audience are also much engaged by the many disguises and cross-dressing that take place in the carnival atmosphere.

Firstly the theme of disguise is vitally important in establishing the carnival setting of the play. Carnival represents to the characters a day in which debauchery and pleasure can take place before the period of religious fasting (Lent). The masquerade and costumes employed by Behn are therefore very significant, giving Naples a sense of fun and festivity, confirmed by Willmore's declaration '*Fun and mirth are my business in Naples*.' The carnival is also a particularly enthralling and relevant setting in terms of audience engagement as they will recognise Lent as similar to the interregnum where Puritans ruled and activities such as the theatre were banned. In comparison, the carnival is lively, flamboyant and great fun, much like the Cavalier values of Charles II. In addition, the costume changes, allowed by the setting of carnival, enable the various characters of different classes to merge and take opportunities for action which were impossible before, shown by Hellena's excited exclamation '*Let's ramble!*' This creates an always busy stage, full of action, given an additional sense of drama and chaos by the recently invented front stage lighting and pulleys in order to change scenes quickly. All of this creates a wonderfully fast pace, emphasised by the repetition of '*Tomorrow!*' to remind the audience of the impending deadline of Lent. This fast pace is arguably the most fundamentally important aspect of the play in allowing the sub-plots of disguise and mistaken identity to take place. Although in some cases the idea of disguise gives characters new opportunities, at other times the idea of disguise adds only danger, an example being the ever-present threat of the rape plot caused by the '*licensed lust*' allowed by the carnival. Hence, disguise in the carnival setting allows pace and dramatic tension to be built for the audience watching the play.

A thoughtful and relevant introduction, well-expressed.

Disguise as a vital part of the carnival setting is explored: its contribution to the play's pace, but also to the dangerous, edgy quality of the play. Perhaps there is an opportunity here to mention the comic elements.

Furthermore, disguise is crucial in allowing the appearance vs reality themes to be magnified and exemplified. Most of the characters change costumes regularly in order to maintain a disguise which benefits them, aiding them to accomplish their ultimate aims. The masculine characters for example, ear masks in order for their actions to have not repercussions – '*our own may not be obliged to answer 'em*' – a policy with strong resonances of cavalier and to a large extent, libertine, values. Willmore however differs

▶

Appearance and reality as an important theme is discussed and valuable (brief) contextual points are made.

Key Critical Term: Feminist Criticism

The twentieth century has seen a much greater emphasis on the unbiased presentation of women in literature. Feminist literary criticism uses the principles and ideology of Feminism to inform the analysis of language and especially female characterisation in literature. You will find a section on Schools of Literary Criticism in Section 3 of this book

This is explored further in relation to the female characters and the way in which they are categorised as being of quality or of 'easy virtue'.

Further development of the theme of disguise in relation to female characters' opportunities and the special case of Angellica. If time permitted, she is a character worth further discussion.

A thoughtful and apt summing up of the argument of the essay.

slightly from this in that he wears his '*own clothes, vizard in hand*' as he has no need to disguise his physical attributes, owing to his use of language. He is able to manipulate his language to suit his surroundings, changing between blank verse to match Angellica's language and prose and witty repartee when in the presence of Hellena. His language gibes him all the disguise he needs concealing his true motives in subversions within his speech.

Perhaps most prominent though is the angel-courtesan duality present in the female characters. This is the ultimate case of appearance vs reality as the ladies of quality dress as '*gipsies*' creating a blurring of distinction. Depending on how well they utilise this power, they experience varying levels of success. Hellena convinces Willmore (who previously exclaimed '*What the devil would I do with a woman of quality?*') and at the play's conclusion marries him, hence winning dominance over him. On the other hand, Florinda is put in danger as Willmore drunkenly stumbles upon her. His priorities are clearly expressed when he says '*A female! By this light, a woman. I'll be a dog if it's not a very wench*' – in other words, gender first, then age of maturity, then what social standing she is. The threat of rape is therefore imminent for Florinda and would have been a real issue for women of the time as legally women were unlikely to receive justice and their value in the marriage market is based entirely on their virginity. Overall the theme of disguise allows the characters to change or conceal their true identity, enabling them to achieve their freedom , but it can also pose a threat which would be felt as tension by a modern audience and perhaps more comedically by an audience of Behn's time.

Finally, the role of disguise in exploring feminine identity within the play is vital as it acts as an opportunity for the female characters to achieve their true desires, an act which is almost impossible in ordinary society. At the start of the play, each female character has their own space established. Hellena, for example, is a '*maid designed for a nun*', the idea of '*designed*' a particularly telling one, suggesting a lack of control on her part, coupled with an obvious unwillingness expressed in her pejorative tone on the subject. Florinda is destined to marry old Vincentio and Angellica is '*exposed for sale*'. The use of '*exposed*' is especially revealing of the vulnerability of women at the time to the economics of the marriage market. However, through disguise, two of them manage to gain some, if limited, freedom. Hellena is the perfect example of this, with frequent costume changes symbolising her fluid identity. She even enters dressed '*as a boy*' (the '*breeches part*'. Hence the use of disguise allows her to escape the hypocrisy of the patriarchal society of the time. In contrast, the courtesan Angellica is not given a happy ending and hence is not present on stage in the closing scene. Although Angellica begins as a promising powerful female character who uses her treatment as a commodity to her advantage, allowing Willmore to dominate her leads to her ultimate downfall. As a woman of easy virtue, her position is inescapable. The use of the portraits demonstrates this. They are open for the male '*gaze*' and illustrate her lack of uniqueness as a commodity. Her delusional attempt to became a wife to Willmore is inevitably unsuccessful as she is worthless to the marriage market due to lack of chastity. Despite this she tries to fool herself and the audience, describing herself as having a '*virgin heart*'. Even her name is ironic: '*Angellica Bianca*' carries strong connotations of purity which is very different from her role in the play. Therefore the use of disguise allows Behn to explore with the audience the idea of female identity and how women may be able to escape the boundaries placed on them by a male-dominated society.

In conclusion, Behn's use of disguise not only adds to the plot by deepening it, quickening the pace and creating tension and suspense, but it also allow the audience to question and consider the idea of perceived identity in relation to truth and femininity.

COMMENT

This is a well-organised essay, skillfully expressed and illustrated. The writer considers the themes seriously but could perhaps say more on the comic effects of masks and disguises in the play. An audience is not just thinking about themes – they are also reacting all the time to the comic potential of a play.

Reflection: Think about masks, especially full-face ones, and discuss their effects with your classmate. Covering your face not only hides your own real identity, but the new face you put on gives you another one. If you think no-one knows who you are, it might affect your behaviour. What plays have you studied where masks are used? (*Romeo and Juliet*, perhaps.)

FURTHER STUDY

Watching some of the trailers for the Royal Shakespeare Company's production of *The Rover* shows clearly that the director is making the most of the visual spectacle, action and comedy. What the members of the audience say is also revealing – note how they don't talk about the serious themes of the play; they say how much they enjoyed it. You are a serious student and have to discuss the writer's concerns, but you always need to keep in mind the effect of a play on an audience in a theatre.

Waiting for Godot by Samuel Beckett

ACTIVITY 26.3

Read the following student essay on Samuel Beckett's *Waiting for Godot*, the 20th-century existentialist and absurdist play. It's a famous play, since it encapsulates very effectively 20th-century loss of faith and meaning, yet it is entertaining to watch.

Once again, highlight the audience response comments.

Essay: *A 'tragi-comedy'. How far is this an apt description of the play?*

KEY CONCEPTS

Theatre of the absurd: drama that abandons conventional dramatic forms and focuses on the futility of human efforts in a senseless world.

KEY TERM

Existentialism: a philosophy that emphasises the isolation of the individual in an indifferent universe, and stresses freedom of choice and responsibility.

STUDENT RESPONSE

A 'tragi comedy' is traditionally a play which combines elements of tragedy (such as downfall, waste and death) with comedy (which may have complex comic complications but ends happily, often with marriage.) It is a genre often used to describe plays such as Shakespeare's *The Winter's Tale*. Is it an apt description for a play such as '*Waiting for Godot*'? It was the playwright's own subtitle for the play. Theatre critic Kenneth Tynan aptly said when it first came out: '*It has no plot, no climax, no denouement; no beginning, no middle and no end*'. It is thus clearly not an example of a traditional tragi-comedy, but it certainly combines the suffering of everyday life and its inevitable pointlessness with elements of comedy in the form of farce, slapstick and music hall, so the audience can see some tragic and some comic features.

The introduction defines the term and uses a helpful critical comment evaluation of which could be emphasised and employed in the argument. The essay title is engaged.

There is comedy to be found in the repetitive routines of the two tramps. Throughout the play there are repeated or almost repeated sections both structurally and in the dialogue and the audience will find this amusing. From the very start their exchanges are drawn out with the end of one line being echoed by the beginning of the next so that they never really reach a conclusion ('*In a ditch / A ditch?*'; '*Where? / Over there*'; '*Beat you? / Beat me*' and so on)This use of language, paired with the cyclical structure where whole sections of conversation are repeated throughout the course of the play is certainly comic for the audience. Throughout the play there are also name games like '*Pozzo, Bozz Gozzo*' and name ▶

calling such as '*punctilious pig*', puns, and rude humour. This resembles vaudeville or music hall banter and can include physical slapstick, especially if the director focuses on this and highlights it. Estragon can be played as Vladimir's feed, for example, like a pair of old-fashioned comedians. When Pozzo and Lucky enter in Act 2 and the whole ensemble end up piled upon one another on the floor, trying to pull each other up, which can add light relief. Other comedic moments come when Vladimir and Estragon talk about hanging themselves and at the end of the play try to use Estragon's belt, which merely results in his trousers falling sown and he shuffles off with the trousers round his ankles as they try to find somewhere to spend the night. Such moments are very comic for the audience and give the director and the actors a great deal of opportunity for comic presentation if they wish to take it.

The comedy is discussed, with textual examples and some awareness of comedy genre.

Yet, this very repetition highlights the tragic quality of the play. The trousers fall down because they are trying to commit suicide with Estragon's belt. Waiting endlessly for something that never comes, having no point or meaning to one's existence, suffering the petty irritations of everyday life such as pain or minor illness: these are exemplified throughout the play and suggest a bleak vision of life. There are a number of references to more serious suffering and violence such as Lucky going dumb and Pozzo being struck with blindness as well as Estragon's foot pain and Vladimir's prostate , as well as his frustrated inability to remember. Some of these offer a moment of comedy to the audience, but overall it is a bleak vision. In order to pass the time they indulge in irrelevant, meaningless activity. The element of farce is easily forgotten and the miserable condition of human beings dominates.

The serious themes of the play are addressed.

Estragon and Vladimir are waiting pointlessly. They do not know who Godot is. They are not sure about the time or about the place of their appointment. They don't even know what will happen if they stop waiting. They are totally impotent and powerless. All they can say is "*Nothing to be done*". Theirs is a world of negation in which inactivity is the safest course; as Estragon says: '*Don't let us do anything, it's safer*'.

Specific focus on the two tramps.

So in my view it's the tragic elements that drive the play and resolutely stay with the audience after watching, even if the moments of comedy make it bearable to watch in the wait for Godot to appear. Beckett seems to undercut the traditional definitions of tragedy and comedy with the play, as there is no grandeur or nobility in the tragedy and the comedy is short lived. Perhaps his subtitle was intended to be ironic.

A clear summing up with a personal response to the play.

COMMENT

This is a well-organised essay with scope for further reflection and illustration. The audience is kept in mind throughout.

Reflection: Think about some of the plays you have studied and the interplay of serious and humorous elements within them. Could any of them be described as 'tragi-comedy'? Can you think of any serious plays which have no comic elements at all? How does this affect an audience?

FURTHER STUDY

There are many filmed versions of parts of the play to be found online.

FURTHER ESSAY QUESTIONS

1. Discuss the role and significance of the travelling players in the play *Hamlet*.
2. In what ways is jealousy presented in the play *The Winter's Tale*, and with what effects?
3. Compare the characterisation of Marlene and Joyce and its importance to the play *Top Girls* as a whole.

Self-assessment checklist

Reflect on what you've learnt in this unit and indicate your confidence level between 1 and 5. If you score below 3, revisit that section. Come back to this list later in your course. Has your confidence grown?

	Confidence level	Revisited?
I am fully alert to the importance of the word 'dramatic' and what it implies for essays		
I appreciate complex characterisation and audience response		
I can understand the power of disguise and how it affects an audience		
I can define tragi-comedy in the 20th century		

Unit 27
Drama – passage questions

Learning objectives

In this unit you will:

- consider the subject of kingship in Shakespeare and relate to the passage on Henry V
- acknowledge different interpretations and their validity
- study sample responses and make discriminations between specific and general critical points in passage-based answers
- complete text boxes and a table linked with a passage containing a larger number of characters, exploring subtle interactions of words and actions.

KEY CONCEPTS

Language, form, structure, genres, context, style, interpretation, critical reading.

Before you start

- Revise the drama units in the first section of the book.
- Review the essay on Caliban in the previous unit and especially the points about the character of Prospero, who is ruler on the island (and in that sense like a king). This will be relevant for *Henry V*, the subject of the first exercise here.
- Prepare for the exercises by studying the printed passages carefully. You may like to research the writers before starting, although you are familiar with Shakespeare of course.

Section A: Shakespeare

The following two Shakespeare essays are from plays with important individuals as main characters. Henry is the eponymous hero ('eponymous' means the title of the text is the main character's name); Iago and Roderigo are talking about Othello, the main character. Willy Loman is an ordinary man (thus his name Low-man), and the Irish sisters are poor country girls, but the audience is just as engaged by all of them.

Reflection: Refer to the advice given on answering passage questions in Unit 30 of this book.

Henry V

ACTIVITY 27.1

Read carefully the following extract from the end of one of Shakespeare's most well-known History plays, *Henry V* (Act 5, Scene 2). Of course, it would be helpful if you could act it out with two classmates, but you will need a good actor for the part of Henry! Then, with a friend, answer the questions that follow, which are preparation for answering a passage question on the play, and study the two sample responses on it.

Shakespeare's Histories are all concerned with the subject of Kingship – what are the qualities of a good king? Some of the questions he explores are:

- The effect being king has on the character and psychology of the individual person
- Whether a successful ruler can combine efficiency with a humane and sensitive attitude to life
- The nature of power and political complexity

- Ambition
- Cunning and unscrupulous behaviour to advance oneself, cynicism, hypocrisy and manipulation

Keep these points in mind. The scene is right at the end of the play and you could argue that it isn't necessary – after all, Henry has already defeated the French and part of the conditions of the treaty are that the French princess Katharine will become his wife; yet in this scene, he is persuading her to marry him. In a sense, then, the wooing of Kate is an artificial pretence since the result is a foregone conclusion. How will an audience respond to this? You will be exploring the passage and relating it, if you can, to the rest of the play.

Your passage question would be:

a *Write a critical analysis of this passage showing the ways in which it adds to our understanding of Henry's character* OR

b *Paying close attention to the language and action of this scene, discuss how effectively the playwright explores the king's behaviour and attitudes.*

This passage gives you an excellent opportunity to see how two different interpretations can be valid. (Alice is Katharine's lady in waiting, as a young princess would not be permitted to talk to a man – even a king – on her own. Shakespeare makes her bi-lingual which is helpful for the scene.) Read the scene and then answer the questions which follow.

King Henry V: Fair Katharine, and most fair,
Will you vouchsafe to teach a soldier terms
Such as will enter at a lady's ear
And plead his love-suit to her gentle heart?

Katherine: Your majesty shall mock at me; I cannot
speak your England.

King Henry V: O fair Katharine, if you will love me soundly with your French
heart, I will be glad to hear you confess it
brokenly with your English tongue. Do you like me, Kate?

Katherine: Pardonnez-moi, I cannot tell vat is 'like me.'

King Henry V: An angel is like you, Kate, and you are like an angel.

Katherine: Que dit-il? que je suis semblable a les anges?
[What is he saying, that I'm like the angels?]

Alice: Oui, vraiment, sauf votre grace, ainsi dit-il.
[Yes, save your Grace, that's what he's saying]

King Henry V: I said so, dear Katharine; and I must not blush to affirm it.

Katherine: O bon Dieu! les langues des hommes sont pleines de tromperies.
[Good Lord, men's words are full of
deceptions]

King Henry V: What says she, fair one? that the tongues of men
are full of deceits?

Alice: Oui, dat de tongues of de mans is be full of deceits: dat
is de princess.

▶

King Henry V: The princess is the better Englishwoman. I' faith, Kate, my wooing is fit for thy understanding: I am glad thou canst speak no better English; for, if thou couldst, thou wouldst find me such a plain king that thou wouldst think I had sold my farm to buy my crown. I know no ways to mince it in love, but directly to say 'I love you:' then if you urge me farther than to say 'do you in faith?' I wear out my suit. Give me your answer; i' faith, do: and so clap hands and a bargain: how say you, lady?

Katherine: Sauf votre honneur, me understand vell. [Save your honour, I understand well]

King Henry V: Marry, if you would put me to verses or to dance for your sake, Kate, why you undid me: for the one, I have neither words nor measure, and for the other, I have no strength in measure, yet a reasonable measure in strength. If I could win a lady at leap-frog, or by vaulting into my saddle with my armour on my back, under the correction of bragging be it spoken. I should quickly leap into a wife. Or if I might buffet for my love, or bound my horse for her favours, I could lay on like a butcher and sit like a jack-an-apes, never off. But, before God, Kate, I cannot look greenly nor gasp out my eloquence, nor I have no cunning in protestation; only downright oaths, which I never use till urged, nor never break for urging. If thou canst love a fellow of this temper, Kate, whose face is not worth sun-burning, that never looks in his glass for love of any thing he sees there, let thine eye be thy cook. I speak to thee plain soldier: If thou canst love me for this, take me: if not, to say to thee that I shall die, is true; but for thy love, by the Lord, no; yet I love thee too. And while thou livest, dear Kate, take a fellow of plain and uncoined constancy; for he perforce must do thee right, because he hath not the gift to woo in other places: for these fellows of infinite tongue, that can rhyme themselves into ladies' favours, they do always reason themselves out again. What! a speaker is but a prater; a rhyme is but a ballad. A good leg will fall; a straight back will stoop; a black beard will turn white; a curled pate will grow bald; a fair face will wither; a full eye will wax hollow: but a good heart, Kate, is the sun and the moon; or, rather, the sun, and not the moon; for it shines bright and never changes, but keeps his course truly. If thou would have such a one, take me; and take me, take a soldier; take a soldier, take a king. And what sayest thou then to my love? speak, my fair, and fairly, I pray thee.

▶

Katherine: Is it possible dat I sould love de enemy of France?

King Henry V: No; it is not possible you should love the enemy of France, Kate: but, in loving me, you should love the friend of France; for I love France so well that I will not part with a village of it; I will have it all mine: and, Kate, when France is mine and I am yours, then yours is France and you are mine.

Katherine: I cannot tell vat is dat.

ACTIVITY 27.2

1 Look first at the characters of Alice and Kate. What does Alice's presence add to the scene?
2 Do you think Kate is a meek and passive character? Find evidence from the passage for your view.
3 What do the short pieces of dialogue in French add to the scene? (Although I've translated them for you, Shakespeare does this himself by having the characters do so to each other.)
4 Henry's first four lines are in verse (iambic pentameter), but the rest of his speech here is in prose. What effect does this have on the atmosphere of the scene and his approach to the wooing? (Incidentally, these speeches give the lie to the idea that prose is only used for common folk in Shakespeare!)
5 Henry claims he is glad Kate doesn't speak very good English because if she could, she would find him *such a plain king that thou wouldst think I had sold my farm to buy my crown.* In addition to comparing himself to a farmer, Henry presents himself in various modest and low-key ways. Look carefully at his long speech and find examples of him saying he is:
   - Not a typical lover
   - Physically strong
   - Not very good looking
   - Not very eloquent
   - A soldier
   - A good-hearted, constant person
   - Someone who loves her and her country
6 How many times does Henry use the word *plain* and how many times the word *soldier* to describe himself? How many times does he use the word *king*?
7 How many compliments does he pay to Kate and how many lines do they take up compared with his talking about himself?
8 See how many examples of wordplay you can find, where Henry is punning, being clever or playing on words. (The scene carries on in a similar way!)
9 What examples can you find of Henry's use of climax, building his argument by adding incremental phrases? (Incremental means adding elements in a series for effect.)

ACTIVITY 27.3

Now that you have looked closely at the scene, try answering question a) in Activity 27.1 and then read the following contrasting sample responses.

Essay: *Write a critical analysis of this passage showing the ways in which it adds to our understanding of Henry's character.*

KEY CONCEPTS

The ability to show that you can see the possibility of different interpretations of the same passage or whole text. This is an A Level skill and one of the key concepts.

SAMPLE RESPONSE 1

In this delightful and amusing scene, Henry shows another side of himself. Up to this point, the audience have seen him as a firm and skilful ruler and administrator, an excellent soldier and as a common man who is able to talk to other men – as we saw when he went disguised through the camps to hear what the ordinary soldiers thought. For the first time in the play, he is a lover, wooing for the French princess's hand. Under the eye of her chaperone Alice (who in an earlier comic scene has been teaching Kate English), he woos Kate and reassures her that he is a good and honest person, a *plain king* who is more of a *soldier*, but he is of *plain and uncoined constancy. Clap hands and a bargain* sounds very unromantic, like a business proposition between men, which adds to the sense of his honesty. He claims not to be eloquent *I cannot…gasp out my eloquence, nor I have no cunning in protestation*, yet he wins her through his long and convincing speech. He builds to a climax of persuasion in the words *A good leg will fall; a straight back will stoop; a black beard will turn white; a curled pate will grow bald; a fair face will wither; a full eye will wax hollow: but a good heart Kate is the sun and moon.* Later in this scene, he says that it would be a lie to say that if she refuses him he will die, showing his honesty again to the audience. He is witty as well as eloquent, answering her concern about loving an enemy of France by saying that when France belongs to him and he belongs to her, then she is keeping France anyway. Kate understands more than she seems to, and there is an atmosphere of flirtation in the scene. Audiences enjoy this final proof of Henry's good character and the sequence helps to round off the play and give it a happy ending. Elizabethan audiences would enjoy the sight of the English king defeating the old enemy France and modern British audiences have often seen this as a very patriotic play.

SAMPLE RESPONSE 2

Henry has proved himself throughout the play to be a manipulative and shrewd ruler. This scene, far from showing another side to his character, shows that he is the same clever and devious Henry the audience has seen before. He makes many long and persuasive speeches in the play, such as the angry one in response to the Dauphin's tennis balls in Act 1, his damning of the traitors Grey and Scroop in Act 2, the stirring encouragement to the troops before Harfleur at the beginning of Act 3 (*Once more unto the breach, dear friends, once more*) and then the vivid and threatening persuasion to the governor of Harfleur to surrender or risk terrible reprisals (*the blind and bloody soldier with foul hand; your naked infants spitted upon pikes*, and so on). He can be ruthless too, as in the order for all the soldiers to kill their prisoners. We expect him to be able to persuade Kate and he uses all the rhetorical tricks of flattery and false modesty and wordplay to do so. He is particularly skillful in the use of incremental phrases to create a persuasive climax: *A good leg will fall;*

▶

a straight back will stoop; a black beard will turn white; a curled pate will grow bald; a fair face will wither; a full eye will wax hollow: but a good heart Kate is the sun and moon; He denies that he is eloquent and gives the impression he is a simple man (the word is used several times), more like a farmer and certainly more of a soldier than a king. But his ambition is clear. The final speech of this extract has the telling line *for I love France so well that I will not part with a village of it; I will have it all mine:* Winning the French princess is just another stage in realising his kingly ambitions.

FURTHER STUDY

The scene from the film adaptation of Henry V, with Kenneth Branagh and Emma Thompson, will help you to visualise this excerpt from the play. This particular interpretation is a very serious one: the princess seems very anxious and there is no sense of flirtation between her and Henry. The scene can be played in a more light-hearted way, with Henry's false modesty being part of his charm. See if you can find another version online which brings out the possible humour of the scene.

Othello

ACTIVITY 27.4

Look closely at the following passage and sample response on Othello. The interweaving of critical commentary and wider reference is a useful example of this technique.

Note: Iago has persuaded the wealthy Roderigo, who earlier made an unsuccessful bid for Desdemona's hand, that he should wake Brabantio, Desdemona's father, and tell him she has secretly married Othello, a black African army general. This is the end of a very lengthy scene in which Brabantio has appealed to the Duke and Senate about the marriage, but both Othello and Desdemona have defended their love for each other and subsequent elopement.

Essay: *Write a critical appreciation of the following scene, discussing what it contributes to your understanding of the play as a whole.*

Roderigo: Wilt thou be fast to my hopes, if I depend on the issue?

Iago: Thou art sure of me. Go, make money. I have told thee often, and I retell thee again and again, I hate the Moor. My cause is hearted: thine hath no less reason. Let us be conjunctive in our revenge against him. If thou canst cuckold him, thou dost thyself a pleasure, me a sport. There are many events in the womb of time which will be delivered. Traverse. Go; provide thy money. We will have more of this to-morrow. Adieu.

Roderigo: Where shall we meet i'th' morning?

Iago: At my lodging.

Roderigo: I'll be with thee betimes.

Iago: Go to; farewell. Do you hear, Roderigo?

▶

Reflection: Following your close analysis of the language of the scene, consider and discuss with your classmate which of these two interpretations you favour – the more positive one, or the more critical one. Henry loves talking, and he gets results by using his eloquence. Is this a bad thing? Further, think about kingship. Does the king have to be devious and persuasive to be successful? Is being a manipulator part of being a king? Relate what you have studied here to your own reading of the Histories, or any plays with kings, princes and rulers.

Roderigo: What say you?
Iago: No more of drowning, do you hear?
Roderigo: I am changed.
Iago: Go to; farewell. Put money enough in your purse.
Roderigo: I'll sell all my land. [*Exit* Roderigo]
Iago: Thus do I ever make my fool my purse;
For I mine own gain'd knowledge should profane
If I would time expend with such a snipe But for my sport and profit. I hate the Moor,
And it is thought abroad, that 'twixt my sheets
He's done my office: I know not if't be true
Yet I, for mere suspicion in that kind,
Will do as if for surety. He holds me well:
The better shall my purpose work on him.
Cassio's a proper man. Let me see now;
To get his place and to plume up my will
In double knavery. How, how? Let's see.
After some time, to abuse Othello's ear
That he is too familiar with his wife;
He hath a person and a smooth dispose
To be suspected, framed to make women false.
The Moor is of a free and open nature,
That thinks men honest that but seem to be so,
And will as tenderly be led by the nose
As asses are.
I have't. It is engendered. Hell and night
Must bring this monstrous birth to the world's light.

Shakespeare *Othello* Act 1 Scene 3

In the following response, I am going to mark in bold those elements that relate to the rest of the play, showing knowledge and understanding beyond the passage. The essay exemplifies the skilful incorporation of wider comments while analysing the passage closely. We are never in doubt that the writer knows the play well.

SAMPLE RESPONSE

This is a very significant scene, **coming as it does at the end of a public display of Othello's and Desdemona's affection for each other**, as well as confirmation from the Duke and Senate of Othello's **pride, reputation and status** as a general. The scene gradually narrows down from the **busy, formal, public scene** to a dialogue between Iago and Roderigo, and finally a soliloquy – **Iago's first in the play**, and one in which he is apparently open about his motives and his view of other characters.

Roderigo is wealthy and not very perceptive. He **has been fooled by Iago** and **keeps asking** for reassurance, as we see in the first line *Wilt thou be fast to my hopes . . .?* He seems very dependent on Iago and **has been threatening in the dialogue** to kill himself because of his unrequited love for Desdemona. We don't take him very seriously, and the short dialogue in lines 12–18 seems enough to reassure him that he should find more money and stop threatening to drown himself. **His role in the play is never dominant; he is used and abused by Iago throughout and dies in Act 5, attacking Cassio without very good reason, urged on by Iago: *Tis but a man gone: forth my sword, he dies*. He remains a shallow character throughout, although as a minor character he has the function of paralleling Othello in his gullibility and reinforcing our impression of Iago's persuasiveness.**

Iago's soliloquy begins with some very dismissive comments about Roderigo. He is a *fool*; a *snipe*, whom Iago would not bother with except for *sport and profit*. But he is wealthy and easily led and Iago takes advantage of this. Iago is perceptive about the characters of others too: he thinks Othello is *of a free and open nature* and thus easily fooled; Cassio is handsome, *a proper man*, the sort of man *framed to make women false*.

In this first soliloquy, and **in the earlier persuasion to Roderigo, we get a sense of Iago's motives for his hatred of Othello.** He says *my cause is hearted* – full of vitality – and he cites simple hate. He says he may be a cuckold: people think Othello has been to bed with his wife: *he's done my office*. Fear of cuckoldry is a major theme in many of Shakespeare's plays, so we could take this seriously. **We have already seen that he feels slighted because Cassio, a great arithmetician and not a good soldier (*mere prattle without practice*) has been promoted over him.** His is the resentment felt by all who have been passed over for promotion by someone whom they consider has lesser qualities than themselves. Perhaps he is envious of Cassio's attractiveness to women too. His pride has been hurt on all these counts. **We have also seen his racism from the very beginning of the play – his crude physical descriptions to Brabantio: *an old black ram / Is tupping your white ewe*, for example.** All in all, there is enough here to explain his hatred. But interestingly, his plan against Othello is not yet fully formed. In the final lines, he says it is *engender'd* or conceived. It will take time before the birth lines, he says it is or conceived. It will take time before the birth of the plan comes to pass. He has already said to Roderigo: *There are many / events in the womb of time which will be delivered.* Here he calls it a *monstrous birth* which will depend on *Hell and night* to bring it out. These metaphors of conception and birth are a travesty of what new life normally brings and show his twisted, bitter nature.

▶

The language of this extract is revealing in other ways too. First of all, there are a number of repetitions in Iago's prose speech to Roderigo, mostly concerned with his money. He also tells Roderigo what to do, in contrast with which Roderigo asks many questions for reassurance. The extract moves from prose to verse, as Iago begins his soliloquy. There is more emotional intensity now that he is on his own, reflecting and scheming, and his utterance is expressed in blank verse. The short line *As asses are* suggests a pause for thought before the final couplet, ending the scene and the act with a rhyme on *night* and *light*: enhancing the sense that **the play has good and evil as a theme.** Iago is thinking as he speaks: he says *Let me see* (*Let's see*) twice, and *How, how?;* finally, he says *I ha't – it is engender'd:* his plan has been conceived and time will develop it.

One of the most obvious themes here is Iago's jealousy. **We know that he will later use Othello's jealousy to lead him on,** but he himself is obviously envious of Cassio's good looks and fears his wife had been to bed with Othello. Over the centuries, critics have debated whether Iago has a motive or not. For example, critic Samuel Taylor Coleridge called him a *motiveless malignity.* **However, this soliloquy, ending Act 1, prepares the audience for his willingness to do anything to take revenge on Othello and Cassio in *double knavery.* His persuasion of Roderigo is proleptic of his tragic persuasions of Othello later on. We cannot help feeling that intelligence and determination used for such villainous purposes will have a tragic outcome. Othello does indeed believe him and is taken in relatively easily. Only at the very end of the play, after the death of the innocent Desdemona, is the truth revealed.**

ACTIVITY 27.5

Take one of your own passage essays and underline the comments in it which relate to the rest of the play. Is your essay a convincing analysis of the passage as well as a wider comment? If you've underlined almost the whole essay, you are not giving enough attention to the printed passage, and if there are hardly any underlinings, you haven't incorporated wider reference.

Arthur Miller (1915–2005).

Section B: post-1900

Death of a Salesman by Arthur Miller

ACTIVITY 27.6

Read the following essay on the passage from *Death of a Salesman* by Arthur Miller, the 20th-century tragedy of the common man. When you've read the passage and the essay, go through with your highlighter and indicate the parts which refer to 'the play as a whole.'

Essay: *Write a critical appreciation of this passage, relating it to Miller's methods and effects in the play as a whole.*

Willy: [*Driving.*] So tell me, he gave you a warm welcome?

Happy: Sure, Pop, sure!

Biff: [*driven*] Well, it was kind of—

Willy: I was wondering if he'd remember you. [*To Happy*] Imagine, man doesn't see him for ten, twelve years and gives him that kind of welcome!

Happy: Damn right!

Biff: [*trying to return to the offensive*] Pop, look—

Willy: You know why he remembered you, don't you? Because you impressed him in those days.

Biff: Let's talk quietly and get this down to the facts, huh?

Willy: [*as though Biff had been interrupting*] Well, what happened? It's great news, Biff. Did he take you into his office or'd you talk in the waiting-room?

Biff: Well, he came in, see, and—

Willy: [*with a big smile*] What'd he say? Betcha he threw his arm around you.

Biff: Well, he kinda—

Willy: He's a fine man. [*To Happy*] Very hard man to see, y'know.

Happy: *[agreeing]* Oh, I know.

Willy: [*to Biff*] Is that where you had the drinks?

Biff: Yeah, he gave me a couple of—no, no!

Happy: [*cutting in*] He told him my Florida idea.

Willy: Don't interrupt. [*To Biff*] How'd he react to the Florida idea?

Biff: Dad, will you give me a minute to explain?

Willy: I've been waiting for you to explain since I sat down here! What happened? He took you into his office and what?

Biff: Well – I talked. And—he listened, see.

Willy: Famous for the way he listens, y'know. What was his answer?

Biff: His answer was—[*he breaks off, suddenly angry*]. Dad, you're not letting me tell you what I want to tell you!

Willy: [*accusing, angered*] You didn't see him, did you?

Biff: I did see him!

Willy: What'd you insult him or something? You insulted him, didn't you?

Biff: Listen, will you let me out of it, will you just let me out of it!

Happy: What the hell!

Willy: Tell me what happened!

Biff: [*To Happy*] I can't talk to him!

▶

Dialogue analysis

A passage such as this gives opportunity for close analysis of conversational dialogue. You could consider whether characters are seeking in their dialogue to confirm (like Happy) or challenge (Willy)what each other says; at what point they might be trying to repair or re-direct the conversation (Biff) and why. You could look for adjacent pairs of words where one character pick up a word previously used by another and does something with it (for example 'explain' here).

A single trumpet note jars the air. The light of green leaves stains the house, which holds the air of night and of a dream. Young Bernard enters and knocks on the door of the house.

Young Bernard: [*frantically*] Mrs Loman, Mrs Loman!

Happy: Tell him what happened!

Biff: [*To Happy*] Shut up and leave me alone!

Willy: No, no! You had to go and flunk math!

Biff: What math? What're you talking about?

Young Bernard: Mrs Loman, Mrs Loman! *Linda appears in the house, as of old*

Willy: [*wildly*] Math, math, math!

Biff: Take it easy, Pop!

Young Bernard: Mrs Loman!

Willy: [*furiously*] If you hadn't flunked, you'd've been set by now.

Arthur Miller *Death of a Salesman* (1949)

SAMPLE RESPONSE

Note: This passage is part of the restaurant scene, which is near the climax of the play. Biff has told Happy what happened when he went to see Oliver for a job and is determined to try to have it all out with his father. His attempts are thwarted – Willy doesn't listen and tells the boys he has been fired before this sequence begins. The structure of this extract is a gradual build-up to Biff's trying to talk honestly to his father and his frustration and anger when he fails to do so. The end of the sequence is one of Willy's memories intruding, a memory of Biff's failure to pass his maths at school, to which Willy attributes all Biff's failures, desperately trying to convince himself that it was not caused by the hotel trauma with the 'other woman'.

The dialogue follows a pattern which by now is familiar to the audience. Biff is trying hard to take the initiative, but is beaten down by Willy. Miller's stage directions at the beginning of the extract shows that Willy is *driving* and Biff is immediately disadvantaged: *driven*. Throughout the first part of the extract, Biff's sentences are incomplete: *Well it was kind of—; Pop, look—; Well, he kinda—*, until the point where he gathers enough strength to say *Dad, will you give me a minute to explain?* Willy's optimism about the meeting builds incrementally on his own exaggerations, as can be seen in his second speech: *I was wondering if he'd remember you. (To Happy) Imagine, man doesn't see him for ten, twelve years and gives him that kind of welcome!* (First, he probably wouldn't remember him, then it's ten years, then it's twelve years, then it's *gives him that kind of welcome*.) This is typical of the alternative idealised reality Willy creates about himself and the boys through the play. As Biff tries at last to explain, Willy makes the assumption that Biff has ▶

somehow insulted Oliver and their communication breaks down. Biff says to his brother: *I can't talk to him!* Interestingly, when Willy asks if he had a couple of drinks with Oliver, there is a moment where Biff seems to be drawn back into the old bravado, and talking up of every situation when he says *Yeah, he gave me a couple of* – before regaining his sense of purpose and saying *no, no!*

Happy's responses throughout this sequence are typical of him – he goes along with everything his father says and just makes affirmative comments: *Sure, Pop, sure; Damn right; Oh, I know.* He is not strong enough to help Biff to explain anything to his father: his own immaturity and illusions about himself and his capabilities are suggested in the one line about his *Florida idea*, Florida: the symbol of the *promised land* through the play. It is, however, a chilling moment when Happy rejects his father and claims not to know him a little later in this scene (*No that's not my father. He's just a guy*). Willy is so determined to believe his own fantasy about Biff's capabilities that he rides over Biff's attempts to communicate, imagining his own view of Oliver and what he would like Oliver to have behaved like. At first, his wishful thinking dominates the conversation: … *he gave you a warm welcome?; Imagine, man doesn't see him for ten, twelve years and gives him that kind of welcome!; Because you impressed him in those days; Betcha he threw his arm around you*. It is no wonder Biff cannot communicate with him, faced with this barrage of determinedly positive comments. Although this is a very naturalistic conversation, there are two ironic moments in Willy's comments on Oliver: *Very hard man to see, y'know.* Willy has no personal experience of this, but has to believe that a man in Oliver's position must be like that. We can also see the irony that this applies metaphorically to Willy himself; equally ironic is: *Famous for the way he listens, y'know.* Willy also wants to believe this, but it, too, is highly ironic because Willy himself hasn't listened to Biff at all. It is at that point that Biff comes in angrily with *Dad, you're not letting me tell you what I want to tell you!* When it all goes wrong, Willy's angry assumption is that it was all Biff's fault and that he has somehow insulted Oliver. Neither of his extreme positions is the right one. His fantasy about Biff being welcomed is as invalid as his fantasy that it all went wrong because of Biff's insulting Oliver. The truth is that Oliver didn't remember Biff, and why should he? Biff was never his salesman and left under a cloud because of the missing basketballs years before, whatever story Willy has built up in his own mind, and Biff had to wait for six hours before he managed to see Oliver for *a minute*. Biff's desperate words: *will you let me out of it, will you just let me out of it!* seem to refer to Willy's designated role for Biff, which has tragically limited both of them all their lives. The critic Susan Abbotson claims that Willy's apparent ordinariness should not blind us to his tragic stature, but Biff too has some claim to a tragic role in the play.

Willy's memory then cuts into the scene and the final moments interweave the old memory of Bernard coming with the news that Biff failed maths and the two sons anxiously trying to understand in the present what their father is talking about. (Bernard and Charley are used in juxtaposition to contrast the Lomans throughout the play – realists rather than dreamers, sensible and hard-working.) Miller's use of the memory technique runs through the play and creates a kind of stream of consciousness effect. Willy's present conversations are underpinned by his memories of earlier events and concerns. A little after the printed sequence, the climactic moment where the younger Biff comes into the hotel room where Willy

▶

has been in bed with a woman is played out in Willy's memory; the audience see the roots of Biff's disillusionment with his father and Willy's guilty despair.

All three men are trying to escape from an unworkable life-model imposed on them: Happy, with his unrealistic dreams of Florida, from grinding tedium and meaningless relationships; Biff moving to the country but still with a sense of his own failure to grow up; and most of all Willy, self-deluding to the last, clinging to his ideas about business and capitalism even though he is really a nature lover and *a happy man with a batch of cement*, not a successful salesman. His ambiguous feelings about Biff come through in this scene as they do throughout the play: that Biff is fine and heroic; or that Biff has ruined his life because of failing maths; or, underlying it all – but not able to be admitted fully – that Willy is actually partly to blame because he has failed to live up to his own projected image to his sons of what a decent man is.

KEY CONCEPTS

I have included this play not only because it is very popular on syllabuses and in coursework, but because many students write about the failure of the American Dream (the chance of freedom, opportunity and wealth) that they see in it. Valid though this is, I hope that looking closely at the dialogue in this passage will remind you of what a master craftsman of the family drama Miller is, a quality seen in many of his other plays too. As with the previous sample essay, it is clear that the play as a whole is very well-known and the response shows insight into Miller's writing of this scene.

FURTHER STUDY

Search online for the filmed version of the whole play starring Dustin Hoffman and John Malkovitch. The part of Willy is one of those key roles that all actors want to play.

Dancing at Lughnasa by Brian Friel

ACTIVITY 27.7

The next exercise is connected with a domestic drama, *Dancing at Lughnasa* by Irish playwright Brian Friel. It's set in the rural Irish area of Donegal in summer 1936. The family is poor and consists of five young women and their frail older brother Jack, who has just returned from being a Roman Catholic missionary in Africa. One of the girls, Chris, has an illegitimate son of seven, fathered by Gerry Evans who has never supported them or visited them very much, in spite of making promises to do so. Note that the family are devoted Roman Catholics, so their use of language about Jesus is as a result of strong emotion, not careless swearing. I've chosen it to end this unit because it has a large number of characters – the five sisters – and their actions, making for a lively scene with implications for theme and character that lie below the surface of the words. You need to take actions into account as well as the dialogue.

In order of age, the sisters are:

- Kate: the older sister (the only one with a job – a teacher)
- Maggie: the housekeeper
- Agnes: does knitting at home to make a little money
- Rose: also does knitting at home – she is rather 'simple'

- Chris: the boy's mother – has no income
- (Woodbines are strong, cheap cigarettes.)

Read the passage from the play *Dancing at Lughnasa* by Brian Friel (1990)

If you can, it would be very helpful to get some friends or classmates together and act out this little scene as it will fall into place much more clearly. Then answer the questions, working with one friend. Aiming towards a passage question essay, your passage question would be:

Essay: *a) Paying close attention to stage directions and dialogue, write a critical appreciation of the following passage, showing what it contributes to your understanding of Friel's methods and concerns.*

or possibly

b) Paying close attention to stage directions and dialogue, write a critical appreciation of the following passage, showing what it contributes to your understanding of Friel's characterisation.

Maggie: Come here till you see! Look who's coming up the lane!

Agnes: Who's coming?

Maggie: I only got a glimpse of him – but I'm almost certain it's –

Agnes: Who? Who is it?

Maggie: (to Chris:) It's Gerry Evans, Chrissie.

Chris: Christ Almighty.

Maggie: He's at the bend in the lane.

Chris: Oh, Jesus Christ Almighty.

[The news throws the sisters in to chaos. Only Chris stands absolutely still, too shocked to move. Agnes picks up her knitting and works with excessive concentration. Rose and Maggie change their footwear. Everybody dashes about in confusion – peering into the tiny mirror, bumping into one another, peeping out the window, combing hair. During all this hectic activity they talk over each other and weave around the immobile Chris. The lines overlap]

Kate: How dare Mr Evans show his face here.

Maggie: He wants to see his son, doesn't he?

Kate: There's no welcome for that creature here.

Rose: Who hid my Sunday shoes?

Maggie: We'll have to give him his tea.

Kate: I don't see why we should.

Maggie: And there's nothing in the house.

Kate: No business at all coming here and upsetting everybody.

Rose: You're right, Kate. I hate him!

▶

Maggie: Has anybody got spare shoelaces?

Kate: Look at the state of that floor

Maggie: Maybe he just wants to meet Father Jack.

Kate: Father Jack may have something to say to Mr Evans. *[Of the ironing.]*

Agnes, put those clothes away.

[Agnes does not hear her, so apparently engrossed is she in her knitting]

Maggie: My Woodbine. Where's my Woodbine?

Rose: He won't stay the night, Kate, will he?

Kate: He mostly certainly won't stay the night in this house!

Maggie: Have you a piece of cord, Aggie? Anybody got a bit of twine?

Kate: Behave quite normally. Be very calm and very dignified. Stop peeping out, Rose!

Rose: *[at window]* There's nobody coming at all.

[Silence. Then Agnes puts down her knitting, rushes to the window, pushes Rose aside and looks out.]

Agnes: Let me see.

Rose: You imagined it, Maggie.

Chris: Oh God

Rose: He's not there at all.

Agnes: *[softly]* Yes he is. Maggie's right. There he is.

Rose: Show me.

Kate: Has he a walking stick?

Rose: Yes.

Kate: And a straw hat?

Rose: Yes.

Kate: It's Mr Evans all right.

Brian Friel *Dancing at Lughnasa* (1990)

ACTIVITY 27.8

Look at the speeches of each character and put them together. You could use different colours to highlight each character. Don't omit any of their words – you need them all. Then look closely at the stage directions for each character. (Remember that they are one of the ways the playwright can indicate his ideas about how the scene could be acted on the stage.) Consider each character and what her speeches and actions reveal. From this brief sequence, what can you deduce? Fill in the table.

Character	Evidence
Kate	
Maggie	
Rose	
Chris	
Agnes	

Structure and action

The scene moves very quickly but the attitude of each sister is very clear from their words and movements. The frenetic action to make themselves and the room look tidy contrasts strongly with Chris's immobility and Agnes's pretence at unconcern.

i. When Rose says there's no-one outside, what happens to the tone of the scene?

ii. What do you think is the most dramatic moment?

Themes

Find evidence from this sequence of the following concerns. Write in the table:

The family's poverty	
Their attempts at respectability in spite of this	
Their solidarity and support for each other	
Passionate feelings repressed	

Now try writing the essay! You are not required to relate to the rest of the play, so you can do it by studying the evidence here.

FURTHER STUDY

1. Read or watch any other plays by Brian Friel set in Ireland.
2. Irish short stories about rural communities by Frank O'Connor, for example.
3. Other plays about sisters; for example, Chekov's *The Three Sisters*, Shakespeare's *The Taming of the Shrew*.
4. Many scenes from the film of the play *Dancing at Lughnasa* starring Meryl Streep (1998) are available on the internet.

Reflection: Characters in plays come from all walks of life. Shakespeare histories and tragedies are most often concerned with important figures such as kings and generals, but many modern dramas show the intense relationships of families who are socially insignificant, but whose interactions strike a chord with audiences because they can identify with them. Reflect on a play you are studying and consider your response to complex individual characters and how the playwright has presented them to an audience.

Self-assessment checklist

Reflect on what you've learnt in this unit and indicate your confidence level between 1 and 5. If you score below 3, revisit that section. Come back to this list later in your course. Has your confidence grown?

	Confidence level	Revisited?
I recognise the importance of this Shakespearean theme and can see its validity in other drama		
I value the importance of different interpretations using the evidence of the text		
I know how to distinguish between scene-specific and general points - Shakespeare		
I know how to distinguish between scene-specific and general points – modern drama		
I can understand and complete this exercise		

Unit 28
Drama – close analysis

Learning objectives

In this unit you will:

- engage in active learning: reading and acting scenes with friends
- focus on detail and answer directed questions on a wide range of drama excerpts, as scaffolding for unseen essay responses
- recognise the value of broadening your range of drama experience.

KEY CONCEPTS

Language, form, structure, genres, context, style, interpretation, critical reading.

Before you start

- Revise the A Level close analysis poetry and prose units.
- Prepare for the exercises by studying the printed passages carefully. You may like to research the writers before starting.
- See if you can gather a few friends who are willing to act out the sequences with you, so that you can experience the drama first hand.

The following exercises have been chosen to represent a range of different eras and types. You may do them as complete unseens or you can answer the questions at the end of each one as a help towards close analysis. The first is from another Shakespeare play, *The Tempest* (1610–1611) (1606); the second from Richard B. Sheridan's play *The Rivals* (1775); the third from John Galsworthy's play *Strife* (1909); and the fourth a short revue sketch, *Last to Go* (1964), by Harold Pinter (which is complete); the fifth is from *Our Country's Good* (1988) by Timberlake Wertenbaker, and is intended for class discussion.

Each one of these plays has something of value to communicate about the human condition: about authority and family life; about social attitudes and our conventional responses to them; about working people and their masters and trade unions; and about the ordinariness of daily life and its inconsequentiality. The final passage reminds us of the value of theatre.

Passage 1: from *The Tempest* Act 1 Scene 1 and 2

ACTIVITY 28.1

Read the following passage and study the comments and questions that follow. Stop reading when you come to the unseen alert if you intend to try this entirely unseen.

Passage 1

Scene 1 [A tempestuous noise of Thunder and Lightning heard: Enter a Shipmaster, and a Boatswain.]

Master: Boatswain

Boats: Here Master: What cheer?

Master: Good: Speak to th' Mariners: fall to't, yarely, or we run our selves a ground, Bestir, bestir. **[yare=quick]**

[Exit Master]

[Enter Mariners]

Boats: Heigh my hearts! Cheerly, cheerly my hearts! Yare, yare! Take in the top-sale: Tend to th' Masters whistle: Blow till thou burst thy wind, if room enough.

[Enter Alonso, Sebastian, Antonio, Ferdinand, Gonzalo and others.]

Alonso: Good Boatswain have care. Where's the Master? Ply the men. **[keep them to their business]**

Boats: I pray now, keep below.

Antonio: Where is the Master, Boatswain?

Boats: Do you not hear him? You mar our labour, keep your Cabins.

You do assist the storm.

Gonzalo: Nay, good, be patient.

Boats: When the Sea is: hence! What cares these roarers for the name of King? to cabin; silence: trouble us not.

Gonzalo: Good, yet remember whom thou hast aboard.

Boats: None that I more love than myself. You are a Counsellor, if you can command these elements to silence, and work the peace of the present, we will not hand a rope more, use your authority: If you cannot, give thanks you have liv'd so long, and make yourself ready in your cabin for the mischance of the hour, if it so hap. Cheerly good hearts: out of our way I say.

[Exit Boatswain]

▶

Gonzalo: I have great comfort from this fellow: methinks he hath no drowning mark upon him, his complexion is perfect gallows: stand fast good Fate to his hanging, make the rope of his destiny our cable, for our own doth little advantage: if he be not born to be hang'd, our case is miserable.

[Refers to a proverb: 'he that is born to be hanged will never be drowned']

[Exit Gonzalo and courtiers]

[Enter Boatswain]

Boats: Down with the top-Mast: yare, lower, lower, bring her to try wi' th' main-course. A plague—
[A cry within. Enter SEBASTIAN, ANTONIO & GONZALO.]
upon this howling: they are louder than the weather, or our office: yet again? What do you here? Shall we give over and drown?
Have you a mind to sink?

Sebastian: A pox o'your throat, you bawling, blasphemous incharitable Dog.

Boats: Work you then.

Antonio: Hang cur! Hang, you whoreson insolent noise-maker! We are less afraid to be drowned, than thou art.

Gonzalo: I'll warrant him for drowning, though the ship were no stronger than a nut-shell, and as leaky as an unstanched wench.

[as a girl whose tears are pouring down]

Boats: Lay her a hold, a hold, set her two courses off to Sea again.

Lay her off.

[Enter Mariners, wet.]

Mariners: All lost, to prayers, to prayers, all lost.

Boats: What must our mouths be cold?

Gonzalo: The King, and Prince, at prayers, let's assist them, for our case is as theirs.

Sebastian: I am out of patience.

Antonio: We are merely cheated of our lives by drunkards. This wide-chopped-rascal, would thou might'st lie drowning the washing of ten tides.

[wide-chopped=big mouthed]

Gonzalo: He'll be hang'd yet,
Though every drop of water swear against it,
And gape at wid'st to glut him. **[glut=to swallow]**

[A confused noise within.]

▶

Voices: Mercy on us.
We split, we split, Farewell my wife, and children,
Farewell brother: we split, we split, we split

Antonio: Let's all sink with the King

Sebastian: Let's take leave of him.

Gonzalo: Now would I give a thousand furlongs of sea, for an acre of barren ground: long heath, browne firs, anything; the wills above be done, but I would fain die a dry death.

Scene 2.

Enter Prospero and Miranda.

Miranda: If by your Art (my dearest father) you have
Put the wild waters in this roar; allay them:
The sky it seems would power down stinking pitch,
But that the Sea, mounting to th' welkin's cheek, **[welkin=sky]**
Dashes the fire out. Oh! I have suffered
With those that I saw suffer: A brave vessel
(Who had no doubt some noble creature in her)
Dash'd all to pieces: O the cry did knock
Against my very heart: poor souls, they perish'd.
Had I been any God of power, I would
Have sunk the Sea within the Earth, or ere
It should the good Ship so have swallow'd, and
The fraughting Souls within her **[fraughting=forming the cargo]**

Prospero: Be collected, no more amazement: Tell your piteous heart there's no harm done.

Unseen alert! If you are doing this as an unseen, do not read on. A typical essay question would be: *Write a critical analysis (or appreciation) of the following sequence, commenting on Shakespeare's methods and concerns here.*

Shakespeare *The Tempest* Act 1

COMMENT

This sequence comes from the very beginning of the play, with the whole of the first storm scene and the beginning of the next scene where Prospero reassures his daughter Miranda. *The Tempest* is probably Shakespeare's last play and it was first produced at Whitehall in London before the King, James I.
On the ship in the storm are the court party – King of Naples Alonso, his son Ferdinand, his brother Sebastian, Prospero's brother Antonio, and Gonzalo, an old counsellor, as well as other attendants.

Dramatic action

The ship being wrecked in the storm is a really exciting way to start the play, with noise, shouting and every stage effect that could be summoned at the time. It contrasts strongly

▶

with the next scene where Prospero, who has caused the storm by magic, reassures his kind-hearted daughter that no-one has been hurt. Later in Scene 2, he goes on to explain the past events that have led him to want to take revenge on his brother Antonio, who has usurped his place as Duke of Milan and banished Prospero and the baby Miranda by setting them onto the ocean in a small boat. Here in Scene 1, vivid dramatic effect is assured, and in Scene 2, the back story is given.

Characterisation, with emphasis on language and tone

- Although the King and his nobles are on board, the King is not in charge. Who is? Why? What does this tell us about authority and command? (Look at the Boatswain's longer speech to Gonzalo.)
- How does the dramatist create the chaotic atmosphere of a storm?
- Although this is a scene of action, characterisation does emerge. What do you notice about the speeches of Gonzalo? Is there anything in their tone that helps you to feel that this will not be the end for these characters?
- Look closely at Antonio and Sebastian's speeches. What sort of characters are they? What expectations do you have of their behaviour later on in the play?
- What do you notice about the form of the speeches in Scene 1 compared with Miranda's speech in Scene 2? What is the effect of this?
- What impression do you get of Miranda's characterisation from her speech here?
- How does her description of the storm help to create atmosphere?
- What does her reference to 'Art' suggest about her father's capabilities?
- How would you describe the relationship between the father and daughter here?

Proleptic irony

- Gonzalo's positive attitudes and the savage dismissive speeches of Antonio and Sebastian are ironic in the light of their survival on the island where they will be subjected to a series of tests and challenges by Prospero.
- Gonzalo's description of the boat being like a wench who cannot stop her tears foreshadows the pity we see in Miranda in the next scene.
- Miranda's reference to Prospero's 'Art' introduces the idea of magic power.
- Miranda thinks the ship has 'some noble creature' in her. This is true, but it also has some wicked people including those who tried to drown her and her father when she was a baby.

KEY TERM

Prolepsis: sometimes called foreshadowing or adumbration, looks forward to what is going to happen; the opposite is **analepsis** – looking backwards in a story.

Reflection: Read some summaries of the action of Shakespeare's last plays and reflect on how they relate to others you have studied. All contain tragic events, either within the play (as in *The Winter's Tale*) or as part of the back story (as in *The Tempest*), which are reconciled within the action of the play to create a happy ending. The good brother/evil brother motif is seen here, just as it was in *Hamlet*, but the consequences are not so dire. Have you read or studied any other works in which the younger generation are the agents of hope and reconciliation?

ACTIVITY 28.2

Read the following passage from *The Rivals* (1775) by Richard B. Sheridan and study the comments and questions that follow. This play is a comedy of manners.

Note: Sir Anthony is Jack Absolute's father, and has arranged to marry him off to a wealthy young lady. Jack is already in love, so the two quarrel violently.

KEY CONCEPTS

Don't forget that when you are studying a specific passage, the rest of the play is just as much a context for the scene as social background is. Every Shakespeare scene contains within it hints of the major concerns of the play in question. Close analysis can yield much insight.

Passage 2: from *The Rivals* by Richard B. Sheridan

ACTIVITY 28.3

If you have been able to persuade some friends to read the scene with you, talk to them about how you would present this scene on stage and what themes and effects you would try to bring out. Your teacher will help to organise this with you.

Passage 2

[Enter Sir Anthony Absolute.]

Absolute: Sir, I am delighted to see you here; looking so well! Your sudden arrival at Bath made me apprehensive for your health.

Sir Anthony: Very apprehensive, I dare say, Jack.—What, you are recruiting here, hey?

Absolute: Yes, sir, I am on duty.

Sir Anthony: Well, Jack, I am glad to see you, though I did not expect it, for I was going to write to you on a little matter of business.—Jack, I have been considering that I grow old and infirm, and shall probably not trouble you long.

Absolute: Pardon me, sir, I never saw you look more strong and hearty; and I pray frequently that you may continue so.

Sir Anthony: I hope your prayers may be heard, with all my heart. Well, then, Jack, I have been considering that I am so strong and hearty I may continue to plague you a long time. Now, Jack, I am sensible that the income of your commission, and what I have hitherto allowed you, is but a small pittance for a lad of your spirit.

Absolute: Sir, you are very good.

Sir Anthony: And it is my wish, while yet I live, to have my boy make some figure in the world. I have resolved, therefore, to fix you at once in a noble independence.

Absolute: Sir, your kindness overpowers me—such generosity makes the gratitude of reason more lively than the sensations even of filial affection.

Sir Anthony: I am glad you are so sensible of my attention—and you shall be master of a large estate in a few weeks.

Absolute: Let my future life, sir, speak my gratitude; I cannot express the sense I have of your munificence.—Yet, sir, I presume you would not wish me to quit the army?

Sir Anthony: Oh, that shall be as your wife chooses.

Absolute: My wife, sir!

▶

Sir Anthony:	Ay, ay, settle that between you—settle that between you.
Absolute:	A wife, sir, did you say?
Sir Anthony:	Ay, a wife—why, did not I mention her before?
Absolute:	Not a word of her, sir.
Sir Anthony:	Odd so!—I mustn't forget her though.—Yes, Jack, the independence I was talking of is by marriage—the fortune is saddled with a wife—but I suppose that makes no difference.
Absolute:	Sir! sir!—you amaze me!
Sir Anthony:	Why, what the devil's the matter with the fool? Just now you were all gratitude and duty.
Absolute:	I was, sir,—you talked to me of independence and a fortune, but not a word of a wife.
Sir Anthony:	Why—what difference does that make? Odds life, sir! if you have the estate, you must take it with the live stock on it, as it stands.
Absolute:	If my happiness is to be the price, I must beg leave to decline the purchase.—Pray, sir, who is the lady?
Sir Anthony:	What's that to you, sir?—Come, give me your promise to love, and to marry her directly.

Richard B. Sheridan *The Rivals* (1775)

COMMENT

Characterisation

Jack

- Comment on Jack's use of *sir* to his father. What impression does this give?
- How would you describe the tone of Jack's first few speeches to his father?
- *I pray frequently that you may continue so*: what might be an audience's reaction to this line? What figure of speech is this?
- *such generosity makes the gratitude of reason more lively than the sensations even of filial affection*. Comment on Jack's diction here. What effect does this have? How might an audience respond to his tone?

Sir Anthony

- *Jack, I have been considering that I grow old and infirm, and shall probably not trouble you long …*

  Well, then, Jack, I have been considering that I am so strong and hearty I may continue to plague you a long time.

  What do these two sentences tell us about Sir Anthony? What effect do they have on the audience?
- Do you believe Sir Anthony's claims to want to give Jack more of an allowance and a large estate? Why not? In what tone would the actor speak these lines?
- Sir Anthony starts to call Jack *sir* towards the end of the passage. How does his tone differ from the way in which Jack uses *sir* earlier?

COMMENT

Structure

- Which line is the turning point in the scene? How does Jack's short reply emphasise the point?
- What is the effect of the repetition of the word *wife*?
- To whom is *Why, what the devil's the matter with the fool*? addressed? What effect does this have?
- What effect does the juxtaposition of lengthy complex sentences with short phrases have here?

Themes

- What can we deduce about Sir Anthony's attitude towards marriage from what he says? Find two illustrations to support your view.
- Although today's audiences pride themselves on being egalitarian, the idea of a wife as livestock always gets a big laugh in the theatre. (See **Stock figures and responses** in the 'key concepts' box.)
- How do you respond to the following exchange? *Pray, sir, who is the lady? What's that to you, sir?*

As with many comedies, love, marriage and money are major issues. Sir Anthony is arranging Jack's marriage, but we are sure that, being a comedy, the young people will have their own way eventually after various obstacles are overcome. (Arranged marriages can of course be a serious subject, especially in prose works.)

KEY CONCEPTS

Stock figures are familiar types. We see them in jokes, clichés and comedy; here the severe father who refuses to allow a child (often a daughter, but here a son) to marry the man/woman she/he pleases. (We are reminded of Egeus in *A Midsummer Night's Dream*.) Other stock figures include the wife who wears the trousers, the hen-pecked husband, the dimwit, the servant who is very quick and clever who helps his master, and so on. Characters such as this in comedy will produce a stock response too – audiences know that this is a character or situation to laugh at.

TIP

Writing about comic scenes is not easy. You need to be very alert to the sharpness of the dialogue and the tone of voice in which it is spoken, as well as any implications for stage business, gesture and movement. There is a kind of tennis match effect here where the ball is lobbed across the net from side to side in a quick, even pattern of witty exchange that is very enjoyable for the audience.

FURTHER STUDY

You can find and watch online the whole play performed on the stage by a famous British company (Bristol Old Vic) and just a few minutes' watching will give you the right atmosphere straight away!

Passage 3: from *Strife* by John Galsworthy

ACTIVITY 28.4

Read the following passage from *Strife* (1909) by John Galsworthy and study the comments and questions which follow. Stop reading when you come to the unseen alert if you intend to try this entirely unseen.

Note: Anthony is Chairman of the Board, Edgar is his son, Wilder, Scantlebury, Wanklin, Tench and Underwood are members of the Board. Harness is the Union representative. The Board of the Company has been meeting to discuss the strike of the men that has been going on for some time

Passage 3

Frost: [*TO* ANTHONY] Mr Harness from the Union, waiting, sir. The men are here too, sir. [ANTHONY *nods.* UNDERWOOD *goes to the door, returning with* HARNESS, *a pale, clean-shaven man with hollow cheeks, quick eyes, and lantern jaw*—FROST has retired.]

Underwood: [*Pointing to* TENCH's *chair*] Sit there next the Chairman, Harness, won't you? [*At* HARNESS'S *appearance, the Board have drawn together, as it were, and turned a little to him, like cattle at a dog.*]

Harness: [*With a sharp look round, and a bow*] Thanks! [*He sits—his accent is slightly nasal.*] Well, gentlemen, we're going to do business at last, I hope.

Wilder: Depends on what you call business, Harness. Why don't you make the men come in?

Harness: [*Sardonically*] The men are far more in the right than you are. The question with us is whether we shan't begin to support them again. [*He ignores them all, except* ANTHONY, *to whom he turns in speaking*]

Anthony: Support them if you like; we'll put in free labour and have done with it.

Harness: That won't do, Mr Anthony. You can't get free labour, and you know it.

Anthony: We shall see that.

Harness: I'm quite frank with you. We were forced to withhold our support from your men because some of their demands are in excess of current rates. I expect to make them withdraw those demands to-day: if they do, take it straight from me, gentlemen, we shall back them again at once. Now, I want to see something fixed upon before I go back to-night. Can't we have done with this old-fashioned tug-of-war business? What good's it doing you? Why don't you recognise once for all that these people are men like

▶

yourselves, and want what's good for them just as you want what's good for you [*Bitterly*] Your motor-cars, and champagne, and eight-course dinners.

Anthony: If the men will come in, we'll do something for them.

Harness: [*Ironically*] Is that your opinion too, sir—and yours— and yours? [*The Directors do not answer*] Well, all I can say is: It's a kind of high and mighty aristocratic tone I thought we'd grown out of—seems I was mistaken.

Anthony: It's the tone the men use. Remains to be seen which can hold out longest—they without us, or we without them.

Harness: As business men, I wonder you're not ashamed of this waste of force, gentlemen. You know what it'll all end in.

Anthony: What?

Harness: Compromise—it always does.

Scantlebury: Can't you persuade the men that their interests are the same as ours?

Harness: [*Turning, ironically*] I could persuade them of that, sir, if they were.

Wilder: Come, Harness, you're a clever man, you don't believe all the Socialistic claptrap that's talked nowadays. There's no real difference between their interests and ours.

Harness: There's just one very simple little question I'd like to put to you. Will you pay your men one penny more than they force you to pay them? [WILDER is silent.]

Wanklin: [*Chiming in*] I humbly thought that not to pay more than was necessary was the A B C of commerce.

Harness: [*With irony*] Yes, that seems to be the A B C of commerce, sir; and the A B C of commerce is between your interests and the men's.

Scantlebury: [*Whispering*] We ought to arrange something.

Harness: [Drily] Am I to understand then, gentlemen, that your Board is going to make no concessions? [WANKLIN and WILDER *bend forward as if to speak, but stop*]

Anthony: [*Nodding*] None. [WANKLIN and WILDER *again bend forward,* and SCANTLEBURY *gives an unexpected grunt*]

Harness: You were about to say something, I believe? [*But* SCANTLEBURY *says nothing*]

Edgar: [*Looking up suddenly*] We're sorry for the state of the men.

Harness: [*Icily*] The men have no use for your pity, sir. What they want is justice.

John Galsworthy *Strife* (1909)

COMMENT

What do you notice about the playwright's stage directions? Find some examples of direction involving the actors' appearance, words or movements and think about their effect.

Characterisation

Who are the dominant characters in the scene?

Anthony

In what tone does Anthony speak throughout the scene? Find some examples that reveal his authority.

Harness

Harness has the longest speeches here. Consider his repetition of the word *gentlemen* – what effect does this have? Find examples of his use of rhetorical question, antitheses, first-person prefaces to remarks. How does he use speech to dominate? Do you have sympathy for his viewpoint? Is he presented sympathetically? Is he any more than a mouthpiece for socialist views? Does he represent the workers? Support your views with textual reference.

The Board

Look closely at the second half of the passage. Find examples to show how the Board members are reacting to what is going on (you may find the stage directions helpful here). Are they differentiated from each other?

Edgar

Edgar has only one line. In what ways is it important?

Structure

In what ways and how effectively does this extract move towards a climax?

Themes

This is clearly a drama of issues. The characters here are antagonists and there is not much differentiation of their speech. (If you read the play, you will find the working men don't speak very differently either: they just say *ye* instead of *you* and drop the 'g' from *-ing* words.) Giving realistic-sounding dialogue to characters came later in the 20th century! The dispute between masters and men is the writer's main concern, which is expressed in the conflict of powerful personalities.

A concern with how far the Union represents the ordinary workers is also suggested here. Young and old values are contrasted, with Edgar representing a softer, more sympathetic line than his father. Characters have representative functions.

There are other playwrights who use almost novelistic detail in stage directions (George Bernard Shaw, for example, or Eugene O'Neill). See if you can find some examples and consider their effectiveness.

KEY TERM

Fourth wall: the invisible wall; we imagine this across the proscenium arch of a conventional theatre through which an audience watches the play. It is usually a naturalistic convention, as the actors carry on as if the audience is not there and we are able to look in on something private.

KEY CONCEPTS

Although this is a play with obvious political concerns, there is no evidence of any 'distancing' effect. It strives to show the characters as being 'real' people, some of whom are more sympathetic than others. The audience here form the **fourth wall** to the scene.

Passage 4: *Last to Go* by Harold Pinter (an early revue sketch)

ACTIVITY 28.7

Read the following sketch *Last to Go* (1959) by Harold Pinter, and study the comments and questions which follow. If you want to try it as an unseen, stop when you reach the unseen alert.

Passage 4

A coffee stall. A barman and an old newspaper seller. The barman leans on his counter, the old man stands with tea.

Silence.

Man: You was a bit busier earlier.

Barman: Ah.

Man: Round about ten.

Barman: Ten, was it?

Man: About then.

Pause.

Man: I passed by here about then.

Barman: Oh yes?

Man: I noticed you were doing a bit of trade.

Pause.

Barman: Yes, trade was very brisk here about ten.

Man: Yes, I noticed.

Pause.

Man: I sold my last one about then. Yes. About nine forty-five.

Barman: Sold your last then, did you?

Man: Yes, my last 'Evening News' it was. Went about twenty to ten.

Pause.

Barman: 'Evening News', was it?

Man: Yes.

Pause.

Man: Sometimes it's the 'Star' is the last to go.

Barman: Ah.

▶

Man: Or the … whatsisname.

Barman: 'Standard'.

Man: Yes.

Pause.

Man: All I had left tonight was the 'Evening News'.

Pause.

Barman: Then that went, did it?

Man: Yes.

Pause.

Man: Like a shot.

Pause.

Barman: You didn't have any left, eh?

Man: No. Not after I sold that one.

Pause.

Barman: It was after that you must have come by here then, was it?

Man: Yes, I come by here after that, see, after I packed up.

Barman: You didn't stop here though, did you?

Man: When?

Barman: I mean, you didn't stop here and have a cup of tea then, did you?

Man: What, about ten?

Barman: Yes.

Man: No, I went up to Victoria.

Barman: No, I thought I didn't see you.

Man: I had to go up to Victoria.

Pause.

Barman: Yes, trade was very brisk here about then.

Pause.

Man: I went to see if I could get hold of George.

Barman: Who?

Man: George.

Pause.

Barman: George who?

Man: George … whatsisname.

Barman: Oh.

▶

Pause.

Barman: Did you get hold of him?

Man: No. No, I couldn't get hold of him. I couldn't locate him.

Barman: He's not about much now, is he?

Pause.

Man: When did you last see him then?

Barman: Oh, I haven't seen him for years.

Man: No, nor me.

Pause.

Barman: Used to suffer very bad from arthritis.

Man: Arthritis?

Barman: Yes.

Man: He never suffered from arthritis.

Barman: Suffered very bad.

Pause.

Man: Not when I knew him.

Pause.

Barman: I think he must have left the area.

Pause.

Man: Yes, it was the 'Evening News' was the last to go tonight.

Barman: Not always the last though, is it, though?

Man: No. Oh no. I mean sometimes it's the 'News'. Other times it's one of the others. No way of telling beforehand. Until you've got your last one left, of course. Then you can tell which one it's going to be.

Barman: Yes.

Pause.

Man: Oh yes.

Pause.

Man: I think he must have left the area.

Harold Pinter *Last to Go* (1959)

Unseen alert! If you are doing this as an unseen, do not read on.

ACTIVITY 28.8

Read the sketch in Passage 5 carefully and answer the questions, then discuss with your classmates. Bearing in mind that this is a complete short play, does any action take place on the stage?

- What topics are raised?
- How many of them are repeated?
- Is there any discussion of these topics?
- The time is frequently referred to. What effect does this have?
- Are the two characters differentiated in any way? Do they have anything in common?
- In what ways, if any, does the Old Man appear older than the Barman?
- How many pauses can you find here? What effect do they have?
- Does either character interrupt the other?
- How do you interpret the different attitudes to George?
- What, if any, is the significance of the title of this sketch: *Last to Go*?
- Consider the tone of the play – is it humorous? Where might an audience laugh? Does it have pathos? Is it menacing or sinister? (These are adjectives which have been used for Pinter's later work.) Could you argue that it is ambiguous in its effect? What evidence would you use to do so?

KEY TERM

Phatic communication: a kind of small talk that is used socially, not for ideas or information but to establish a familiar atmosphere. This kind of communication is often trivial and inconsequential but usually repetitive and affirmative, never exploiting differences of opinion but moving on from them to safer ground. Do you find this in the play, or do you find it more unsettling?

COMMENT

Themes

Work, time passing, being busy, purposeful but ultimately pointless travel, gossip about common acquaintances, illness; none of these is discussed – merely referred to and repeated. These are the basic problems of just being alive which we all experience.

Pinter's work is not easily categorised – it is as if he has thrown away all the dramatic categories we are familiar with, such as comedy, tragedy, farce and so on. This dialogue is very close to everyday conversation of the kind we call **phatic communication**.

KEY CONCEPTS

Pinter has been associated with **Theatre of the Absurd**, but this passage is an interpretation of naturalistic speech. It also has poetic qualities, with its repetitions of words and phrases, its rhythms and pauses.

Reflection: When you've read this little play (remember it is a complete one), discuss with your classmate whether you find any parts of it humorous. Do you think an audience would laugh, or do you think it has sinister, mysterious qualities? Or perhaps both of these things? Some of the points you considered when studying *Waiting for Godot* will also be valid here.

FURTHER STUDY

Search online for '*The Last To Go*, Kenneth Williams' for an audio version of the play worth listening to.

KEY TERM LITERARY CONTEXT

Theatre of the Absurd: a form of drama that began in the 1950s and emphasises the absurdity of existence. It uses disjointed, repetitive, meaningless dialogue. The situations shown are often confusing and inconclusive and the characters remain uncertain and sometimes tormented. The plots have little development. The effect on the audience is very disturbing, as you can imagine. Examples of the form include plays by Samuel Beckett – including his best-known play *Waiting for Godot*, which you looked at in Unit 26 – and by Eugène Ionesco.

Passage 5: from *Our Country's Good* (1988) by Timberlake Wertenbaker

ACTIVITY 28.9

Unseen exercise (for class discussion).

Read the following passage from *Our Country's Good* (1988) by Timberlake Wertenbaker and study the comments and questions that follow.

Because of the relatively large number of characters involved here, reading aloud – with different students taking a role each – will clarify your discussions of each character's attitudes.

Background Note: In the 1780s, convicts and Royal Marines were sent to Australia as part of the first penal colony there. The convicts, who had often committed minor crimes in England such as stealing a loaf when they were hungry, were treated with the utmost harshness. In this sequence, the officers are discussing the idea of the convicts putting on a play, *The Recruiting Officer* by George Farquhar, a Restoration playwright. Phillip is the governor, Ross is a major, Collins a judge, Tench and Campbell are captains, Johnson a vicar. The rest are lieutenants. Sergeant Kite and Captain Plume are characters in the proposed play.

Passage 6

Rev. Johnson	What is the plot, Ralph?
Ralph:	It's about this recruiting officer and his friend, and they are in love with these two young ladies from Shrewsbury and after some difficulties, they marry them.
Rev. Johnson	It sanctions Holy Matrimony, then?
Ralph:	Yes, yes, it does.
Rev. Johnson	That wouldn't do the convicts any harm. I'm having such trouble getting them to marry instead of this sordid cohabitation they're so used to.
Ross:	Marriage, plays, why not a ball for the convicts!
Campbell:	Euuh. Boxing.
Phillip:	Some of these men will have finished their sentence in a few years. They will become members of society again, and help create a new society in this colony. Should we not encourage them now to think in a free and responsible manner?
Tench:	I don't see how a comedy about two lovers will do that, Arthur.
Phillip:	The theatre is an expression of civilisation. We belong to a great country which has spawned great playwrights: Shakespeare, Marlowe, Jonson, and even in our own time, Sheridan. The convicts will be speaking a refined literate

▶

language and expressing sentiments of a delicacy they are not used to. It will remind them that there is more to life than crime, punishment. And we, this colony of a few hundred, will be watching this together, for a few hours we will no longer be despised prisoners and hated gaolers. We will laugh, we may be moved, we may even think a little. Can you suggest something else that will provide such an evening, Watkin?

Dawes: Mapping the stars gives me more enjoyment, personally.

Tench: I'm not sure it's a good idea having the convicts laugh at officers, Arthur.

Campbell: No. Pheeoh, insubordination, heh, ehh, no discipline.

Ross: You want this vice-ridden vermin to enjoy themselves?

Collins: They would only laugh at Sergeant Kite.

Ralph: Captain Plume is a most attractive, noble fellow.

Rev. Johnson He's not loose is he, Ralph? I hear many of these plays are about rakes and encourage loose morals in women. They do get married? Before, that is, before. And for the right reasons.

Ralph: They marry for love and to secure wealth.

Rev. Johnson That's all right.

Tench: I would simply say that if you want to build a civilisation there are more important things than a play. If you want to teach the convicts something, teach them to farm, to build houses, teach them a sense of respect for property, teach them thrift so they don't eat a week's rations in one night, but above all, teach them how to work, not how to sit around laughing at a comedy.

Phillip: The Greeks believed that it was a citizen's duty to watch a play. It was a kind of work in that it required attention, judgement, patience, all social virtues.

Tench: And the Greeks were conquered by the more practical Romans, Arthur.

Collins: Indeed, the Romans built their bridges, but they also spent many hours wishing they were Greeks. And they, after all, were conquered by barbarians, or by their own corrupt and small spirits.

Tench: Are you saying Rome would not have fallen if their theatre had been better?

Ralph: [very loud] Why not? [Everyone looks at him and he continues, fast and nervously] In my own small way, in just a few hours, I have seen something change. I asked some of

▶

the convict women to read me some lines, these women who behave often no better than animals. And it seemed to me, as one or two – I'm not saying all of them, not at all – but one or two, saying those well-balanced lines of Mr Farquhar, they seemed to acquire a dignity, they seemed – they seemed to lose some of their corruption.

Timberlake Wertenbaker *Our Country's Good* (1988)

KEY CONCEPTS

This play is a useful example of late 20th-century inter-textuality. Based on a novel entitled *The Playmaker* by Thomas Keneally, and also on the diaries of real officers who sailed with the First Fleet, it is clearly rooted in historical facts about the penal colonies. Its post-colonial concerns are evident even in this short extract. However, it is also a play about staging a play, so that Restoration drama – in the form of *The Recruiting Officer* – is also incorporated. (If you are familiar with Shakespeare's *Hamlet*, you will know that it has a group of travelling players and a play within a play.) Above all, *Our Country's Good* claims that the arts, represented here by the theatre, have a humanising, civilising, egalitarian effect on people: *We will be watching this together*, as Phillip says.

ACTIVITY 28.10

Read Passage 6 and discuss the extract from the play by Wertenbaker. Here is a checklist of discussion points.

- Characterisation: what attitude to the play proposal, and to the convicts, does each speaker have?
- What does this suggest about each of the speakers? What are their main concerns?
- Look closely at the way each man speaks. How does their use of language vary?
- What would you say is the main theme of this passage?
- How does the discussion of the classical theatre add to it?
- What is the difference, if any, between Phillip's and Ralph's attitude to the play proposal?
- Highlight the most significant points made in the discussion and justify your choice.

TIP

Probably the most useful activity you can undertake to enhance your study and revision of drama is to go to the theatre. There is nothing like seeing live theatrical performance: no polished re-takes, no dubbing, no distance. Real live actors speaking and doing things in real time in front of you – wonderful! If you can't manage this, try to act out some scenes from a play with your class. Learn the lines, get some rudimentary costumes and props together – and enjoy yourselves!

Self-assessment checklist

Reflect on what you've learnt in this unit and indicate your confidence level between 1 and 5. If you score below 3, revisit that section. Come back to this list later in your course. Has your confidence grown?

	Confidence level	Revisited?
I can entirely appreciate the value of reading and acting with friends		
I am conscious of the dramatic and thematic effects of this first scene of a play (*The Tempest*)		
I recognise the stock comedy situations here (*The Rivals*)		
I can understand the power of two opposing groups being depicted (*Strife*)		
I can recognise the depiction of ordinary conversation and action in a modern play (*Last to Go*)		
I fully endorse the value of theatre as depicted in this play about Australian convicts (*Our Country's Good*)		

Part 3
Essay skills, techniques and problem solving – for AS and A Level

Introduction

This section of the book is for you to refer to for advice and information throughout your course whenever you need advice on writing techniques for assessment. Remember to refer to your course syllabus for precise guidance on how you will be assessed.

Here are the units and what they contain:

Unit 29: Writing a good critical essay
• Reminders
• Discourse markers
• Successful quotation from the text
Unit 30: Tackling a passage question
• Approach to analysis: Type 1 (not requiring wider reference: poetry, prose and drama) and Type 2 (requiring wider reference: two methods)
Unit 31: Unseens
• Poetry
• Prose
• Drama
Unit 32: Unseen comparison
Unit 33: Writing longer essays/coursework
• Text selection
• Managing your material
Unit 34: Using critics
• Advice on using other sources
• Examples of using critics' comments
Unit 35: Command words and typical essay terminology
Unit 36: Troubleshooting: How to remedy common essay problems!
• Relevance to the question: five problems discussed
• Problems of essay structure: four problems discussed
• Handling the material: three problems discussed
• Contextual matters: three problems discussed
• Using the critics: three problems discussed
• Coursework essay pitfalls: six problems discussed

Unit 29
Writing a good critical essay

Reminders

Here are some reminders for you of how to prepare and then write your essay.

1 **Research** Begin the essay-writing process by reading and studying your set text or texts thoroughly. Your own personal response comes from immersing yourself in the text, and good knowledge will give you confidence too. Later, you can see what other critics say about the work. You will also have the views of your classmates and teachers to help you formulate your ideas. Later in this section, there is also some advice about using critics.

2 **Brainstorm** Think carefully about the essay title you've been given. Highlight the key words in it. You may like to use a spider plan or mind map; you may prefer to jot down notes in a more linear fashion. Do what works best for you. However, if you use a non-linear form such as a spider plan, you need to arrange the ideas in preparation for writing the essay, which is a linear form. You could number your points.

3 **Organise** Look closely at your ideas and decide how to organise them. Some are more important than others. Write a **topic sentence** for each paragraph which sums up that stage of the argument and consider what would be the most convincing order for them. Try different orders and see what the effect is. Try to formulate your overall argument in answer to the essay question in one sentence.

4 **Detail** For each of these main ideas expressed in a topic sentence, find examples to support the ideas and what you want to discuss about them. You could have up to three or four bullet points for each paragraph, which will be further thoughts on that topic prompted by the examples you've chosen. You may find that some cannot be fitted in logically and should be excluded. Be brave! Sometimes they are points you have revised, but they just aren't really relevant to this topic.

5 **Introduction** Now start the essay. The introduction should relate closely to the wording of the task and suggest the argument you are going to present. Try not to present your ideas in a simple list. Look at Unit 36: Troubleshooting for some examples of introductions that don't work very well.

KEY TERM

Topic sentence (sometimes called 'focus sentence'): makes the main point of the paragraph in one sentence. The rest of the paragraph develops the idea or gives examples of it. A topic sentence can appear anywhere in the paragraph but as it controls the ideas and examples in the paragraph, it is most often found at the beginning or as a summing up at the end of the paragraph.

TIP

If you have followed this advice during the course, it will seem like second nature under test or exam conditions. Don't spend too long planning – about five minutes should be enough. Some lucky students can just sit down and write, but they do have a plan in their head!

1 **Main body** Each individual paragraph should be focused on a single idea expressed in each topic sentence, developed and supported with textual evidence (see later in this unit for advice on this) and linked to the next paragraph with clear signposts. You are using your detail from point 4.

2 **Discourse markers or signposts** Paragraphs should be linked with appropriate words or phrases that show the direction the argument is taking.

3 **Write clearly in complete sentences and try to use appropriate literary terms where relevant** Practice makes perfect, as the old saying goes. The more you write essays and

act on the advice of your teachers, the more fluent your work will become. However, don't over-use obscure critical terminology in the hope that it will impress the examiner. There are literally hundreds of critical terms and figures of speech; your essay is not an exercise in including as many as you can! Knowing the right word is useful, but even more important is being able to discuss the writer's effects.

4 **Critical ideas** If you have quoted the ideas of others, such as critics, they must be placed in quotation marks and attributed properly, not just 'many critics argue …' (see Unit 34 for more advice on this). If you have more critical quotations in your essay than quotations from the primary text, then you are probably not giving sufficient weight to your own ideas and responses.

5 **Personal response** Assessment Objectives often highlight informed personal response. You naturally respond to a text that you know well and this will show in your essay. However, it must be 'informed' by knowledge and study of the text. You don't need to keep putting 'I think' or 'I feel that…' If you do, use this feature sparingly. When tackling an unseen, it may be appropriate to discuss your personal response to it after you have read and analysed it.

6 **Conclusion** Your conclusion should sum up your argument and round it off clearly. You may have come to a definitive conclusion; however, in our subject, it could be a more tentative one because you have explored different interpretations of a work.

7 **Checking** Proofread your work for technical errors. Don't rely on a computer's spell check! If you are writing by hand, make sure your handwriting is clear.

8 **Read over your whole essay** Does it answer the question? Does the argument follow on clearly?

TIP

See Unit 36: Troubleshooting for avoiding common pitfalls.

Discourse markers

These are the useful signposts between paragraphs which show the reader where your argument is going.

- **Order** If you want to show the order of things, you can say: 'firstly', 'secondly' and 'thirdly', but this does seem rather mechanical if you over-use it. (You may end up like Dogberry in *Much Ado About Nothing* with his *Sixth and lastly*!) If your ideas are well-ordered, it will be obvious. 'Next' is a helpful word, of course.
- **Continuation** If you want to show that your argument is continuing, you can use: 'in addition', 'also', 'too', 'another aspect', 'similarly', 'furthermore', or 'moreover'. Make sure that your next point really is similar if you use 'similarly', otherwise it will confuse the reader. 'Moreover' is a continuation word, but it has quite a strong effect – it's a little like 'and another thing' in a verbal argument.
- **Linking paragraphs** If you are writing an essay about three poems, and each poem is discussed in one paragraph, make sure that there is a link between them, or each paragraph will seem like a mini-essay. You can use something like: 'Another poem that shows the poet's concern with (theme), or use of (contrast) is …' You are trying to find links and should show this in the structure of the essay.
- **Introducing a new point** If you want to show that you are now introducing a different point of view in the argument or qualifying it to some extent you will need: 'however', 'on the other hand', 'in spite of this', 'yet' or 'nonetheless'.
- **Conclusion** When you come to your conclusion you can say: 'finally', 'in conclusion', 'to sum up', 'lastly'. You may want to say 'on one hand' and 'on the other' here if you feel there are different ways of judging the essay topic and the essay title suggests it. Avoid 'Thus we see that …' at the beginning of your conclusion.

Successful quotation from the text

1 The purpose of quotation is to give evidence that you know the text really thoroughly, to support detailed points in your argument and to show that you appreciate how the writer's use of language and style contributes to the effect. It is essential for the well-made essay.
2 You do not need to quote at length. Two lines is the absolute maximum for poetry; a few words would be better. Try to integrate the quotation within your own sentence. See the following examples of this.
3 Brief, indirect references to the text are fine if you can't remember the exact words in a closed book test.
4 Make sure that your quotations really do support the point you're making and are not just scraps that you remember which aren't quite relevant.
5 You may have heard of the formula **PEE** – point, evidence, explain. Of course, it's good to have evidence to support your points, but be careful not to explain things in a paraphrasing kind of way. I suggest you make an analytical comment rather than giving any explanations, and make your final E for Explore. There is another formula that involves L for 'Link back to the question'; this is part of point 4 about remaining relevant.

Examples that illustrate effective use of textual support

1 This is from an essay on Edith Wharton's novel *The Age of Innocence*. The main character, Newland Archer, is engaged to be married to May, the conventional 'right choice' for him, although this does not turn out well. Look at how neatly apt references are tucked into the writer's sentences:

STUDENT RESPONSE

Newland is trapped by society and by May. Although he recognises that May is the embedded image of the family and is ripening into a copy of her mother, he is not put off by this at first. The blameless domesticity tempting prospect at this stage, and though her naïvety annoys him (that's the only target she'll ever hit). May is just the wife he was brought up to desire.

2 The following example is from a passage question on Harold Pinter's play *The Room*. Again, the references are skilfully incorporated into the sentences.

STUDENT RESPONSE

Although the language seems ordinary enough, the tone at first seems a little tense. The fact that Rose never goes out makes her seem defensive and this is contrasted with Mr Sands who is dominant and tends to finish her sentences. (I don't know–You don't know exactly where he hangs out). Gradually a sense of fear and paranoia colours the whole scene.

3 This example is from an unseen poetry exercise: the lines are quoted and their implications explored.

STUDENT RESPONSE

In *Ancestral Poem* by the Caribbean poet Olive Senior, the poet emphasizes her father's harsh and endless work rituals in the following lines: the centuries of dirt / beneath his fingernails / encased in the memories / of his race. This hyperbole is effective in expressing her father's unending toil in the sense image of dirty fingernails, but it also links his efforts to the identity of his whole race and their enslavement.

4 Here is an example of successful indirect reference to the text from an essay on *Ode to a Nightingale*: instead of quoting *I cannot see what flowers are at my feet or in embalmed darkness guess each sweet* . . ., the answer has:

STUDENT RESPONSE

The poem is full of sense imagery but sound is the most important. Keats imagines standing in the darkness and just listening to the nightingale singing. He can't see but he senses all the spring flowers around him, which he can smell. The effect is very evocative – the reader can imagine being there.

5 The following is an example which shows that you can discuss the structure of a novel in detail but without actual quotation.

STUDENT RESPONSE

The three sections of Woolf's To the Lighthouse do not follow a conventional structure. 'The Window' takes up a third of the novel but is based on a single day, as is the final chapter 'To the Lighthouse'. These two sections are joined by a structurally shorter section which covers the passing of ten years. This allows Woolf to deal with human feelings and with objective reality in different areas of the novel....

This makes us confident that the writer knows the novel well, but is also fully aware of the conventions that exist in narrative structures.

Unit 30
Tackling a passage question

A passage question in an exam includes a printed poem, part of a novel or short story, or a section of a drama, and asks you to write on it. There are two common types of passage question.

For the **first type**, you have to focus on the given text and write a commentary on an aspect of it (such as creation of atmosphere, main concerns, characterisation, use of a particular kind of language, and so on. You have examples of this in the relevant units on poetry, prose and drama).

For the **second type** (usually at a more advanced level), you must write a critical appreciation of the text and then relate it to the rest of the work – more poems by the poet or stories by the short-story writer, other parts of the novel or play.

With the second type, you have the advantage that you are familiar with the work in question, so your commentary is not an unseen. However, for both types of question, all the close analysis work you do on unseens will be helpful to you. For the second type of passage question, you have the challenge of writing a good, well-structured essay which both focuses on the appreciation **and** incorporates wider reference.

How to choose: You are faced with a choice between a) a critical essay, and b) a passage question. Which will you opt for – a) or b)? You may feel secure because you have the poem or piece of prose or drama printed in front of you, so you don't need to worry about remembering quotations. On the other hand, you will have to have plenty of detailed points to make about the printed extract, as well as referring to the whole work, if the question asks for wider reference. The critical essay would allow you to range more widely, using references chosen by you from what you know best. Only you can decide, but give it a moment or two of careful thought. However, do not choose a poem that you don't know very well and treat it like an unseen! Don't be tempted to use a prepared answer, either.

Approach to analysis

Type 1: Passage questions (not requiring wider reference)

You are familiar with the work because you have studied the set text.

Poetry

You are asked a particular question, so your analysis must be focused on that. Make sure you look at the structure and verse form; the rhythm, rhyme and pace; the language: figures of speech, images of the senses, the diction (the kinds of words used), sound effects such as alliteration and assonance. It may be relevant to talk about the atmosphere, and certainly the tone: the speaking voice of the poem. The question may specifically ask you to look at this. All your analysis must be focused on the particular question asked, so don't be mechanical in your application of checklists. Structure the essay clearly, with a topic sentence for each paragraph.

Prose

You are asked a particular question, so your analysis must be focused on that.
A common requirement is to consider particular **characters** – you will need to look closely at the language used to present them. You will be able to identify the main concerns (or themes) of the set passage if you are asked for one of these. You know the **themes** of the novel as a whole, but not all of them will be evident in the passage. Read carefully and don't make assumptions – always relate your answer to the question asked.

Identify **relevant imagery** and **figures of speech**, discussing their effect. Consider any noteworthy **diction**.

The writer's **tone** is an important feature of any piece of writing, whether in prose or poetic form. Finally, the **atmosphere** created in the prose passage is just as worthy of discussion as it may be in a poem though, again, make sure this is relevant to the question asked.

When analysing a prose passage, you will need to look at its division into paragraphs and sentences. Do they vary between shorter and longer? Look at any longer passages of description and reflection. Is there a climax in the passage? Look at the dialogue if there is any. What effect does it have?

TIP
Revise the Part 1 and Part 2 units on poetry, prose and drama where detailed advice is given.

Drama

You are asked a particular question, so your analysis must be focused on that.

1 **Plot and context** How is the story, or plot, developed in the passage you are given? Remember that although you will never be expected to tell the story in an advanced essay, it is an essential foundation for all your understanding of, and response to, the play. Note the context of the passage in the play as a whole, and consider how it fits into the wider structure, but relate to this briefly.
2 **Themes** What major concerns of the work as a whole are developed in the passage? How are the play's issues expressed and further explored?
3 **Characterisation** Are any new characters introduced? If so, how do they fit into the picture so far established?
4 **Dramatic action** What is going on in the sequence in front of you? The action is one of the most difficult aspects to consider when you are writing an essay; you will need to use your imagination to understand this aspect well. Make use of the stage directions – they will help you.
5 **Audience Response** Always try to envisage the reactions of the audience to the scene in front of them. You have been focusing on this throughout the drama units in Parts 1 and 2 of this book, so you have had plenty of practice.

Type 2: Passage questions (requiring wider reference)

Look at the points made here as they continue to apply at a more advanced level, then consider how to structure your essay. Here are two methods of approaching the advanced type of passage question (requiring wider reference).

Method 1

1 **General introduction**.
2 A **critical appreciation**, following guidelines for poetry, prose or drama. This may take three or four paragraphs.
3 A **wide-ranging paragraph** that links to the points made under point 2 and relates to other poems or the rest of the relevant parts of the novel or play.
4 **Conclusion:** highlighting the relationships between the printed passage and the general comment.

Method 2

1 **General introduction**.
2 A **critical appreciation**, following guidelines for poetry, prose or drama. This may take three or four paragraphs. **At the end of each paragraph**, relate the points you have made to other works by the poet, or the sections of the novel or play, depending on the question asked. You may be able to make these linking comments **within** each paragraph. There are detailed examples in Part 2 of this book.
3 **Conclusion:** highlighting the relationships between the printed passage and the general comment.

TIP

There isn't one right way to do this. Try both methods and see how you get on – choose what works best for you.

Check the balance of your essay by underlining all the comments in your essay that relate to the rest of the text rather than the passage. There should always be *more* on the printed passage. You will find examples of this in Units 20, 23 and 26.

Unit 31
Unseens and close analysis

Being able to look closely at and analyse a poem or passage of prose or drama you have never seen before is an essential reading skill that will always be useful. It is also a crucial work skill for your future life, in whatever field, although usually in the form of prose. (Not many bosses use blank verse for their reports!) Recap the diagrams in Part 1 of this book (Figures 5.1, 11.1 and 18.1) to remind yourself of the essentials.

Here is a checklist:

Poetry

1. Who is speaking, and who are they speaking to? (Look for personal pronouns: 'I', 'you', and so on.) What situation are they in? Are they doing anything in the poem?
2. What does the poem seem to be about? Themes or main concerns? (You will need to keep this in mind at all times when considering language effects.)
3. Language: figures of speech and diction, images of the senses.
4. Structure: how is the poem organised? Where does it begin, what happens next, how and where does it conclude? Does it work up to a climax of some sort or become more philosophical, moving from the particular to the general?
5. Verse form, metre, rhyme if there is any. Pace. Special sound effects such as alliteration, onomatopoeia, and so on.
6. Linking with point 1, what tone of voice is the poem's speaker using?
7. What sort of atmosphere is created through the words, images and tone used?
8. What is your own personal response?

Prose

1. What is the subject matter? Is it descriptive? Does it concern people, and if so what are they doing?
2. What are the main concerns of the writer? (You will need to keep this in mind at all times when considering language effects.)
3. Language: figures of speech and diction, images of the senses. Prose can be just as rich in imagery as poetry. There may also be longer passages of description or reflection than you find in poetry.
4. Structure: how is the passage organised? Where does it begin, what happens next, how and where does it conclude? Does it work up to a climax of some sort or become more philosophical, moving from the particular to the general? Although it will not be a complete work, it will have been chosen carefully to be cohesive.
5. Narrative position: is it first or third person? Is it focalized on one character? Is there any direct speech or free indirect? What tense is it written in? What effects does this create?
6. Linking with point 5, what tone of voice is the narrator using?
7. Sentence structure: how varied is it and what effect does this have?
8. What sort of atmosphere is created through the words, images and tone used?
9. What is your own personal response?

Drama

The words are in prose or poetry, so some of these questions apply to dramatic dialogue.

1. What is happening? What do the stage directions indicate? Can you visualise what happens in the scene? Remember the audience!
2. Who speaks and what do they say? Make a note of all the characters and consider what they might be doing if they are not speaking. Are they contrasted with each other? Do they conflict in any way?
3. Dramatic action: does it develop during the extract? Don't neglect the second half – it is just as important as the first.
4. Look out for changes of tone. A scene can move quickly from humour into seriousness or vice versa. Sometimes the action moves to a climax, and afterwards there is a change of tone. This is more common in staged plays than in film.
5. What are the main concerns of the dramatist in this extract? Don't imagine for a moment that domestic situations such as filling a kettle or making the bed are just 'filler' actions to keep the stage looking busy. They may have important symbolic significance (e.g. the wife always makes the tea because she is subservient; the bed has just been slept in by one of the children's friends who has slipped away early so as not to be seen, and so on) Equally, serious political themes may be being played out.

Your unseen paper at AS level does not involve comparison. However, even if you don't need to do comparison exercises under exam conditions, they are really helpful for sharpening your critical reading skills as well as providing an extra stretch and challenge for you.

When you come to write your comparison, you are faced with a choice of essay structures. Are you going to talk about poem A first and then bring in poem B? Or are you going to try to comment on both simultaneously as you go through your paragraphs? Bear in mind that the instruction given is to 'compare' or 'compare and contrast', so you must be seen to be answering the question from the word go. ('Compare and contrast' is a favourite formula – it just means discuss the similarities and differences. Even if you just have the word 'compare', you should still also contrast.)

How to choose: The best way is the way that works for you – so that you are able to write your most confident essay. There are advantages and possible pitfalls in each method.

Method 1

1. An **introduction**, with reference in general terms to both poems/passages – perhaps to a similar theme or subject matter.
2. The main body of the essay is organised **thematically**, with a topic for each paragraph that refers to both poems/passages and compares them from the outset (for example, use of extended metaphor, complex repetitive structure, verse form/rhyme, and so on).
3. A **conclusion** that sums up the comparative argument.

The **advantage** of this more sophisticated method is that the whole essay is relevant to the comparison; its main **disadvantage** is that some students find the continuously interweaving reference to both texts confusing and the essay structure becomes muddled. For these students, Method 2 may be advisable.

Method 2

1. An **introduction**, with reference in general terms to both poems/passages – perhaps to a similar theme or subject matter. (The same as Method 1.)
2. The **first paragraph** of the essay deals with the first poem/passage, referring to all the elements of language, structure, tone, and so on. The **next paragraph** deals with the second poem/passage, comparing with the first as it goes, and from that point on, the essay is entirely comparative. It is possible to move from one piece to the other in successive paragraphs, but you must give equal weight to each and you must compare and contrast.
3. A **conclusion** that sums up the comparative argument.

The **advantage** of this method is that you feel confident that you have the material under control, dealing first with one and then with the other, making comparative interpretations and evaluations only as you get into the second poem/passage. The **disadvantage** of this method is that you might get carried away with poem/passage A and then not write much about poem/passage B; or forget to compare and write two almost separate mini-analyses with very little comparison.

TIP

Create a table for comparison of poems or prose passages using this method. It can be very helpful. See Units 22 and 25 for examples of this.

The Cambridge International AS & A Level Literature in English syllabus (9695) for examination from 2021 does not include coursework or an extended essay assessment, but this advice may help for other subjects and you will also find it useful later on for university essays. First, you need to make quite sure that you know what you are aiming for. If you are submitting coursework, you may have, for example, 2000–3000 words for two essays, or up to 3500 for one essay, or an alternative word count, so make sure you know the rules before you begin the work. Note that quotations and bibliography are often not part of the word count – but check your syllabus to be sure.

Text selection

If you need two texts for your coursework, check whether they must be in different forms (poetry, prose and drama). Also check if you need to select main texts and subsidiary texts, and if they can be in the same form (all novels for example). Consider whether you need to make a comparison of them.

Usually your chosen works must be literary texts and they should normally be as demanding as the texts on a timed exam paper (one or two poems won't be enough, for example, to count as a text, unless it's a long text like *Paradise Lost*).

Make sure that your chosen texts are not used elsewhere on the syllabus, as there is often a rule about this (although the individual writers may be reused; for example, a different Shakespeare play would be acceptable).

Check whether your texts should all have been written in English – on many syllabuses, no translations are allowed.

Managing your material

Get the balance right.

- Think about your word limit. If you imagine a typical paragraph to be around 200 words, that's about five paragraphs for a 1000-word essay, eight paragraphs for a 1500-word essay and 17 paragraphs for a 3500-word essay. Take away the introduction and conclusion and you will see how many paragraphs you need to write for your coursework essay. You can adjust this by looking at your own work. How many words do you have in one of your typical paragraphs in a shorter essay? Make the adjustment and work out the number of paragraphs. This is just a rough guide, of course, but it does give you a sense of the overall structure of your essay.
- Follow the rules for essay writing in Unit 29. Make sure that you link your paragraphs well. If you are writing on poetry and use four poems, for example, have you said enough to relate them to each other?
- If you need to write about main texts and subsidiary texts, it is usual to write an introduction to all your texts, then make reference to both main texts within each paragraph, or if you devote a paragraph to one text only, bring in the second text in the next paragraph. Don't go for pages and pages on only one of your texts; this is a more

common problem than you would think! It's often clear to the reader that one of the texts is favoured over the others.

- Some students refer to all of their texts in each paragraph of the essay. You don't have to do that with your subsidiary texts: a few well-discussed paragraphs relating them to your main theme would be enough if your comments show clearly that you have studied them and know how they relate to the main texts. One or two sentences on each work in a long essay are not enough.

Don't forget to comment on form, structure and language.

- In any literature essay, you are analysing the writing, not just the ideas. Be careful if you've chosen texts, often novels, where you can easily forget about this because you are fascinated by the theme; say, the idea of the future created in a science fiction topic, or the notion of an 'American Dream'. How is it done? What literary means does the author use? Close analysis of language is always important.

Use critical material but always attribute it.

- Background material and critical reading may be very helpful, but other people's ideas and words must be attributed, placed in quotation marks and footnoted. The work should be cited in your bibliography. This includes the 'Study Guide' sort of material, with which we are familiar both in print form and on the Internet. Failure to acknowledge the words of others can lead to plagiarism, which has dire consequences. See Unit 34 for further guidance on this.

Stay within the word limit.

- Quotations, bibliographies and footnotes do not usually count towards the word limit.
- Don't go over your limit and don't include in your footnotes large amounts of discursive material that should be in the main body of the essay. Footnotes are intended to be brief references to page numbers and the like.

Unit 34
Using critics

Personal response is always valued in responses to literature, particularly when it is 'informed' by knowledge and understanding of texts. However, syllabuses also highlight the importance of being able to appreciate and discuss varying opinions.

You have opinions – so do your classmates, and your teacher guides you with her or his opinion too. There are probably helpful notes in your textbook and a wealth of other material in books and online. These all suggest ways of looking at your texts and interpretations that you may not have thought of yourself. Reading literary criticism can be an inspiring, enriching and enjoyable experience. New ideas about your old favourites still have the power to thrill and energise your brain. Always take the opportunity to go to the theatre to see plays, if you can. Every new production produces new insights. Why do so many directors continue year after year with Shakespeare productions? Because each one offers some new perceptions for us to think about.

Literary criticism is a well-established genre and there are many 'schools' of criticism. However, you will find that some more recent literary theorists may seem more like philosophers than professors of literature and thus more difficult to read and understand; you should not be discouraged by this. Many older critics have valuable insights in an accessible style. Be guided by your teacher and by your own trial and error.

The new requirement at A level to 'evaluate' critical perspectives involves a more active approach to the critics you cite. How far do you agree with what they say, and why? Just because someone has asserted a particular view doesn't make it sacrosanct. Engage with it and extend the range of your essay.

TIP

Books in print have usually been through strict editorial processes and are likely to contain accurate and helpful information. In addition to useful material, the internet also has many unreliable sources that cannot be trusted and may be very unhelpful – for example from bloggers who put their views online as if they were established literary critics. You may also find 'self-published' works, which can be unreliable. You need to be very selective. Ask for your teacher's advice if you are not sure. Just because it's there doesn't mean it's true or dependable.

Major Schools of Literary Criticism (critical perspectives)

Historical critics see works of literature as the reflection of an author's time and place. They believe it's important to know about the work's political, sociological and economic context in order to truly understand it. (This approach can be very helpful in overall understanding and appreciation but should not be considered a substitute for close reading of the text itself. It also demands a breadth of research)

Biographical critics seek to interpret by placing the work in context of the author's life, times and influences. They believe it is important to understand the author's life events and relationships in order to assess their impact on the content and meaning of the works. (This approach can become shallow, simplifying as it does the creative process and is useless where the author's life, or even identity, is not known. Very popular at the moment perhaps because of 'celebrity culture')

Psychoanalytical critics view the work through the lens of psychology, scrutinizing the motivations of characters often by relation to Freud's theories such as the id, the ego and the superego; eros and thanatos; or Jungian theories such as the collective unconscious. (Some works invite this sort of critical approach more readily than others; however, subtle characterisation can be limited by being subsumed into a psychological pigeon hole)

Marxist criticism depends upon Marx's view of the class-based structure of society, emphasising power differentials between the haves and the have-nots.
(Can be very useful when discussing the novel, but it is not as helpful for analysis of lyric poetry)

Feminist criticism assesses the presentation of gender in literary works. Like Marxist critics, feminist critics believe that a powerful dynamic underlies all social conditions, but where the Marxist critics focuses on class-related forces, the feminist critic looks to the unequal distribution of power between genders. (Very illuminating; one can read works in an entirely different way, but it's important to keep a historical perspective on what were givens at the time of writing.)

Late 20th 21st Century Criticism is post-modern, emphasising deconstruction, disunity and intertextuality.

Advice on using other sources

Be discriminating – take care with some of the readily available study guides and 'Notes' series, both in print and online. Some of them tell the story, paraphrase or describe rather than analyse and are thus not illustrating advanced skills.

Read widely, but make sure you have studied your primary text well first so that you understand the thrust of any critical argument from another source.

Make notes of interesting ideas and critical statements that you feel could be useful in an essay of your own, always remembering to attribute them.

Watch DVDs or filmed versions – making a literary text into another form such as a film is, in itself, an act of literary criticism, since the film-maker will have to exclude, include and adjust material, which will change the original in many ways. Enjoy these versions but always remain aware of their potential for distortion. Film is a different medium, and Film Studies is a discrete subject.

However, you can incorporate the pleasure of watching a film into the classroom by deliberately comparing the handling of different sequences. It is probably helpful if you know the **original** text reasonably well, so that you don't get muddled when writing about the original novel or play (for example, saying something about a character's red dress being a symbol of blood when it's not mentioned in the novel at all). A filmed version of Jane Austen's *Pride and Prejudice* showed Mr Darcy (a well-known actor) plunging into a lake on his estate to have a swim and emerging like a pin-up with a wet shirt. This has been quoted and repeated many times and is, of course, not in the book at all and not really in tune with the characterisation of Mr Darcy, who would never behave in that way.

- Read a section – watch the scene on film.
- Find examples where the words on the page have been used to create a background or atmosphere.
- Consider whether any dialogue has been directly used from the original work or adapted significantly.

- Are any characters omitted? Why do you think this might have been done?
- Compare different filmed versions of the same work. This is particularly helpful for Shakespeare and especially for a favourite such as *Romeo and Juliet*. I enjoy all the different filmed versions of this play and think they can each offer a thought-provoking interpretation.
- Search YouTube and other Internet sites for individual scenes for consideration and comparison.

Personal Response Your own response to what you read is all-important. Give yourself the best chance by reading carefully and without distractions. Ask yourself if you have considered all the evidence in the text and not jumped to conclusions.

TIP

Writing the words of someone else as if they were your own (plagiarism) is a very serious offence with serious consequences. Never do this.

Write your own essays in your own words. If someone else expresses a great idea really well, then quote it, put it in quotation marks and attribute it in a footnote or bibliography. Search engines can readily identify plagiarised sentences and even phrases, so do not be tempted. Plan carefully, use your time well, and take pleasure in your own achievement.

Examples of using critics' comments

You will find that many of the sample essays in Part 2 of this book have at least one critical comment to enhance the argument and highlight 'evaluation'. Here are some others:

1 On *Othello* (from a passage question on Act 4 Scene 1)

STUDENT RESPONSE

Critic Gamini Salgado writes: whatever pity we have for him now is inextricably entangled with horror and disgust at his behaviour to his wife, and I agree with this assessment. Even though we have watched Iago working his poisonous thoughts into Othello's mind, the words and action here stun the audience.

The student elaborates on the point and introduces audience reaction directly.

2 On *Measure for Measure* (from an essay which discusses Isabella)

STUDENT RESPONSE

Isabella is, however, not a sympathetic character. At the beginning of the third act, her scorn of Claudio's weakness has been described by E.M.W. Tillyard as *dramatically definitive and perfect* while his pleas are considered *pathetic*. One cannot argue with the dramatic quality of the scene, but an audience's sympathies are more with Claudio who is a much more likeable, less extreme character, so I am not convinced by Tillyard's view.

The student has strong feelings about these two characters and is not afraid to challenge the critic.

3 On Larkin's poetry (from an essay which includes *An Arundel Tomb*)

STUDENT RESPONSE

Nicholas Marsh has described what he calls the comic elements in An Arundel Tomb, but this is a distortion of the tone of the poem. It is ironic, but this is part of a serious exploration of life and death.

The student only uses two words of the critic, but to very useful effect, reminding you that quotations do not need to be long.

4 On Pinter's plays (from a passage question)

STUDENT RESPONSE

Martin Esslin coined the term Theatre of the Absurd and used it to describe Pinter's bizarre conversational sequences. Within the first ten lines of this extract we can see an example of this style.

This student shows knowledge of particular terminology and uses a few words of definition and description to apply to the passage.

5 On Arundhati Roy's *The God of Small Things*

STUDENT RESPONSE

Amit Chaudhuri has argued that the novel is a reworking of *To Kill a Mockingbird* by Harper Lee and it does have some elements in common, such as the two children in the small town, the History House like Boo Radley's house and the black man accused of rape.

Here the critic's views are clearly mentioned and agreed with, but without direct quotation. This is perfectly acceptable.

6 On Virginia Woolf's *To the Lighthouse*

STUDENT RESPONSE

Jane Goodman has described the novel as '*elegaic in mood*' and Hermione Lee similarly as a work '*full of loss and grief*'. I agree with both these critical statements, but feel they are one-sided. Lily and her painting represent the overwhelmingly positive force of Art.

Two critics are quoted here saying something similar, but the student has the confidence to disagree with them. Note that once again the quotations are brief and easily remembered.

Unit 35
Command words and typical essay terminology

In this unit, examples from poetry, prose and drama questions at this level are illustrated with helpful comments on what is required.

1 Discuss ...

The word 'discuss' is often used for essays at this level. Discussion of a topic means that you must consider all the important aspects of it, analysing and debating the issues that you think are important. Occasionally the word '**Consider**' is used and it requires the same thoughtful analysis as '**Discuss**'.

COMMENT

Essay: *Discuss Shakespeare's use of images of light and darkness in Macbeth.*

You will need to cover what the images are, how they are used in specific situations and what they add to the play overall. Some consideration of the contrast between them would be helpful too. You should be able to quote several examples directly, and analyse them, as well as making more general points.

COMMENT

Essay: *Discuss [the writer's] presentation of [character/setting/ idea] and what it adds to the [novel/play] as a whole.*

You would not be given the first part of this question without the second, because you might otherwise be tempted just to describe the person, place or theme, without showing its importance in the whole work. For example, a character could be used to contrast with the main character; a setting could be used to symbolise a particular culture or way of life; and an idea might be one of the writer's main concerns in that work. 'Presentation' means how the writer has used language, tone and structure to represent the character, setting or idea.

2 How far ... or To what extent ...?

'**How far** ...' and '**To what extent** ...' give you the freedom to pitch your response on an imaginary scale: it could be completely, not at all, or something in between.

COMMENT

Essay: *How far do you agree that Emma is self-centred?*

You are free to argue as you wish: that Emma is selfish; that she isn't; or that she partly is and partly isn't; or that she is at first, but becomes less so. You will need to argue carefully to support your case from the novel, but there is not a 'right' answer here. An essay arguing that Emma is selfish and controlling can be as strong as an essay arguing that she has never had the chance to develop her real character, which emerges as the novel proceeds and she learns from her mistakes.

3 In what ways … (or By what means …) and How effectively …?

'**Ways**' and '**means**' are the methods used by the writer to communicate her/his ideas. If they are effective, then the reader is moved to realisation, understanding or appreciation of the idea.

COMMENT

Essay: *In what ways and how effectively do two poets in your anthology write on the passage of time?*

You need to look closely at the poetic methods used and decide if you find them effective for communicating the ideas to you.

4 What importance or significance …?

The question is asking you to argue how far and in what ways an episode, character or idea adds meaning to the work as a whole.

COMMENT

Essay: *Discuss the significance of ideas and images of religious faith in the poems of Christina Rossetti in your selection.*

A selection of ideas and images must be analysed and discussed and a judgement made as to their importance.

5 Comment closely/Comment in detail with close reference to the text, focusing on …

Analyse the language of a passage or poem, looking closely at …

6 Concerns

'**Concerns**' are themes or ideas.

7 Methods

'**Methods**' are the means used by the writer such as imagery, symbol or characterisation – all the aspects of style that have been covered throughout this book.

COMMENT

Essay: *Comment closely on Hughes's concerns and methods in the following poem.*

Don't neglect any aspect of the themes and style of the poem.

8 Effects

'**Effects**' result from the writer's employment of particular methods.

COMMENT

Essay: *Looking closely at the effects of the dialogue and other narrative methods, show how this passage helps you to understand Maggie's characterisation in the novel The Mill on the Floss.*

You need to look closely at how you respond to the way George Eliot at times offers dialogue without authorial comment, and at other times comments as an omniscient narrator. Perhaps there is use of reported speech too. You will need to refer to the novel as a whole by using judicious, wider examples.

9 Dramatic

The word 'dramatic' is used to remind you that you are studying a play, with action, tension and dialogue. '**Dramatic significance**' means importance to the play as a whole; '**dramatic contribution**' means contribution to the play; '**dramatic effects**' are, for example, action, climax, characters in conflict, sudden changes of scene, surprises or denouement for the audience. Don't be frightened by the word 'dramatic' – plunge into the passage and look for the excitement!

COMMENT

Essay: *Discuss the dramatic function of the witches in Macbeth.*

You will have your own ideas about the function of the witches; for example, as instigators of Macbeth's downfall. Make sure that you also give plenty of evidence of their effectiveness on the stage: refer to their stirring the cauldron and producing the apparitions, as well as their parallels/contrasts with Lady Macbeth and their ambiguous, riddling speeches.

10 Language, imagery, tone, atmosphere

Although imagery is part of language, it is often highlighted separately in the question to remind you to look for figures of speech, such as metaphor. Don't forget images of the senses, such as sight, hearing, touch, taste, smell and movement. If you are asked to comment on tone in a passage of drama, it suggests that there are significant features of tone for you to identify: someone is angry, another is evasive, someone else is trying to calm them down. If the passage is a poem, perhaps the poet's tone is striking in some way: especially sad, or aggressive, or nostalgic. Prose can be satirical or ironic in its presentation of characters' behaviour, too. Atmosphere is created by all the many effects of language in a poem, play or novel. If you have analysed closely, you will absorb the atmosphere and will be able to refer to it.

COMMENT

Essay: *With close reference to the language and tone of this passage, discuss how effectively …*

To answer this well, you will need appropriate examples from the printed text in front of you.

11 Paying particular attention to…

This phrase in an essay question reminds you that you must focus on this in the essay.

COMMENT

Essay: *Paying particular attention to the imagery, discuss the poet's depiction of the city at night.*

There will be other points to make but the imagery is very important and mustn't be neglected.

12 Here and elsewhere in the novel/play…

Is a phrase attached to a passage question. You need to discuss the printed poem or passage, but you also need to relate it to other parts of the work.

COMMENT

Essay: *Discuss the manipulation of Othello by Iago, here and elsewhere in the play.*

You will need to know the play well so that you can analyse the printed sequence but also find examples from the rest of the play.

13 What might be the thoughts and feelings of an audience?

Is an audience-focused requirement that allows you to consider how the audience is likely to think and to feel about a scene from a play. It is likely to be a scene with strong ideas and characters that the audience can think about, but also one with emotional power that will make the audience feel. It's an open question which allows you full rein in your response. You could consider different audiences here, too, for example, 'an Elizabethan audience' compared with a contemporary one.

COMMENT

Essay: *What might the thoughts and feelings of an audience be as they watch this, the final scene of the play?*

Unit 36
Troubleshooting

TIP
Don't become discouraged as you go through this unit – most students don't write like this most of the time! It's here to be a helpful reminder of what **not** to do.

All students would like to write better essays, especially under exam or test conditions. This unit is to help you to identify some of the pitfalls of writing under the pressure of time and how to avoid them.

I've divided the problems into different categories (A–F) to help you see where you might have been at fault in essays you've done before. There are examples to help you identify each problem precisely. Categories D and E may not apply to your exam, but they are worth looking at for future reference. Category F is about particular pitfalls encountered with coursework. In many cases, it would be helpful to discuss these examples with a friend.

A Relevance to the question asked

Problem	How to resolve it
1 Not answering the question, for whatever reason.	Always highlight the key words of the question and ask yourself if each paragraph is to the point. Keep checking back.
2 Writing another essay, perhaps using familiar material which is not quite relevant.	You may have done a mock exam with a similar question. Take care that you use your known material carefully and in a focused way. It is hard to omit something you have revised carefully, but you must do so if it is not relevant to the question asked.
3 Being mainly relevant but having passages that drift away from the main focus.	Plan and ensure that each paragraph relates to the question.
4 Focusing on a character at the expense of other features.	Don't allow a fascinating character to unbalance your essay. For example, if you are studying *The Return of the Native*, students are often obsessed with the character of Eustacia Vye (understandably as she is a very compelling character) and write too much on her when it is not strictly relevant. The same is true of Iago in *Othello* and Edmund in *King Lear* as well as Heathcliff in *Wuthering Heights*. If the essay title is about a main concern or theme of the work, such as the passage of time, then the characterisation is only one aspect of it. You may need to explore the effects on the natural world presented by the writer, or on society as a whole.
5 Not choosing the most suitable material to illustrate your answer.	Don't, for example, write on poems that do not really fit the question asked just because you know them. Be ready for all possibilities by studying thoroughly. This is a very common pitfall under exam conditions and appears in many examiner's reports. Irrelevant quotations are also very unhelpful.

B Problems of essay structure

Problem	How to resolve it
1 No clear argument.	Plan, and use suitable discourse markers (see Unit 29).
2 Repetition of ideas.	Planning should help this too. Develop a sense of whether you have made a particular point before.
3 No introduction, or one that doesn't introduce any relevant ideas.	See the following exercise on introductions.
4 No conclusion.	Even if you are pressed for time, try to sum up what you have argued in your essay.

More on B: problems of essay structure

Introductions

COMMENT

Look at the following examples of introductions and discuss with a classmate which is the most effective. If you find yourself being critical of one, justify your feelings and see whether you could improve it.

Essay: *In what ways, and with what effects, does the novel Americanah present the time frame of the narrative?*

STUDENT RESPONSE

Introduction 1

Chimamanda Adichie is a novelist from Nigeria, who now spends some of her time in the United States and some in her native Nigeria. She won the Orange Prize for fiction for her novel Half of a Yellow Sun and Americanah has also been widely acclaimed.

STUDENT RESPONSE

Introduction 2

Americanah is a novel which crosses three continents and many lives. However, it is not told in a chronological way, and the reader moves backwards and forwards in the lives of the main characters.

STUDENT RESPONSE

Introduction 3

I am going to write about the different time frames of the novel. I will then write about the main characters' youth and their older selves. I will consider the writer's methods.

STUDENT RESPONSE

Introduction 4

The love story of Ifemelu and Obinze is a long and complex one. Americanah does not present the story in a chronological way, but moves backwards and forwards, focusing at times on their youth, at times on their mature adult selves, and taking a narrative point of view focalized first on one and then on the other, as young people and as more mature people, against a social and political backdrop. This allows a wide range of points of view, giving the novel scope for historical and sociological comment as well as exploration of characters and relationships.

COMMENT

The first example is simply a biographical introduction which is irrelevant to the essay. NEVER begin an essay in this way. Could you salvage it at all or would it be best to start again? The second is apt and focused but a little sketchy. Could you say something useful to add to it? The third is a statement of intention rather than an introduction to the ideas of the title (and rather dull in its expression). The fourth covers a lot of ground and is effective because it moves away from simply character towards the social and political background of the novel, which is just as affected by time as the characterisation is.

Essay: *Discuss some of the features of Brontë's presentation of marriage in Jane Eyre.*

STUDENT RESPONSE

Introduction 1

In the novel *Jane Eyre* by Charlotte Bronte, Jane's two love interests, Edward Rochester and later St John Rivers are both keen for Jane's attention, but it's Rochester she marries. They are opposite characters, and this tells us a lot about Bronte's view of marriage, which is that it should be a partnership.

STUDENT RESPONSE

Introduction 2

At the heart of the novel, it is a story of the protagonist Jane whose search of home happiness and love brings her through various trials and tribulations. It is at Thornfield Hall where Jane appears to have found a partner in Rochester, yet the terms of inequality in which the two stand compels Jane to leave him. It's only on attaining financial independence that Jane returns to Rochester, who has been humbled by his loss of wealth and then the two can join in a relationship of equals, which seems to be Bronte's main point. regarding marriage.

STUDENT RESPONSE

Introduction 3

The novel *Jane Eyre* tells the story of the protagonist Jane and her relentless quest for happiness. One striking element of this quest is that of marriage and the expectations of marriage in Victorian society are noted by the reader. Bronte shows that spiritual equality is more important than class.

STUDENT RESPONSE

Introduction 4

The novel *Jane Eyre* is a bildungsroman, a story of growing up and development; Jane's growth while searching for the perfect marriage is a significant feature of the novel, but she is a free spirit and desires a marriage between equals so that she can remain free and independent. Her journey towards such a marriage is presented in her rejection of two unequal and destructive proposals of marriage before finally returning to one of them on a more equal footing and achieving happiness. The novel also presents other marriages of convenience which have a destructive effect as well, showing that the idea of 'happily ever after' is not necessarily easy to achieve.

COMMENT

This is a complex topic, and all the introductions here have something worthwhile to offer as an opening to the essay. It is interesting that they all refer to equality within a relationship. The first one is clearly character-based and almost sounds as if it is going to be a comparison of Rochester and Rivers, although the idea of partnership suggests a useful line for the essay to pursue. The second introduction has a narrative quality which must be avoided. Never tell the story or come near to doing so. Again, the final sentence suggests a valid point to develop in the main body of the essay. Rochester's loss of wealth is not a completely convincing point. His loss of eyesight is a more important feature, but better not go into such detail in the introduction, anyway. The third introduction is concise and relevant, with an awareness of the Victorian context too, although a little more content would be helpful to suggest where the essay is heading. The distinction made between class and spiritual qualities suggests an interesting trajectory (or path) for the essay. The fourth introduction uses a valid critical term – **bildungsroman** – and makes a useful point about Jane's characterisation. However, it reaches into more abstract areas with its comments on the potential destructiveness of marriage and the necessity for equality. On the whole, the last introduction promises most.

C Handling the material

Problem	How to resolve it
1 Telling the story.	See the following, detailed examples.
2 Describing rather than analysing; paraphrasing.	See the following, detailed examples.
3 Writing too generally without textual support.	See the following, detailed examples.

More on C: handling the material

1 Telling the story: a problem with prose and drama essays

Students are always advised that telling the story is not an advanced-level skill, so a whole essay narrating the plot is very unusual. Nonetheless, there are moments in essays where telling part of the story creeps in: for example, when that part of the story seems really important, or where critical ideas are fading and it may seem better under test conditions to write anything rather than nothing. Here are two examples. The first is from an essay about the Ghost in *Hamlet*.

COMMENT

Essay: *'The Ghost of Hamlet's father is forgotten once the main drama at court begins.' How far do you agree with this comment on the function and effect of the Ghost in the play?*

STUDENT RESPONSE 1

(Introduction): I disagree with this comment. The Ghost of Hamlet's father is the mainspring of the action and therefore he cannot be forgotten. His command to his son to take revenge is an almost impossible request, so Hamlet's inaction throughout the play arises clearly from it. The Ghost is a reminder of the past and a comparison with his evil brother Claudius and this also remains throughout the play. If these were not enough reasons to disagree with the comment, there is also his chilling report of his existence after death which adds to the atmosphere of the play and confirms mortality as one of its main themes. Additionally, he appears later in the closet scene between Hamlet and his mother.

This is a clear and relevant introduction with a strong sense of the importance of the Ghost both thematically and as a contributor to atmosphere and characterisation – there are many ideas to develop. Now, what happens in the next paragraph?

(Main body 1.): A ghost has been seen on the battlements of the castle in Elsinore and soldiers on guard such as Marcellus tell Hamlet that it looks very like his father, old Hamlet. They are frightened by its appearance wearing armour. Hamlet decides he will go there at night and try to get the Ghost to speak to him. In a very exciting scene, he does just that and the ghost tells him in a thrilling speech of how Claudius his own brother poisoned him and that Hamlet must now revenge his 'foul and most unnatural murder.'

After an introduction packed with potential critical ideas, the essay degenerates into telling the story, almost as if the writer is taking a break from thinking! Telling the story of the first scene of a Shakespeare tragedy is more common than you would think: Antony and Cleopatra's relationship and the division of the kingdom in King Lear are cases in point.

This student is not short of ideas, but must now keep focused on the topic and attend to the thread of the argument, not the events of the story.

The first paragraph of the main body of this essay does not need to repeat the events of the beginning of the play. One of the points made in the introduction now needs to be discussed, illustrated and developed, after which another point can be explored in another main body paragraph. The writer makes two references to the exciting atmosphere, so a way of rectifying this paragraph could be to focus on the supernatural atmosphere created at the beginning of the play and the frightening depiction of the world beyond the grave, introducing the theme of mortality that runs throughout the play. Another possibility would be to focus on the speech in which old Hamlet describes the poison administered by Claudius taking over his body; in this speech, an extended metaphor of the body as a castle being attacked is used, reminding us of the sanctified nature of the king as representative of the 'body politic' (the governance of the land), making Claudius's crime – the murder of the king – even more terrible.

The next example is from the middle of an essay on *Emma* about Emma learning and becoming more mature. The essay has already discussed Emma's interference in the life of Harriet Smith and her own shock at being proposed to by Mr Elton. The essay is going on to discuss Emma's mistaken assumptions about Jane Fairfax and Frank Churchill.

STUDENT RESPONSE 2

(Main body): Emma shares her suspicions about Jane's love life with Frank Churchill, who encourages her in them and, in fact, makes some quite open hints and insinuations himself. When a piano arrives in Highbury as a gift for Jane, it is thought to be from the Campbells.

Frank, however, suggests that it is a gift from Mr Dixon, a gift to show his continuing affection for her even after his marriage to her friend. Jane's response is one of confusion, suggesting that it may indeed be a gift from a secret admirer.

Novel plots are often quite complex, as you can see from this if you don't know the novel *Emma*. However, telling the reader what happens is not productive.

What to do here to avoid storytelling

There are useful points to be made here about Emma, Jane and Frank Churchill. Emma is flattered by Frank Churchill's attentions to her and continues to make unfounded assumptions about others – here, apparently, Jane Fairfax. The text suggests the latter's discomfort and confusion, but Emma plunges on wilfully and blindly. In a kind of double irony, Frank Churchill's own collusion with Emma's misunderstanding is because he himself has a secret relationship with Jane and is trying to create a smokescreen so that people won't suspect what's going on between them. So you avoid telling the story by focusing on the **themes** of arrogance and misunderstanding, the **characterisation** of the three characters involved, and the **continuing ironies** exploited by the novelist in her development of Emma's education.

2 Describing rather than analysing

Describing is a little like telling the story, saying what qualities something has rather than analysing. It may take the form of paraphrase, which means putting the passage into your own words; again, not analysis. A common flaw in essays on *The Wife of Bath's Prologue and Tale*, for example, is to describe the Wife's first four marriages before getting to the analysis of the important fifth one.

Read the extract from Tennyson's poem *Ulysses,* then consider the example that follows from an essay on Tennyson's creation of personae in his poetry.

It little profits that an idle king,
By this still hearth, among these barren crags,
Matched with an agèd wife, I mete and dole
Unequal laws unto a savage race,
That hoard, and sleep, and feed, and know not me.
I cannot rest from travel: I will drink
Life to the lees: all times I have enjoyed
Greatly, have suffered greatly, both with those
That loved me, and alone; on shore, and when
Through scudding drifts the rainy Hyades
Vexed the dim sea: I am become a name;
For always roaming with a hungry heart
Much have I seen and known; cities of men
And manners, climates, councils, governments,
Myself not least, but honoured of them all;
And drunk delight of battle with my peers,
Far on the ringing plains of windy Troy.

Tennyson *Ulysses* (1843)

STUDENT RESPONSE

Ulysses is a famous classical hero, also called Odysseus, who was away from home (Ithaca) for about twenty years, fighting at Troy before journeying home and having various adventures en route. Tennyson shows him as someone and having various adventures en route. Tennyson shows him as someone who longs for further adventures and is dissatisfied with the domestic life and duties of a king. He wants to live fully, to *drink life to the lees* which means to drink his wine right down to the dregs and leave nothing in the glass.. He dreads having a dull life where he does nothing: *to rust unburnished, not to shine in use.* Tools and weapons rust when they are not used, but they shine when they are polished for use. He wants more adventures, even though he is old: *this grey spirit yearning in desire*; he doesn't want to *store and hoard myself*. He doesn't want to cut himself off and keep himself to himself. Tennyson is commenting on old age and how many old people don't want to slow down, especially if they have had a fulfilling life.. They want to keep having experiences.

What to do here to avoid description and paraphrase

Omit the introduction to *Ulysses*: the marker knows the story and the poem. Don't explain what *drinking life to the lees* means: comment on how the metaphor works and whether it is effective. (What does such a comparison tell us about Ulysses's character and habits, for example?) Don't describe the actions of rust; discuss, again, what impression it makes that Ulysses compares himself to a sword. Analyse similarly his comparison of himself to a commodity being kept in a store.

There is, of course, more to say about *Ulysses*; being more analytical about the language referred to in this sample could take you back to the poem where you might notice further points; for example, how important his self-image is to him: *I am become a name*. The race that he rules *know not me*; he has been among the heroes and *honoured of them all* – these references show his concern for his reputation. Ironically, becoming a *name* means that Ulysses is now past history; his life of dramatic exploits and widespread fame is over. He doesn't want to *hoard* himself – he wants to be out in the open, known to all, still being the main man, the hero. This dramatic monologue is more revealing of a complex character if the imagery and tone are examined more closely.

Ulysses is a famous hero with many exploits, but great insight can be given into more domestic matters by a good poet. Read this poem by Elizabeth Jennings and the student's analysis of it, which is largely paraphrase and description.

She kept an antique shop – or it kept her.
Among Apostle spoons and Bristol glass,
The faded silks, the heavy furniture,
She watched her own reflection in the brass
Salvers and silver bowls, as if to prove
Polish was all, there was no need of love.

And I remember how I once refused
To go out with her, since I was afraid.
It was perhaps a wish not to be used
Like antique objects. Though she never said
That she was hurt, I still could feel the guilt
Of that refusal, guessing how she felt.

Later, too frail to keep a shop, she put
All her best things in one narrow room.
The place smelt old, of things too long kept shut,
The smell of absences where shadows come
That can't be polished. There was nothing then
To give her own reflection back again.

And when she died I felt no grief at all,
Only the guilt of what I once refused.
I walked into her room among the tall
Sideboards and cupboards – things she never used
But needed; and no finger marks were there,
Only the new dust falling through the air.

Elizabeth Jennings *My Grandmother* (1968)

STUDENT RESPONSE

In the first stanza the poet describes her grandmother who used to own an antique shop full of 'faded' silks and 'heavy' furniture, where she used to polish up all the metals objects so well that they were like a mirror: 'she watched her own reflection in the brass' and she gets rid of the fingermarks. She has Apostle spoons and Bristol glass which are both collectible valuable antiques. In the second stanza, the poet describes how when she was a child she refused to go out with her and even now feels guilty because of it. She thought the grandmother treated her like one of the valuable objects. In the third stanza she becomes old and too frail so, all the antiques were crammed into one '*narrow room*', narrow like her life and 'the place smelt old', also like her. There was nothing then 'to give her own reflection back again'. When she dies eventually (4th stanza) and goes back to dust herself, the room goes to dust as well 'the new dust falling through the air'. The poet writes in a regular verse form of six-line stanzas with a rhyme ababcc, which has a definite feel about it.

What to do here to avoid description and paraphrase

This comment on the poem is at times an observant one, but paraphrase is always a temptation when you go through a poem stanza by stanza.

- **Emphasise features of structure:** Make sure you relate each stanza to the development of the poet's thought – here, the grandmother's devotion to her objects cannot prevent her increasing age and frailty, and her life narrows, with her eventual death. Juxtaposed with this is the poet, or persona of the poem, who is now grown up but still feels the guilt that began when she was a child and she still cannot really love her grandmother. The motif of dust links the first and last stanzas – it is the dirt which must be cleaned from valuable objects, but it is also what we will return to, noted by the writer. These recurrent ideas are not helped by a chronological approach to the poem.
- **Explore the implications of the diction:** the words quoted also need to be explored to interpret the poem and its meaning without just describing and paraphrasing. The Apostle spoons and Bristol glass mentioned by the student are used by the poet to show the grandmother's pride in her antiques – they are not just any old spoons or vases, and this point could be emphasised. This is a poem about people's attachment to objects and inability to relate to other people, even those they should be close to. The student has noted *faded* and *heavy* describing the antiques and these both relate to the grandmother herself, in what is known as a 'transferred epithet' (you will remember this from Unit 20); the descriptive words *old* and *kept shut* have the same function. She has become completely identified with the valuable objects she looks after: they give her identity and significance. Another way of expressing this would be to say that the objects are symbolic of the grandmother. The fingermarks she tries to clean off represent human hands touching, but she doesn't want that, either physically or metaphorically. Here, the student has observed, but not fully explored the words quoted. The final lines of the student response nearly get to this but don't quite develop it enough.
- **Consider the theme and the relationships depicted.** This poem is not a criticism of the grandmother – just as she is rather cold and lacking in friendly feeling, so the poet herself is guilty of not being more loving and reaching out. It's a very thoughtful poem about

communication, or lack of it, and our relationship with the material world of objects: 'things she never used but needed'. The word *polish* is ironic, as it means rubbing the surface of something to make it shine, but it is also used for people who have a gloss of good manners or sophistication. Perhaps the grandmother would like the granddaughter to be more well-behaved and polite! Loving people is a natural activity, but one that there is not much evidence of in this poem, on either side. Taking the dust off surfaces doesn't prevent us from going back to dust ourselves eventually, so perhaps we should be more nurturing of the people we know rather than what we own. The writer of the response has noticed but not developed points about language. Jennings' word choices are always meaningful and effective.

- **Relate verse form to meaning**. Additionally, the student has noted the regular verse form and rhyme scheme of the poem but hasn't related it to the effects in the poem. Although the rhyme is ababcc, there are many half-rhymes that give a sense of incompleteness and awkwardness, mirroring the relationship, which is not fully in tune; for example, put/shut; room/come. However, the final lines of the poem have full rhymes, giving finality to this relationship, which is now closed with the death of the grandmother.

Read this extract from a passage question on Pinter's play *The Homecoming*.

STUDENT RESPONSE

Halfway through the passage we are introduced to Sam, Lenny's uncle, and the interaction between them seems to be quite pleasant.. Lenny and Sam talk. Hullo. How are you, Uncle? Lenny is more friendly when he speaks to his uncle: Well, I think you're entitled to be tired, uncle, after Sam has had a long day at work. The relationship between Sam and Lenny seems to be more friendly, whereas the relationship between Sam and Max seems to be more distant. We see this when Max says: I'm here too, you know, implying that he is expecting a greeting. However, he does not get one as Sam just looks at him and does not fully acknowledge him. Sam only says: I know you're here. There is another pause after this.

What to do here to avoid description and paraphrase

Look closely at this passage of writing. It seems to me that only one point is being made, with description and repetition. Try writing one sentence to express this point. You do not need to labour a point by repetition and description. Analysing the language and tone is all-important. Usefully here, the tone of the speakers could be examined more closely. The idea of being entitled to be tired could be expressed in a sardonic way, which doesn't suggest friendliness. In what tone does Max say his line? How does the pause contribute to the atmosphere?

3 Writing too generally without textual support

What you say may be valid, but support from the text is essential to make your claims convincing.

Read this paragraph from an essay on a drama unseen.

STUDENT RESPONSE

As a theatre piece, I feel this scene is rather effective because there is a lot of detail squeezed in, yet the pauses and silences help draw it out. There is a lot of action in the piece, most of it unjustified. His [the playwright's] stage directions and sound cues help, and the readers feel pathos towards the main character.

What to do to support this paragraph from the text

Examples are needed of: *detail squeezed in*; *pauses and silences*; *action*; and *stage directions and sound cues*; and considered evidence of why the reader would feel sympathy towards the main character. Additionally, the claim that the action is *unjustified* seems inexplicable without further discussion. It is not a successful paragraph and saying *I feel* doesn't enhance it. Considering 'the readers' rather than 'the audience' suggests too that awareness of theatrical qualities is not entirely secure.

Read the following paragraph from an essay on Keats and beauty, which has more to say than the paragraph yet still fails to support its ideas from the text.

STUDENT RESPONSE

La Belle Dame Sans Merci is written within a framework of the cruelty of nature, The knight is lost and it is evident that he has no purpose to his life. In the centre of the poem there is a moment of intense beauty and the language becomes rich and erotic. However the moment ends and the knight is left alone. Keats leaves the reader with the idea of how to reconcile a moment of beauty with brutal reality. When it is over you are once again in a world of suffering.

What to do to support this paragraph from the text

Whether you know the poem or not, you can see that the ideas remain general and vague. The following points could be illustrated and discussed: framework; nature's cruelty; the knight's purposelessness; the moment of beauty with language becoming rich and erotic (we would only know that a woman is involved from the poem's title!); the juxtaposition of beauty and suffering. Some evidence of the verse form could be useful here too.

TIP

Under timed conditions, when you do not have a text to hand, it is acceptable to illustrate indirectly. If you can't remember the exact quotation, refer as directly as you can to the images you remember. Looking at the example shown here, you could say that no birds are singing and the vegetation is bare because summer is over; the knight is wretched; the lady is like a fairy's child and moans with love for him; she gazes at him and sighs with love, but he is soon left on the cold hillside. These would all show a close familiarity with the poem. If you are studying Keats, find exact quotations from the poem to illustrate these points.

D Contextual matters

Problem	How to resolve it
1 Over-emphasis on the writer's life.	Details of the writer's life story are best avoided altogether. Concentrate on the text.
2 Bolt-on paragraphs of historical or social material.	Try to incorporate this material relevantly within paragraphs about literary qualities.
3 Forgetting the other contexts, such as the domestic, cultural and literary.	Many answers consider all 20th-century material to have been affected by the First and Second World Wars. This may seem an easy solution, but it is often irrelevant. 'Culture' is not just history. Family contexts exist in every era and are understood by every reader.

Here are some examples of poor use of context:

STUDENT RESPONSE 1

'Victorian women were all meek and subservient, so her behaviour here is out of character.'

This is such a generalisation about a Victorian novel character that it is bound to be simplistic.

STUDENT RESPONSE 2

'She wanted to write a novel to exorcise the memory of her parents' (of Woolf's To the Lighthouse)

The creative imagination of a great writer is a very complex entity. To suggest that all their work relates simply to their own life events is reductive and uncritical. Remember T.S. Eliot's poem *The Love Song of J Alfred Prufrock*, written with great empathy about an elderly man, but when the poet was himself young.

STUDENT RESPONSE 3

'Shakespeare's son had just died so he wrote Hamlet, which is full of images of death.'

Like Student Response 2, this straightforward cause and effect explanation omits all the artistry of the great writer.

STUDENT RESPONSE 4

'Larkin was a known misogynist and never married, so his view of relationships in Dockery and Son is very limited.' Another narrow presumption here.

Close observation and imaginative sympathy are more important for a writer than some life events.

This is true, but will only move beyond an encyclopedia-style definition if the text being discussed is shown to have typically Romantic features and this is relevant to the essay title.

STUDENT RESPONSE 5

'The Romantic movement took place in the late-18th and early 19th centuries and was a revolt against classicism and neo-classicism'.

E Using the critics

Problem	How to resolve it
1 Making sweeping generalisations about critics' views without naming them.	Try to remember the name of the critic whose ideas you are quoting.
2 Using quotations from critics without thinking.	Don't just put in some words you've learnt. Do you agree/disagree with the ideas expressed? How have they helped you to understand the primary text? For example, when the editor of an edition of the *Wife of Bath's Prologue and Tale* says *the Wife of Bath bursts upon the pilgrimage with the unexpectedness of a bomb*, think carefully before you quote it. It's easy to remember, but how entirely apt is this metaphor? A bomb may be 'unexpected' (although not if it's a war situation) and it's totally destructive – is this true of the Wife? Always evaluate what you read and quote.
3 Relying on the words of one critic so that your own personal response is smothered.	Some critics can be very persuasive in their views. It is a good idea to read other points of view as well to get a balance of opinion, and of course your own personal response is even more important.

F Particular coursework essay pitfalls

- If you are choosing your own title, try not to be too ambitious. You haven't got enough time to discuss the whole of American drama in the second half of the 20th century, but you have got time to do a close analysis of some plays that were written then.
- Dwelling on the writer's life can easily become biography rather than literary criticism, so be sparing with these details, which, used selectively, can be helpful as contextual background.
- Related to this, trying to work out the writer's intentions is unproductive (this has been called 'the intentional fallacy'). What matters is what has been written in your texts and what effects this has.
- Characters being viewed as real people, rather than as constructs of the author, is a danger to be avoided at all costs.
- Always discuss and analyse – don't just illustrate!
- Make sure your paragraphs develop an argument and are linked carefully with discourse markers.

Glossary

Act and **scene:** divisions within a play to show change and development. An **act** is a larger unit, a **scene** is a smaller part of an act. However, it should be noted that some recent playwrights do not use them at all.

Action: what is happening at any given moment in the story, what people are doing. (The plot is the completed series of actions making up the whole story.)

Alexandrine verse: a line of iambics with six feet – 12 syllables in all.

Alienation effect: *see* **Distancing effect**

Alliteration: the repetition of consonant sounds especially at the beginning of words.

Alter ego or 'other self': a character who is similar to another in the text, or one who represents the author in some way, or, as here, a different aspect or side of the character being presented.

Ambiguity: being open to more than one meaning or interpretation.

Analepsis: *see* **Prolepsis**

Anapaest: this is another rising rhythm, but the pattern here of two unstressed syllables followed by a stressed one (˘ ˘ ¯) is called an anapaest (or anapaestic foot).

Anaphora: introductory phrases that are repeated.

Anti-climax or **bathos** *see* **Climax**

Antithesis or contrast: places contrasting ideas next to each other for effect; often they are in balanced phrases or clauses. This placing can also be termed **juxtaposition**. You will find many examples of this throughout the book.

Assonance: the repetition of vowel sounds within words that have different consonants.

Augustan: the name given to a style of literature written in the period between around 1690 and 1744 (the year Alexander Pope died). Writers imitated classical models and emphasised order and rationality. It is sometimes referred to as the Neo-classical Age.

Back story: a set of events leading up to the main plot – background information that can be revealed during the main narrative.

Bed trick: the substitution of one actor for another pretending to be someone else in bed in the dark.

Blank verse: written in iambic pentameter but has no rhyme at the end of each line. Make sure that you don't muddle 'blank verse' with 'free verse'.

Caricature: a depiction of a person whose main features are simplified and exaggerated. Some of Dickens's minor characters are caricatures.

Caesura: The slight natural pause in a line. Most lines of poetry, unless they are very short, have such a pause. Sometimes this is emphasised by a punctuation mark to indicate where you might take a breath if you were reading.

Characterisation: literally 'making a character'; the writer has chosen words and tones to create a particular effect.

Chronological: following the order of events as they actually happen.

Climax: (from a Greek word meaning 'ladder'): the point of highest significance which is gradually reached; for example, *to strive, to seek, to find and not to yield* (Alfred Lord Tennyson). Its opposite, **anti-climax** or **bathos**, suddenly undercuts the climax (and may be humorous); for example, from a poem describing the survivors of a shipwreck (the cutter is the ship carrying foodstuffs): *they grieved for those that perished with the cutter/and also for the biscuit casks and butter* (Lord Byron).

Colonial and post-colonial literature: written in English from a number of societies that were governed in the past by Britain as a colonial power. Post-colonial works explore the issues of personal and national identity and displacement, often using particular narrative techniques to do so.

Comedy of manners: concerned with social conventions and what lies behind them; satirises the manners and affectations of a particular social class who are often represented by stereotypical stock characters.

Coming-of-age or **growing-up novel:** (sometimes called the *bildungsroman*): has a young person as its main character. It may be in either first- or third-person form.

Conceit: an extended metaphor, which is often ingenious and sophisticated. A persona is a role adopted by the poet for effect.

Concrete poem: a poem arranged in such a way that the words on the page form a distinct recognisable shape which adds to the poem's meaning.

Consonance: identical consonants but different vowels.

Cross-dressing: this takes place when characters of one gender dress as the other. In Shakespeare's day, all the parts were played by men and boys, so a boy could be dressed as a girl who then disguises herself as a man. This reminds the audience of the complexities of human sexuality.

Dactyl: the pattern here is known as a dactyl (¯ ˘ ˘) and these are dactylic feet. It has a falling rhythm which seems to suit very well the meaning of the poem's lines here, reflecting on a suicide: doomed and melancholy.

Denouement: comes from a French word which means 'untying' and is used in relation to unravelling or resolving the complexities of the plot.

Dialectical: a format of question and answer, or opposing voices, to present ideas. This form was favoured by the Metaphysical poet Andrew Marvell.

Diction: the writer's choice of vocabulary. (You may also come across the word lexis, which is a term from the field of Linguistics.) Not to be confused with diction meaning style of pronunciation in speaking.

Direct speech: a character's speech in its original form as the character says it. In quotation marks.

Distancing or alienation effect: a feature of some plays in which the familiar is made strange, so that the audience see characters and events differently and are surprised into thinking about them rather than simply identifying with or accepting.

Dystopian fiction: (the opposite of 'Utopian' which deals with ideal societies) focuses on societies which are frightening and oppressive. The main characters of such works are often shown in opposition to their society, or at least deeply affected by its restrictions.

Ear-rhyme: a true rhyme when spoken aloud, but looks as if it shouldn't be by its spelling.

End-stopped line: a line that expresses a complete thought. The second line, although it makes sense on its own, needs the third line to complete it and is therefore an open line.

Enjambment (from a French word meaning 'straddling' or getting its leg into the next line): a run-on line where the meaning crosses a line break

Epiphany: a moment of sudden realisation or illumination. These often happen at the climax of a short story or novel.

Eponymous: the title of the text is the main character's name.

Existentialism: a philosophy that emphasises the isolation of the individual in an indifferent universe, and stresses freedom of choice and responsibility.

Exposition: the early part of the play in which the audience receives background information about setting, events, characters and possibly themes, so that they understand what's going on.

Extended metaphor: is where the identification of similar qualities is elaborated over a number of lines, and may run throughout a poem or paragraph of prose.

Eye-rhyme: a rhyme that looks as if it should rhyme from the spelling but doesn't.

Farce: comedy full of exaggerated situations and improbable twists and turns of plot. The humour is often very physical.

Feminine rhyme: a rhyme on two syllables.

Feminist criticism: assesses the presentation of gender in literary works. Like Marxist critics, feminist critics believe that a powerful dynamic underlies all social conditions, but where the Marxist critics focuses on class-related forces, the feminist critic looks to the unequal distribution of power between genders.

Figures of speech: don't be put off by the fact that many words for figures of speech are unusual, often deriving from ancient Greek. This shows that using them has been an essential feature of language from since ancient times. There are literally scores of them, but the list on page 10 gives you the most common.

Focalization: the limited point of view of one character in the story without using the first-person narrative approach.

Foot: where two or three syllables recur in a pattern to form a metrical unit of rhythm (the plural is feet).

Foreshadowing: A writer will sometimes give a hint of what is to come in the play or novel.

Fourth wall: the invisible wall; we imagine this across the proscenium arch of a conventional theatre through which an audience watches the play. It is a usually a naturalistic convention, as the actors carry on as if the audience is not there and we are able to look in on something private.

Frame device: means giving a narrative the same beginning and end, within which the main narrative takes place – sometimes the finding of a manuscript or a letter, for example.

Free Indirect Speech: (as used in literary works): a mixed form where it is difficult to separate the voice of the narrator from the voice of the character. Some parts will sound like indirect or reported speech, but others sound very close to the voice of the character.

Free verse: does not have a regular metrical or rhyme scheme, but linking devices such as repetition, parallelism and the careful use of very short lines, enjambments, direct speech and sound effects make it as careful a construct as a rhymed iambic pentameter. Make sure that you don't muddle 'free verse' with 'blank verse'.

Half-rhyme: repeats the final consonant sound in words without the vowel sound corresponding. You may also come across the terms imperfect, near, oblique, off and slant rhyme – they mean the same.

Hemistichomythia: this device is where half-lines of verse are uttered by alternate speakers.

Hyperbole: is exaggeration – an over-statement, used for effect. It isn't used to disguise the truth, but to emphasise. It can be an ingredient of humour too; for example, *An hundred years should go to praise thine eyes* (Andrew Marvell, praising his lover).

Iambus: this foot (˘ ¯) is known as an iambus or you can call it an iambic foot. It has a rising rhythm.

Imagery: refers to the images of any of our senses (sight, hearing, touch, taste, smell) produced in the mind by descriptive language. These images are often being compared with something else, so frequently associated with specific figures of speech.

Imagists: a group of early 20th-century poets who believed that experience was most effectively communicated through images of the senses. This approach is an important element in appreciating *what* a poet is expressing by considering *how* it is expressed. Sense images do not have to be metaphors. The senses are sight, hearing, touch, taste and smell; to these we can add the 'sense' of energy or movement, which could be termed the kinetic sense.

Incremental repetition: the name given to an effect of repeated lines recurring again and again, as here. Ballads often have repeated lines of this kind. Incremental means 'adding' and 'adding to the effect'.

Indirect speech: a character's speech told by someone else and doesn't have to be word-for-word. Not in quotation marks.

Internal rhyme: when words within the same line rhyme.

Inter-textuality: the shaping of a text meaning by another text. The older word for a similar language effect is allusion.

Irony of situation: an event or occasion in which the outcome is very different from might have been expected. Seen in plays and novels.

Irony: in its simplest form, irony involves a discrepancy between what is said by a writer and what is actually meant, or a contrast between what the reader expects and what is actually written. More complex forms of irony are dealt with in Part 2 of this book. The word **sarcasm** refers to speech rather than writing, though it would be appropriate for a character speaking in a play.

Juxtaposition: the skilful placing of elements side by side so that they illuminate each other by contrast. The elements can be words, concepts or characters. It can be used in discussing poetry, prose and drama.

Litotes: is an understatement used for effect, often using a double negative (such as *not bad*); for example, Wordsworth uses *not seldom* to mean 'quite often' in *The Prelude*.

Marxist criticism: depends upon Marx's view of the class-based structure of society, emphasising power differentials between the haves and the have-nots.

Masculine rhyme: a rhyme on one syllable only.

Metafiction: narrators comment on their own writing in a self-reflexive manner, or play games with the readers, reminding them that writing a novel is a process, and the end result is not real life. The finished article is a construct of the writer.

Metaphor: is the most important and widespread figure of speech. It is a comparison in which unlike objects are identified with each other so that some element of similarity can be found between them. Here a comparison is made by identifying one thing with another, but without using *as* or *like*. In its identification of one thing with another it goes further than a simile.

Metre: the name for the organisation of rhythms into regular and recurring patterns, such as you find in poetry.

Mirroring: a useful term for the symbolic reflection of one thing in another.

Mistaken identity: where characters disguise themselves, pretend to be what they are not, act or put on a show and behave hypocritically.

Motif: a recurrent element in a text. It is a word used in relation to music as well.

Narrator: the person who tells the story – not the author.

Neologism: a newly coined word or expression.

Omniscient narrator: see definition on page 68.

Onomatopoeia: words whose sound seems to imitate their meaning, so that the sound reflects the sense of the word.

Oxymoron: see **paradox**

Pace: a word used to denote the speed at which a verse moves.

Paradox: often an important feature of more demanding texts. The writer is aware that nothing is as simple as it seems, e.g. life is short, beauty may be fleeting, but this makes the pleasure in them more intense.

Paradox: two apparently contradictory ideas placed together which make sense when examined closely; for example, *the child is father of the man* (William Wordsworth). If the contradiction is expressed in words in close proximity, it is called an **oxymoron**. In Shakespeare's *Romeo and Juliet*, Romeo makes a whole speech using them (e.g. *Feather of lead*, *bright smoke*, *cold fire*, *sick health*).

Parallelism: a device in which parts of the wording of a sentence are the same, repeating or paralleling each other for emphasis.

Pathetic fallacy: the term used to describe the literary presentation of inanimate objects in nature as reflecting human feelings.

Persona: comes from a Latin word meaning 'mask' and is the 'I' who speaks in a novel, short story or poem: the writer's own identity is hidden by the mask of the chosen narrator.

Personification: is a form of metaphor in which the qualities of a person are transferred to non-human things or abstract qualities, to 'humanise' them and make them easier to understand; for example, *the street lamp muttered* (T. S. Eliot): the environment is just as alive as the person walking down the street.

Phatic communication: a kind of small talk that is used socially, not for ideas or information but to establish a familiar atmosphere. This kind of communication is often trivial and inconsequential but usually repetitive and affirmative, never exploiting differences of opinion but moving on from them to safer ground.

Platonic: perfect, ideal.

Plot: the series of events and actions that occur in a story.

Post-colonial literature: see **Colonial and post-colonial literature**

Prolepsis: sometimes called foreshadowing or adumbration, looks forward to what is going to happen; the opposite is **analepsis** – looking backwards in a story.

Register: the language used for a particular purpose or in a particular social setting.

Repetition: extremely common for emphasis; the word **parallelism** is used for similar structures, phrase or clauses placed together.

Rhyme: the agreement in sound between words or syllables. These words rhyme: *night*, *sight*, *fight*; so do these: *flying*, *dying*, *implying*.

Rhythm: the measured flow of words and phrases in verse or prose as determined by the relation of long and short or stressed and unstressed syllables.

Sarcasm: the use of a mocking or scornful tone of voice. If analysing a writer's tone you should use the word irony, but a character's direct speech can be called sarcastic.

Satire: a genre in which the follies, vices and shortcomings of humankind are held up to ridicule. Satire criticises society and individuals, using wit and irony to point the criticism. It can vary from vicious attack to gentle, humorous disapproval.

Scansion: the analysis of poems into stanzas, lines and pauses. This includes rhythm and rhyme, and the effects of sound and pace.

Scene: *see* **Act**

Simile: is a figure of speech (really a kind of metaphor), in which two things are compared using *as* or *like*. A good simile will be clear and economical, but also suggestive; for example, *My love is like a red, red rose* (Robert Burns): beautiful, with soft skin like petals.

Soliloquy: a dramatic convention in which characters are alone on the stage and speak their thoughts aloud to the audience.

Sonnet: a 14-line poem with particular variations of rhyme, rhythm and structure.

Spondee: an occasional foot with two stressed syllables.

Stage business: activity with props (properties), which are employed for extra dramatic impact (notes, letters, cleaning materials, length of rubber hose).

Stage space: used to create an illusion of the setting the playwright wants to create.

Staging: the whole process of realising a dramatic work for performance.

Stanza: an Italian word that means 'room', a place to stop. Poetic stanzas can be irregular as well as regular.

Stichomythia: single lines of verse uttered by alternate speakers.

Stream of consciousness: writing that tries to express the very complicated thoughts and feelings which pass through the mind at any one time. Virginia Woolf and James Joyce are famous examples of writers in this form.

Surrealism: a movement originating in the visual arts, but when applied to writing it means combining realistic details with unlikely dreamlike images.

Symbol: a physical object that represents an idea or abstract concept. For example, a heart or rose may conventionally represent romantic love.

Synaesthesia: describing one sense in terms usually used for another; for example, 'melodious plot' (auditory and visual).

The Metaphysical poets: This term groups together certain 17th-century poets whose work is characterised by intelligence and an energetic style, often using witty, unusual comparisons known as conceits. Their subject matter was often religious, although some also wrote passionate love poems.

Theatre of the Absurd: a form of drama that emphasises the absurdity of existence. It uses disjointed, repetitive, meaningless dialogue. Situations shown are often confusing and inconclusive and the characters remain uncertain and sometimes tormented; plots have little development.

Topic sentence: (sometimes called 'focus sentence'): makes the main point of the paragraph in one sentence.

Transferred epithet: a descriptive word that qualifies something other than the thing it is describing. 'Melodious plot' [of trees] in *Ode to a Nightingale* is a transferred epithet – it's the bird that is melodious, not the plot of trees.

Tricolon: a series of three parallel words, phrases, or clauses, which can be very persuasive in both speech and writing.

Trochee: a metrical foot consisting of a stressed syllable followed by an unstressed one.

Universal: that everyone can relate to the experience.

Unreliable narrator: one whose views can't be fully trusted by the reader, perhaps because the narrator is too young to understand events fully, or is biased in some way, or doesn't know everything, or is perhaps a liar or exaggerator. You may sometimes find the term 'imperfect' narrator.

Utopian fiction: *see* **Dystopian fiction**

Verisimilitude: a useful word meaning the 'likeness of a narrative to real life'.

Verse: the regular unit of structure within a hymn, song or rhymed poem.

Villanelle: an old medieval form, with five stanzas of three lines followed by a quatrain. The rhymes are interwoven and there are only two of them throughout. The first and third lines of the first stanza are repeated as refrains at the end of each of the following stanzas alternately and then together in the final quatrain.

Volta: a change of idea or mood in a sonnet, usually at line 8 or line 12.

The author and publishers acknowledge the following sources of copyright material and are grateful for the permissions granted. While every effort has been made, it has not always been possible to identify the sources of all the material used, or to trace all copyright holders. If any omissions are brought to our notice, we will be happy to include the appropriate acknowledgements on reprinting.

'In a station of the metro' from *Personae* by Ezra Pound, reprinted with the permission of Faber and Faber Ltd; 'The Thai-Chi Man' by Ong Teong Hean from *Poems Singapore and Beyond*, Ethos Books, reproduced with the permission of the representatives of the Estate of Ong Teong Hean; 'Egrets' from *Collected Poems* by Judith Wright reprinted with permission of HarperCollins Australia; 'Whitecaps on the Bay' from *Haiku: This Other World* by Richard Wright, reproduced with the permission of John Hawkins & Associates and Arcade Publishing, an imprint of Skyhorse Publishing, copyright © 1998 Richard Wright; 'Words Between Us' was first published in *A Little Bridge* by Debjani Chatterjee et al, Pennine Pens, 1997, reproduced with the permission of Debjani Chatterjee; Excerpt from 'The Midsummer' (poems XVll and XXVl) from *Selected Poems* by Derek Walcott. Reprinted by permission of Faber and Faber Ltd and by The Estate of Derek Walcott from Farrar, Straus and Giroux; 'Metaphors' from *The Collected Poems of Sylvia Plath* Edited by Ted Hughes, copyright © 1960, 1965, 1971, 1981 by the Estate of Sylvia Plath. Editorial material copyright © by Ted Hughes. Reprinted by permission of HarperCollins Publishers, and Faber and Faber Ltd; 'The First Breakfast: Objects' by Dilip Chitre published in *The Bloodaxe Book of Contemporary Indian Poets*, edited by Jeet Thayil, poem used by permission of Jeet Thayil; 'The Germ' from *Candy is Dandy: the Best of Ogden Nash selected by Linell Smith and Isabel Eberstadt* Copyright © 1935 by Ogden Nash, renewed, reprinted by permission of Curtis Brown Ltd. and Carlton Books Ltd; 'An Arundel Tomb' by Philip Larkin reprinted with the permission of Faber and Faber Ltd; 'Enemies' from *The Collect Poems* (Carcanet Press) by Elizabeth Jennings reprinted with permission of David Higham Associates; 'Preludes' from *Selected Poems* by T S Eliot reprint with the permission of Faber and Faber Ltd; The poem 'Boxes' by Sampurna Chattarji, taken from *The Bloodaxe Book of Contemporary Indian Poets* (2008), is reprinted with the permission of the author; excerpts from 'Esther's Tomcat' and 'The Jaguar' from *Selected Poems 1957-1994* by Ted Hughes, Copyright © 2003 by The Estate of Ted Hughes, reprinted by permission of Farrar, Straus and Giroux, and Faber and Faber Ltd; Excerpts from 'The Skunk', 'The Otter', 'Clearances II' and 'Clearances III' from *Opened Ground: Selected Poems 1966-1996* by Seamus Heaney, Copyright © 1998 by Seamus Heaney, reprinted by permission of Farrar, Straus and Giroux, and Faber and Faber Ltd; Excerpt from 'An Englishman's Home' from *The Complete Short Stories* by Evelyn Waugh (Penguin Classics 2001) Copyright © the Estate of Laura Waugh, 2011, reproduced with the permission of Penguin Books Ltd and The Permissions Company on behalf of Hachette; Excerpt from *Martha Quest* by Doris Lessing, Copyright © 1952 by Doris Lessing, featured by kind permission of Jonathan Clowes Ltd., London, on behalf of The Estate of Doris Lessing and by permission of HarperCollins Publishers Ltd; Excerpt from *The God of Small Things* by Arundhati Roy reproduced with permission of HarperCollins Publishers Ltd.; Excerpt from 'Of White Hairs and Cricket' by Rohinton Mistry from *Tales from Firozsha Baag* (Penguin Books Canada, 1987, McClelland & Stewart, 1992, 1997). Copyright © 1987 Rohinton Mistry, used with permission of the author; Excerpt from The Namesake by Jhumpa Lahiri, Copyright © 2003 by Jhumpa Lahiri. Reprinted by permission of Houghton Mifflin Harcourt Publishing Company and HarperCollins Publishers Ltd.; Excerpt from *The Third Policeman* by Flann O'Brien (Copyright © Flann O'Brien, 1968) Reprinted by permission of A.M. Heath & Co Ltd.; Excerpt from *Americanah* by Chimamanda Ngozi Adichie, copyright © 2013 by Chimamanda Ngozi Adichie. Used by permission of Alfred A. Knopf, an imprint of the Knopf Doubleday Publishing Group, a division of Penguin Random House

LLC. All rights reserved, and by permission of HarperCollins Publishers Ltd. And by permission of Penguin Random House, Canada; Excerpt from *Cat's Eye* by Margaret Atwood, copyright © 1988 by O. W. Toad, Ltd. Used by permission of Doubleday, an imprint of the Knopf Doubleday Publishing Group, a division of Penguin Random House LLC., all rights reserved, and with permission from Bloomsbury Publishing Plc; Excerpt from *We Need New Names* by NoViolet Bulawayo published by Chatto & Windus. Reproduced by permission of The Random House Group Ltd. ©2013, and The Permission Company on behalf of Hachette; Excerpt from *A Grain of Wheat* by Ngugi wa Thiong'o, copyright © 1967, 1986 by Ngugi wa Thiong'o. Used by permission of Penguin Books, an imprint of Penguin Publishing Group, a division of Penguin Random House LLC. All rights reserved; Excerpt from *World Without End* by Helen Thomas is reproduced with the permission of Mrs RBH Vellender; Excerpt from *The White Tiger, A Novel* by Aravind Adiga, Copyright © 2008 by Aravind Adiga. Reprinted with the permission of The Free Press, a division of Simon & Schuster, Inc., all rights reserved, and permission from Atlantic Books; Excerpt from 'The Third and Final Continent' from *Interpreter of Maladies* by Jhumpa Lahiri, Copyright © 1999 by Jhumpa Lahiri, reprinted by permission of Houghton Mifflin Harcourt Publishing Company, all rights reserved, and by permission of HarperCollins Publishers Ltd.; Excerpt from *Absurd Person Singular* by Alan Ayckbourn; Excerpts from *Death of a Salesman* by Arthur Miller, copyright © 1949, renewed copyright © 1977 by Arthur Miller. Used by permission of Viking Books, an imprint of Penguin Publishing Group, a division of Penguin Random House LLC. All rights reserved, and with permission by The Wylie Agency (UK) Limited; Excerpt from *The Club* by David Williamson, copyright © David Williamson, First published by Currency Press in 1978, reproduced by permission from Currency Press Pty Ltd, Sydney Australia www.currency.com.au; Except from *The Road to Mecca* by Athol Fugard reprinted with the permission of Faber and Faber Ltd; Excerpt from *A man for all Seasons*, Robert Bolt, 1960 © Robert Bolt, published by Methuen Drama, used by permission of Bloomsbury Publishing Plc; Excerpt from *A View From The Bridge* by Arthur Miller, copyright © 1955, 1957, 1960, renewed © 1983, 1985, 1988 by Arthur Miller. Used by permission of Viking Books, an imprint of Penguin Publishing Group, a division of Penguin Random House LLC., all rights reserved, and permission by The Wylie Agency (UK) Limited; 'Rhapsody on a Windy Night', 'The Hollow Men', 'The Waste Land' and 'The love song of J. Alfred Prufrock' from *Collected Poems 1909 -1962* by T.S. Eliot, Copyright 1936 by Houghton Mifflin Harcourt Publishing Company. Copyright © renewed 1964 by Thomas Stearns Eliot. Reprinted by permission of Houghton Mifflin Harcourt Publishing Company, all rights reserved, and permission of Faber and Faber Ltd; 'The Sports Field', 'The Diver' and 'The Surfer' by Judith Wright from *Judith Wright Collected Poems* Fourth Estate 1994. Reprinted with permission of HarperCollins, Australia; 'Home is so Sad', 'Mr. Bleaney' and 'Water' from *The Complete Poems of Philip Larkin by Philip Larkin*, edited by Archie Burnett, Copyright © 2012 by The Estate of Philip Larkin. Reprinted by permission of Farrar, Straus and Giroux, and Faber and Faber Ltd; 'The Letter' from *Against Certain Capture* by Miriam Lo, Five Islands Press, used with permission; 'Private Ground' by Sylvia Plath from *The Collected Poems Of Sylvia Plath Edited by Ted Hughes*, copyright © 1960, 1965, 1971, 1981 by the Estate of Sylvia Plath. Editorial material copyright © by Ted Hughes. Reprinted by permission of HarperCollins Publishers, and permission from Faber and Faber Ltd; 'Ancestral Poem' by Olive Senior; Excerpt from 'Villanelle' by William Empson from *William Empson Collected Poems*. Reproduced with the permission of Curtis Brown Group Ltd, London on behalf of the Estate of William Empson, Copyright © Estate of William Empson, 2000; 'Grief' from *Rapture* by Carol Ann Duffy, Picador 2005. Reproduced with the permission of Pan Macmillan; 'The Empty Song' from *A Choosing: selected poems* by Liz Lochhead. Reproduced with permission of the Licensor through PLSclear; 'The Shell' by James Stephens from *Modern British Poetry*. Reproduced with the permission of The Society of Authors as the Literary Representative of James Stephens; 'The Relic' from *Selected Poems 1957-1994* by Ted Hughes. Copyright © 2003 by The Estate of Ted Hughes, Reprinted by permission of Farrar, Straus and Giroux, and Faber and

Faber Ltd; Excerpt from *The Courthouse* by Tahmima Anam. Copyright © 2006, Tahmima Anam, used by permission of The Wylie Agency (UK) Limited; Excerpt from *Disgrace* by J.M. Coetzee, copyright © 1999 by J.M. Coetzee. Used by permission of Viking Books, an imprint of Penguin Publishing Group, a division of Penguin Random House LLC. All rights reserved, and David Higham Associates; Excerpt from *The Lives of Others* by Neel Mukherjee, published by Chatto & Windus. Reprinted by permission of The Random House Group Limited and W. W. Norton & Company, Inc. © 2014 by Neel Mukjerjee; Excerpt from *The Remains of the Day* by Kazuo Ishiguro Published by Faber & Faber, 1993. Copyright© Kazuo Ishiguro, Reproduced by permission of the author c/o Rogers, Coleridge & White Ltd., 20 Powis Mews, London W11 1JN, and permission from Faber and Faber Ltd; Extract from 'Commission' by Tim Winton from *The Turning*, 2005, published by Penguin Random House, reproduced with permission; 'Heartsongs' From *Heart Songs and Other Stories* by E. Annie Proulx. Copyright © 1988, 1995 by E. Annie Proulx. Reprinted with the permission of Scribner, a division of Simon & Schuster, Inc. All rights reserved; Excerpt from *The Boat* by Nam Le, copyright © 2008 by Nam Le. Used by permission of Alfred A. Knopf, an imprint of the Knopf Doubleday Publishing Group, a division of Penguin Random House LLC., all rights reserved, and permission from Canongate Books Ltd.; Excerpt from *In Custody* by Anita Desai, published by Vintage, 2001. Copyright© Anita Desai. Reproduced by permission of the author c/o Rogers, Coleridge & White Ltd., 20 Powis Mews, London W11 1JN; *Dancing at Lughnasa* by Brian Friel reprint with the permission of Faber and Faber Ltd; *Last to go* by Harold Pinter reprint with the permission of Faber and Faber Ltd; *Our Country's Good* by Timberlake Wertenbaker, reproduced with the permission of The Agency; 'My Grandmother' by Elizabeth Jennings from *The Collected Poems* (Carcanet Press) by permission of David Higham Associates.

Thanks to the following for permission to reproduce images:
Cover Natalia Lavrenkova/Getty Images; *Inside*

Ellinor Hall/Getty Images; Thomas Marent/Minden Pictures/Getty Images; DeAgostini/Getty Images; UniversalImagesGroup/Getty Images; Glasshouse Images/Getty Images; Print Collector/Getty Images; Russell Kaye/Sandra-Lee Phipps/Getty Images; FPG /Getty Images Bettmann/Getty Images; Fred Stein Archive/Getty Images; Reg Innell/Getty Images David Levenson/Getty Images; Egor Krasnoborov/EyeEm/Getty Images; Arcaid Ltd - Corbis/Getty Images; DEA / W. BUSS/Getty Images; Education Images/Getty Images; Lipnitzki/Getty Images; A.F. ARCHIVE/Alamy; James Osmond/Getty Images, Images from BarbAnna/Getty Images, Colin McPherson/Getty Images; Mark Sykes/Getty Images; Dan Kitwood/Getty Images; Everett Collection Inc/Alamy, Robbie Jack /Getty Images; MathijsDelva/Getty Images; DEA / BIBLIOTECA AMBROSIANA / Getty Images;Tunbridge /Getty Images; Hulton Archive/Getty Images; Alexandre Schneider/Getty Images;

Chaloner Woods/Getty Images; Juan-Carlos Munoz/Getty Images; Wouter_Marck/Getty Images; Dan Kitwood/Getty Images; Hulton Deutsch/Getty Images, Jacques Pavlovsky/Getty Images; whitemay/Getty Images; UniversalImagesGroup/Getty Images; Time Life Pictures/Getty Images; Hulton Archive/Getty Images; David Cleveland/Getty Images; Vstock LLC/Getty Images; Christoph Wagner/Getty Images; Hulton Deutsch/Getty Images; United Archives GmbH / Alamy Stock Photo; www.galerie-ef.de/Getty Images; Russell Monk/Getty Images; Rene Frederick/Getty Images; Nadieshda/Getty Images; Guy Corbishley/Alamy Stock Photo; vkbhat/Getty Images; ullstein bild/Getty Images; John Snelling/Getty Images

Alfred Eisenstaedt /Getty Images; AF archive/Alamy Stock Photo; Monica Riveiro / EyeEm/Getty Images